D0867644

SUBJECT

The Integrated Circus

The New Right and the Restructuring of Global Markets

M. PATRICIA MARCHAK

McGill-Queen's University Press
Montreal & Kingston • London • Buffalo

© McGill-Queen's University Press 1991
ISBN 0-7735-0845-7 (cloth)
ISBN 0-7735-1149-0 (paper)
Legal deposit third quarter 1991
Bibliothèque nationale du Québec

Printed in Canada on acid-free paper
First paperback edition 1993

This book was first published with the help of a
grant from the Social Science Federation of Canada,
using funds provided by the Social Sciences and Humanities Research Council of Canada.

Canadian Cataloguing in Publication Data

Marchak, M. Patricia, 1936–
    The Integrated circus: the New Right and the restruc-
turing of global markets
Includes bibliographical references and index.
ISBN 0-7735-0845-7 (bnd)
ISBN 0-7735-1149-0 (pbk)

1. Free enterprise. 2. Conservatism. I. Title.

HM211.M37 1991   330.12'2   C91-090099-X

This book was typeset by Typo Litho composition inc.
in 10/12 Palatino.

Contents

Tables

Acknowledgments

My dear partner, Bill Marchak, made many meals and managed to exude good humour as I puzzled my way through this project. I thank him for that kindly companionship.

Kelly Littlewood, my secretary, was not obliged to type this manuscript, but without her talent in keeping the department running it would have been a much tougher undertaking.

I would also like to thank the University of British Columbia and the Social Science and Humanities Research Council of Canada for making it possible for me to take a year off from my teaching duties in 1984. Both organizations extended trust, since my project was then ill-defined, and I spent much of the time travelling. The travels had other spin-offs, some now published, but more particularly they enabled me to see the global economy from other perspectives. While most of the data cited in this book are from documentary sources, my understanding of them derives more from the journeys of that and the following years in Asia and Latin America.

Finally, my thanks to two anonymous reviewers who were generous in their assessments, to Kathy Johnson for her superb copy-editing, and to my publisher for taking on a book that is most unlikely to serve as a money-making text.

Preface

When F.A. Hayek and Milton Friedman received Nobel Prizes for economics in 1974 and 1976, their views were little known by the general public and they had few outspoken disciples. Selected versions of Keynesian economics had been accepted as self-evident truths for three decades, and conservative parties had long since adapted their platforms to the preservation in perpetuity of the welfare state. Few individuals and even fewer political parties in the liberal democracies would have labelled themselves right-wing. Democracy was good; whatever proposals politicians or economists might offer for improving economies or the quality of social life, no serious contender for public office suggested that democracy itself was expendable.

Yet by the mid-1980s the American and British governments were led by political parties claiming to be followers of supply-side economics and proclaiming the virtues of laissez-faire free enterprise of a kind not witnessed since the mid-Victorian age in Britain. Throughout the world, groups, institutes, and media were established and well funded to disseminate the theories of what had become known as the new right. Keynesian ideas were widely debunked. The welfare state was under attack. In Britain especially it was being dismantled. It became acceptable to blame the poor and the unemployed for their poverty and lack of employment, and politicians began to question publicly the value of liberal democracy. "Unemployment insurance creates unemployment," said the new right, and "welfare for single mothers creates single mothers." "There is an excess of democracy," said the Trilateral Commission. Heresies these were in the mind-set of the post-war era, yet suddenly acceptable in the 1980s.

To its opponents the new right was a reactionary, possibly fascist, retreat from progressive social democracy; to its supporters it was a welcome relief from the excesses of Keynesian liberalism. I will argue that neither assessment is adequate, because each treats the new right as a purely ideological phenomenon existing in a void. Ideologies never exist in a void; they have deep structural roots, but as they emerge and flower into social movements or political parties, they are fashioned and refashioned to fit many interests and numerous agendas. So with the new right.

My two objectives are to consider the train of events that brought about this remarkable change in public thinking, and to analyse the consequences that followed from it in the 1980s. It is not my intention to argue a line-by-line case against the new right on either moral or logical grounds (though I discuss some of the arguments advanced by others, and I do not pretend to admire the philosophy). Ideologies by their nature are bundles of not especially coherent beliefs, and their importance lies in their effects rather than in their truth or falsity.

This ideology emerged with the deterioration of the Pax Americana. Its roots lie in the restructuring of a global economy that began in the mid-1960s and reached fruition towards the end of 1980s. My argument is that the political movements and parties of the new right, promoted by corporate leaders who funded the think-tanks and participated in the crafting of their strategies, provided the ideological framework for the restructuring of the global economy.

That restructuring had several dimensions. One was technological, as integrated circuitry became the basis of new forms of production and new service industries. Another was spatial, as capital developed fully global composition and applications. No industrial process was untouched by the technological changes, and these changes fundamentally altered the composition and nature of labour. Spatially, capital moved quickly and relentlessly around the globe, probing new markets, establishing new labour supplies, and bringing in new resources, while simultaneously relinquishing old markets, abandoning old labour supplies, and leaving exhausted resources.

A third dimension was political, as governments structured along Keynesian lines were pushed aside in a series of bloodless coups. A fourth was sociological, as the institutionalized patterns of behaviour that had developed over the post-war period were systematically disrupted.

Great wealth was generated under the Pax Americana, and great poverty. As the new technologies, the global strategies, and the new right agenda became embedded in the world economy, wealth and poverty grew hand in hand. The debt crisis and fortunes made through leveraged buy-outs and speculative investments occurred together; wars both sustained and ultimately destroyed the victors. The insistence on free markets enslaved the populations of under-developed countries, and market economies finally required more authoritarian government. These were the ineluctable paradoxes of the time; none was resolvable through free market ideology. The world of the integrated circuit was also an integrated circus in all three senses of the word: it resembled at once the Barnum and Bailey three-ring travelling show, the competitive spectacle of ancient Rome, and the organized chaos of the Piccadilly underground train exchange.

The new right's proselytizing has faded somewhat since Margaret Thatcher and Ronald Reagan first took office. By the end of the 1980s the new right was already on the wane, much of its ideology debunked. Electorates appeared to be moving back to more traditional politics. Now, at the beginning of the 1990s, one can begin to unravel the sequence of events that led to the successes of the new right. It is possible too to examine the changed political world that the new right created. Privatization, deregulation, downsizing of public sectors, and a more general removal of the state from welfare functions are features of this change, but so are apparently opposite trends: the creation of larger political units with more centralized power, the increased regulation of private monopolies, and the growth of an international public sector. What was previously known as the Third World is now divided into industrializing and underdeveloped groups, both increasingly marked by great gaps between rich and poor, and increasingly ruled by military juntas or army-backed dictators.

The agenda of the new right was created in a period of transition. There was much that it did not address or addressed so superficially that no political solutions emerged. By the end of the decade the movement had lost some of its appeal and exhausted its program, but these problems remained. They included, for example, continuing environmental destruction, a debt crisis that burgeoned during the 1980s, widening gulfs between rich and poor countries and between rich and poor within the industrial countries, and unemployment rates that seemingly could not be reversed. The world moved into the 1990s with somewhat restructured nation-states and the framework for larger territorial units, but without solutions to its most pressing and no longer avoidable issues. The new right waned, but there was no obvious successor ideology, movement, or leadership.

It is not my intention (and in any case it is not within my limited powers) to suggest solutions to the problems of the 1990s. The stunning international events of 1989–91 have fundamentally altered the global arena. What I attempt here is a sociological analysis of the conditions that brought us to this point and that created the context for the new right of the 1980s.

INTEGRATED CIRCUITS:

1 Two or more transistors embedded in silicon or gallium arsenide chips that constitute complex information storage devices; also known as semi-conductors.

2 Metaphorical: transnational corporations embedding complex communications and production operations on a global scale; might also be known as semi-conductors.

CIRCUS:

1 Enclosed space designed for exhibitions of acrobatics, exotic trained animal shows, clowns, and other amusements; originated in Rome; featured combats between beasts and men; Pompey the Great is said to have slaughtered some 500 lions and 20 elephants in one five-day circus in 55 BC; the phrase "bread and circuses" (*panem et circenses*) derives from this period.

2 Modern circus dates from 1770s, with English travelling shows. The Barnum (American) circus, c. 1870s, was billed as "the Greatest Show on Earth." Its successor, Barnum and Bailey, was so large it had three rings.

3 Busy intersection and train station, where travellers move in all directions and create the impression of organized confusion; especially, the Piccadilly Circus in London.

CHAPTER ONE

Introduction

The new right is an ideology and a political agenda that became popular in the industrial democracies between the mid-1970s and the mid-1980s. It rejects the Keynesian consensus of the post-war era, and extols the virtues of free enterprise and entrepreneurship. It expresses dissatisfaction with democracy, equality, social welfare policies, collective bargaining, and other citizens' rights achieved throughout the previous three decades. By the end of the 1970s this ideology was adopted by the British government, and within the next few years it influenced the political policies of most of the world's governments. The questions I address in this book are why this ideology emerged and flourished at this particular time, and what its consequences are.

I argue that it was a response to economic changes already under way by the late 1960s. The Keynesian consensus was based on steel industries, mass production and mass consumption, nuclear families, and nation-states. Its components included mildly interventionist government; "free enterprise" tempered by some regulation of markets; labour protections and acceptance of workers' rights to engage in collective bargaining; welfare provisions and some redistribution policies; and a fairly widespread agreement that some goods were properly protected from market forces. The steel industries, assembly-lines for mass production, wages for mass consumption, nuclear families, and nation-states were all disappearing or in jeopardy by 1970 as mobile capital and the silicon revolution reduced the limitations of space and time.

International business leaders initiated many of these changes, but as capital became global they discovered national trade barriers, government resistance, labour legislation, investment rules, and welfare systems impeding the full development of a global economy. They initiated policies and funded the dissemination of publications with a radically different approach to social organization. As their views became known through these publications, other groups with a more libertarian perspective took up the cause of destroying Keynesian ideas. The new right, a label used by the British and subsequently adopted by other followers of this approach, succeeded in fundamentally altering the terms of the public debate over welfare, citizens' rights, equality, public property, and the nature of work.

As the new right grew into a social movement, its adherents included members of fundamentalist religions who understood it as a means of recovering a lost innocence and clear values; many of the well-funded institutes published both economic treatises and religious tracts. For the first time in post-war history, traditional social democratic and other left-wing parties were viewed as reactionary: the new right had become the radical vanguard of a new social order.

The political agenda of the new right was partially achieved by the end of the 1980s. International capital encountered fewer barriers as new trade and investment agreements were established, and governments privatized numerous social services and utilities. Smaller business interests had opportunities to compete for contracts to perform services no longer performed by the state. Unions were smaller and struggling to survive with less collective bargaining power. The education systems of industrial democracies were becoming more directed towards serving industry. Welfare and health costs were not rising as rapidly, though taxes had not been reduced. Yet there were still many unresolved issues for which the new right was unprepared. These included the debt crisis of underdeveloped countries, environmental disasters, the growing poverty at the core of industrial societies, unanticipated spin-offs of the technological revolution, militant fundamentalism in unexpected places, and, most spectacularly, the dissolution of the Russian empire.

I will examine the economic and political context of the rise and development of the new right up to 1990, and present an interpretation of contemporary history as it is linked to the new right agenda.

THE ARGUMENT I WILL make is embedded in this sequence of events:

Pre-1945: The theories of Adam Smith and John Locke had accompanied the development of industrial economies since the eighteenth century. The particular theory of laissez-faire or free, unfettered markets, had flourished under the Pax Britannica and declined during the Great Depression of the 1930s. Keynesian modifications of free market theories were introduced between the depression and the end of the Second World War.

1945–1965: The United States emerged the victor of the European War. It implanted new management in the forms of the International Monetary Fund (IMF), the World Bank, and numerous other international agencies. Its oil companies became quasi-state agencies, and the distribution of control between them and the government was never altogether settled. Its military forces became international peacekeepers.

Already in place in America were mass production corporations in steel-age industries. They had overcapacity once war production ceased, and their expansion involved the creation of both the American domestic market and new markets abroad. For the latter, open borders to investment and trade were required, and the American state made that demand in the language of free markets and free enterprise.

Although the ideology of free enterprise was adopted in Europe, the reality was that state governments undertook the major reconstruction tasks. State-owned properties in steel and utilities were features of all European societies in the 1950s and 1960s. There was no alternative, since privately owned production organizations had been effectively destroyed in the war, and huge corporations, near or actual monopolies, were the most efficient vehicles for mass production. Only the United States could sustain private sector monopolies.

The cost of maintaining the monopolies and the hegemonic regime was the establishment of a powerful military force in the United States. The military became the prime purchaser of technology, the major employer of technically skilled workers, and a significant propaganda agency charged with much of the task of rooting out communists at home and abroad.

Throughout this period the United States was a society of self-proclaimed individualists. Private happiness, private liberties, private salvation, and private property were its ideological props. Their monopolistic corporations notwithstanding, Americans viewed themselves as entrepreneurs in a high-risk world where little people fought honestly for their rightful rewards.

Mass production rests on mass consumption by masses of workers. To turn workers into consumers, wages in excess of bare survival and reproduction were required, and state cushions were put in place to reduce their vulnerability to economic downturns. The Keynesian revolution became conventional wisdom in all the industrial countries. At the domestic level it consisted of state monetary policy to facilitate the growth of consumer power, combined with numerous protections and aids for the working population. Potential labour unrest was contained within an implied social contract whereby unions bargained collectively and ensured a steady, contractually secure labour force between negotiations.

The public sector expanded, and the range of issues negotiated in the political sphere also expanded. The idea of the citizen's right to income and to decent housing, equal employment opportunities, and equitable wage distribution became embedded in industrially advanced states; these rights ultimately challenged the rights already assigned to property and investment capital. As governments became more powerful, the market became less powerful in regulating such rights. In the United States social rights were phrased in the language of individual rights; elsewhere, similar demands were expressed in more collective terms.

The economically weaker states were defenceless from their inception. Created arbitrarily by colonial governments, often ethnically and linguistically heterogeneous, their survival depended on their relationships with industrial states and transnational capital. But the industrial states were concerned with these regions as resource reservoirs, not as separate and independent societies with their own survival interests. The instruments of resource procurement were multinational corporations, and the industrial states supported them through enforced open borders and conditional loans for the dependent states. These policies prevented the growth of democracy, in some cases actively displaced democratic alternatives, and inhibited the capacity of the weaker states to operate primarily in the interests of their citizens. Poverty, famine, and the absence of civil rights cannot be divorced from the affluence of a handful of industrial countries.

The problem was not trade itself; the problem was the freedom of capital to pursue private ends irrespective of the social good, and the absence of countervailing power. Only in the industrial countries had a modicum of countervailing power been put in place in the interim between Smith and Keynes, enabling democratic political institutions to constrain national capital in its behaviour towards labour.

Expansion of the industrial economies proceeded for about two decades thereafter. Europe was reconstructed, Japan revived, Taiwan propped up, Latin America sustained; during this time the United States remained dominant in the political and economic arenas, encountered virtually no serious competition, and was recognized everywhere as the hegemonic power of the age. The USSR, and subsequently China and Cuba, were thorns in the American side, in American versions; they were necessary enemies in the version suggested here. They served as bogeymen to frighten anyone who imagined that free enterprise might not be the ideal means of converting poverty into wealth.

1965–75: A series of transformations occurred simultaneously. These were not causally connected in any simple way; the process was like a bowling game in which one pin knocks down another, and a chain reaction takes place. The original ball was silicon chip technology. The silicon chip was an outgrowth of technical developments during the war, and in the United States much of the early technological growth occurred under the aegis of military institutions. In its early stages economists and industrial leaders did not anticipate that this technology would fundamentally alter industry and indeed the whole of industrial society; industrialists and politicians assumed that the chip, like most new developments in the post-war period, would provide incremental advantages to production sequences already established.

But the pace of change was rapid. The transistor became the integrated circuit, and the applications of the circuit became microelectronics, computers, satellites, and an infrastructure for the reorganization of every other industry.

Some industries, taking advantage of improved air transportation and the new communications technologies, moved their labour-intensive operations offshore, largely to capture low-cost labour and favourable tax benefits. They then imported the finished products to sell on the domestic markets of the industrial countries. The silicon chip manufacturers also moved offshore, partly for the same reasons, and partly to avoid the stifling business hierarchies and financial constraints of established corporate America.

Other companies fell by the wayside. Some declined because they could no longer offer their goods at competitive prices if they used the relatively costly labour of the industrial centres. Some, the subsidiaries of the same companies that moved offshore, could not compete with their own parent and sibling firms; they were closed to make room for the "competition." Others were victims of their own hierarchies; their ambience was inhospitable to innovative science. The biggest losers, however, were not the companies but the disemployed, the unions, the unskilled workers, and the dependent communities in industrial countries.

Despite its lead and its use of cheap labour elsewhere, the United States failed to capture all the downstream benefits of the silicon revolution. Japan, organized on a different state-capital axis, endowed with a different cultural history, unencumbered with a military-industrial complex, and greatly aided by the American military exercises in Korea and Vietnam, became a serious contestant for industrial supremacy. The most significant difference between the American and Japanese societies was the emphasis in Japan on social organization. The themes of private happiness, private rights, individualism, and free enterprise as defined in the United States were missing. Japan also established offshore operations, and gradually re-created an Asian economic empire with trade ties centred on Japan. The monetary regime spluttered and finally splintered: the American dollar could no longer sustain it.

There followed some random hits. The rebellion of the oil-producing regions fundamentally altered American power over allies and changed the cost-benefit ratios for steel-age industries. Apparently the underdeveloped countries could, with organization, alter the balance of power. The defeat in Vietnam challenged America's political leadership and raised doubts about the effectiveness of the military establishment. It also changed the culture of the United States. When societies become prosperous through plunder, or through more contemporary forms of economic imperialism, they pay an internal price. As Britain's experience has shown, the costs of imperialism are extraordinarily high. If (as Marx is too often quoted) the underdeveloped see their future reflected in the face of the centre, then today in America, as yesterday in Britain, that face is pocked by the ravages of war, maimed by gluttony, and crushed by internal class cleavages and racism.

The Vietnam debacle raised the crucial issue: it was not clear that the war was essential to defend corporate interests in the region. On economic grounds, one might argue that the war was the outcome of the military-industrial complex within the United States. Even if that were the instrumental explanation, the US politicians' enthusiasm for entry into a civil war appears to have rested on an ideological conviction that American interests were threatened by any group, anywhere, that called itself, or could be labelled, communist. That conviction was embedded in an almost religious devotion to the idea of free enterprise, an idea that considerably exceeded the relatively simple theories of free markets enunciated in an earlier age.

With the OPEC challenge, the Vietnam defeat, and the loss of control over the world monetary system, the United States was also encountering opposition throughout the developing countries, which increasingly viewed its private banks and the IMF as hostile institutions. The United Nations became a forum for the articulation of complaints that in an earlier age might have had no mass audience; now, the media of the industrialized countries made known the new struggles and claims. The struggles became more poignant and more pressing with the droughts in Africa and the declining agricultural markets for developing countries generally. The "Green revolution" had been touted as a solution to famine, but its main beneficiaries were the chemical companies of the industrialized countries.

American hegemony going down, the leaders of the industrial countries met frequently in OECD, IMF, World Bank, summit, and other forums. One of these was the privately financed Trilateral Commission, established in 1972 with the explicit objective of devising strategies for managing the post-hegemonic global economy. While the decline in America's fortunes had some benefits for Europe and Japan, many new problems were presented by the end of a hegemonic regime. No nation was capable of taking on the tasks of global policing, global financing, and global energy provision. The unification of Europe was underway, and Japan had created her own trade zone. The objective of many of these meetings was to establish the real value of an artifically high American currency so that the global market could be sustained. While the less developed countries (LDCs) called for a new international economic order, the developed market economies (DMEs) continued to argue that economic growth elsewhere depended on their own continued accumulation of new wealth.

1975–1985: Change was unavoidable once the technological revolution was underway and the global marketplace was established. How it was to be achieved and at whose expense was yet to be determined. The interest groups we now call the new right grasped the historical situation and provided the rationale for a particular kind of change. In this they were greatly aided by the other great technological device of the age, the television set.

The new right was not a passing convention of amateurs, nor was it, despite the temporary popularity of supply-side theorists and libertarians, a utopian movement. It was a well-funded global political organization. Business leaders of the OECD countries had an agenda long before the agenda became known as the new right's; already, in the establishment of the Trilateral Commission and several think-tanks throughout the industrial countries, corporate capital was organizing forums for disseminating its message.

I do not offer a conspiracy theory, for the "conspirators" did not meet clandestinely and did not deceive; on the contrary, they announced their intentions publicly. They published extensively, bombarded the media with information and interpretations, and aggressively sought out audiences for their messages.

The label "the new right" was adopted by a second group for the political movement that emerged in the mid-1970s with the explicit intention of breaking the post-war consensus of the welfare state. Under that label it sought to reorganize politics to facilitate a fully competitive free market economy. Its popularizers were champions of small business, entrepreneurialism, and nationalism, and it may seem unjust to argue that global corporations and the new right movement shared common objectives. However, the agenda of the Trilateralists, and ultimately of transnational capital, could not be implemented until the existing structure of states was dismantled, and that task could be advanced through the libertarian ideology adopted by the second group. Its funding came in large part from the corporations that in other arenas promoted not a fully competitive economy but a selected free market system which still had at its core strong, yet internationally organized, governments. These governments were to be shorn of many social service functions, and of nationalized industries where they existed, but they were to be authoritarian instruments for the protection of private property.

Both versions opposed the welfare state, the middle class attached to the state, and the moral climate of the late American era. That moral climate included the excesses of the 1960s, the drug culture, permissive child-rearing, college drop-outs, widespread divorce, demands for equality by minorities and women, great expectations followed by broken dreams. The solution for many at the private level was salvationist religion, and at the public level a denunciation of the governments and the public sector middle class that somehow had caused the eclipse of the American age.

Free enterprise as an idea had always protected property rights, and alternative versions of the good society had always attacked them. Thus there developed a bipolar world of ideological opposites: the free enterprise system versus communism. That the vast majority of economic transactions fitted neither version did not deter ideologues. Proponents of the free market deemed it essential to sustain the belief that there were only two possible systems, each characterized in absolute terms. The bipolar world was retained and even intensified in new right ideology. The détente of the early 1970s was rejected, and hostility was renewed.

Yet the Japanese model offered an alternative – capitalism co-ordinated by a strong state. Since Japan continued to pay homage to the language of free enterprise, its deviance was not deemed unacceptable by libertarians, and its capacity to harness its population in the drive towards constant accumulation of capital was envied.

Ideology alone would not have changed the world. But ideological explanations for why the world has changed can be powerful instruments for restructuring societies, and that is what the new right provided. One would be foolish to dismiss the power of words, especially words that are assiduously propagated and well funded. The messages of the new right became vital carriers for the restructuring of the 1970s and 1980s.

By the mid-1970s the integrated circuit was swiftly changing the way business operated. The production of the chip itself could be automated, and the advantages of cheap labour in developing countries were declining. Threatened protectionist legislation, especially in the United States, dictated relocations in the industrial countries, but the relocations involved numerous pools of capital from diverse sources. American capital returned to the United States, but in combination with Japanese and European capital; and while European companies became stronger, they too were now financed by global pools of capital.

The new technology, combined with the restructuring of industries, provided the basis for transforming services into commodities. Financial services had always been commodities, but they could now be expanded on a global scale, provided that they could jump borders without penalty. Management services also became exportable as companies developed new strategies of decentralization and contracting out to deal with labour and unpredictable changes in technology. The emerging new service sector was created in part by a redefinition of "service"; in part by the reorganization of industry from single monopolies to central firms surrounded by contractors surrounded by subcontractors; and in part by genuinely new services embedded in telecommunications technologies.

Many services, especially in Europe, Canada, and Australia, were supplied primarily by the public sector. The management of hospitals, extended care centres, medical laboratories, and educational institutions was included in the cost of government. New private sector companies, already established in the United States, were now able to export and more actively trade such services. Utilities, including transportation, communication, energy infrastructure, and highway construction, were becoming potentially profitable services.

The major steel-age industries, however, were becoming obsolete. Either their production machinery and labour organization impeded their capacity to adapt to new technology, or the products they made were technically outmoded, or both.

The restructuring of the industrial and service sectors was contingent on changes that even in the United States ran counter to the existing moral understanding of the social contract and the role of

government. If government was the negotiated outcome of a pluralistic society, where all interests were equal, it could not itself undertake or even tolerate the unilateral restructuring that major
companies and investors perceived as necessary. New political conditions were required if these companies and investors were to
achieve their agenda.The first political condition was the private
right to disinvest and move capital elsewhere. This right already
existed within the free enterprise ideology, but it had been delimited
by long-term obligations to labour enforced by union contracts and
state legislation. It was also morally constrained by a history of
grants, taxation holidays, and government-provided infrastructures
and resources intended to induce companies to locate in particular
regions. The second right was to non-discriminatory national treatment, by which was meant the obligation of governments to treat
non-national and national companies alike in competition for state
contracts.

Where the state owned or participated in industries, as throughout
Europe, Canada, and Australia, it was the state that had to disinvest.
This too required political changes, since the state, like private cap-
ital, had obligations to labour and to regions.

With the new technologies in communication and transportation,
capital could be transferred instantly. The banking system had to
be altered to accommodate this change on a global scale. Deregulation at the state level would be required, and states would have
to relinquish their capacities to manage the monetary affairs of their
territories.

To mount the changes proposed and anticipated by investors, the
power of unions, the power of public sector workers, and especially
the power of the Keynesian solution were all attacked in strong moral
terms. In their place a new international order to regulate monetary
exchanges and "transnationalized" capital would be established.
This was the new right agenda, which now appeared as part of the
policies of new right governments.

1985–1990: As the industrial countries began to now practise what
the new right preached, the underdeveloped countries became increasingly indebted. The debt crisis had its beginning in the absolute
dicta of the IMF and World Bank conditions for loans. Many of the
conditions could be implemented only by absolutist governments,
and the 1960s and 1970s were marked by the overthrow of fledgling
democracies by military juntas and dictators whose willingness to
accommodate the demands of foreign capital was assured. Direct
investment was followed by influxes of private bank loan capital.
As deregulation and the growth of the service sector proceeded in

the industrial countries, these loans, including Eurobonds, carried with them new conditions that could be met only if the recipients quickly became massive industrial powers. The oil crisis decreased their ability to industrialize on the old model, and only a handful of newly industrializing countries (NICs) were in a position to create a new model. In the others poverty was intensified, populations increased, cities were crowded with hungry and unemployed families, and governments became more repressive.

The debt crisis was not a one-way disaster, though its consequences were vastly more severe in the indebted countries. In the lending countries the major banks were overextended, and exports of commodities that needed a middle class of consumers in the recipient countries were sharply cut back.

In the NICs foreign direct investment had created enclaves in free trade zones. The high technology of the age became the assembly line, which released young female workers from the age-old bonds of patriarchy even as it chained them to a new regime of production. The new centres received the bulk of foreign aid, external military support, and direct investment, but in American eyes they were the models of free enterprise. Even in the last year of the 1980s *Forbes* could note, in reviewing a Peruvian critique of Latin American statism, that the "few developing countries that have embraced capitalism – South Korea and Taiwan, for example – have shot way ahead of the others in wealth and well-being."[1] The two NICs cited as models are both statist, both recipients of large quantities of foreign capital and foreign aid in their initial development, and both inextricably tied to American and Japanese strategic interests in Southeast Asia.

Statism itself was not the problem. Taiwan remains statist, if by that term we mean that there is a large degree of state participation in the economy. All of Europe was statist at least until 1980, and necessarily so. Japan was statist throughout the three decades following the war, and in many respects continues to be; without the state's long-term planning and investments, private capital would never have succeeded in leap-frogging over the United States with commercial applications of microchip technology. Even the United States is statist in the central role of its military and in its agricultural policies after 1972. Its industries were publicly regulated, though not publicly owned. The term "statist" is meaningless outside ideology, but at that level it is vital because it provides a contrast to the ideological purity of free enterprise.

For countries such as Peru, the state has undoubtedly been a problem, but not because it wilfully prevented the growth of free enterprise. There, as elsewhere in Latin America, the prolonged strength of oligarchies and the sustenance of military institutions were related to the one-eyed policies of global capital and markets. Even honest politicians (and presumably some were) and leaders with sincere intentions to redistribute land and generate benign growth found it impossible either to develop industry at an indigenous level or to develop their societies while accommodating foreign capital.

1990–: The ecological dimension of a global marketplace had been gradually emerging as an issue throughout the 1980s, but it was the middle of the decade before public awareness of something called global warming and something else called the greenhouse effect erupted in political arenas. Environmentalists had been dubbed "ecofreaks" and "back-to-the-landers" by both politicians and corporate leaders, but hard scientific evidence was not so easily dismissed. By 1990 public opinion polls showed that citizens throughout the industrial countries believed that the polluted environment was the most serious issue of the time. This prodded politicians to seek ad hoc technical solutions to specific problems. But the solutions failed to quiet public fears. The new right's nostrums offered no comfort; indeed, it was becoming clear that market forces would not clean up the air or the water or save the tropical and temperate rain forests.

The image-makers of new right governments had boasted of their ability to mould public opinion. Throughout the 1980s they had one success after another; Ronald Reagan appeared as the father-figure. Margaret Thatcher as everybody's mom. The agenda of the new right had been implemented in numerous ways, and the Keynesian revolution was superceded. But the environmental crises had not come out of the new right package, and the debt crisis could not be shelved by new right slogans. As the European Community became a reality, Thatcherism in Britain faded. Reaganism declined more gradually once its chief was out of office. The agenda remained but the rhetoric diminished, and by 1990 there were new and unpredicted issues on the world's menu.

In the midst of the debate over environment and markets, contemporary history suddenly, astonishingly – some would say miraculously – took a new turn. Communism, or more accurately, centrally managed economies in Eastern Europe, collapsed. Within the calendar year 1989 the political map of Eastern Europe was fundamentally changed, largely without force or revolution. East Germans tore down the wall, and in October 1990 the two Germanies were unified. Poland, Hungary, Romania, Czechoslovakia, the Baltic states, and Albania and the internal provinces of Russia were rapidly introducing market forces and private property rights – were even, finally, flirting with parliamentary democracy and new forms of civil rights.

These swift changes bolstered the new right's claims about the superiority of markets over central state management, but even so they were not entirely welcome. For the first time in post-war history, the "free world" was obliged to confront the turmoil of contemporary events with no counterfoil. The "evil empire," as Reagan had called the Soviet bloc, had rather quietly, and for the most part voluntarily, ceased to exist. Now the new right appeared as a caricature of capitalism: it was all there was, and it was organized chaos.

CONTEMPORARY SCHOLARLY works on the problems of the new global economy begin with the general premise that the world has passed through a hegemonic crisis whereby key institutional arrangements were destroyed and superceded. Giovanni Arrighi, for example, has noted three elements of the change: the reconstruction of the world market, the transnational expansion of capital, and the spread of the mass production methods of the advanced countries.[2] Market competition emerged, superceding the American control of international trade in the immediate post-war period. This analysis accepts that general premise. It is also informed by the arguments of American political economists who charted the deindustrialization and disinvestment,[3] the "paper entrepreneurialism,"[4] and the wasted industrial capacities in the United States of the 1970s and early 1980s.[5] They have argued that a major immediate cause of the United States loss of hegemony lay in the hierarchical structure of risk-avoiding, vertically integrated corporations, and in the investment class that gave industrial organizations neither loyalty nor leadership. They have documented their case well, and I accept it (it is summarized in chapter 4). I depart from these interpretations when their concern becomes excessively geocentric or their policy pronouncements are devoted to reinventing American supremacy. I also depart from them in interpreting the trends. Their analyses, published in the 1980s, were already somewhat dated. They were concerned with disinvestment from the core industrial regions, but by the mid-1980s reinvestment was already underway, if under new auspices and in new forms.

My analysis is further informed by the general theory of regulation as advanced by the European scholars Alain Lipietz and Michael Aglietta.[6] In their view, capitalism has regular cycles of declining profits as its methods of regulating labour exhaust the potential for improving profits on a given model of industry or regime of accumulation. Fordism (mass production and mass consumption systems) combined with Taylorism (scientific management of labour and, more generally, a political and social organization appropriate to the given mode of accumulation) began to reach the exhaustion level in the mid-1960s.

This model has an international aspect involving the extraction of resources from underdeveloped countries for use in the factories of the central manufacturing countries on unequal terms of trade. The exhaustion level involves technical and social limits which cannot be overcome through the same methods; for example, Fordism required the continual adaptation of mass consumption to productivity gains brought about by intensive accumulation (itself brought about through constant changes in mechanization). Continued improvements in productivity and continued upward consumer demands for mass-produced goods reached impasses by the 1960s, yet it was not possible to reduce wages; in any event, reduced buying power created recessions and further decreased profitability. Capitalists (accumulators) sought alternatives, as they have done in the past.

They argued that new labour pools provided an alternative that lowered the wage costs and gradually created a new consumer population; as well, they permitted capital to close factories and (through absence rather than through socially impossible alternatives) reconstruct the labour force in industrial countries. This was the extension of Fordism to new regions, together with the introduction of a new production process (mode of accumulation and of labour regulation suitable to it) in the industrial centres.

Folker Fröbel argues that capitalism uses other social modes of production (the peasant economy and feudal and patriarchal systems) as it advances, unevenly incorporating them to tap surplus labour value.[7] In the process, the international division of labour is constantly revised. Thus, in earlier phases of capitalism, industrialists brought rural populations within their own nations into wage-labour production. As this labour force became entrenched, it reached its limits for production of surplus value, and capital (as merchants, companies, industries, and banks) penetrated the peripheries under colonial regimes. Eventually this process reached the underdeveloped countries either in post-colonial regions or in new regions, pulling the rural populations into the orbit of accumulation.

In Fröbel's view, the objective during the colonial phase is to obtain raw materials, and indigenous labour is used in the extraction phase. In the post-colonial phase, labour is brought under direct supervision in manufacturing goods to be exported. This process is dictated by the rising cost of labour and by class conflict in the centres already controlled by capital. Expansion abroad and disinvestment in the core regions are modes of regulating labour and reducing its ability to negotiate improved terms of employment. In the late 1950s and early 1960s the social contract with labour in the industrial countries, combined with the corporate expansion, led to the reduction in a reserve army of potential workers whose existence would otherwise exert pressure against rising labour costs. Full employment thus led to increasing wages, and (perhaps more important) to greater labour organization and political demands for the social wage inherent in the welfare state. Capital's move to the less developed countries (LDCs), transforming them into NICs, was a response to this pressure at home.

In the NICs, Fröbel argues, capital has access to an almost inexhaustible supply of labour power at low wages. These workers put in longer hours than workers in the industrial countries; they can easily be replaced because of the enormous pool of reserves both in their own countries and in other disadvantaged countries; and they are given little protection by government or unions. The precise timing of this move to the NICs was partly contingent on the development of appropriate technologies that would allow production using a largely unskilled and often illiterate labour force.

This general approach is appreciated and selectively adopted in what follows, though I am sceptical about the particular explanation for a decline in profits. While I agree that restructuring has occurred, I do not see it as a shift away from either mass production or mass consumption in the industrial countries. I also insist that there are cultural features of societies that filter economic change; in the United States, that feature is extreme individualism. Much of the disenchantment with the 1960s was centred on the consequences of this individualism: the broken marriages, the drug-taking schoolchildren, the overwhelming anomie in American cities.

In much of the world, by contrast, kinship is still the central organizing principle, and economic transactions, political action, and interpretations of social structure are filtered through kin relations and obligations. The theory of the free market fails to appreciate these fundamental cultural differences, and much of the critical thinking about the export of Fordism similarly ignores the cultural filters in the transmission of technology and market behaviours.

Capitalism does have cycles of growth and decline, and the trough of that cycle in the late 1970s and early 1980s was both deep and prolonged. While it affected the industrial centres, there was some movement to new regions. Still, the total movement to NICs was not massive; indeed, throughout the entire period most investment continued to be lodged in the industrial countries. While the new technologies reduced the advantages of economies of scale within production units and removed the steel-age industries from their dominant place in the industrial spectrum, mass production did not cease, and mass consumption was still an essential ingredient for growth. The crucial dilemma, indeed, was how profits could be made from the new technologies under conditions of overproduction and high unemployment. The high unemployment was not primarily due to offshore production; it was due to the intrinsic nature of the new technologies.

The output of the five largest industrial economies grew by 3 per cent in 1983, by 4.2 per cent in 1984, and by 2.8 per cent in 1985, and rates of inflation in those economies had dropped sharply.[8] OECD countries as a whole continued to grow, with rates of 3.3 per cent in 1987 and 4.1 per cent in 1988.[9] What remained was high unemployment in all industrial countries and trade deficits for the United States and most European countries.

American growth rates in the late 1980s were slightly lower than those of Japan, Britain, and Canada, but still very high (at 3.8 per cent in 1988). In comparative terms, purchasing power in the United States and other industrial countries had actually improved relative to the rest of the world. The per capita income in the United States was second only to that of Switzerland throughout the 1980s, and both they and the next five countries – Norway, Luxembourg, Sweden, Japan, and Canada – were still vastly richer than the rest of the world.

As to the argument that the state had provided the appropriate mode of labour regulation for the mass production, mass consumption era, there are several caveats. One, noted by Lipietz but frequently ignored in much of the subsequent literature, is that different states were involved. Not all provided the forms of regulation adopted in either Europe or the United States. Japan and Argentina, two obvious examples, took quite different approaches (one considerably more successful than the other). Even within the general Keynesian state structure there were important differences between the forms adopted in the United States, West Germany, the United Kingdom, France, the Scandinavian countries, Canada, and Australia. The differences were due to many factors that cannot be instrumentally reduced to a preconceived notion of appropriateness; they certainly include the level of union organization and the history of labour-management relations in the 1940s and 1950s. These differences carried over to the process of restructuring and the state's contribution to it.

Both the British and the American states, while exercising hegemonic power in the world theatre, took on independent momentum. In both cases the ideological premises, which originally provided a moral basis for the accumulation of capital, became the moral basis for the advancement of independent state interests. Laissez-faire and free enterprise became state ideologies, but protectionism in both cases followed economic decline. Protectionist legislation and the threat of it became part of the complex global economy by the 1980s. In both cases, as well, military strength grew with the state, creating yet another centre of power with independent momentum, draining national revenues. These conditions need to be attended to at the level of theory, and existing theories of capitalism are not well attuned to them.

Nor are those theories attuned to the simple fact of corruption. Capitalism is only partly a rational system of investment and decision-making. Individuals do pocket funds, forge documents, and engage in stock market manipulations that are inexplicable in terms of either neo-classical or neo-Marxist theories.

Apart from corrupt practices, the critical theorists attribute to capital both a homogeneity and a rational purposiveness that are difficult to justify in view of American investment habits. This is a perplexing problem, and it can be solved only by assuming that with each restructuring some agents take control of the overall system, while others lose power. Restructuring is as much a contest between powerful groups as a means of ultimately saving the system.

The term "capital" refers diversely to agents – managers, corporate exectives, stockbrokers, and bankers – and to shareholders who are not now individual families, and not, in any event, families closely attached to any one corporation. It also includes capital in diverse categories – transnational, national, and local, large and small. It therefore includes members with different property rights and highly varying occupational niches.

Corporate decision-making capacity rests in ordinary human beings occupying executive offices (both public and private) with the mandate to make profits. These people have greatly enhanced powers of foresight by virtue of their organizational context: corporations are systematic ways of pooling a spectrum of specialized skills and permitting the group to do what no single individual could manage in the way of calculating probable outcomes of various strategies. But even powerful corporations do not control all the variables in a global economy, and the corporations themselves are so complex that their ability to define long-term interests is constrained by the numerous and contradictory private and organized interests of their own members.

Forbes, a magazine devoted to the adulation of American capitalism, analysed its "100 largest firms" lists over the seventy-year period between 1917 and 1987. [10] Only 22 per cent of the firms had survived, and half of the survivors had been taken over. Among the drop-outs from the élite were Bethlehem Steel, Chase Manhattan Bank, Marathon Oil, Union Carbide, and F.W. Woolworth. Anaconda Copper, at fourteenth position in 1917 and still strong with its investments in Chile through the 1960s, was acquired by Atlantic Richfield and stripped of its assets in 1985. US Steel, first on the list in 1917, had dropped to fifty-fifth place and was still on the way down. Such a record does not support the notion that these companies are endowed with great foresight or prescience.

Without doubt, a successful strategy for reducing costs will be used and copied (for example, shifting labour-intensive production offshore), but the net results of such activities are surely beyond anyone's calculations. Corporations invest in technological research and development with a view to changing both products and production processes, but radical transformations are not predictable, their applications are rarely anticipated, their side effects are unknown, and only in retrospect can we see their introduction as a historical process. Genuinely new technologies can have devastating impacts on those who were privileged in a previous organization.

The evidence on corporate long-term planning is ambiguous at best. Indeed, the case studies examined by American social scientists and the continuing documentation in financial publications on leveraged takeovers, closures, joint ventures, aborted investments, overproduction problems, and rapid declines in fortunes suggest that a very different assumption should be entertained: namely, that both investment practices and American corporate behaviour are typically dictated by relatively short-term interests. This would make sense in view of corporate executives' relatively short life spans and their high intercorporate mobility. It would make sense in human terms: the executives do not own the properties they play with; their stakes in any one corporation are not inheritable by their children; and, in the individualistic culture they have created, wealthy families are not established "houses" as they are in most of Asia. Finally, technology so rapidly changes the profit margins that long-term strategies are possibly pointless, and in any case are unlikely to be adopted by executives whose payoffs depend on very rapid returns on investment.

For Asian executives the cultural context is clearly different. The Suharto family, for example, rules Indonesia; brothers, uncles, sisters, and aunts are all brought into the dominant enterprises by virtue of their connection to the president. Long-term strategies are designed to protect families, not individuals. The powerful military establishment supports these strategies, and nepotism is endemic to a degree that shocks North Americans. The kin-organized society has its own defects; the point is that capital is not disembodied from its social context.

Taking that fact as a point of departure, we might say that American corporations sought short-term profits and tried to evade both unions and welfare state legislation when they moved to low-wage labour regions. There followed a period of intense competition during which some of them, along with the labour force they left behind, suffered decline. Shareholders, with no particular loyalty, traded shares, invested, disinvested, and joined new alliances. American investors, perceiving the greater profitability of Japanese-managed firms, sought out joint venture arrangements. Japanese firms, which did not operate on the same short-term motivations and which were able to count on greater loyalty from shareholders and managers, also sought out joint venture arrangements to evade protectionist legislation in the United States and Europe.

The continuing technological change, together with increasing fuel costs and other conditions, reduced the advantages of cheap labour in the NICs. The advantages were greater for some industries and firms than for others, depending on the nature of their production system, their sources of funding, the growth of new markets in the NICs themselves, and changing political conditions. Overall, however, reinvestment in industrial centres now took form.

My scepticism about capital's prescience refers to the notion that capital held all the cards. But I would not preclude deliberate attempts to alter the course of events, or at least to seek preferred outcomes. There can be little doubt that during the 1970s and 1980s business and political leaders engaged in extensive planning and deliberate public relations campaigns within the numerous think-tanks, OECD organizations, Groups of Five, Six, and Seven, the IMF and the World Bank, and the Trilateral Commission. In part this activity was by way of avoiding imperialist rivalries with Japan. Its aim was to restructure governments both spatially and directionally, and for that purpose Japan became a useful model.

There was a profit decline, it was contingent on a changing technology, and it could not be reversed without some changes at the private and public levels. The changes at the private level involved reorganizing labour. In the United States and Europe though not in Japan, this was accomplished by abandoning existing industrial organizations, producing goods elsewhere until unions were weakened and the labour climate changed, and then returning in changed form. The changes at the public level were brought about by a concerted public relations campaign and by pressure on governments to decrease expenditures, reduce public services, and privatize public properties.

These actions were not undertaken by separate national pools of capital, as they might have been in an earlier era. By the early 1970s international capital had become conscious of itself as a specific entity independent of its national origins. The self-destructive behaviour of American investors and corporations began to threaten international capital and the system itself. The American government and military could not sustain the global operations; indeed, they themselves had become obstacles. International (or, more accurately, transnational) organizations appeared or became stronger so as to cope actively with a new kind of global economy. That economy still rested on mass production and mass consumption, but it was no longer separated into national units (even if national cultures affected its behaviour), its technological base was no longer the steel-age industries, and it encompassed, if most unevenly, the entire globe.

For the NICs, and even more for other less developed regions, the costs of restructuring were greater than for the industrial countries. By the end of the 1980s, with the advantages of cheap unskilled labour much reduced and with capital now moving back towards the industrial countries (and within them to the industrial heartlands), many countries experienced even greater poverty than before. Several of the NICs had developed some independent capacity for industrial production and competition with transnational capital originally sourced in North America, Europe, and Japan, but the majority of poor nations were not so lucky.

For the LDCs their share of world trade as a whole (though with variations between OPEC countries, NICs, and others) declined steadily after 1950, their dependence on single raw material commodities intensified, and the price of commodities declined relative to the price of manufactured products. The tariff structure so favourable to the industrial countries worked against them, allowing exports of raw materials but inhibiting value-added goods.[11] Their share of the consumer price for raw materials declined and in virtually all cases was, even at its best price share, very small.[12]

The strong American dollar and the high American interest rates intensified the debt crisis in poorer countries, and further inhibited their ability to sustain democratic governments. In real dollar terms, average incomes even for the NICs were lower in 1983 than in 1973. This increasing disparity between the have and the have-not countries was the legacy of the restructuring that had propped up the United States, rejuvenated Europe, and permitted Japan to assume its place as a major power in the now multipolar global economy.

The debt crisis also had an impact on the industrial countries. If Latin American debt was repudiated, or if the nations continued to decline to the point that they could not repay their debts, several large American and European banks would crash with them. This precarious situation does not fit into the general theories of Fordism and post-Fordism; the accumulators have created their own dilemma, and there is no obvious solution to it. There is also no new right nostrum available; the problem was studied but not resolved by the corporate leaders who financed the new right think tanks and tolerated the simple-minded analyses of the unproductive Third World.

Finally, there is the problem of separating the system and the agents. Capitalism operates on identifiable principles. Rational decision-making towards achievement of known goals is its hallmark. The agents of capitalism, however, are influenced not only by the general cultural conditions of their society, but also by the mass media, the appeals of mass movements, and world events. It was not economic rationality that dictated the exclusion of women from corporate boardrooms, but a variety of prejudices and historical developments; when the feminist movement gathered force, the corporate world, eventually began to soften its stance. Similarly, corporate attitudes towards the environmental aspects of business are affected by new information and social pressures that are not embedded in the system of economic rationality. American businessmen (the term is accurate; it is the practice, not the word, that is sexist) studied engineering, accounting, and business on their road to the boardrooms; in the 1990s they are recruiting students of philosophy, sociology, history, literature, and science. Economic rationality is not enough, it appears, and it is not unreasonable to anticipate a substantial change in the way capitalism operates in the twenty-first century.

IN WHAT FOLLOWS, events and ideology have been intertwined to show how each affected the other and with what consequences in different social contexts around the globe. Chapter 2, beginning Part one, provides a background discussion of classical theories of property, the state, and markets, because it was these that so influenced the way the new world of North America developed, and it was to them that the new right popularizers turned in the crisis.

From the third chapter onward, the book is about the American age. Chapter 3 considers international organizations following the Second World War, the post-war reconstruction, the working out of American hegemony, and the sociological fabric of the period to about 1965. Chapter 4 describes the gradual disintegration of the Pax Americana. Chapter 5 examines the institutions and ideas of the new right as it emerged through the final stages of the American era.

Part Two examines the global economy of the 1980s, providing where necessary some of the historical antecedents. Chapter 6 begins with the silicon revolution and its relationship to the growth of Japan's industrial power. Chapter 7 considers the situation of labour, especially in the free trade zones of the NICs, during the heady period of offshore investment by Japanese and American companies. Chapter 8 focuses on the "globalization" and the technological changes in automobile production, using Canadian materials by way of illustration. Chapter 9 addresses the development of the European Community, and includes a section on the British new right experiment from 1979 to 1989. Chapter 10, which concludes the section, is concerned with the dilemmas of the countries that did not benefit from the restructuring but instead became immersed in a growing debt crisis, unable to extricate themselves from external pressures or internal chaos.

Part Three is about the problems that cannot be solved by market forces. It begins, in chapter 11, with an examination of the debates between North and South in United Nations forums, identifying another dimension of the new right agenda and the attempts by the poor nations to change it. Chapter 12 considers the environmental crisis and, more specifically, the ecological and human impacts of global agribusiness and industrialization on underdeveloped countries The final chapter summarizes the arguments, reconsiders the theories discussed, and then examines the prospects of the 1990s, which will see the new right agenda partially in place but with a new and unanticipated world order rapidly undermining its designs.

PART ONE

Free Markets

CHAPTER TWO

The Invisible Hand:
The Legacy of Smith,
Locke, and Their Critics

Market theories, originally articulated in Britain's imperial age, were adapted to new conditions as the United States took over world leadership in the immediate post-war era. The adaptation, known generally as Keynesianism, introduced a substantially enlarged role for national governments and international organizations. However, the ideology of free markets was not modified by the adaptations. Whatever its correspondence to economic and political reality, this ideology remained strong, and when America's fortunes declined, it was the Keynesian modifications that were blamed.

This chapter provides a background history of the classical theories of property, the state, and markets, and their development up to the end of the Second World War. The revived versions in the rhetoric of the new right are encountered in chapter 5 and more generally throughout the book.

THE ISSUES HAVE not changed in the three centuries since John Locke (1632–1704) and Adam Smith (1723–90) wrote their treatises on government, property, and markets. They were and still are about the respective rights of private persons and communities, or "the public." Does an individual have the right to own land? If so, what constitutes a right? Does the right to own land include the right to the labour of others? Does it include the right to sell land and to use it for private benefits that disinherit others? What are the responsibilities of governments vis-à-vis property? Should governments have the authority to curb property rights? What, ultimately, is the public interest? What, besides land, constitutes property?

John Locke provided a rationale for private property exempt from state control. He argued that when a man mixed his labour with natural materials to create something new, that new thing became his private property. "As much land as a man tills, plants, improves, cultivates, and can use the product of, so much is his property."[1] Locke assumed that there was plenty of land for everyone, and the right to an unlimited amount of private property, provided only that labour was joined to it, was viewed by him as a natural right. From this proposition he concluded that the only function of the political state was to preserve property rights. Adam Smith assumed the existence and legitimacy of private property rights, and pursued the logical next question: how could these rights be translated into general prosperity through market exchanges?

It matters that Smith was concerned primarily with a domestic system of markets.[2] The actors in his markets were local artisans, and the property they traded, like that understood by Locke, consisted primarily of goods they themselves manufactured or cultivated. But Smith's words were not so interpreted over the next two centuries: his theory became a disembodied, ahistorical version of the marketplace. The arguments were (1) that human beings by nature have a propensity to "truck, barter, and exchange"; (2) that in the process of exchanging, they develop a division of labour, so that a complementarity of capacities is created; (3) that each person goes into the exchange with a view to improving his material situation, and his transactions are entirely self-interested; (4) that the value of goods exchanged will be determined by the relative supplies and demands in the marketplace, provided there is no external (state) interference. This is so because each person seeks personal advantage, each can sell more or at higher prices if the demand exceeds the supply, and thus each will adjust his supplies in nature and quantity to the potential market demands. If the marketplace is not subjected to regulations on price, supply, and demand, there will be a tendency towards equilibrium as sellers and buyers anticipate supplies and demands and regulate their own activities accordingly. This behaviour is understood here as rational. With all actors behaving in such rational self-interest, all production and consumption should equal one another (restated later as Say's Law, 1803) because prices and wages will always respond to supply and demand conditions; and (5) that the net effect of this commercial market unhindered by state regulation will be constant growth in the nature and quantity of goods, increasing division of labour, and overall prosperity.

The metaphor of the invisible hand's replacing state regulations describes the theorized propellant of economic growth. The important moral message embedded in this theory is that people acting entirely in their self-interest are better able to produce the good society than governments purporting to act in the public interest. Smith put it this way: "It is not from the benevolence of the butcher, the brewer, or the baker, that we expect our dinner, but from their regard to their own interest. We address ourselves, not to their humanity but to their self-love, and never talk to them of our own necessities but of their advantages. Nobody but a beggar chooses to depend chiefly upon the benevolence of his fellow-citizens."[3]

Embedded in this theory are important assumptions about labour and property. Smith advanced the idea that labour was the source of value in commodities exchanged in the marketplace: "The value of any commodity to the person who possesses it, and who means not to use or consume it himself, but to exchange it for other commodities, is equal to the quantity of labour which it enables him to purchase or command. Labour, therefore, is the real measure of the exchangeable value of all commodities."[4] This view of value rests on the understanding that each person owns his labour and whatever his labour produces. For Smith the market, populated by local artisans, was not a place dominated by large, organized trading companies selling goods manufactured by a paid labour force. Nor was it a local manifestation of a global system. It did, however, involve the sale of goods manufactured by local wage labour, and labour had to be treated as a commodity on the market like other goods.

Smith noted that once land becomes private property, the landlord demands a share of the produce raised by the labourer.[5] In the absence of a worker's right to combine bargaining power, the landlord or master is in the stronger position; further, landlords and masters are generally better able to combine against rising wages. Smith argued that a minimum wage is actually inherent in the market for labour because labourers must be maintained and reproduced in the next generation. Beyond that, labour can bargain when labour demand exceeds supply, and this occurs when an economy is expanding. In the long term it is to the benefit of private property holders, landlords and masters alike, to maintain wages above subsistence level so that workers can work and reproduce workers, and thereby expand production in a flourishing economy. In such an economy masters will invest in labour-saving technology, and productivity will increase while the demand for labour decreases. But in these circumstances, employed labour will receive higher wages from the master in response to rising productivity and prices, and the division of labour will increase to include higher numbers developing new technologies. Over the long run, then, the market will constantly restructure labour, and with rising economic fortunes will provide each stratum with improved conditions.

In this version the state retains only one function: to protect property so as to ensure stability and security for the traders. To deal with the theory of the free market, then, we have to suppose that private property rights already exist and that a system of laws and political governance is in place to guarantee those rights.

In fact, private property rights have not always existed, and where they did (or do) exist they were not universally alike. In hunting and gathering societies anthropologists have noted a range of property rights, including the rights of craftsmen to a share of the catch made possible by their arrows, the rights of families to their own songs and dances, and the rights of chiefs to particular feast rituals and ceremonial garb. Historically, such societies normally inhabited general territories where neighbouring tribes were not welcome, and to the extent that neighbours accepted them, the claims could be understood as property rights held in common by members of the tribe or band.

Agricultural societies typically defined property rights in territory more precisely, and mixtures of communal and private rights emerged. Within the complex system of property designations that developed in Europe some lands remained common property, or commons. On these lands individual families, defined as members of a specific community, could graze cattle, raise geese, and sometimes farm. Such properties were strictly regulated by the community, just as fishing territories were regulated by native communities throughout much of the world. In both cases the produce from the commons was used directly by the producers for their subsistence. This remained the case in Europe until extensive markets for wool and beef were established, when the more powerful landlords evicted the tenant farmers from the common properties and replaced them with sheep and cattle destined for markets. These forces of change were underway even as Locke and Smith were writing, and it was precisely such forces that elicited defences of private property right from those most likely to benefit.

It is worth noting here that Barrington Moore, in his celebrated study of the origins of democracy and dictatorship, attributes to the English commons the preconditions for the emergence of democracy. In his view, "despite considerable variation, the main idea connected with these arrangements stands out very clearly: every member of the community should have access to enough resources to be able to perform obligations to the community carrying on a collective struggle for survival."[6] From this, he argues, the notion of a public or community interest emerged, and where this did not occur within feudalism, democracy did not emerge.

The growth of commodity markets was a gradual, though uneven, development throughout Europe from at least the fourteenth century.[7] European merchants were also engaged in extensive interregional (and subsequently international) trade from an early date, and the exploitation of resources far from European soil was commonplace in the fifteenth century. The labour market, complete with supply and demand fluctuations, likewise appears to have been well entrenched by the fourteenth century.[8] Fernand Braudel documents this, showing that regular marketplaces, hiring-fairs, and personnel services were in place throughout much of Europe in the late thirteenth and fourteenth centuries. The selling of labour was not peculiar to a fringe urban population: it was normal for farm populations to sell their labour to landlords, and even to travel long distances in search of wages to supplement their family's food supply. Unmarried persons frequently travelled in search of work, and unmarried women sought domestic wage work in villages and early towns and on estates. In Tudor England, by Braudel's account, as many as two-thirds of all households received part of their income in wages. Merchants and shops became a substantial part of the urban world during this period, well before industry was established beyond the artisanal level.

As towns became more populated, the number of goods sold increased. Agricultural produce became more of a commodity, since an urban population had to purchase its food. Peasants became entrepreneurs, selling surplus farm produce to merchants. In time, the commercial possibilities of land became attractive to urban merchants. They bought up real estate and began to develop commercial crops. The British gentry joined with merchants in developing the wool trade, gradually erasing the distinctions between the two classes. Wealthy peasant farmers (the yeomanry) also became commercially adept, and it was this group even more than the gentry that dispossessed tenant farmers of their rights to common lands for pastures and subsistence crops.[9] The commercialization of agriculture diluted the traditional rights and obligations of both lords and peasantry. Commercialized agriculture, the markets, and the transportation and communication systems that serviced them required a supply of labour on more than a seasonal or happenstance basis, and the labour market became as fixed a feature of the society as commodity markets.

The shift from rural to urban society, from landed relations of production to market relations, did not occur everywhere at the same time. In fact, a paradoxical consequence of these developments was a renewal of serfdom in Eastern Europe in the sixteenth century. Compulsory labour was imposed on the free peasantry in Poland by 1500, and continued throughout the region over the next three hundred years. Grain, wood, livestock, wine, and other goods were produced for distant markets. The markets and the merchants who mediated them operated on increasingly rationalistic calculations of profit and investment, but the landed nobility did not adapt or themselves become merchants; instead, they used the land and labour available to them as crude materials for sales to others. [10]

As private property rights expanded, political philosophy and economics became distinct branches of literature, both strongly supportive of private property and the marketplace. Jeremy Bentham (1748–1832) created a new basis for the theory, abandoning the natural rights thesis. Property, he said, "is nothing but a basis of expectation; the expectation of deriving certain advantages from a thing which we are said to possess, in consequence of the relation in which we stand towards it." [11] The law must protect property so that industry can develop, since no one would exert energy in enterprise toward industry if expectations of advantage could not be realized. Property rights, in his view, provide the greatest happiness to the greatest number: "If all property were equally divided, at fixed periods, the sure and certain consequence would be, that presently there would be no property to divide. All would shortly be destroyed. Those whom it was intended to favour, would not suffer less from the division than those at whose expense it was made. If the lot of the industrious was not better than the lot of the idle, there would be no longer any motives for industry." [12]

Bentham's argument became pivotal in subsequent theory because it provided the basic justification for inequality in property rights: industriousness. While John Stuart Mill (1806–73) did not entirely accept the Benthamist position, his defence of property on the grounds that it enhances liberty built up an additional defence of inequality. Mill was aware of the problem, and noted several times that while the institution of property rests ultimately on the right of persons to the fruits of their own labour, the question remains: how far can property rights be defended when they involve the labour and skill of others? Finally, however, he concluded that "the right of property includes then, the freedom of acquiring by contract. The right of each to what he has produced, implies a right to what has been produced by others, if obtained by their free consent; since the producers must either have given it from good will, or exchanged it for what they esteemed an equivalent, and to prevent them from doing so would be to infringe on their right of property in the product of their own industry."[13]

The defence of private property throughout the eighteenth and nineteenth centuries was not simply an academic exercise; it emerged in conjunction with the rapid expansion of markets. Land as the basis of wealth, and the landed agrarian society, passed into European history as new urban industrial classes emerged. Urban merchants and industrialists demanded economic freedom, and in England especially this freedom was perceived not only as a natural right but as the basis for carrying out the will of a god who favoured industriousness.[14] Freedom of economic action was the basis of market transactions, and not surprisingly the defences of property and of free economic transactions were simultaneously advanced.

The free market theory has very little to say about raw materials. With Smith, earlier physiocratic theories attributing value primarily to land passed into history. There is a subtheory about resource rents and what happens if the state captures them to excess, and there is a debate about the Malthusian proposition on population pressures and scarce resources, but nature itself is treated quite simply as a resource reservoir for industrial activity. Since industrialism and colonialism appeared to solve the Malthusian dilemma and technology appeared to be capable of enlarging the reservoir or inventing substitutes, it seemed that the economic pie could expand forever; nothing in nature limits human greed.

THE MOST CONTENTIOUS features of classical economic theory throughout the nineteenth century were its belief in the legitimacy of private property rights and its faith in the justice of labour's wage relationship to capital. Jean-Jacques Rousseau (1712–78) offered an early objection; he said that unlimited property rights could not be justified because they inevitably deprived most people of owning any property.[15] Much of this debate involves different versions of human evolution and the state of nature. As C.B. Macpherson points out[16], Rousseau introduced the notion that humans had developed many artificial wants far removed from any state of nature, and Locke's ahistorical version of natural rights was based on an unchanging human nature.

Rousseau declared: "The first person who, having fenced off a plot of ground, took it into his head to say *this is mine* and found people simple enough to believe him, was the true founder of civil society. What crimes, wars, murders, what miseries and horrors would the human race have been spared by someone who, uprooting the stakes or filling in the ditch, had shouted to his fellow-men: Beware of listening to this impostor; you are lost if you forget that the fruits of the earth belong to all and the earth to no one!"[17] Property rights do not consist of mere possession. Ultimately they rest in a community that recognizes their legitimacy and is prepared to enforce that recognition. Property rights are relations denoting power; they are not things, though they normally pertain to things. As relations of power, property rights are nothing more than a description of the social hierarchy existing in a society at any given time. There is nothing "natural" about them; they are socially constructed. If this is so, then the marketplace, where private property rights are exchanged, is only a social arrangement whereby power is negotiated.

Karl Marx (1818–83) took Rousseau's theories further. The particular forms of property that emerged with capitalism represented for him the exploitation of the many by the few. In the *Communist Manifesto* he chided the defenders of property:

We Communists have been reproached with the desire of abolishing the right of personally acquiring property as the fruit of a man's own labor, which property is alleged to be the ground work of all personal freedom, activity and independence.

Hard-won, self-acquired, self-earned property! Do you mean the property of the petty artisan and of the small peasant, a form of property that preceded the bourgeois form? There is no need to abolish that; the development of industry has to a great extent already destroyed it, and is still destroying it daily.

Or do you mean modern bourgeois private property?

But does wage-labor create any property for the laborer? Not a bit. It creates capital, i.e., that kind of property which exploits wage-labor, and which cannot increase except upon condition of getting a new supply of wage-labor for fresh exploitation. Property, in its present form, is based on the antagonism of capital and wage-labor.[18]

Capitalists (those with property rights) accumulate wealth by employing labour to produce goods valued in excess of wages and the costs of plant and raw materials. All wealth is attributable to the value added by labour. In addition, capital controls a market for both resources and goods, and establishes global exchange values. There are built-in contradictions in the capitalist system which lead to periodic crises and will ultimately lead to a breakdown of the system, but capital is none the less systematic and rational in its pursuit of profit.

For Marx and for his followers in the next century, the institutions of private property and market relations were understood as the rights of one class to the labour of others. Mill's assumption that the workers freely exchange their labour for wages is, from this perspective, naïve at best.

Later non-Marxist critics added new dimensions to the debate. Thorstein Veblen (1857–1929) drew attention to the modern corporation with its capacity for coralling financial as well as productive property, and its increasing ability to superimpose corporate interests over all others:

Ownership of natural resources – lands, forests, mineral deposits, water-power, harbor rights, franchises, etc. – rests not on a natural right of workmanship but on the ancient feudalistic ground of privilege and prescriptive tenure, vested interest, which runs back to the right of seizure by force and collusion. The owners of these natural resources own them not by virtue of their having produced or earned them, or on the workmanlike ground that they are making use of these useful things in productive work. These owners own these things because they own them. That is to say, title of ownership in these natural resources is traceable to an act of seizure, legalised by statute or confirmed by long undisturbed possession. [19]

Further criticism was advanced by R.H. Tawney (1880–1960), [20] who found modern corporate property rights indefensible. Like Marx, Veblen, and Rousseau, he recognized a distinction between the small properties of farmers who worked their own land and the vast claims of those who used the labour of others to accumulate wealth. In his opinion the only defence of property was its functional contribution to society; in the case of modern corporations, no positive contribution to creativity or social harmony could be detected.

In the twentieth century Morris Cohen[21] and later C.B. Macpherson[22] emphasized that property was a set of socially enforceable rights connecting persons to one another and in reference to things, and therefore property denoted a system of power between persons. Cohen found a limited property right to be defensible, arguing that the state was entitled to impose limits on behalf of the public interest. This defence brings us back to the theory of the free hand of the marketplace and its relationship to the state; this is the realm of political as well as economic theory.

IT TOOK FOUR centuries for the more than five hundred separate political units of Europe to become twenty or so that existed at the beginning of the twentieth century. According to Charles Tilly, virtually all of the many state-building attempts that failed (far more than succeeded) involved military defeat.[23]

If the boundaries of European states were determined by force rather than by cultural homogeneity, there is no reason to suppose that early states had ethnic integrity. Linguistic differences roughly coincided with the boundaries of new states, but this was never a perfect relationship. Where there were identifiable minority cultures, the solution was either absorption or exclusion, and both occurred throughout the nation-building process. The phenomenon of statelessness became commonplace in Europe by the eighteenth century.[24] Through the processes of absorption and exclusion, and through the development of common institutions (including the state itself as a separate political system), the other side of that phenomenon was created: the emergence of citizens. Citizens, unlike the stateless, had specific locations, rights, and obligations.

The European states were dominated by one or a few cities, but it was the conjoining of agricultural estates with market and financial centres that characterized the nation-state. National boundaries were drawn (or fought over) to maximize the potential of commercial agriculture for those groups able and eager to control production and markets. Markets, both local and distant, were well entrenched as the process of nation-building took place.

Nations were market organizations, but they were also political states. The state was vital to the growth of the markets, and thus to the accumulation opportunities of those who were most active in them. The state's monopoly on military force ensured that the whole territory was protected from external threat, and that competing internal groups were unable to exert force against one another. The state's other functions included the active development of conditions favourable to the expansion of commercial activity beyond the territory, the development of rules for operation inside the territory, and the creation of infrastructure, labour policies, and resource procurement conditions suitable for commodity production. These conditions, applied to or usable by all competing interest groups, were vital to the maintenance of nation-states.

Absolutist principles of political governance were contrary to the impersonal, market-oriented society. By the seventeenth century this was evident in Britain, where the monarchy was identified as an impediment to the independent commercial activities of gentry and bourgeoisie. Since the monarch also failed to protect the peasantry, the Puritan Revolution was an outcome that arose not so much from class war as from a straightforward and widespread disenchantment with a particular form of political rule.

The British Revolution of 1688, the much more violent French Revolution a century later, and the American War of Independence (for which the Declaration was signed just as Adam Smith was publishing *The Wealth of Nations*) were landmarks in the evolution of property laws and of political rights within national units. The early establishment of a Parliament in Britain is important not because it meant democratization – clearly it did not, since the franchise was restricted to those with property, and Parliament was inhabited by the landed aristocracy until well into the nineteenth century – but because an institution and its laws took precedence over individuals and groups. Such a concept was entirely consistent with a market society, where goods are sold on an impersonal basis through the medium of impersonal coinage, and where supplies and transportation are negotiated by contract rather than kinship principles, and where the state is an impersonal government rather than an individual.

Political theories propounded between the sixteenth and twentieth centuries refined the concepts of law, political rights, civil rights, and property. They interpreted government as the creature of a contract between individual citizens. The contract defined the rights of property and the limitations of the state in relation to property. Locke's 1748 thesis laid much of the groundwork for subsequent examination. Men had a "natural right" to property, property rights took precedence over civil law, and the purpose of government was the preservation of that right.[25] The state was enjoined to be "above" particularistic interests, to govern in the public or national interest but without infringing on property rights, and to leave the market free to operate with its own supply and demand equations.

The arguments of the eighteenth century remained tied to national markets. By the middle of the nineteenth century national markets were in place, and theorists turned their attention to international markets. Their theories were extensions of earlier ones, with Smith's conceptual framework now removed from its original context and turned into a set of propositions stated as universal truths. Where Smith eulogized the division of labour at a local level, the emerging science of economics developed the law of comparative advantage or the division of labour in an international economy. Investors in each nation would determine what their comparative advantage might be in the market, whether to trade cotton or gin in return for whatever might be sold by investors elsewhere, calculating the advantages one nation might have over another in production of each good. Over time, each nation should find its best combination of market goods, and a roughly balanced exchange would occur. The market would be self-correcting. Wages would tend to increase with sales, thereby making the same goods from a lower-wage area more attractive in relative terms; the trade would move to the more attractive seller; wages would then decline in the first region because the goods would not sell, and that region would then gradually build up new sales with its lower-cost labour. And so on, with the system always re-creating the balance.

This theory of international trade had much the same function at a global level that Smith's theory had at the national level: it provided a justification for the elimination of trade barriers for those most able to benefit from it. Not surprisingly, the theory was advanced most strongly in Britain as British imperialism and merchant trade became dominant on the world stage.

Theory notwithstanding, governments were always involved in economic activity. Merchant companies, engaged in Asian trade and later in North American trade, were chartered by European monarchs. In return they were obliged to pay for their charters through taxes or, more commonly, through levies imposed whenever the state ran into difficulties or wars while protecting their interests. Domestic merchant activities were supported or undermined by states through the granting of monopolies, the opening of new market possibilities, the provision of grants for the setting up of factories, or the imposition of rules pertaining to labour and land. Further, the state was necessarily involved in providing the infrastructure of roads, railways, and eventually public schools that was essential for the expansion of economic enterprise. On empirical grounds, the theories were disjunctive with reality.

On ideological grounds, however, they were most significant, because they absolved investors of social responsibility and reined in the state so that it could not impose unwanted responsibilities. Investors were free to use labour, tap resources, sell commodities, lend money, and buy properties wherever they wished, irrespective of social consequences. The state, contrary to the theories, was then obliged to become more than the protector of properties. It was forced to take on the social functions never accepted by the bourgeoisie and no longer performed by an aristocracy: the protection of labour and community.

The theories of free markets and social contracts assumed a single bounded territory governed by one political system. In nineteenth-century Europe this was an appropriate assumption. Imperialists annexed nearby territories or created colonies rather than establishing new nations elsewhere. England controlled the peripheral regions of Scotland, Ireland, and Wales, thereby obtaining wool, coal, and labour; it obtained other raw materials from other colonies. It was entirely to the advantage of Britain to pronounce on the superiority of free trade with the colonies, since this allowed British manufactured products to enter the markets of its weaker trading partners without barriers. Property rights in Britain were protected from the state as well as by it, but the British state, like other European nations, was fully engaged in exploiting resources elsewhere. In Hannah Arendt's view the (European) state became "a tremendous business concern."[26]

Karl Polanyi, examining the history of markets in the mid-twentieth century, argued that the entire theory of free markets and the natural human tendency to truck, barter, and exchange was a function of the development of markets themselves: that is, it was not that humans had any such natural tendency, but rather that a market had emerged, which gave rise to the rationales for its existence.[27] Further, he argued, these markets were inextricably tied to a particular kind of political power. Far from actually involving a laissez-faire state, European market societies depended absolutely on the growth of strong interventionist states. In particular, states such as nineteenth-century Britain intervened to create and sustain labour supplies for capital.

Karl Marx and Friedrich Engels also viewed the state as the instrument of capital. Marx was the more ambiguous of the two. He noted the contradiction between universal suffrage and private property, and pointed out that the political realm provided an arena for the struggle against private property rights.[28] Elsewhere, however, he treated the state as nothing more than the executive for managing the long-term interests of the bourgeoisie.[29] It is that sentiment, rather than the more difficult argument on universal suffrage, that is recalled in many contemporary neo-Marxist analyses. Democracy and capitalism in Marxist analysis as in libertarian theories are ultimately incompatible, but are seen to be temporarily conjoined during a phase in which labour passivity could be facilitated and mass production and consumption advanced by the appearance of political democracy. As ideology, democracy has made the capitalist state appear to be neutral and above class interests. As practice, democracy is a trade-off between the classes: workers have accepted partial political answers to their demands along with an acceptable standard of living, and in return they have not attempted to displace capitalism. The roots of this argument are found in Engels: "In order that these antagonisms, classes with conflicting economic interests, shall not consume themselves and society in a fruitless struggle, a power, apparently standing above society, has become necessary to moderate the conflict and keep it within the bounds of 'order'; and this power, arisen out of society, but placing itself above it and increasingly alienating itself from it, is the state ... the modern representative state is the instrument for exploiting wage labor by capital."[30]

While the critics were less baffled than the classical theorists by the continuing expansion of the state's role in economic affairs, the Engels version of an instrumental alliance cloaked by the pretence of neutrality had its own defect. Throughout the following century the state played double agent, simultaneously advancing the interests of capital and protecting labour from extreme exploitation. To adopt Engels's approach, the critic was obliged to do precisely what classical theorists did: reduce all non-economic phenomena to the apparent material interests of capital. Rational capital, it was imagined, manipulated the state in such a way that it would always advance the long-term interests of the bourgeoisie even as, in the short term or for the sake of appearances, it gave a few benefits to labour. Much of the activity of real states in real societies was thus either ignored or relegated to economic motivations.

Missing is the social community that contains both markets and states. For an obvious example of the importance of that community and the moral nexus of its operation, one might consider the lingering notion of *noblesse oblige* that still affected the aristocracy in the parliaments of industrial nineteenth-century Britain. That class retained a notion of its duties towards the rest of British society that influenced its legislation on working hours, the rights of workers to a fair wage, the use of child labour, and, finally, the extension of the franchise. The expanding institution of the state reflected both its basis in private property and its role as a custodian of something more than property, something that, in many ways, it created: the public interest. Legislation, the justification for legislation, the creation of public schools and public transportation – these nurtured the public interest, and, with that, a dimension of being "above particularistic interests" that was no longer (if it ever had been) just a masking of the instrumental interests of a dominant class.

THE ASSUMPTION in both the Smithian and the Marxist literature that labour is the source of all value is also problematic. Human beings' view of themselves as masters of the earth, made in the image of gods, with dominion over nature, has an ancient history and cannot be attributed solely to market theories. In the past, powerful taboos accompanied this hubris. To take on the aspects of gods was to incur their wrath and to court disaster. Yet attitudes towards the gods themselves were ambivalent. In Greek mythology the gods were exposed as lascivious and self-seeking. Judaeo-Christian mythology has fashioned God in man's image as vengeful and intolerant. The themes of Eden play incessantly through time: human folly brings on the wrath of a god, expressed as the loss of innocence through knowledge: carefree access to the means of survival is lost while the technical capacity to create subsistence without nature's intervention is gained. The myth of the Ark recurs again and again, dramatizing man's control over animals, his ability to save them from the wrath of the gods, remaining strong in the face of nature's force if not actively conquering it.

The myths are ancient, but the means of conquering the earth are recent. As roaming hunters or gatherers, humans could inflict only limited damage on their world. Not until we were concentrated in large numbers with the capacity to produce more food than we needed and to engage in market transactions did the idea of dominating nature become an obsession. Transportation and communication infrastructures were essential to our use of nature as a commodity beyond simple subsistence.

Paradoxically, it was the liberation of human minds that made the conquest of nature both possible and acceptable. The secular universities established by the fourteenth century gave birth to modern science when they encouraged free inquiry. Humanity's notion of the universe and of our place in it took on a different aspect. Nature, which had been regarded as a context for humans and other forms of life, and in most cultures also as a deity or a manifestation of a deity, became an object to be studied, and very quickly an object that could be manipulated and controlled. Scientific inquiry led to an expansion of survival options by providing the knowledge necessary for the production surpluses of food sufficient to maintain urban populations.

The theories of social contract, of the invisible hand of the market, of humanity's inalienable right to pursue happiness, theories that ultimately justified private and national greed, grew in tandem with the notion that humans had the right, even the unique and holy mission, to bring nature under control. A society living on limited resources necessarily constructs a moral reality that recognizes the finite range of behaviour appropriate to survival.[31] But moral limitations on greed in an ever-expanding world have a declining effect on individual aspirations. Moreover, if it can be demonstrated that individual greed results in an expansion of options, little seems to be gained by social limitation. Thus, as European society secularized knowledge it also secularized the moral order, infusing it with the market analogy. Demystified, God could no longer impose strictures against greed. Indeed, a separate, secular body of social knowledge became established which explicitly justified individualism in pursuit of profit – the science of economics.

By the seventeenth century, with markets becoming core systems of national societies, the "commoditization" of crops, of animals, of textiles and household goods, of metals from the ground and fish from the sea, was a general process. The fear of the tree of knowledge was now turned into a craving for its fruits, as Ludwig Feuerbach observed approvingly in the mid-nineteenth century: "Natural science has therefore no other goal than to more firmly establish and extend the power and domination of men over nature. But the domination of nature rests solely on art and knowledge."[32]

This and other affirmations of the ideas promoted by Francis Bacon rest on such elegantly phrased arguments as this: "Only let the human race recover that right over nature which belongs to it by divine bequest, and let power be given it; the exercise thereof will be governed by sound reason and true religion."[33] William Leiss points out the subtle shift towards secularization in Bacon's writing, where mastery of science (eating the fruits of the tree of knowledge) becomes the means of human advancement, while the religious mythology Bacon draws on to substantiate this argument is concerned not with knowledge but with morality.[34]

The argument advanced by Bacon and expanded throughout the next three centuries is an amalgam of Christian teachings on original sin and redemption, Hobbesian views of human nature, and economic views of rational free market economic behaviour. Humans are by nature savage, their lives in nature short and brutish; yet they are capable of learning, and through their mastery of the secrets of nature they will learn to live in peace with one another in universal prosperity. In Leiss's view there was a gradual shift from nature as the focal point of this undertaking to science and technology; the latter eventually came to be seen as the source of marvels and conquest, while the former became the passive object of the enterprise.[35] Werner Heisenberg contemplated the transformation of inquiry into nature since Aristotle: "One was not so much interested in nature as it is; one rather asked what one could do with it. Therefore, natural science turned into technical science; every advancement of knowledge was connected with the question as to what practical use could be derived from it."[36]

The virtues of science perceived by its admirers include its sceptical, relativistic, pragmatic mind-set: it would free the minds of humans and civilize them. But one must distinguish between these characteristics of the scientific enterprise and the objectives towards which scientific inquiry is directed. Science itself promotes scepticism, but the technologies developed by science appear to encourage a new kind of faith and an appetite for material things that has not freed our minds at all. By the nineteenth century the proclaimed virtues of science had expanded to include the elimination of classes and national animosities. Yet the history of a world guided by science and the free market of "rational" economic humans has revealed no inclination whatever to eliminate such conflicts. The gulf between rich and poor within nations and between rich and poor nations has grown in direct proportion to the growth of science, technology, and the mastery of nature. And while humans have pursued their goals in free markets, the commoditization of nature has created a condition where humans risk their very survival in enacting so-called rational behaviours.

Marx was sensitive to the commoditization of nature, to the insatiable desires of humans in marketplaces designed for endless consumption. None the less, he offered the labour theory of value, a theory that attributes all value to the exertions of human beings. Nature's bounty was taken for granted. By the mid-nineteenth century a market was already well established for industrial products, a bourgeoisie was firmly in place, the university had dislodged the monastery, and the industrial mode of production as well as capitalist control of it were all features of the social world. Not surprisingly, Marx conceived of science as his contemporaries did: as a mode of actively intervening in natural processes for the purpose of changing the human condition. For him the world was a machine set in motion by laws of history, ultimately predictable, and subject to manipulation.

What is the mode of production if not a mode of thinking about the natural world? What is the industrial mode of production if not a mode of thinking that justifies and then provides the means for intervening in that world? To call this the capitalist mode of production is to add a dimension of power: it is the industrial mode of production under the direction and control of a particular group. Marx did not question whether human beings should control nature; he assumed that they should. His concern was with the property rights, not the propriety, of industrial modes of production. As it turns out, the same industrial mode of production under the control of a state bureaucracy is but a variation on a theme; eliminating a class that has formal property rights does not eliminate the central dilemma, and the social relations of production turn out to be similar whether the surplus is destined for private profit or public investment.

As ideologies, as ways of organizing reality and dealing in an evaluative way with its contradictions, capitalism and socialism have shared a mental universe in which humanity is divorced from nature and nature is treated as something to be consumed or transformed in production. This outcome warns us that although the free enterprise ethic is not the single cause of our disdain for nature, the larger part of the world is governed by that ethic, and its origins lie in the market society. It is here, in market relations, that we confront the issue most directly.

What transpired is not the "fault" of science itself: there is no reason for science, a method of inquiry which has greater self-correcting mechanisms embedded in it than any other method, to produce the environmental crisis we face in the twentieth century.[37] Scientific inquiry could be directed at any number of subjects and towards the development of a range of subsistence goods very different from those produced by contemporary corporations. And science today does in fact produce both the causes of pollution and the critique of those production methods. The particular ends to which science has been put have more to do with capital than with science: the research and development of technical means of producing substantive results is a costly endeavour.

Science is a time-consuming activity. It engages the passions while it demands a scepticism of mind that inhibits dogmatic adherence to ideologies other than science itself; it cannot be pursued intermittently; and it rarely attracts practitioners whose interest is in domination of people. It also has a tendency to be very narrow: the majority of scientific undertakings involve very specific questions about a limited range of problems, and scientific work rarely poses for the practitioner value-issues, context-meanings, or political implications. Someone engaged wholly in science cannot be simultaneously engaged in pursuing capital (one of many reasons for regarding as naïve the "new right" demand that everything be measured by its entrepreneurial component).

The consequence of this organization is that technology is not simply a neutral outcome of a value-free science; it is frequently a selected outcome by dominant groups with particular values. Whether by conscious intent or through the relatively impersonal working of industrial systems, science and technology have become means of conquering not merely nature (indeed, only incidentally nature) but humanity. Nature becomes a series of resources – food, coal, oil, hydroelectric-power, minerals, wood – to be processed through industrial production organizations. What is not commoditized – the air, the oceans – becomes waste or a context for production.

Not only do economic theories justify this use of nature, they provide quantifiable measures of its contributions to the affluent lifestyles of humankind. We learn that when a resource becomes scarce, its price will increase; as its price increases, its extraction rate will decline, and thus, magically, the hand of the market will save nature – when it is nearly exhausted. As well, when resources become scarce, technology will come to the rescue: for everything we use there will eventually be a substitute. Nothing in classical economic theory suggests that nature is anything other than a series of resources. That trees are essential for oxygen, for example, is irrelevant to their economic value in the marketplace. That trees are related to wildlife and fisheries is relevant only when wildlife and fish are equally recognized as potential commodities.

Nature is not evenly distributed across the earth. Fuels, minerals, forests, fish, agricultural lands, and fresh water, as they became resources for industry, incited envy in those who wanted but did not have easy access to them; the boundaries of the nation-state were insufficient to contain the economic interests of the dominant classes and organizations engaged in industry. Conquest of other nations or economic penetration of their territories was an inevitable outcome of the commoditization of nature. The means of conquest became increasingly tied to further commoditization. Finally, the development of mass production techniques, profitable when combined with mass consumption societies, is the outcome. Only through the constant exploitation of nature, and through a market valuation system that treats its products as copious and therefore cheap, were these techniques and these societies possible.

HISTORY IS A GAME of leapfrog. One country becomes dominant by developing a particular technological infrastructure. Its dominance may last a long time if that technology remains the most effective and efficient means of producing necessities. Another technology is eventually developed – sometimes within the same country – but the dominant power has so much invested in its earlier infrastructure that it cannot disengage rapidly. Its social and political organization and its culture are integrated into that first technological condition. It cannot adapt, and it is usually slow even to recognize the need to adapt. There are powerful groups within its borders who strongly resist change, and its people, so used to being the dominant power, cannot restructure their society or develop alternatives as fast as others who were never as strongly tied to the first technology.

Biology and anthropology have posited zigzag theories of evolution. Marshall Sahlins and E.R. Service proposed, for example, a "leapfrog law" of evolution: "The more specialized and adapted a form in a given evolutionary stage, the smaller its potential for passing to the next stage."[38] In their view, a given social organization does not give rise to a new form, either through its internal contradictions or through progress and reform. It is simply by-passed by other forms at that stage where it is less able to meet some external requirements, or to feed its members, or to maintain itself on the resources it is organized to exploit. One might examine Egypt, Rome, Spain, or Britain in the light of the leapfrog law. Spain never got over its dependence on new world gold; like a high-school hero, it remained in a bygone era.

In the mid-nineteenth century Britain was far ahead of other countries as a result of her early adaptation to steam-powered industrial development and trade. At the end of the century, drawing on the resources of empires and manufacturing commodities through the technologies of the industrial revolution, Western Europe as a whole accounted for about 90 per cent of world industrial production.[39] But the social fabric that couched this high productivity was frail. Furthermore, it had spawned impossible conflicts between the separate nation-states, each with imperial extensions. There seemed to be nowhere to go, no new way of expanding except by eliminating one another. And while they contemplated a return to the means by which they were created, the United States had overtaken them all. A second industrial revolution spurred its growth as its industries established mass production lines. Britain remained strong in textiles but fell far behind in steel, automobiles, electricity, chemicals, and the new consumer goods that were based on those technologies. Growth rates for the period from 1870–1913 are estimated at nearly 5 per cent for the United States, 4 per cent for Germany, and just over 2 per cent for Britain.[40] The first European war of the twentieth century did not resolve the conflicts of imperial powers or arrest the decline in economic power.

The free market ideology waned with the decline of the Pax Britannica. It no longer served the political agenda of the dominant European classes; for them, protected markets and state interventions were essential for survival. Nor did it serve the bourgeoisie of America in the early twentieth century, for while the United States was showing greater growth rates than European states, it did not yet have a hegemonic role in world affairs. It could not control world trade, and its interests were best served through highly protectionist arrangements to prevent European manufactured goods from competing on domestic markets.

Mass production technologies and organization altered the dynamics of European and North American societies. Such production could result in profits only if there were masses of consumers. Those potential consumers were workers. They would have to receive wages sufficient to purchase what they produced. Left to the mechanisms of the marketplace, wages did not miraculously rise to meet the occasion. By the 1930s, the gap between purchasing power and productive capacities had contributed to a widespread depression in the industrial countries. There were also gaps between the restructuring of industry around the new technologies and labour force skills and distribution. The old order of laissez-faire policies broke down: every country, including Britain and the United States, imposed protective barriers around its manufacturing and agricultural industries. The international trading market became a tangle of barriers as European nations attempted to destroy one another in the second war of the century.

Both the international system and the domestic regulation of mass production industries were dramatically restructured after the war. The economic theories that had prospered with Britain's prosperity and declined with its decline were shelved during the Great Depression of the 1930s. The market economy did not reach equilibrium as orthodox economists believed it would; indeed, the assumption that rational behaviour characterized investment and consumer decisions, depending as it did on the reasonable predictability of outcomes, had become untenable. Between Michal Kalecki and John Maynard Keynes, the basic arguments on wages, marginal productivity, and prices were refuted.[41] By 1945 governments in the industrial countries were prepared to introduce a series of reforms to regulate domestic economies in at least the general direction advocated by the new school of economics.

Keynes and Kalecki argued that wage rates were primary determinants of prices. Workers without wages or with subsistence wages could not purchase goods above their level of disposable income, so that an unemployed labour force necessarily caused a drop in prices or a crisis of overproduction and underconsumption. Governments could interrupt the process of declining prices by injecting purchasing power into the economy through public works, minimum wage laws, welfare provisions, and unemployment insurance schemes. These would increase effective demand, which in turn would stimulate supply and revive flagging economies.

Smith's argument, and in particular the version known as Say's Law, had it that the volume of savings determines the rate of investment. Keynes argued that savings levels varied with income levels and with uncertainty about future income levels. Again, the solution for savings that were not applied to investments in productive capacity and savings that were not used in the consumption of goods involved government intervention.

The policy outcomes of these and further arguments included a vastly expanded state role whereby the state was expected to stimulate demand through monetary policy, active labour market supports, public works expenditures, and taxation. At another and more psychological level, the Keynesian revolution included a considerably changed understanding of human nature and social responsibilities. The Smithian invisible hand had been expected to lead to the optimum social welfare outcome not because of a preconceived moral theory but because the sum of private interests would achieve mutually beneficial results. Now the invisible hand needed guidance because economic activity turned out to be grounded in a moral universe, and because the condition of the social fabric reduced the rationality of the actors. Investors especially turned out to have a distinct tendency to withdraw capital from circulation when the investment climate was undertain.

These outcomes were evident in the United States as well as in other industrial countries; indeed, the New Deal had been the initial experiment. That notwithstanding, over the post-war era the welfare state never became as entrenched in the United States as it did in Europe, Australia, New Zealand, and Canada. This, like the policies of state ownership and nationalization elsewhere, was in part an effect of the vast differences in affluence and productivity between the United States and other countries in the immediate post-war period. It was also linked to the American fixation on free enterprise and property rights.

THE ARGUMENT, then, is this: the free market theory, as Polanyi observed, is a function of a particular social development rather than an accurate depiction of that society or any other. Economic rationality is a response to specific social relations of production and consumption within market societies of a certain kind, rather than a "normal" and universal human characteristic. The European market society developed in tandem with a particular attitude towards nature and human intervention in the natural world. It gave rise to a view of human nature which its theorists then embedded in theories they or their descendants believed to be universally applicable.

Their theories had a political agenda: to create political units suitable for the advancement of a class of merchants and industrialists on a national and later an international scale. Their agenda was achieved, but that did not mean that the political units were like the states imagined in the theories; real states had strategic functions in the development of the "free market" societies, even if those functions were different from those against which the rising bourgeoisie originally struggled. Markets are social institutions that develop in particular ways according to the social context of their time; they change the social context and are changed by it. This process was manifest in the rise and fall of the doctrine of laissez-faire.

CHAPTER THREE

Pax Americana, 1945–1965

As the undisputed victor of the European wars, the United States emerged with excessive productive capacity and an appetite for world reform. Historians may debate far into the future which of these exerted the greater influence on its foreign policy.

American production had increased by 50 per cent between 1939 and 1945,[1] and its companies sought market outlets. The United States had nothing to fear from its diminished allies if it opened its own borders to imports, and it had much to gain by insisting that other countries open theirs. It did this not merely as a means of advancing its economic fortunes, however. For the United States this was a spiritual crusade. The objective was to refashion a world in its self-image, a world of peaceful trading nations under American leadership. Thus was ushered in the second era of laissez-faire, now rephrased as free enterprise, free trade, and the free world.

Even so, the rhetoric and the reality were disjunctive. In Europe and Japan private monopolies capable of re-establishing enormous mass production steel-age industries had been crushed. Only the United States had such companies in place. Elsewhere, the only institutional means of re-creating competitive capacities was the state. State organizations and nationalized industries were established outside the United States by both conservative and labour or social democratic governments throughout the period from the 1940s to the 1960s.

In Europe, as in Taiwan and Japan, American foreign aid, troop locations, military procurement policies, oil controls, and direct investment established the terms of reconstruction. Though the American government itself did not own or manage state properties, it was heavily engaged in facilitating these elsewhere. The reasons for this lay in the understanding that conquered nations continued to be enemies if they were not reconstructed (Germany had proved the case), and American products would not find consumers if the American government failed to re-create an international trading system. As the cold war became embedded in American policies, America needed strong allies. The growth of the welfare state was also disjunctive with the theory of free enterprise and free markets. Keynesian reforms were put in place in the United States, albeit to a lesser degree than elsewhere. Government had become a guardian of the public interest, and the definition of that interest continued to expand throughout the post-war period.

The new era had six prominent institutional features: a system of international agencies, agreements, and alliances; an arrangement between the American government and private oil companies that ensured fuel supplies to allies; the global expansion of private corporations; a shift in international investment patterns from government loans and portfolio financing to private direct investment; a crusade against communism and a growth in military expenditures and alliances to sustain it; and reconstituted national governments based on a variant of Keynesian economic ideas. The era was brief – about a quarter of a century following 1945 – but in that short time was born a global economy.

In this chapter I will discuss the international institutions of the post-war period, and the ways in which European, Japanese, Taiwanese, and American governments and companies managed their respective economies within the framework of the post-war international order.

AT THE INTERNATIONAL level, the United States offered vital benefits to European nations in return for their allegiance to its hegemonic leadership. These included a stable international monetary system, liberalized trade, and access to cheap oil; all were proclaimed at the time, and in the ensuing two decades, to be manifestations of the virtues of free enterprise, and all required the development of international regulations and co-operation between states for which the existing theories of the market were inadequate underpinnings.

The Bretton Woods Agreement of 1944 established the International Monetary Fund (IMF) and the International Bank for Reconstruction and Development (IBRD), better known as the World Bank. It also recognized the American dollar as the central currency, though gold was maintained as the official standard for international transactions. It set out the framework of rules and regulations for the central banks of national units and their governments.

The IMF was established as a reserve bank to extend short-term credit for the development of infrastructure and technology to increase productive capacity. Countries borrowing from the fund were required to meet numerous conditions for the use of credit and for repayment. Directors of the fund (in the language of the agreements and civil discourse) worked with the governments of indebted countries to help them reduce their debt or pay it off without pushing themselves into a major depression. The overt objective was to retain flexibility and stability in the international trading arena. After the 1960s the IMF began to exert pressure on the creditor countries to revalue their currencies, lower tariff barriers, reduce export subsidies, increase foreign aid, and otherwise remove some of the burden of flexibility and stability from the debtor countries.

The World Bank was intended to provide long-term loans to countries in much the same way as private banks provided loans (at interest) to individuals. It was owned by the member countries, whose voting rights were proportional to their shareholdings. The United States held approximately two-fifths of the shares in the 1940s. No dividends or interest were paid to members, and members guaranteed World Bank debts so that the bank could obtain favourable borrowing terms in world financial markets. Recipient countries paid interest at commercial, but favourable, rates.

The World Bank co-ordinated the financial arrangements of other banks and funding agencies, generally providing the original appraisals of proposed projects. It lent money under stringent conditions for projects it approved to countries that satisfied the lenders that they were capable of eventually repaying the loans. Its component parts expanded in the next two decades to include the International Finance Corporation (IFC) and the International Development Association (IDA). The IFC component was created in 1956 to provide loans to private corporations, and the IDA, established in 1960, was intended to provide special development funds for Third World countries.

Keynes, the intellectual architect of much of this system, recognized that it had political implications, and that if the post-war institutions imposed constraints on the uses of borrowed funds, they would necessarily infringe on the sovereignty of nations. But in his view this was both inevitable and not wholly undesirable, and in line with the need for all countries to develop "a greater readiness to accept super-national arrangements." The IMF might become "the pivot of the future economic government of the world."[2] A global economic government implied (and this did not escape Keynes) an international police force with the "machinery for enforcing a financial blockade." If such a system was to remain independent of national politics and the aspirations of groups within the dominant countries, it would have to be established in such a way that the dominant countries could never veto or exert unilateral influence over the operations. Such a possibility may have been envisioned by Keynes, but the reality never achieved that arm's-length purity.

The structure of the IMF and the World Bank favoured the industrial nations, which between them held some 80 per cent of the voting power, and the voting mechanisms especially favoured the United States, which held 30 per cent of the votes in the early years.

The General Agreement on Tariffs and Trade (GATT) was signed in 1947 by twenty-three nations (their number has since expanded). The GATT established some basic rules for international trade. The long-term objective was to reduce import barriers (including but not restricted to tariffs) and generally to liberalize trade. Among the means of liberalizing trade were provisions for non-discrimination. This meant that special favours previously granted to selected or "most favoured" trading partners would be extended impartially to all trading partners. Multilateralism, another GATT formula, meant that all signatories would accept a certain loss of sovereignty in favour of global regulation of trade and finance.

Industrialized countries enjoyed much success over the next two decades as tariffs declined steadily from an average 20 per cent in the late 1940s. None the less, GATT never achieved the status its architects had envisioned. It was intended that an international trade organization, charged with the responsibility of enforcing GATT rulings, would be established. The United States was frightened off, and the Senate refused to ratify the treaty setting up the organization in 1950. The GATT operated on the basis of social and (ineffective) economic sanctions, voluntary obedience, and considerable ambiguity. This was not problematic for the industrial countries as long as the post-war boom lasted.

The areas covered by liberalized trade agreements were selective. Agriculture was virtually omitted. Numerous areas in processed products and small manufactures were scarcely affected. These omissions had the greatest impact on the underdeveloped countries; the lack of an effective sanctioning body able to act impartially when the interests of the underdeveloped countries were pitted against those of the industrial countries was a serious shortcoming.

The United Nations, established under the terms of the peace treaties, inherited the ideas that had been promoted but never advanced in the League of Nations after the First World War. Nominally, the World Bank and its component parts, together with the IMF, were linked and subordinate to the United Nations. In fact, the financial agencies always had considerable independence and privileges. The United Nations itself gave birth to numerous subsidiary bodies, including the Food and Agriculture Organization (FAO), the World Health Organization (WHO), the United Nations Educational, Scientific, and Cultural Organization (UNESCO), the United Nations Industrial Development Organization (UNIDO), and the United Nations Development Program (UNDP). From time to time the United Nations sponsored meetings for the purpose of resolving international issues, including numerous and prolonged conferences on the law of the sea (UNCLOS) and on trade and development (UNCTAD). The United Nations also maintained a peacekeeping military force to be deployed only with the weighted voting agreement of participant nations. The number of participants in UN deliberations increased steadily over the post-war period as colonial territories gained formal independence.

An explicit aim of the UN Charter was that all countries would enjoy full employment; the trading system was subject to countries' creating policies consistent with that aim. In the two expansionist decades after the war the aim was achieved only in the industrial countries. Much of the underdeveloped world could not even measure unemployment, since most nations were still embedded in feudal land relations or in transitional phases with masses of hungry and impoverished city-dwellers.

Other organizations were formed. The Organisation for Economic Co-operation and Development (OECD) was established in 1961 by the industrialized nations to monitor their internal relations and trade. This was an expansion of the Organisation for European Economic Co-operation established in 1948.[3] The relatively rich member countries also shared in military alliances in varying degrees and combinations, and the élite of the two dozen nations formed "executive committees". Their meetings came to be known as the "summits."

With the exceptions of the specifically military alliances and the peacekeeping forces of the United Nations, the post-war institutions were not designed for imposing order by force. Agreements reached in international forums were negotiated. Even so, this framework for the post-war order was powerful. Countries accepted conditions of membership in the international community, and the costs of non-compliance were high. To fail to observe the conditions could result in the withdrawal of international funds and in trade and other sanctions that could effectively strangle the economic life of a country. Beyond the institutions there was always the American military capacity and the military alliances, particularly the North Atlantic Treaty Organization (NATO) and the North American Air Defence (NORAD), to enforce compliance.

Within this framework of international agreements and institutions, American capital moved abroad in numerous forms, including unconditional grants and tied or conditional foreign aid for the reconstruction of war-torn economies, loans made through the World Bank and the IMF or other agencies and banks, and private investment. Two-thirds of the major multinationals in the mid-1960s were American corporations with production units in Canada and Europe and extraction units in the rest of the world. The remainder were mainly European corporations whose growth had been made possible by the post-war reconstruction regulations. The world's economy was built around these organizations throughout the era of the Pax Americana, just as it was built around the British merchant houses in the era of the Pax Britannica.

The non-industrial countries were not included in the original agreements; in 1945 most were scarcely included in the world trading arena. Japan was also excluded, though it became a member of GATT in the mid-1950s.

FREE MARKETS AND the freedom of capital to locate outside its national borders were blocked by centrally managed economies of Eastern Europe. In much of this region market economies had never taken root, or had existed only in marginal fashion under the control of merchant-landowners. The prolonged rule of the Russian czars impeded the full growth of capitalism before the 1917 revolution. The establishment of an oligarchy under the label of communism extended central control of the economy and subordination of the peasantry to its new overlords. When hostilities ended in 1945, the Russian state expanded into neighbouring territories, aided to some degree by their internal communist parties. During the war, communism in these states was as much a label denoting opposition to German fascism as a positive theory of economic and social development.

This region became the counterfoil to American expansion. Persistently, it provided the alternative of state management. That was hardly what Marx had meant by communism; he had envisioned a transition state entrusted with the task of self-destruction. But states do not intentionally self-destruct, and the Eastern European states expanded their bureaucratic control of populations under their jurisdiction. These strong states became the enemy in an industrial world otherwise dominated by markets; how much of the enmity was engendered by their own activities and how much was due to US policy is open to debate.

In any event, these countries were excluded from the world trading arena as constructed under the Pax Americana. Initially, they had participated in the planning of these organizations, but withdrew by 1947 and remained outside until the mid-1950s. Between 1955 and 1965 the smaller Eastern European countries gradually reentered the world trading system through GATT. However, the organizations were by that time oriented towards the priorities of the United States and European countries. The impact of Eastern European countries on policy and trade during this period was minimal.

OIL DISPLACED COAL as the major fuel for industry about a century ago. Its production and marketing in the United States and in Canada were very quickly brought under monopoly control by the Rockefeller companies. In the 1920s the United States had also secured access to oil in Turkey, Syria, and Iraq, areas at that time dominated by Britain and France. There were major oil discoveries in Texas, and then in Saudi Arabia, in the 1930s. Before the end of the Second World War the US president announced that Saudi Arabia was eligible for American lend-lease assistance. This would be available in return for an oil reserve, from which the United States could obtain supplies at prices below those of the world market. There followed an internal struggle for control of this oil between the State Department, which advocated US state ownership through a Petroleum Reserves Corporation, and the major oil companies, in particular the predecessors of Exxon and Mobil. A compromise proposal involved what amounted to an Anglo-American cartel explicitly designed to prevent "uncontrolled competitive expansion."[4] The proposal failed to pass in the US Senate. According to one scholarly account, a major reason for this failure was the traditional opposition in the United States to government interference in the free market.[5] Another reason was the opposition of small operators in the United States, whose fears of cheap imported oil were not unreasonable. A central plank of the proposed policy was to conserve domestic oil while exploiting reserves offshore.[6]

There followed a period of general scrambling for control of the Saudi oil. This culminated in the American policy of supporting the expansion of private corporations rather than developing an American government presence or an intergovernmental arrangement. Either way, American control would have been the outcome. The question was merely whether the control would be in private or state offices. The state, though not the owner, became the essential provider of security to the oil companies, and attempted by negotiations, aggressive actions, and threats to prevent British oil interests from obtaining larger shares of the markets and producing countries from obstructing American oil company expansions. Control of cheap oil supplies was a central component of the Pax Americana.

The difference between the oil component of the post-war arrangements and the trade and exchange agreements was that the former was not subjected to or influenced by international institutions. Robert O. Keohane notes that on this ground it may be stretching the point to talk of "the oil regime," but the informal rules and the private agreements between oil companies, the weak producing nations, the buyers, and the State Department operated until the mid-1960s in a manner similiar to the regimes of trade and monetary relations.[7]

THE INSTITUTIONS established at Bretton Woods were not immediately successful. This was partly because European nations were unable to reconstruct their economies without greater access to American goods and currency. The us negotiators were at some odds with us business concerns, which finally squelched proposed plans for the international trade organization on the ground that it failed to oblige governments to maintain liberalized trade conditions. The alternative was the massive Marshall Plan initiated in 1947, and the establishment of a European Payments Union (EPU) in 1950. Marshall Plan aid consisted of grants, not loans, and was generous in both the material and the visionary sense: it provided the basic necessities for European reconstruction, and it bound Europe to American interests in a relatively gentle fashion. The EPU offered a means of balancing accounts on a multilateral basis, and was enthusiastically supported by the United States as a way of promoting intra-European trade and eventually attaining multilateral liberalized trading relations. In fact, the EPU served in the short term to allow European nations to discriminate against American exports, thereby causing considerable agitation in the United States. By the mid-1950s, with European currencies firmly re-established, the union was dissolved and more multilateral trade was undertaken.

The separate nations of Europe used their state machinery for reconstruction. The United States called this free enterprise, but in reality strong states took up monopoly positions in strategic industrial sectors, especially in the automobile, steel, and heavy machinery industries. In Britain the state became dominant in communications, transportation, energy, steel, shipbuilding, and aerospace. In France the state owned major coal-mining operations, power stations, and chemicals. An arm's-length management arrangement was established for the state-owned Renault Car Company. In Italy the state controlled communications and transportation, and held shares in steel, other engineering, textile, and chemical companies. The Scandinavian states had social democratic governments in place, and already were actively managing their domestic economies.

As Leonard Tivey argued for the British case,[8] the technology of the time made single-firm monopoly production more efficient than competitive production. When private sector monopolies were absent, as they were in most of the steel industries of Europe following the war, the state took on centralized planning, research and development, direct investment in manufacturing, and provision of the social and physical infrastructure essential to both societal maintenance and private capital's growth.

The theory of laissez-faire was forged in imperial Britain, and became a successful tool for maintaining European supremacy. In Germany the divided kingdom, the longevity of agrarian classes, and the absence of coalitions between classes had impeded industrial development. Yet once its internal barriers were broken down, Germany demonstrated a capacity for industrial production that challenged Britain and led the two countries into the first war. Intense nationalism, bred in the inter-war depression, fuelled German resentment; major industrial companies promoted hostilities and provided financial support to fascism. Germany's ideology at that time was not laissez-faire; on the contrary, it was statist in the sense that the state actively intervened, managed, and controlled the economy. The military was a central actor. At the time, this was advantageous to German capital, which was denied entry to other markets by tariff and other barriers. The major consumer of large industrial products was the German state. (Indeed, some observers have wryly noted that perhaps it was Hitler, not Keynes and Kalecki, who demonstrated the importance of the state in a capitalist economy.)

It was to West Germany (also known as the Federal Republic of Germany or FRG), now defeated, that American capital moved after the war. American forces were stationed there and needed supplies; in addition, the German industrial capacity could be quickly rejuvenated through capital investments, and Germany could become a major consuming nation. Beyond those economic concerns, however, there was another, more ideological, interest in West Germany:

it bordered on communist countries, and its eastern section was occupied by Russian forces.

Reconstructed with substantial aid from the United States and shielded by American bases and forces on its territory, West Germany was already becoming the strongest national economy in Europe by the mid-1950s. Again, the state, though not now as a fascist state, was the propellant for growth.

During the 1950s international trade doubled, then more than doubled again in the 1960s. Most of this trade was transacted between OECD nations. This growth was similar to that which occurred between 1870 and 1913, when total trade volume had increased at an annual rate of 3.4 per cent. By contrast, between 1913 and 1939 trade volume had grown at a rate of less than 2 per cent a year. Over the whole period from 1870 to 1945, the relative positions of the top three nations had changed, with Britain steadily declining, West Germany improving, and the United States steadily climbing to the top. Yet given the aid programs and successful reconstruction, European nations together had a higher proportion of the world's exports (38 per cent) than the United States (21 per cent) or North America as a whole (27.4 per cent) in 1953.[9] The strength of the rejuvenated Europe vis-à-vis the United States was still diluted by national divisions, but the figures indicate the remarkable change already underway.

The EPU and the Benelux Union (established in 1947 by Belgium, the Netherlands, and Luxembourg) explored the possibilities of a more general trading block in Europe. The European Coal and Steel Community (ECSC) was established in 1951 by France, West Germany, Italy, and the three Benelux Union countries. The ECSC included a supranational body that administered the two industries. Tariff barriers between members were abolished. The experiment was successful, and production of crude steel and end products expanded over the next twenty years.

In 1957, under the Treaty of Rome, agreement was reached by the same six countries on initial forms of economic integration, including the dismantling of tariffs, a customs union, free movement of labour, goods, services, and capital, and common policies on transportation, industry, energy, and agriculture. In 1959 the European Free Trade Association (EFTA) was formed by the United Kingdom, Norway, Sweden, Denmark, Portugal, Switzerland, and Austria. This was a weaker association, but it secured tariff reductions between the seven who were not then members of the European Economic Community.

The establishment of the Common Market was based on the assumption that through unification European nations might regain their trading strength. No single nation could provide the aggregate demand for consumer goods in its domestic market that would permit it to reduce the proportion of GNP that went to exports. No nation had the sheer quantity of raw resources within its borders to compete with the United States over the long run, or the range of combinations of resources and manufacturing that a country the size of the United States could put at the disposal of its industrialists. None of the countries was in a position to maintain colonies or pursue imperialist ambitions in a global economy so overwhelmingly dominated by the United States. What was envisioned was the creation of a super-nation equivalent to the United States in size and internal market, with numerous urban centres, large rural regions, extensive resources, and a full range of specialized manufacturing capacities: in short, the twentieth-century expansion of the nation-state model.

The United States supported the development of a united Europe in line with its general support of trade liberalization. This support continued even as it became clear that the union actually evolving would become an instrument for discrimination against imports from outside the federation, including (perhaps especially) American products. It may be that by the late 1950s American companies were well established in Europe, and trade discrimination against imported and competitive commodities posed relatively little threat. In any event, American devotion to trade liberalization and strong trading countries was genuine. The whole of US foreign policy in this period was coloured by the anti-communist crusade, and policies on both Europe and Japan were directed towards the creation of strong, anti-communist trading partners.

Trade figures are useful vital signs, but by themselves they tell only part of the story. Unlike small nations or nations without industrial capacity, advanced industrial nations with large domestic markets are not dependent on exports. Until the 1950s the United States exported only 5 per cent of its GNP, while both European and less developed nations depended on a much higher level of exports to enable them to import basic machinery, commodities, and agricultural products. In 1955 Germany's exports as a percentage of GNP constituted 20 per cent, Britain's 21.5 per cent. The figures for these two countries, and for France and Italy, remained between 15 and 26 per cent throughout the post-war history, while those for the United States remained below 10 per cent until 1980.[10] Throughout the period of American hegemony the United States traded about 5 per cent of its GNP, an amount of no consequence; free trade in the classic sense of exchange of goods was not the critical element in American economic activity. Import statistics followed the same pattern. Free trade, meaning borders open to foreign investment, had entirely different effects on European nations and the United States.

Trade figures also mask the effects of direct investment. One of the features of the post-war period was a substantial change in types and patterns of foreign investment. Up to that time most investment by Europeans, in Europe or elsewhere, took the forms of government bonds or portfolio loans. The extensive loans to colonies by Britain, for example, were of this type. American companies were more inclined from the beginning to purchase assets directly, and to use bank loans (often secured from sources in the host country) as capital. Before 1914 most American investment was in Mexico and Canada, and most of that was direct investment by companies. After the war, American direct investment in Europe increased, along with bank loans, international institutional loans, direct government loans to other governments, and aid grants.

The formation of the EEC provided a common, tariff-free market for all companies operating within its jurisdiction, and tariffs were imposed against imports from other countries. The union also provided incentives for US companies to establish subsidiaries inside the common market. Trade data reflect both the growth of domestic economies and the growth of foreign subsidiaries operating within them. In the 1950s and 1960s, the "cousins," as John LeCarré called the Americans, moved into Europe. The medium was the same kind of multinational company that had moved a generation earlier into Canada – a parent firmly established in a dominant country, with subsidiary offshoots elsewhere.

When companies establish subsidiaries in foreign countries, they initially bring in funds, provide employment, and produce commodities behind tariff barriers for local consumption. However, they also tend to import their machinery and other manufactured components, thus affecting the balance of trade for the host country; they preclude the development of local competing companies because they have world-wide supply and transportation facilities, greater financial resources, and international markets. As well, they tend to bring in their own management personnel and to repatriate profits and dividends to their own shareholders in their home country. It was for these reasons that Europeans in the 1960s expressed the fear that they were being taken over by American corporations. Jean-Jacques Servan-Schreiber was especially concerned with France, though in fact the larger part of American direct investment in the late 1950s and 1960s went to West Germany. He wrote, "Already, in the ninth year of the Common Market, this European market is basically American in organisation."[11]

WITHIN TWO YEARS of the war's termination, the Truman doctrine proclaimed the United States to be the leader of the free world.[12] Stripped of its ideological trappings, "the free world" meant all countries whose borders were open to American investment. The free world soon included dictatorships, military juntas, propped-up monarchs, and oligarchies. But the phrase still implied a world of free citizens, democratic governments, and civil rights, in contrast to the unfree world of communism.

The cold war dictated American policies in Asia. In Korea, China, and Indochina revolutionary forces were changing the international map and threatening the expansion of American capitalism. The original objective in Japan had been to demilitarize, to democratize, to defang the economic power of the leading merchant houses (the *zaibatsu*) and integrate the Japanese economy within the American orbit. Cold war strategies redirected American energies towards ensuring that Japan would become a staunch ally in the crusade against communism and would serve as a base in the Pacific. The Japanese people, still stunned by defeat, their cities in shambles, their society paralysed by inflation, unemployment, and hunger, accepted the formal machinery of democracy and the prohibitions of the new constitution on the use of arms for pursuit of national objectives as imposed by the Supreme Command of the Allied Power under General Douglas MacArthur. Early in the occupation the GHQ ordered the dismantling of over a thousand industrial plants. These were to be transported as reparations to Southeast Asian countries and to China. Mitsui, Iwasaki (Mitsubishi), Sumitomo, and Yasuda houses were to be purged, and all executives in these and other leading firms were to be dismissed. But with cold car strategies taking over from Second World War emotions, the dismantling was much less extensive than had been intended. Mitsui and Mitsubishi lost some of their properties, but the banks were not diminished; they were able to reassemble many of the former firms into new groups, even retaining the former house names. The Japanese, who had co-operated in most other reforms initiated or ordered by the Americans, resisted the dismantling of the large houses, and after the signing of the peace treaties in 1951 they ignored various provisions of the anti-monopoly laws that had been promulgated in the Diet while it was under American control.

The Korean War was, in the words of Japan's premier, Yoshida

Shigeru, a godsend to post-war Japan. The United States began to purchase provisions from Japan for the war in the neighbouring country. Some $1.7 billion in special procurement revenues was paid by the United States to Japan. Okinawa became a major supply base. Exports rose, foreign currency reserves increased, and companies began producing a range of consumer goods, especially textiles and, gradually, machinery, in response to American market demand. The peace treaty with Japan, signed in 1951 with the Korean War as its context, brought Japan into the American orbit as a military ally in an anti-communist offensive, and obliged the Tokyo government to support the Kuomintang in Taiwan.[13]

At the end of the Korean War, Japan experienced a recession. Its idle, energy-intensive industries were in need of large quantities of raw materials, which, along with oil, had to be imported, for Japan was endowed with little more than forests and ports. The Ministry of International Trade and Industry (MITI) surveyed the industrial spectrum and initiated a number of long-term strategies to increase self-sufficiency. For a few years the primary offshore investments were to be in raw materials and energy. The government and the trading houses (especially the *sogo shosha*, described below) carried out this plan together, and succeeded in pulling Japan out of the post-war recession. The country's economic growth between 1953 and 1970 was enormous. The immediate reconstruction period was followed by the "modernization" period, when the growth of the machinery, petrochemical, automobile, and electric appliance industries was emphasized. MITI and other government agencies promoted the growth of the large companies through regulations permitting mergers, a relaxation of the anti-monopoly rules, subsidies, and planning. Government agencies combined with the large houses to procure raw materials and establish sales agencies abroad that combined the interests of several companies and researched foreign consumer habits and cultures.

The success of Japanese exports depended on the differential world price for raw materials and manufactured goods. Japan could import coal, oil, and minerals at low prices and export finished products at high prices. The country's one natural advantage was its harbours, which were reconstructed to accommodate the tankers and freighters that carried the raw materials. The chemical and steel plants were built adjacent to the harbours to decrease transportation costs.[14]

Socially, Japan remained in the pre-war era. Taxation rates were the lowest among the leading industrial countries long after Japan's economic growth had outstripped that of Britain and other European countries. Social welfare programs were never instituted, although education, which had long held a special place in Japan, was supported. Learning had gained high status in the feudal period when the *samurai* codes of behaviour and emphasis on knowledge influenced the larger culture. After the Restoration, education conferred prestige, and the educated person was assured of employment in one of the great houses. After 1945 this long-standing emphasis on learning was renewed with vigour. The government established a university in every prefecture, and by 1950 there were 70 state universities and 105 private universities throughout the country; by 1980 there were 443 universities in all. Nearly 95 per cent of all junior high school graduates enrolled in senior high school, and 40 per cent of high school graduates entered higher educational institutions of one kind or another.[15] Education became the avenue of upward mobility. It also created a deadly competition between students as acceptance into the higher-ranked universities became the essential route to top jobs. (The organization of Japanese companies is described in a later chapter).

LIKE JAPAN, TO which it owed its colonial heritage, Taiwan was of military and strategic importance to the United States, and received large amounts of foreign direct investment and aid. The flow of US aid through the 1950s to mid-1960s was very high, ranging from more than one-half of gross investment in 1955 to about 10 per cent in 1964.[16]

Much of Taiwan's infrastructure had been put in place by Japanese investors and colonial administration in the pre-war period. The Kuomintang, which had been ousted by Chinese rebels in 1949, constituted an alien military force in Taiwan, occupying the country and imposing land reforms, an educational system, and economic development almost as a by-product of its military designs on China. Land was parcelled out between small owner-operators and tenants, and agriculture was rapidly commercialized.[17] Surplus gained through commercial agriculture was invested in industry under strict controls, which involved high land taxes and compulsory rice sales to the government at lower-than-market prices. Land bonds in public enterprises in exchange for compulsory divestiture of their holdings permitted some landlords to become successful industrialists. This forced change in class structure and property rights was possible because the ruling junta was neither ethnically nor historically integrated into Taiwanese society.[18] Latin American and African societies were less flexible because their ruling classes were also composed of the landlords.

Though persistently praised by the United States as a model of free enterprise, Taiwan industrialized through the extensive use of government monopolies, first with an import-substitution policy and later through exports. Those monopolies included the power company that set the price for electricity, the single oil importer that regulated the price of fuel, the sugar company that controlled the island's main cash crop, the aluminum, fertilizer, gold, copper, salt, and shipping companies, and the airports, railways, and telecommunications sectors.[19] Foreign financing was essential to the development projects, the nuclear power plants, and the petrochemical plants, and took the form of loans from international and private agencies and the private sector. General Electric and Westinghouse were and still are major recipients of contracts connected to such projects. The American government, through the us Aid Mission, provided support for Jiang Jie-shi (Chiang Kai-shek) and his authoritarian military government.

THE AMERICAN CRUSADE against communism can too easily be reduced to American expansionary interests abroad. Obviously, the interests of American capital were threatened by communist advances, and American businessmen had cause to fear further expansion of both the military forces of the USSR and the idea of communism. But to appreciate the magnitude of the crusade, one has to go beyond immediate property interests. Americans saw themselves as individualists; they were obsessed with the word "freedom," which had deep roots in their culture. Their fictional heroes were Huckleberry Finn, the quintessential hustler, and Superman, the infallible fixer. Entrepreneurial, independent, innovative, and imaginative, Huckleberry never permitted trivial facts to get in the way of truth. He came from nowhere, had no family credentials, lied according to intuition and circumstance, and generally saw through the posturings and bombast of what for him was the old order. He also slew the dragon of racism, though his lead was not followed in the next century. He emerged at the end of the nineteenth century, offering Americans a self-image of a people forged by the turmoils of Europe that had overcome European élitism and had a clear, unreflectively protestant understanding of good and evil. Dukes and kings held no courts in America; therefore there were no classes, and equality was in place. Superman too had a simple yardstick of good and evil, and possessed the superhuman physical power to combat evil wherever it appeared.

As rural society dissolved, the community and then the family became impediments to fortune. Like Huckleberry Finn, everyone came from nowhere, belonged nowhere, had no roots, no family, no permanence. The theory of "human capital" became credible only in the context of a mass society, where each component individual was isolated. "Individualism" became not a mark of courageous character so much as a measure of disengagement from vital ties to communities and lifelong social relations. In spiritual terms, the American sought individual salvation. Neither enlightenment nor service to God and humanity had the same attractions for individuals so divorced from the communal roots of earlier societies. The same processes were occurring in Europe, but there the class structure was less permeable, and mass production could not be as quickly adopted as it was in the relatively unstructured, relatively simple American context.

The United States had leaped past Europe through the efficiencies of scale in mass production, mass consumption, mass accommodation, mass transportation, and mass communication. All of this was within the market framework: everything and everyone had a value determined in the market; every idea was the equivalent of every other until it was sold; only one value had pre-eminence – the absolute value of freedom.

In the 1940s and 1950s the Huckleberry Finn ideology meshed easily with the anti-communist crusade. Individualism was expressed in the everyday world through the right to bear arms, a right justified on the ground that they might be needed should the government become oppressive. Though the mass society encouraged anonymity and produced the isolates whose violence reflected their frustration in an achievement-oriented mass society, it was not within the American credo to reconsider such a basic individual right. Communism, equated in the minds of Americans with strong government and the absence of individual rights, was an absolute evil. Yet nationalism flourished, as it had in pre-war and Nazi Germany. This was the nationalism of the mass society, a jingoistic glorification of the abstraction "America," which allowed its individual members to see themselves as a chosen people.

The Keynesian approach resulted in a substantial growth of the interventionist state, encouraged by theory to stimulate and deflate economies as needed and to implement policies of full employment. To deal with this "mixed" system without violating the American version of free enterprise, American political theorists adopted the idea that the state (in fact, that term went out of fashion, and was replaced by "political system")[20] was a forum in which interest groups negotiated political outcomes to arrive at the public and national interest.[21] The interest groups were voluntary, and the final arbiter of the public interest was always the individual citizen who expressed preferences through voting and supporting groups, much as consumers expressed preferences through purchases.[22] Society was understood as an aggregation of individuals, each expressing a personal preference, loosely bound by a hypothetical social contract. All human action boiled down to rational choices about investments and consumption, and this was as true of political as of economic behaviour. The quality of individual life was determined by the quantity of goods and the money available to buy them.

Definitions of democracy are influenced by judgments of the results. Robert Dahl, an American sociologist who took the pluralist perspective and in general approved of the results, defined democracy as a system in which all citizens have the free opportunity to express their preferences, to take individual and collective action to inform governments and others of these preferences, and to have their preferences equally considered in the conduct of government.[23]

That version may be understood as an idealized picture of American government in the 1960s. A large portion of the American black population was still disfranchised at that time, and although citizens were free to express many opinions, a favourable opinion of communism would not be tolerated. To argue that all individuals had equal influence on the conduct of government was to ignore the reality of corporate power – indeed, of economic power generally. None the less, as an ideal this version was compelling, and it was very much part of what Americans believed to be their "free world," part of what gave them a special right, a special duty to combat communism.[24]

The precise role of government remained unclear despite the growth of political science as a standard part of an American education. Governments could concern themselves vaguely with "the public interest," but were not supposed to engage in long-term planning or active participation in the economy. Governments could support corporations through military interventions, special taxation arrangements, funding for research and development, and even offshore plants, but were not supposed to use tariffs, trading regulations, or other means of protecting them from competition. Governments could run unprofitable enterprises such as post offices, but could not compete actively in profitable sectors as producers of goods or services. Governments could plan social services such as education, but could not plan the economy.

The free enterprise ideology extended to the labour market. Workers should be free to seek whatever employment they could command, anywhere; conversely, employers should be free to employ whom they wished on any terms and conditions. This understanding went through a considerable battering in the post-war period as unions challenged the rights of employers by pressuring governments into passing minimum-wage laws, anti-discrimination legislation, safety conditions, unemployment insurance schemes, and employment standards acts. There was still a competitive labour market, but it operated for small businesses and the service sector much more than for multinationals, where the unions were most strongly embedded.

This was fair enough: the multinationals themselves operated in a considerably less than fully competitive market. They had little serious international competition, they functioned in an oligopolistic market, they often had oligopsonistic control of resources, their industrial production systems were vertically integrated, and they preempted much of the competition before it got started. By the early 1960s a very few, very large corporations dominated every industrial sector, and of the world's corporations American-based multinationals were in the majority and at the top of the heap.

Though communism was identified as the enemy, capitalism was a rarely used word. Contemporary society and economy were designated as "modern," in contrast to backward "traditional" societies. Modern societies were perceived to have certain characteristic values that provided the framework for democracy, including a belief in equality of opportunity and the right to participate in social decision-making; a high regard for individual achievement; a tolerance for diversity; and rationality. Wilbert Moore argued that rationality is institutionalized in modern societies, in the sense that individuals operate on the expectation that objective information and rational procedures will be used in pursuit of utilitarian goals.[25] Traditional societies are based on non-rational criteria such as kinship obligations or religious beliefs, which impede economic development and also democracy. Rostow's theory, for example, saw underdevelopment as a result of internal blockages.[26] Traditional societies would eventually "take off" into industrialization when they modernized their cultures. Whether implied or stated openly, the white man's burden of the Victorian era had now become America's burden.

The steel and oil age, as this era may be characterized, had at its core the automobile. Roads and service stations carved up communities. Family holidays, Sunday outings, kinship arrangements, shopping, public meetings, the location of schools, and the eating patterns of North Americans were all organized around the family car. And the two biggest industries, whose companies topped *Fortune*'s and *Forbes*'s lists every year, were oil and automobiles.

Industry, following the lead of the automobile sector, was characterized by the assembly line: mass production made possible through economies of scale. Indeed, the form was so widespread that it was later labelled "Fordism" by its critics. The dividing-line between labour and capital was manifest in every factory, but was blurred in the suburbs of car-oriented North America where the unionized, employed workforce enjoyed, along with the managerial class, private homes, a plethora of personal possessions, three weeks' holiday a year, and one, two, or three automobiles with which everyone became instantly and continually mobile.

Poverty persisted in the inner cities, where the unemployed and, in greater numbers, the marginally employed, the service sector, and the non-unionized and unorganized workers of the affluent society scratched out livings. Yet even among these, and in comparison with the Third World poor, a level of survival above starvation was made possible by the safety net of the welfare state.

To play its leadership role and to protect the world from the chains of communism, the United States built up a vast military establishment. A testing-ground for its effectiveness was provided within a few years in Korea. The Korean War had several important consequences beyond the obvious one of dividing Korea into two camps, capitalist and communist. It gave the United States evidence that could be used in the crusade against communism, and created a fervent cadre of veterans and civilians dedicated to fighting communism wherever it was said to threaten what was religiously called the free world. The Korean War demonstrated to the rest of the Asian nations the penalties to be paid if they followed China's example and struck out on their own. It demonstrated to the Soviet Union that the United States would fight for its stake in Asia. Most important, it gave Japan the opportunity to renew itself as an industrial power. And, contrary to all the arguments on free trade and limited government, it was the springboard by which the American government greatly increased its own momentum and institutions for independent international action.

There were domestic costs to the anti-communist crusade. During the 1950s the intellectual and artistic life of the United States was stifled by the state politics of terrorism known as the McCarthy investigations.[27] Inevitably, this spilled over to affect the way in which the society incorporated a new technology and the scientists who gave that technology birth. The silicon revolution had its beginnings in a massive build-up of armaments, and more and more North American resources and knowledge were meshed with what President Dwight Eisenhower, speaking frankly only as he left office, called the military-industrial complex.

Neither a theory of the free market nor contemporary theories of the state are adequate to the reality of the Pax Americana. Two sets of powerful institutions had emerged, at times operating in concert, at other times diverging and conflicting in their pursuit of power. One set was the transnationals and the banks; the other was the United States government and its political alliances throughout the world. In fact, laissez-faire and free enterprise notwithstanding, both Britain and the United States in their imperial phases were guided by governments that pursued ideological objectives independent of (and in significant instances contrary to) the rational material objectives of their most powerful constituents. Their pursuits were not consistent with the demands or the evident interests of other constituents. Their objectives apparently rested on a power base that could not be reduced to internal interests or negotiations, and were advanced by political leaders with grandiose visions of their role in history. The anti-communist crusade in post-war America undoubtedly had its origins in the interests of capital, but the actions taken by American governments in Korea, Iran, Lebanon, Vietnam, Central America, and Cuba cannot be explained only by reference to these interests. They exceeded the rational pursuit of profits even by the most generous interpretation of long-term property interests. Even more, they inflicted serious and permanent damage on the US economy.[28]

CHAPTER FOUR

The Coca-Cola Stall, 1965–1985

Between 1958, when John Kenneth Galbraith dubbed America the affluent society,[1], and 1973, when the oil-producing and exporting countries (OPEC) mounted an effective opposition to American control of oil supplies and pricing, or at the latest 1975, when defeated American troops finally withdrew from Vietnam, the short era of the Pax Americana ended. During that same period the integrated circuit technology fundamentally altered both the nature of industrial production and its location in a global economy. In this chapter we will investigate some of the links between these events and consider the explanations offered by American social scientists.

JOHN NAISBITT, the author of the popular version of the information society, *Megatrends*, says that the information age began in 1956, the first year in which white-collar workers outnumbered blue-collar workers in the American labour force.[2] Others might point to 1947 as the critical moment. That was the year in which the transistor was invented by AT & T-Bell Laboratories researchers led by the physicist William Shockley. Or 1954, when a Texas Instruments researcher, Gordon Teal, invented the first silicon transistor; or a few years later, when a Fairchild Semiconductor researcher, Jean Hoerni, developed the planar process, which replaced wire connectors with metallic lines diffused into silicon. By 1961 Texas Instruments and Fairchild had developed the integrated circuit, a silicon chip incorporating the properties of two or more transistors.

The silicon chip initiated nothing less than an industrial revolution. Office equipment and industrial production machinery underwent transformations as the new technology was applied and gradually expanded. New service industries were instantly created to realize the potential of immediate communication of information around the globe. Every process involved a reorganization of labour and management, and capital was redirected to capture the benefits of the new technology.

The early development of transistors was meshed with military interests, supported by military contracts, and turned to military uses. Stanford University attracted military research contracts and provided land leases to enable high-technology companies to create a "community for technical scholars." These were attractive to the infant industry, and brought first Shockley in 1954, then many others, to the Santa Clara (Silicon) Valley. Seventy per cent of production in the United States remained tied to military contracts in the early 1960s.[3]

In a process familiar to Americans but alien to their Japanese competitors, Shockley left Bell Labs to set up his own company; in 1957 his own experts left him and created the semiconductor division of Fairchild (known thereafter as "the traitorous eight"). Fairchild's experts eventually quit and founded other firms, including Rheem (Raytheon), Signetics, Amelco (later Teledyne), Molectro (later National Semiconductor), Intel, and Advanced Micro Devices.[4] Loyalty to an employer was not an American habit. Innovative and entrepreneurial scientists and technicians were unwilling to be tamed or to have their discoveries appropriated by someone else. When they were on the verge of a breakthough, they left established firms to start their own enterprises on the cutting edge of the technology.

There was another reason, frequently mentioned, for their swift exits from established companies within the United States. The massive transnational corporations that led the economy were not risk-takers, were not research-oriented, and were organized to meet short-term objectives. This, more than any other single factor, rendered them uncompetitive. (Later on I will examine the semiconductor assembling, computer, electronics, and automobile industries in connection with this argument.)

By the mid-1960s the silicon revolution was in full swing, and American companies that had developed some independent commercial capacities discovered the advantages of moving the labour-intensive sections of their production offshore to underdeveloped regions. The global assembly line was selectively established in countries that had strategic geopolitical positions as well as cheap labour, mostly in former colonies where English was spoken, and in regions that seemed most likely to sustain what was called "a secure atmosphere for investment." These countries were persuaded to establish zones, known as free enterprise zones (FEZs), special export zones (SEZs), or simply free zones, where companies could assemble products for export exempt from local labour laws, taxation, and import-export duties.

Fairchild was the first of the American semiconductor firms to move offshore; it opened an assembly plant in Hong Kong in 1962 and another in Korea in 1966. General Instruments moved to Taiwan in 1964, and others moved to Asia and Mexico within the same few years. General Electric set up a plant in Ireland in 1963, but in 1970 shifted its semiconductor assembly to Singapore.[5] In 1967 two assembly facilities were opened in Mexico,[6] and others were located in Brazil and later in India. These plants provided the cheap labour needed to bond the silicon wafers, which were airshipped from and then back to the United States. Silicon wafers are light, and the total costs of transportation were minimal. Although the salaries of the scientists and technicians in the industrial countries were high, the actual production costs were low.

Following the semiconductor operations were the assemblers of electronic consumer goods. Some electronic firms had already established assembly plants in Hong Kong, and these proliferated throughout the Pacific Basin countries in the 1970s. The firms employing the workers in such places as Hong Kong, Taiwan, Singapore, Thailand, and the Philippines were subcontractors. If labour costs rose or if the workforce became militant, the American, European, and Japanese companies could move elsewhere without any obligation to the local workers or the subcontractor.

American corporations argued that competition from Japan was a major reason for locating plants in Asia. One corporate official told the US Senate Subcommittee on Multinational Corporations, "Our competitors had gone to Korea, some of them, and it was necessary to maintain our competitive position in the world semiconductor market ... [cheaper wages are] a part of it, but also, it is hard to find people in the US to take on that low skilled work."[7] US workers, many of whom were legal and illegal immigrant women, had performed the work before the move to offshore production. Those workers cost more than the female workers in Taiwan and Korea, even if they were relatively cheap within the United States, and unions were beginning to have some success in organizing them.

It was not, however, the semiconductor offshore locations that had the major impact on employment in the United States. First, only the commercial companies had moved (military contracts prohibited offshore production for others); second, these moves were investments in a new industry rather than relocations of existing industries. In fact, offshore production increased overall employment in semiconductors but altered the composition of its "skill content."[8] A relatively small shift in employment for unskilled workers affected women in the Silicon Valley region. More significant than the effect on employment in the United States were the effects on the NICS, where new industrial regions, a new proletariat of female workers, and a growing middle class of consumers were given life. These conditions gradually altered the nature of the world market and global politics.

Offshore production by other industries – electronics, machine tools, steel, and automobiles particularly – had a greater impact on employment in the industrial countries, and it was these, rather than the semiconductor firms, that closed plants and disinvested in their home countries. They moved in search of cheaper labour, just as the chip-makers did, but they had another, perhaps even more powerful incentive: they could not restructure industry to accommodate the new technologies without coming to disagreeable terms with unionized labour. As they relocated plants, disinvesting in order to restructure their production lines elsewhere without labour resistance, they destroyed the social contract between domestic labour and capital. They also entrenched an industrial workforce and supported a national bourgeoisie in some of the developing countries. These grew in dependent form, but they did grow; and technology transfers did take place as the integrated production system was fully established.

Ironically, the liberalization of trade that had so enhanced American opportunities to penetrate these other countries and effectively prevent them from developing their own competitive industries on an import-substitution basis now worked against American interests (though not necessarily against the interests of offshore American companies). Companies elsewhere could ship their goods to the US home market, which was relatively unprotected from competitive goods.

American direct investment in Asia escalated from the late 1960s to the late 1970s. For the major countries – South Korea, Taiwan, the Philippines, Thailand, Malaysia, Singapore, and Indonesia (not including oil investment in Indonesia) – it grew from US$750 million in 1965, to US$3 billion in 1970 and US$10 billion in 1975. The greatest growth was in manufacturing, of which electronics and the garment industries were the leading groups.[9] By the mid-1970s there were eighty-nine US plants in Singapore, Malaysia, Thailand, Indonesia, the Philippines, India, Mauritius, and Central America, according to a US Department of Commerce survey.[10]

This offshore production of manufactured components was critical to the development of these countries and to the globalization of capital. However, we should be careful to remember that the United States' major external investments were still in OECD countries, and OECD countries were the major investors in the United States. Further, some chip producers were unable to move offshore because of military contracts which stipulated that production must take place in the United States or in militarily allied countries; others did not do so because they produced chips primarily for use in their own equipment. I will have more to say about these complications later on.

Private enterprise in the United States was scornful but also wary of the way the Japanese government supported industries. In fact, the US government provided a good deal of aid beyond military contracts, especially in the forms of tax write-offs, offshore production legislation, tariff waivers on third-country-produced imports by American companies, and foreign policies. Exporting companies were helped by a US tariff structure that obliged them to pay only a value-added tax on the reimportation of goods. The quasi-public US Overseas Private Investment Corporation (OPIC) insured offshore investments by US firms against losses from war, civil unrest, and foreign exchange restrictions, so the risks of moving offshore were small. [11]

The international order made loans and offered technical and other aid to countries that facilitated the offshore growth of American and European capital. For examples, the Asian Development Bank lent $11 million to Malaysia for an international airport at Penang in 1972, just in time to serve the electronics industry located there, and the US Export / Import Bank lent $600 million to the Philippines for construction of the Morong nuclear power plant intended to serve the Bataan Export Processing Zone. [12] Since then the United Nations Industrial Development Organization (UNIDO) has provided technical assistance elsewhere for zone construction. The World Bank financed an aerial tramway in Gabon to move manganese from a US Steel mine, and an infrastructure in Mauritania to serve the MIFERMA iron ore mining consortium composed mainly of European steel producers. [13]

But combined state and industry long-term planning was not embedded in American culture. Neither American nor European firms were yet ready to abandon the quick-fix approach to technology. They looked for ways of outsmarting Japanese competition not through long-term strategies, not through investments in basic research, but through relocating offshore their labour-intensive phases of production and other ways of cutting costs and increasing immediate profits. They were slow to develop new designs and to re-engineer the technologies so that they would reap the benefits of second- and third-generation products. When they finally began to recognize that they had lost the edge – especially in the electronics industries, where the Japanese were rapidly taking over whole sectors of second-generation markets – they did what European and American industries had always done: they tried take-overs and partnerships with the competition.

By the mid-1970s small firms could still outstrip large ones in research and entrepreneural talent, but they were outflanked by the big companies in research, development, and marketing funds. In the silicon chip industry the cost-price squeeze was greater than in most others because of the constantly changing ratio between production costs (research and plant as well as labour) and market prices as the chips became smaller and more powerful. The semiconductor industry became intensely competitive, both within countries and between companies in different countries. Demand for chips increased by about 30 per cent each year,[14] but production exceeded demand, and the industry soon developed persistent problems of overproduction. While the power of integrated circuitry increased exponentially, the market prices for single chips (each holding greater capacity) steadily declined, even as the costs of research and plant increased. The United Nations Center on Transnational Corporations reported that the 1981 capital investment cost of producing a 16K memory chip was five times the 1977 cost of producing a 4K chip.[15]

In North America and Europe this inevitably meant that the competitive structure must give way to consolidation. A wave of acquisitions began in 1975 which combined European and American capital. US Philips Trust (Netherlands) took over Signetics; Commodore International bought into MOS Technology; Siemens of West Germany bought shares in Litronix, Advanced Micro Devices, and Microwave Semiconductor; Northern Telecom of Canada bought 24 per cent of Intersil, which was subsequently purchased by General Electric. US Honeywell (Spectronics and Synertek), Exxon (Zilog), Bosch of West Germany (American Microsystems), Schlumberger of France (Fairchild), Nippon Electric of Japan (Electronic Arrays), Sylvania, and Westinghouse were all major players, taking over the innovators and becoming fully established by 1980.[16] Companies such as General Motors developed their own supply firms and began investing heavily in all phases of the semiconductor industries.

The equipment manufacturers were taking over their suppliers, a move identical to the general pattern of vertical integration that had earlier propelled American industry to the forefront. But unlike other industries of the post-war period, this one was technology-driven, and the learning curve still had to be traversed. There were many who suspected it was not ready to be harnessed by companies whose CEOs were lawyers and accountants. The former president of two semiconductor companies warned in 1979 that "the industry is getting the capital it needs, but the price it is paying may well be its long-term world market share."[17]

In Japan an alternative arrangement was struck: the large companies came together with the state to share the costs of long-term research and development, and to share in the results. Japanese scientists were trained in the industrial countries, and Japanese firms purchased technology in order to replicate it and learn from it. But these were not the critical factors that led to Japanese technological advantages. It was co-operative organization and long-term planning that made the difference. Among the long-term plans were decisions about the allocation of research and development funds. The Japanese, lacking the stimulus of military spending, chose to concentrate on quality mass production of specific products in areas where they thought they would have a comparative advantage over American producers. This led eventually to Japanese domination in the production of 64K memory chips.[18]

American companies remained dominant in 1979, with about half of the total market. Their early links with the military and later with the aero-space industry gave them access to research funds and markets. But over time those links became impediments to commercial expansion. The military had a contractual stranglehold on much of the new technology. At a later stage in the development of these technologies, an observer was able to say, "In the United States, the support of the Department of Defense to certain areas of high technology development has become the kiss of death. If commercial interests have something that they think is going to be commercial, the last thing they want is for the Department of Defense to get its finger on it and pre-empt it for military security of the United States. As a result, they would not be able to do anything with it commercially."[19] Between 1978 and 1983 the relative proportions of the market controlled by American and Japanese firms showed a definite trend towards greater market shares for the Japanese. Deducting the captive market in the United States (military production), the ratio of Japanese firms to American firms in market sales was 50 per cent by 1983.

Table 1
World semiconductor production by home country of producing firms
(Millions of us dollars)

Location	1978	1980	1983[1]	1985[2]
UNITED STATES				
IC merchant	3,238	6,360	7,000	10,675
IC captive	1,344	2,695	3,450	5,600
IC total	4,582	9,055	10,450	16,275
Discretes	1,540	2,080	1,970	2,240
Total semiconductor	6,122	11,135	12,420	18,515
WESTERN EUROPE				
IC total	453	710	855	1,240
Discretes	960	910	720	840
Total semiconductor	1,413	1,620	1,575	2,080
JAPAN				
IC total	1,195	2,450	3,910	6,500
Discretes	1,295	1,390	1,640	1,800
Total semiconductor	2,490	3,840	5,550	8,300
REST OF WORLD[3]				
IC total	482	130	190	340
Discretes	985	190	200	220
Total semiconductor	1,467	320	390	560
TOTAL IC	6,712	12,345	15,405	24,355
Total discretes	4,780	4,570	4,530	5,100
Total Worldwide Semiconductor	11,492	16,915	19,935	29,455

Source: United Nations Center on Transnational Corporations, *Transnational Corporations in the International Semiconductor Industry*, New York: UNCTC, 1986, 35.

Note: "IC" refers to integrated circuits. "Captive" refers to military contracts. "Discretes" refers to components for integrated circuits (components may be manufactured separately before assembly).

[1] Estimated value.

[2] Projections.

[3] Excluding CMEA countries but including the People's Republic of China for 1980–5; the 1978 figures include both.

Western European firms had not similarly improved their market share positions, except in cases where they had become, in effect, American firms (see table 1). Individual European governments provided numerous types of support to their own firms, but they were unable to co-ordinate their strategies through the ECC. A plan to jointly fund research on production technology (the European Strategic Program of Research in Technology) in the late 1970s conflicted with separate national initiatives, and no single country succeeded in developing either the mass of technical skills or the aggregate demand to go it alone. Links with American firms further diluted the capacities of the EEC to co-ordinate a specifically European industrial strategy.[20]

JAPANESE OFFSHORE production rarely included chip manufacturing, but electronics consumer goods, textiles, and other labour-intensive operations went offshore from about the mid-1960s. In the chip and other manufacturing industries, Japanese firms steadily gained market shares against American companies despite the American lead in developing the technology. The Japanese were applying the technology to all forms of production, whereas the American firms tried to adapt it piecemeal to their existing organizations. Consumers the world over were discovering that Japanese cars, and indeed Japanese manufactured goods more generally, outstripped North American goods in quality.

It became evident during the 1960s that American goods were no longer priced realistically in comparison with European and Japanese goods. Speculation against the dollar in anticipation of devaluation contributed to the unhinging of the system under American control. In 1972, President Nixon delivered the *coup de grâce* by removing the United States from fixed exchange values.

The US military become even more entrenched, and the economy became ever more dependent on the military's consumption of its products. In many industrial sectors the research and development money that in other countries was being spent on second- and third-generation industrial applications of the new technology was spent on US military hardware. This was justified to the American population in the context of the second Asian war, this time in Vietnam.

The war improved the fortunes of Japan and South Korea, but it was a disaster for the United States. When the US forces withdrew at last (the Paris Peace Accord was signed in January 1973, but the troops did not leave until 1975), it was as a conquered power – conquered as much by the force of world opinion as by the fanatical commitment of the guerrillas. The returning soldiers were bitter, and their war wounds were both physical and spiritual. Many young people had evaded the draft by fleeing to Canada just as American slaves had fled in another age. There was no rejoicing at the end of the war; recriminations, frustrated ideals, losses of sons and fathers, no joy. At home the American government was discredited, and abroad America's political leadership was lost.

The Vietnam War changed the ideological climate. Suddenly there were passionate, tragic films which, unlike the films of the 1950s and 1960s, were about the political world dominated by the United

States. *The Deer Hunter* and *Apocalypse Now* portrayed the legacy of Vietnam, and the costs to Americans; *El Norte* showed Americans their own double standards for Central American migrants and workers; *The Killing Ground* strongly implied the causal connection between American intervention in Cambodia and the rise of the Pol Pot regime. Social science abandoned the value-free universalistic world and began tentatively to explore critiques of capitalism. Liberal theories of market economies and pluralistic theories of democratic governments came under attack. The class divisions of American society were now openly debated. As we shall see, this was part of the context of the emergence of the new right. Among its targets were intellectuals in the media, the arts, and the universities who promoted critical versions of contemporary history.

American hegemony was contested yet again in 1973, this time by the Organization of Oil Producing and Exporting Countries. OPEC had been in existence since 1960, but until 1971 was unable to organize united resistance to the American concessions, the "majors" (the seven largest companies), and the American state. That year OPEC increased prices, and in 1973 quadrupled them without negotiation. Although the United States, like every other country, was faced with increased fuel costs, it had domestic supplies and was confident that it could continue to obtain low-cost supplies from Canada. Two more serious consequences for the United States were the slump in automobile sales as buyers chose the small, fuel-efficient automobiles from Japan, and the clear demonstration that the American oil regime was over. The United States could no longer guarantee cheap fuel to Europe and Japan and could no longer impose prices, transportation, refining, and other conditions on producing and consuming countries. The second oil shock in 1979, a corollary of Iran's rejection of the US-backed Shah, ensured that there would be no backtracking.

AMONG THE CHANGES that the new technologies underpinned was the dramatic growth in the services sector. By the mid-1970s services were becoming major components of international trade, and accounted for an increasing proportion of international investment. Although unemployment rates were growing because of the displacement of industrial production workers, service industries were absorbing new entrants. If occupational statistics are taken at face value, three-quarters of the labour forces of the leading industrial European countries, the United States, and Canada were producing "intangibles" by 1985, and nearly as high a proportion of their GDPS was attributable to the service sector.[21] A Canadian study found that in Ontario, the manufacturing heartland of Canada, a considerably larger number of people were employed in hospitals than in the auto manufacturing and auto parts industries combined, and more were employed in universities and colleges than in iron and steel mills.[22]

Naisbitt's *Megatrends* and a plethora of other books announcing the arrival of the information age waxed eloquent about the benefits of a new service society. Instead of producing goods, the authors imagined, the "post-industrial" societies would produce information. What was not understood in these accounts was the relationship between the production of goods and the production of services. Industrial economies were still industrial at their cores, but the organization of industrial production was no longer contained within national borders, and the goods being produced were transformed by the same technology that was transforming the service sectors. The relationship between goods and services in an international marketplace was underlined in the Canada-us free trade agreement:

It is no longer possible to talk about free trade in goods without talking about free trade in services because trade in services is increasingly mingled with the production, sale, distribution and service of goods. Companies today rely on advanced communications systems to co-ordinate planning, production, and distribution of products. Computer software helps to design new products. Some firms engage in-house, accountants, and engineers, some have "captive" subsidiaries to handle their insurance and finance needs. In other words, services are both inputs for the production of manufactured goods (from engineering design to data processing) and necessary complements in organizing trade (from financing and insuring the transaction to providing installation and after-sales maintenance, especially critical for large capital goods).[23]

The internationalization of manufacturing firms is a precondition to the growth of the international service sector. As manufacturing moves abroad, service firms or service components of the same firms move with them to capture downstream sales and service benefits and to provide financing. Banks, accounting, and tourist services may operate as independent companies; other service agencies are actually industrial companies. Even before telematics, industrials provided many of their own services: oil companies owned tanker fleets and gas stations, and automobile companies provided financial services. With data processing, finance, and technical services becoming vastly greater components of total industrial processes, transnationals may either create huge component service firms or establish long-term servicing relationships with other companies. Service firms in one sector may create spin-offs – for example, airlines that sell packaged holidays or own tourist resorts.

If manufacturing is the key to international expansion of services, then it follows that where the nationals of a country expand their manufacturing units to global proportions, that country's service companies expand. The service sector of American industry expanded up to 1970, then levelled off and slightly declined by 1984, when the United States provided 21.5 per cent of all global services. By then its declining share of world merchandise had dropped to 12.7 per cent, from 15.9 per cent in 1970.[24] The United States had reached its peak in the early 1970s, and thereafter imported more of its merchandise. Its service industries abroad, still able to benefit from earlier investments and international banking transactions, were more resilient through the 1980s. J. Steven Landefeld and Kan H. Young explain the difference between trends in merchandise and service imports this way: "It is easier for overseas manufacturers and financial institutions to export autos to the United States and then to buy US Treasury bonds than it is for foreign construction, accounting, legal, and other firms to sell their services in the United States."[25]

Other industrial nations, meanwhile, developed similar service spin-offs as they became participants in the global merchandise trade (see table 2). Japan increased its share of total foreign investment attributable to services to 52 per cent by 1985, West Germany to 47 per cent. At this stage, Americans imported services worth $33 billion, while foreign firms within the United States sold services worth $125 billion.[26] The United States was still the leader in services, but it was now facing competition in this as in other sectors, and the competition was within America as well as outside it.[27]

The relationship between expansion of manufacturing via foreign investment and establishment of a presence in the services trades is highlighted by Canada's failure to benefit from new services investments. Canada, dominated by foreign-owned companies and having few international companies of its own, experienced a rapidly declining balance of trade in services as the new technologies came into play. Except in the traditional real estate and banking arenas, Canadians had no access to the firms that needed services. Over the 1980s the services share of total foreign investment by Canadians steadily dropped to 29 per cent, much less than in other industrial countries.[28] Canada's payments for international services have exceeded its receipts since 1950.[29] In 1987 the deficit amounted to

Table 2
Stock of foreign direct investment in services
(Value and percentage)

| Country and currency | Year | Value | | Share of services in total FDI (%) |
		Total FDI	FDI in services	
United States of America[1]	1950	11.8	3.8	32
(billions of US dollars)	1957	25.4	7.8	31
	1966	51.8	16.3	32
	1977	147.2	60.4	41
	1985	254.7	111.2	44
Japan	1965	1.0	0.3	29
(billions of US dollars)	1970	3.6	1.4	38
	1975	15.9	5.5	35
	1980	36.5	14.0	38
	1985	83.6	43.3	52
Federal Republic of Germany[2]	1966	10.6	1.1	10
(billions of DM)	1976	49.1	20.0	41
	1980	84.5	36.2	43
	1984	145.4	68.0	47
Netherlands	1973	43.6	5.3	12
(billions of guilders)	1983	119.9	27.2	23
Canada[3]	1973	7.8	2.4	31
(billions of Canadian dollars)	1980	25.8	6.8	26
	1984	41.7	12.0	29
Australia	1978	1.4	0.7	47
(billions of Australian dollars)	1983	3.4	1.6	47
United Kingdom	1971	9.3[4]	2.2[4]	24
(billions of pounds)	1981	45.5	16.2	36

Source: United Nations Center on Transnational Corporations, Foreign Direct Investment, the Service Sector, and International Banking, series A, no. 7 (May 1987), table 5, 26. Data derived from national sources.

[1] Services data include construction, utilities, and services related to the petroleum industry. Investments in finance, insurance, and real estate in the Netherlands Antilles are excluded from data for 1977 and 1985.

[2] Data for 1966 are not fully comparable with those for later years. Figures include construction.

[3] Includes public utilities.

[4] Excludes banking and insurance in countries other than the United States.

$7 billion, double the level of 1981 and ten times the level of 1969.[30]
The bulk of the deficit – $3.9 billion – is attributable to business services. These consist of interest, dividend, and investment income returns; research and development costs; and management, professional, and consulting services associated with foreign-owned firms located in Canada. The balance of trade in services not associated

with foreign direct investment is also in deficit, but that portion has remained constant over the 1980s. Import penetration was found by a task force to be highest in business services, and increased especially in the communications sector from 1961 onwards.

While telematics reduced the importance of space for numerous service functions, particularly for the transfer of capital, many services still had to be located near consumers. Paradoxically, this was especially important for international finance, where physical proximity was highly advantageous when connected to rapid mobility of capital.[31] For the financial companies that offered such services, non-tariff barriers inhibited expansion. Such barriers took the forms of regulations on investment, establishment, foreign exchange, insurance, shipping, and employment. Most countries maintained these barriers, whether directly through public monopolies or indirectly through requirements that public contracts be allocated preferentially to national companies.

GATT referred to services only when they were ancillary to and of lesser value than goods. The new service sector, if it was to expand its global reach and profits, required two new guarantees in the global marketplace: the right to establish, and the right to non-discriminatory national treatment. Both demands became claimed rights of property in the mid-1980s, as the Uruguay Round of the GATT talks, the Single European Act (SEA), and the free trade agreement (FTA) between Canada and the United States came up for negotiation.

In the debates over services, the United States led the movement in favour of the new property rights. The service sector was still providing positive returns, and though the giant had faltered on industrial production, it might still capture downstream benefits if it could establish its presence around the globe.

"THE NEW INTERNATIONAL order" and "the new economic reality" became catch phrases for the world's exit from the Coca-Cola age. The American decline continued through the 1970s and into the early 1980s. The world's newspapers of the mid-1980s reported these events:

The Economist, 2 March 1985: "Japan has emerged as the world's biggest creditor."

The Economist, 4 May 1985: "Trade between North America and Asian countries was almost equal to trade between North America and Europe, Africa, and the Middle East during 1984. By contrast in 1970, trans-Pacific trade was half that of trans-Atlantic trade."

Asahi Evening News (Tokyo), 6 May 1985: The trade surplus for Japan was $45.6 billion in the 1984 fiscal year, up $11.1 billion over the previous year. Japan ran trade surpluses with the United States, Canada, Western Europe except Switzerland, South Korea, Taiwan, Hong Kong, Thailand, China and the Soviet Union. The only countries with which it had trade deficits were mid-Eastern oil states.

Miscellaneous news items: The leading US exports to Japan in the mid-1980s were soybeans, corn, logs, coal, wheat, and cotton. The leading Japanese exports to the United States were cars, iron and steel plates, radios, motorbikes, and tape recorders. Canada exported coal, softwood lumber, fish, and meat to Japan and imported cars, motorbikes, trucks, automomobile parts, telecommunications equipment, and electronic consumer goods. Both the United States and Canada had trade deficits with Japan.

Item by item, these reports documented the shift in economic power from the northeastern United States to Japan, from North America to Southeast Asia, from the Atlantic to the Pacific. American writers of the early 1980s were describing the consequences in closed factories, unemployment, and the growth of poverty. The phrases they coined or popularized – deindustrialization, the wasteland, zero-sum economies, paper entrepreneurialism – became part of the vocabulary of the industrialized nations. Their analyses were picked up or paralleled by European writers who similarly documented the exit of established companies from industrial heartlands, the offshore production of textiles, electronics, and many other products, and the voluminous evidence of a loss of competitive capacity in traditional industrial regions as compared with Japan and with regions now widely called "the newly industrializing countries" (NICS). The newspapers faithfully produced their own evidence of a massive global shift in economic power:

Globe and Mail, 18 December 1984: "Westinghouse Electric Corporation of Pittsburgh and Japan's Toshiba Corporation will establish a joint venture in New York State to produce the electronic tubes used in color television sets and computer display monitors. The new firm will employ about 700 people in a plant closed by Westinghouse in 1977."

Wall Street Journal, 12 April 1985: The US Steel Corporation has negotiated a partnership with South Korea's Pohang Iron and Steel company. US Steel had already reduced capacity by 30 per cent since 1979. The *Journal* speculated that Pohang could gain an equity position in US steel facilities.

Globe and Mail, 25 March 1985: Caterpillar Tractor Company has moved much of its production to France and Scotland to take advantage of lower currency values, and is putting its name on equipment manufactured by suppliers in South Korea in an attempt to meet strong competition from Komatsu of Japan. Komatsu is opening a new production plant in Tennessee.

The Japan Times, 19 May 1985: Nisshin Steel Company, Japan's sixth largest steelmaker, has taken over Thinsheet Metals Co., a major American electronics material maker. The takeover is regarded as part of a strategy to enter the electronics material field. The firm produces 500 tons of material for electronic parts annually.

The Japan Times, 6 May 1985: In 1985, 36 new Japanese joint ventures were established in China, bringing the total to 48, not counting hundreds of technical co-operation and licensing projects or loans and grants. Forty per cent of Japan's steel exports go to China, and Japan not only imports Chinese oil but has established the Japan-China Oil Corporation to finance exploration in China's Bohai Bay. China imported about 60,000 vehicles in 1984 and the market is growing. Japanese auto companies are negotiating joint ventures, as are computer and electrical products manufacturing firms.

Robert Reich provided a popular explanation for these changes.[32] America, he said, gave special preference to developing countries in the form of easy access to international capital through the World Bank and private banks, fluid technology transfers, educational assistance to Third World students, and low-tariff borders for entry into the American market. Companies tended to move towards the lowest-cost regions and to relocate plant and equipment as costs increased in any one place. Japanese companies, which successfully invaded the world marketplace by producing low-cost goods with low-cost labour in the 1960s, produced those goods in the 1970s in Korea, Singapore, and Hong Kong, where labour was cheaper than it was in Japan. The productivity of North American workers used to be a major offsetting advantage for establishing plants in the United States or Canada; now other regions, even those with unskilled local labour, could provide similar productivity ratings because much of the productivity was achieved through investment in automated assembly lines, robots, numerically controlled machines, telematics, and other advanced equipment. This explanation was popular for an obvious reason: it found the United States not only guiltless, but indeed a benefactor whose generosity had been received without gratitude.

Barry Bluestone and Bennett Harrison called the change "deindustrialization."[33] In their view, the disinvestment occurred either because American industry provided technology and management techniques to non-Americans through licences, joint production companies, and direct investment abroad, or because American companies moved elsewhere to establish plants in countries and regions offering lower taxes, lower wages or a non-unionized labour force, lower energy costs, or any combination of these and other conditions that would increase their profitability. They closed plants, laid off workers, dislocated communities, and created economic chaos in their wake. Bluestone and Harrison argued that the competition from Japan was often really competition from American-Japanese companies which undercut the original American companies to the detriment of American workers and taxpayers but to the benefit of their own American investors. For example, General Electric purchased Toshiba stock from 1953 onwards until it owned the majority of offshore shares as well as 40 per cent of a subsidiary firm. These firms were licensed to make GE products for export. Following a 1969 strike against GE in the United States, Toshiba supplied electronic parts to American plants. Similarly, Westinghouse purchased shares in Mitsubishi beginning in 1923, and so decreased competition that it was obliged to face US a Justice Department charges of conspiracy with Mitsubishi to avoid US antitrust laws. [34] These companies sold goods to the United States in such increasing volume that by 1968 imports of electrical products exceeded exports.

Electrical products were not the only area in which American corporations financed their own competition. According to Bluestone and Harrison, between 1975 and 1977 Citibank, Chase Manhattan, and the Chemical Bank of New York made loans totalling over $500 million to the Japanese steel industry. [35] In the same years a number of very large steel plants were closed in the United States; the companies claimed that they could not finance modernization. The banks and steel companies may appear to be independent agencies, and one might conclude that the banks "did in" the domestic firms, were it not for the fact that the steel corporations themselves were investing in overseas operations at that time. US Steel Corporation owned eleven foreign companies, several of which were in receipt of American bank loans. The purchasers of the iron ore, zinc, coal, and other products of the companies owned by US Steel included the Japanese steelmakers, whose growth depended on the same banks.

Japan was not the only region in which American corporations acted against their domestic interests. Goodyear Tire and Rubber, for example, was intimately connected to Michelin of France as well as to Bridgestone of Japan, Dunlop of Britain, and Firelli of Italy.

The list goes on, but the point is always the same: American capital was financing the fall of American capitalism. This version was much closer to reality, and much less popular with corporate capital.

Bluestone and Harrison made a second argument. As profit rates for their home companies declined, American companies began to diversify their American holdings, taking over plants in a wild array of industries they knew nothing about, letting the plants fall apart, then milking them of their cash to finance investments outside the country. They provided evidence that the takeover companies closed plants whose profit margins were below arbitrary levels established by the new parent firms (such as a 20 or 25 per cent return on investment). Such levels would not have been met by most companies even in the heyday of American expansion. Modest returns apparently were no longer acceptable to companies that could realize immodest returns by orgies of buying, merging, taking over, closing, moving from one region to another, and playing tax-evasion games with capital that in an earlier decade would have been productively employed.

This tendency to invest in unproductive takeovers and conglomerates was also noted by Reich, who dubbed it "paper entrepreneurialism." Reich and other social scientists agreed that the hierarchical organization of American industries, the very design that permitted them to produce long runs of standardized goods for mass markets, was a major impediment to their development. They were inflexible, authoritarian institutions within which entrepreneurial talent and innovative intellects were stifled, along with the energy and commitment of production workers. Because they failed to adapt, their capital was put to unproductive uses, and it was their accounting and financial management talent rather than engineering and scientific knowledge that allowed them to survive so long.[36]

Lester Thurow argued in *The Zero-Sum Society* that the United States failed to shift its focus from an international cold war to its own domestic problems and was unable to impose economic solutions.[37] Any group that would be adversely affected by a shift in investment could effectively block reforms. The American population, in his view, was less able to adapt to change in the mid-1980s than in the past. Its faith in politicians had been shaken by Vietnam and Watergate, and its minorities, who used to absorb the economic losses, had become militant. The proportion of disinterested citizens necessary for the proper working of democratic decision-making had shrunk with the growth of government employment and dependence on government welfare programs.

This approach cast government in the role of the (often unintentional) protector of privileges and benefits for groups that might otherwise have lost their economic security. Over the long run and for the society as a whole, this role created barriers to social and economic change. Thus, the energy problems of US industry were seen to be caused as much by protective regulations and subsidies as by foreign cartels, and inflation was created by the energy policies and similar programs of government.

These American economists agreed that the consequence of investment patterns over the 1970s was unused capacity. Samuel Bowles, David Gordon, and Thomas Weisskopf caught the fundamental characteristic of contemporary American industry in the phrase "the wasteland."[38] Together with Reich and Bluestone and Harrison, they argued that the problems – including America's loss of competitive advantage, the growing unemployment and inflation rates, the falling rates of productivity, and troubled Americans in conflict with one another because the economy had failed them – were solvable with a wholly new approach to economic development and industrial production. In particular, they argued, there was a need to inject democratic decision-making into the production plant and worker participation into management decisions.

Canadians, who have always been resource suppliers for American capitalism, were also shocked by the terms of trade with Japan and newly industrialized nations. As the breadlines grew in their cities and the unemployment rate soared, Canadians shared the American unease with what their politicians called "unfair competition."

For the United States, Canada was an essential reservoir of natural resources as well as an important, though small, consumer market. It was a staunch ally in international affairs. Canada had become a peculiar country during the twentieth century. It was a prosperous, stable democracy, but at the same time it possessed scarcely any independent industry, especially outside the heartland of southern Ontario and Quebec. It had the highest level of foreign (mainly American) ownership of industry of any OECD country, the second lowest proportion of GNP invested in research and development (only Belgium had less), and an extremely high dependence on exports. Of these exports, a majority were raw or semi-processed materials, or component parts made for the US-owned firms straddling the border. When the recession hit the United States in the early 1980s, Canada was flattened.

For Canadian business leaders – bankers and financiers, heads of subsidiary firms (whom one researcher called Trojan horses),[39] and companies that wanted to internationalize and greatly feared that increasing protectionist sentiments in the United States would impede their expansion – the solution was what they called "free trade." The free trade agreement between Canada and the United States, when it finally appeared, had less to do with trade than with opportunities for investment, but the slogans carried weight none the less. The FTA was based upon the premise that foreign competition had undermined North American capitalism.

Two Canadian scholars, Bertrand Bellon and Jorge Niosi, repeating the observations of their American counterparts, showed both the decline in American industrial power and the consequences for America's satellites, Canada and Latin America. They demonstrated the decline in Canada's share of international trade, its increasing dependence on the United States for its exports, and its decreasing share of American direct investment and financial control over its industries: "Traditional Canadian industry is just as threatened as its US counterpart by labour-intensive imports from the newly industrializing countries, and it is protecting itself in the same way."[40]

These, then, were the interpretations of the early 1980s presented to North Americans by their leading social scientists. They focused on the United States, and they defined the central problem as the loss of American dominance in the world economy.

There were parallels in the literature elsewhere, because other industrial countries were also experiencing economic decline in the early 1980s. The deindustrialization thesis was advanced in Britain by Frank T. Blackaby and others,[41] and was combined with a theory announcing the "new international division of labour" (but not recognizing that the new division now involved American exports of grains) by German writers, Folker Fröbel, Jürgen Heinrichs, and Otto Kreye.[42] Bill Jordan[43] and Doreen Massey and Richard Meegan [44] published analyses of events in Britain parallel to those of Bowles, Gordon, and Weisskopf. The part of Thurow's argument that criticized the numerous interest groups in democracies and the crippling effects of their pressures on government appeared in a somewhat twisted form throughout the international literature of the new right.

THESE ARGUMENTS ARE helpful in understanding both the structure of the industrial economies and the effects of the globalization of capital. But occasionally they adopted the problematic assumptions of the very system they critically assessed. For the American writers especially, one assumption was that the American economy should grow and Americans should continue to consume a disproportionate share of the world's resources. This assumption was shared by Canadians, whose ties to the United States are cultural as well as economic, and by Europeans, who had enjoyed their own high standards of living under the Pax Americana. It was an assumption that left environmental issues out of economic calculations, and despite occasional sympathetic nods at the poverty and hunger prevalent elsewhere, it suggested no process either for reducing consumption in the developed economies or for peacefully redistributing wealth.

Generally missing in the American appraisals, for example, is a frank recognition of what the United States did as its fortunes declined. Persistently it resorted to GATT for rulings against the competition. It exerted pressure, within its new limitations, on the EEC and Japan to reduce their exports in strategic industries such as automobiles. It continued to impose varying monetary conditions to offset changes contrary to its interests in the international monetary arena. Of particular concern to the poor countries of the world, it introduced new government policies designed to improve the terms of trade in agriculture as well as in manufactured goods. Before 1973 the United States exported foodstuffs in modest quantity; after that year US exports of selected agricultural produce expanded dramatically, and sales to Japan, the EEC, and the USSR became significant components in total US exports. All these responses were inconsistent with the prevailing belief in free enterprise, a belief ever more loudly espoused in reference to the underdeveloped countries yet less evident the United States itself. More seriously, these behaviours, especially the agricultural policies, did real harm to countries that depended on their exports of grains, and upset an already fragile trading arena.

As was suggested in the earlier part of this chapter, the ending of the Pax Americana had a technological context. Because the technology had become attached to military institutions, American commercial applications did not flourish as quickly as they might have. Discussions of the role of military institutions, war preparations, and war itself were absent from most popular analyses of American decline published in the early 1980s. By the end of that decade Paul Kennedy's historical interpretation of the military burdens of hegemonic powers offered an acceptable account, for American consumption, of the relationship between military costs and decline of empires. [45] It was acceptable because it cast the problem in terms of the necessary protective burden that great powers assume. Still missing was a public awareness of how military preoccupations had preempted commercial adaptations of a new technology and of how vertical integration and hierarchical organization of industrial production impeded innovative applications of the technology.

The studies cited above were published in the early to middle 1980s, but they actually described the situation of the middle to late 1970s. By the time they were written the situation had changed again and, while Americans were becoming nearly hysterical about their loss of power, the dilemmas of the 1970s had already been overtaken by new and different circumstances. Investment capital was already returning to the industrial countries, pushed and pulled by further technological change, fuel and transportation costs, and international competition. The international division of labour became more complex. Japanese and European firms located in North America to evade possible tariff walls. New service industries broke down non-tariff walls everywhere. Governments became increasingly active in trying to attract international investment. The Pax Americana was over and would not be revived. But America was still the most powerful single nation, one of the most affluent, and certainly capable of influencing, if no longer determining unilaterally, the course of modern history.

In this same period new studies of Japan were published by business writers. Their overwhelming message was that Japanese corporations had unique organizational features that permitted them to act quickly in response to changing environmental conditions: workers were loyal, governments supported industry, and democratic impulses were restrained. These were the understood reasons for Japan's stunning success. Over the next decade this literature rapidly expanded, and exchanges of business leaders kept the airlines in business. Something new was happening to America and Britain: they were taking an interest in learning from another society. What they learned was highly selective, but it dovetailed with a more general motivation to change the rules of the game. If the Pax Americana was over and a whole new global economy was up for grabs, how could businesses reorganize their own operations and their relationships with governments so as to capture new profits?

CHAPTER FIVE

The New Right Agenda

With the Coca-Cola stall, the invisible hand was recalled from retirement. In what appeared to be a sudden and spontaneous development, business leaders and politicians around the world began using a whole new vocabulary to explain the recession of the early 1980s and to promote a new agenda. They said that government had undercut healthy entrepreneurship through its interference in the free market. The new vocabulary included "privatization," "deregulation," "downsizing," "restraint," and "special export zones." "Free trade" and "free enterprise" took on a new urgency and a more extreme meaning. "Democracy" lost its lustre, and became associated with complaints about excessive and unrealistic expectations.

This apparent spontaneity was underpinned by considerable planning, organization, and funding. The organizations included the Mont Pélérin Society in Geneva, the Kiel Economics Institute in West Germany, and the Club de l'Horloge in France. In Britain, there was the Institute of Economic Affairs, the Adam Smith Institute, the Centre for Policy Studies, the Institute of Directors, and the Aims of Industry. In North America, the counterparts included the Heritage Foundation, the American Conservative Union, Young Americans for Freedom, the Thomas Jefferson Center Foundation, the Reason Foundation, the CATO Institute, the Society for Individual Liberty, and the Fraser Institute. The Trilateral Commission brought together Europeans, Japanese, and North Americans. These organizations united writers, business leaders, and politicians whose common objective was to dismantle the Keynesian welfare state.

The US Libertarian party was established in 1972, and ran John Hospers, a new right advocate and a professor of philosophy, as its presidential candidate. [1] It grew out of an earlier organization, Young Americans for Freedom, whose opposition to the draft had guided members towards opposition to government. By 1980 the party had over five hundred candidates in federal elections and was becoming known as "the tax revolt party." Its counterpart in Australia, the Workers' party (later renamed the Progress party), was established in 1975.[2] Margaret Thatcher became leader of the British Conservative party in 1975, signalling its transition from traditional conservative to new right ideology.

The same phraseology and the same arguments were promoted throughout the world; the same books were published and distributed; public speeches and media events were mounted everywhere at once. Popular magazines spread the message: *Libertarian Review, Libertarian Forum, The Individualist, Public Interest, Plain Truth, Reason, Fraser Currents, The Freeman,* and *The Objectivist.* The *Journal of Libertarian Studies* and scholarly forums brought the intellectuals of the right into universities. Earlier right-wing publications, such as the *Ayn Rand Letter,* were eclipsed: they had viewed communism as the threat to individualism; the libertarians objected to their own governments.

Though the overall message was unambiguous – government was bad, the market was good – the particular arguments were not internally consistent; indeed, even within the same texts contrary ideas were mounted. The extreme libertarian position revealed an authoritarian streak: obedience to impersonal market forces became a shibboleth in a moral crusade. Fundamentalist religious beliefs were interspersed with economic and political arguments extolling freedom. As the movement grew it became evident that there were diverse contributors, and though they shared an anti-democratic ideology their objectives and interests were not otherwise congruent. Even so, they were united in the primary objective: to dismantle the welfare state.

I must emphasize here that this is not a conspiracy theory. The institutes and think-tanks were well funded and the funding sources were publicly listed in annual reports. The international associations, including the one I have selected for special attention, behaved somewhat like an international *zaikai* – a self-conscious core of business leaders whose task is to create an ideological consensus and to influence, if not to direct, public policy.

I use the Japanese term deliberately. Although business leaders in Europe and North America had various organizations in their national arenas, they had never behaved as self-proclaimed leaders of public opinion. Indeed, until the 1970s, business leaders in North America and Europe had argued that business should not be engaged in policy-making or social planning. Their ancestors had eschewed the role of the aristocracy, leaving to government the responsibility for the public interest. Their actions, of course, frequently belied their statements, but they had always publicly refused to undertake the task of shaping opinions.

This chapter describes the views of the libertarian and self-proclaimed new right and of the Trilateral Commission. I argue that though these two major contributors to the new right ideology had divergent interests, they were united in their attack on the Keynesian state. The libertarian wing sought to free entrepreneurs from state restrictions; the corporate wing sought to free investment from national restrictions; both benefited from an ideological campaign against the welfare state.

THE LIBERTARIAN COMPONENT of the new right may have had its origins in the Mont Pélérin Society, whose founding members in 1947 included Robert Nozick, Friedrich A. Hayek, Karl Popper, Milton Friedman, and the West German minister of economic affairs, Ludwig Erhard. Later, Keith Joseph and Enoch Powell of the British Conservative party joined.[3] In this organization, as in others established later, the mutual interest lies in the attack on government, but within the published work of its members there are divergent themes. Extreme individualism, totally free markets, and competition are extolled; yet law and order and a much more disciplined society, even an authoritarian form of government, are also promoted. The economy is to be absolutely free of government intervention, yet government is to remain the protector of property and the enforcer of law and order. In the economic sphere, market order is to supercede government order. The laws of supply and demand will discipline the population.

Andrew Belsey attempted to unravel the contradictions in a study of the British new right. In his view, the five values of neo-liberalism (libertarianism) are, in order or priority, the individual; freedom of choice; market security; laissez-faire; and minimal government. Neo-conservatism has as its core values strong government; social authoritarianism; a disciplined society; hierarchy and subordination; and the nation. Thatcherism is an uneasy combination of all of these.[4] The uneasy combination is due partly to the reorganization of priorities in the British Conservative party; there as elsewhere it is not traditional liberals, but rather conservatives, who support the new right.

While most popularizers of the new right oppose the invocation of any moral ethic external to individual choices (such as the protection of the environment or the well-being of the poor), the theories promote a very particular moral vision. The word "talent," for example, often used in the treatises of the American new right, turns out to mean entrepreneurial skills and nothing else. Certain other concepts have no meaning at all – community; rights other than in traditional properties; or public goods, except where they are purchased by any group of individuals who all agree that they wish to obtain them. The assumption of individual rationality, borrowed from Adam Smith, also promotes a particular moral view. A good society consists only of individuals, each pursuing private interests through rational consideration of preferences, priorities, and alternatives. Democracy is viewed in Tocqueville's terms (but without his context) as the tyranny of the majority.[5] In this analysis, democracy inevitably leads to economic decline and stagnation.

The most celebrated writer in this vein is Friedrich Hayek, who explicitly rejected the term "conservative" for his philosophy.[6] Hayek developed his arguments in the Austria of the 1930s, but his popularity dates from the 1970s. He argues that progress depends on the individual freedom to act, experiment, learn from experience, and benefit from one's own talents. Inequality is both inevitable and necessary – the first because individuals are unequally endowed by nature and circumstance, the second because only through the free actions of the more talented can the mass of people benefit from the entrepreneurial activities those talented ones undertake. This is also true on an international scale: the underdeveloped countries can progress only by learning from the examples of free individuals in free countries. There is a fundamental problem in the concept of majority rule, since the idea contradicts the primary objective of individual liberty: "Liberalism ... is concerned mainly with limiting the coercive powers of all government, whether democratic or not, whereas the dogmatic democrat knows only one limit to government – current majority opinion."[7] Further, "There can clearly be no moral justification for any majority granting its members privileges by laying down rules which discriminate in their favor."[8]

On employment, he argues that the development of a propertyless proletariat was not the result of expropriation but of the growth of a class that could employ others. The problem with democracy, then, is that the employed, who now form a majority, favour policies that guarantee their personal security rather than the longevity of progress and prosperity through the liberation of that class of individuals who are capable of advancing economic development.[9]

Hayek speaks of "the Great Society" in reference to one governed by the order of the market. "The market," he says, "is essentially an ordering mechanism."[10] This, together with various other arguments about the discipline of markets, leads to some contradictory conclusions: liberty is the primary value, yet the rule of markets and market discipline are the central mechanisms for the great society. Individuals are bound by the dictates of markets, ordered hierarchically according to their entrepreneurial success, and subordinated to an abstract set of rules. In Hayek's voluminous writings we find the paradoxical combination of libertarianism and authoritarianism; it is only democratic government that is missing.

Popular versions of Hayek's views are plentiful. Arthur Seldon, once a student in Hayek's classes at the London School of Economics, introduced a collection of essays by self-proclaimed new right writers by observing that what they had in common was the "rejection of the state as the source of the good life."[11] His colleague at the Institute of Economic Affairs, Ralph Harris, created a Life Peer in 1979 as Lord Harris of Highcross, unflingingly refers to himself as "one of Hayek's second-hand dealers in ideas."[12] He specializes in demonstrating the cost, inefficiency, and immorality of government. The immorality lies in governments' tendency to upset the balance of market forces and thus reduce "maximum competition among producers." Harris concedes that governments do have duties, and that a negative income tax may be necessary, but "once government has laid down the ground rules for competition, further interventions should be kept to the minimum. We should not make the poverty or incompetence of a dwindling minority the pretext for denying the growing majority the boon of free choice."[13]

George Gilder is one of the American popularizers. In a celebrated defence of the position, he argues that "the problem of contemporary capitalism lies not chiefly in the deterioration of physical capital, but in the persistent subversion of the psychological means of production – the morale and inspiration of economic man – undermining the very conscience of capitalism: the awareness that one must give in order to get, supply in order to demand."[14] In his view, economic equality "tends to promote greed over giving."[15] For Gilder, much of the problem of contemporary capitalism lies in its subversion of natural leadership: "Leadership is supply and public opinion is demand." Democracy's great flaw is that it reverses the "appropriate direction of influence."[16] Since demand is no more than an artefact of what leaders cause to be supplied, it has no independent reality. People "demand" whatever is created, be it an innovative product or an idea about equality. When governments impose equality, whether through taxation, redistribution, or egalitarian schooling, they oppose nature and bring about the destruction of an otherwise creative society. Equality as an idea is nothing more than a product successfully sold at a particular point in history; the demand for it will pass if entrepreneurs and new right governments market a superior product. "Capitalist creativity is guided not by any invisible hand, but by the quite visible and aggressive hand of management and entrepreneurship."[17]

For this reason, successful management leads inevitably to monopolies in the marketplace. However, monopolies are short-lived if nothing intervenes, since competitors will always seek and eventually find ways of undermining the monopolist. The longevity of contemporary monopolies is caused by government interference. Since demand is an artefact of good management, monopolies will persist only as long as they can create a demand for their product unless governments provide subsidies, protection, and special conditions that oblige customers to buy that product. Otherwise another company will displace the first by persuading potential customers to alter the nature of their demands; then it in turn will become the monopolist. Monopoly is actually "potential competition."

If democracy is nothing more then the vehicle for the expression of demands from the masses, as Gilder argues, then it is not worthy of respect. The masses will demand much more than the system can provide if they are given no leadership; their demands will be random and irrational. To obey such demands or even to give them credence is to abandon government altogether. Finally, since only the creative entrepreneurs produce real wealth, it is they rather than the masses whose interests must be consulted by government. This is the only way the masses can be protected from their cruder instincts.[18]

Irving Kristol is another American popularizer, but his version is more conservative. He acknowledges the reality of classes, and even of class conflict: "There is always class conflict, and the very notion of a possible society without class conflict is one of socialism's most bizarre fantasies."[19] But the unusual feature of capitalism is that "its aim is the satisfaction of 'common' appetites and aspirations," and the most persistent conflict comes not from industrial workers but from intellectuals and the upper middle class. The problem of American capitalism is not class inequality but the lack of a "theoretical – i.e., ideological – legitimacy." Capitalism's power has been usurped by public servants in government bureaucracies.

Most popular writers on the right have little to say about corporate capitalism, since corporations are viewed as extensions of individual entrepreneurship. Kristol, however, defends them. In Kristol's view, corporate capitalism has produced wealth in America and throughout the world. Hunger elsewhere is caused by socialist governments and by hoarding. Deprivation would be overcome and people would be productive if "individual incentives predominate and the free market ... predominates."[20] Agreeing that corporate capitalism sometimes involves corruption or fails to defend itself against the charge of corruption, Kristol suggests that better corporate advertising and a clear corporate code of ethics would solve the problem.

Milton Friedman's fame rests partly on his supply-side theory of inflation, but also on his views about unions (they distort the "natural" wage level and thus become a cause of unemployment) and his advocacy of a negative income tax, education vouchers, denationalization (privatization), deregulation, and abolition of protective legislation on rents, wages, and regional development and of most public spending.[21] Although Hayek and Friedman do not argue the same economic case, their general views on the superiority of market forces and the inherent inefficiency of governments have brought them into the same philosophical camp as the new right.

Robert Nozick[22] and Milton Friedman, though in different ways, offer a utilitarian argument that individual choices determine social outcomes. Any government that imposes its values on a population is necessarily oppressive. If individuals actually want certain social outcomes, the way to obtain them is to band together, to create an explicit contract; when all are agreed, they will achieve the outcome. If they are unprepared to pay the price (in capital, time, or energy) for an outcome, that is a fair indication that they do not assign it a high priority. If, for example, they want education for their children, they should be both prepared to pay for it and able to choose its form; in Friedman's view, education vouchers might be an appropriate mechanism to replace state-funded systems. Nozick carries the argument further: in his view, taxation is theft, and no public demand on private wealth is morally defensible.

In Britain, Enoch Powell produced a libertarian version of utopia in the 1960s, but his critiques of the welfare state were disregarded at the time. Hayek and Friedman influenced his successors of the 1970s, particularly Sir Keith Joseph. By the 1970s there were other sources of anti-welfare, market-oriented thought in the new right think-tanks. The Institute of Economic Affairs (IEA) goes back to 1957, but, like Hayek himself, its numerous publications and leading figures (in particular Seldon and Harris) did not have high profiles until the 1970s. Other institutes were founded in the 1970s and 1980s, some (like the IEA) attacking welfare economics and arguing for a more competitive marketplace. The Social Affairs Unit specialized in denouncing government social services.[23]

The Adam Smith Institute, established in 1977, may be the most influential of the British think-tanks because it is devoted to policy advocacy rather than to analysis. Friedrich Hayek is the chairman of its advisory board, and one of its managers has been quoted as describing the public sector as "inherently evil."[24] Much of the Thatcher government's policy has its roots in the policy pronouncements of the institute, especially the privatization of local and central government services, all nationalized industries, and much of the National Health Service.[25]

The public sector became a self-conscious class during the postwar period. It was unionized in most of Europe, Canada, and Australia, and though it was not unionized in the United States, it negotiated there, as elsewhere, relatively high salaries and tenured job security. It had an explicit, recognized stake in the maintenance of democracy, the expansion of social services, and the growth of government's jurisdiction over the economy. For these reasons, it mounted strong and articulate objections to transnational corporate power. At the same time it provided the central critique of the laissez-faire, market-oriented economic policies promoted by the new right, and was the largest and most active component of social democratic parties. In short, the public sector was anathema to the individualistic, entrepreneurial, free market libertarian, and an obstacle to the full development of the global market promoted by transnational capital. Privatization in Britain and the downsizing of welfare programs in the United States were advanced as means of creating more competitive societies, but much of the frontal attack was against civil servants, who were viewed by the new right as opponents of progress.

Among other effects, the downsizing and phasing out of services has slowed the progress of sexual equality in the workplace. If social services are removed from the public sector, private individuals will have to perform them. Someone must care for the children, the handicapped, and the elderly when no profit-making business can be made of them. Women are being urged to "return to the home." The new right argument is that they never wanted to leave it; they did so only because the high taxes levied to pay for social services obliged them to find paid employment.

Opposition to the new right has concentrated on the moral assumptions of extreme individualism, on the social outcomes of the model for distributional issues, and on the disregard for such externalities as the environment. Critics are located on both the conservative and social democratic ends of the usual political spectrum.[26] They argue that the new right provides a means for the

further concentration of capital and justifies a growing distance between the rich and the poor. All of the arguments mounted since
Rousseau's time (outlined in chapter 2) are restated. The Keynesian
objections are repeated not only by social democrats, but even more
strongly by mainstream economists throughout the world. Other
critics focus on the logical flaws in the new right arguments.[27] A few
of the objections are summarized here, though it is not my intention
to deliberate at length on the logical or moral flaws of the ideology.

Before the new right had advanced its full program, Kenneth
Arrow had argued that individual preferences cannot be translated
into social preferences because there is no logically possible mechanism to accomplish this in a non-dictatorial voting system. Any
combination of individuals cannot achieve a rational decision solely
on the basis of their individual preferences.[28] That argument was
revived against Hayek and Nozick, who advocated social decision-
making through individual preference mechanisms. In the larger
free market argument, the invisible-hand assumption is questioned
on empirical grounds. Individual preferences are not devoid of social
content or social impact, and the preferences of some necessarily
affect the ability of others to express preferences. Consider a west
coast fisher who prefers to catch uncontaminated fish and a pulp
mill owner who prefers not to spend money on pollution controls.
If the pulp mill emits contaminants into the water, the fish become
inedible and the fisher loses her livelihood. Nothing in the new right
arguments overcomes such a problem; there is simply no way that
fishers and pulp mill owners can arrive at a mutually satisfactory
solution on the basis of their respective preferences. Furthermore,
putting the problem in these terms already simplifies it, since the
preferences of many others are also involved, and some of them do
not know the problem exists even though it is affecting them (for
example, they may be eating polluted fish).

The free market answer to such problems sometimes takes the
form of utilitarian solutions: all the participants can offer money to
others, and those who accept money in place of their other activity
indicate thereby how much the activity is worth to them. If at some
point the fishers agree to stop fishing, and if, from the point of view
of the pulp mill owners, the bribe for this outcome is less than the
cost of cleaning up the pollution, then all parties end up with a social
outcome of mutual benefit. Of course, this ignores the differences
in the starting positions of the fishers and the pulp mill owners (the
fishers cannot possibly achieve the opposite result, since they cannot
offer an amount that would make it beneficial for the pulp mill to
cease operations). It also ignores the externalities – uncontaminated

fish as a source of food and as a life-form, an uncontaminated habitat for other life-forms that have not become potential commodities, aesthetic values, and the well-being of the unsuspecting public at large.

The differences between private and public goods are critical to an assessment of the free market argument. The invisible hand may work very well when it governs market choices about private consumer goods. But much of any individual's life is governed by tangible and intangible public goods. A public good, for example, is a system of traffic laws equally applicable to all drivers. Another is clean water. These and many other goods cannot be achieved except by societies and rules that in some respects delimit the freedom of individuals. This may seem obvious when one speaks of traffic and clean water; it is less obvious when the subjects are education, wages, and sexual equality.

On education, the new right argues that its function is to prepare students for the job market. Either all schooling should be privately paid for, in which case the student would be free to choose the form the schooling takes (the Friedman and Nozick argument), or governments should determine what the job market will require and establish funding policies accordingly. In either event, the new right literature advocates a reduction in public spending on education. Fewer students should be encouraged to attend universities; more should be streamed into technical schools and directly into the labour force. Since the new right views the global economy as competitive in high-technology industries, its political leaders selectively fund those areas of applied science that seem most likely to create appropriate technological skills. The new right has no evident interest in the core subjects of a liberal education, and it would not support the notion that the preservation and critical assessment of a cultural heritage are essential to society. If these are valued by the population, then individual citizens should privately sustain them; otherwise the cost of their sustenance is imposed on taxpayers by the educators and infringes on private rights. The opposite argument is that a sound educational system produces citizens with both the knowledge and the wisdom to sustain a healthy society. Such an argument carries little weight for those who recognize no social goods beyond individual preferences.

If, as the new right claims, minimum wage laws are an infringement on the rights of employers and ultimately lead to unemployment, what is the effect of no minimum wage? It is not clear that employment would substantially increase, because, among other things, poverty would increase and profits on consumer products would decline. A substantially enlarged labour force competing for jobs would lower all wages, but the net effect could well be an increase in the number of unemployed and working poor. Andrew Schotter argues cogently that a rational response for low-income workers would be to allocate more of their time to illegal and non-market activities.[29] He argues not so much for minimum wage laws as for ensured and adequate wages (other forms could be implemented); his point is that a free market solution, assuming complete rationality for workers and employers, will not result in the expanded economy postulated by the new right.

Ultimately, these arguments are about human nature, about human rationality and selfishness. But arguments about human nature are puerile if they ignore the cultural and social contexts that condition humans to act in a certain way. The extreme individualism manifest in the United States throughout its history is embedded in a culture that equates rational behaviour with selfishness. From the Japanese perspective, much American behaviour appears strangely irrational and self-destructive. What matters about the new right is that it emerged as a social movement when it did, that its umbrella provided the protection for a swift restructuring of the economies and governments of industrial countries. That task completed, much of the rhetoric diminishes and the industrial countries find themselves with some age-old dilemmas and no easy answers.

AS WE HAVE SEEN, the self-labelled new right is scarcely concerned with corporate capitalism; it sees the world through the eyes of small entrepreneurs. It is not concerned with the world stage; non-industrial countries are relegated to the periphery in its economic analyses. There are organizations, however, that provide the missing dimensions in a way consistent with some features of the new right ideology. They propound the unlabelled doctrines for the more conservative component of the new right.

One of these, and the most important, is the Trilateral Commission, founded in 1973 by David Rockefeller, then chairman of the Chase Manhattan Bank; Zbigniew Brzezinski, then a professor at Columbia University and later, under the Carter administration, a US national security adviser; and a small group of prominent American business leaders and academics. The Trilateral Commission is not normally included in the roster of new right institutions because its members would shun the label, because the self-identified new right members do not usually acknowledge debts to it, and because opponents of the new right do not associate the apparently responsible Trilateralists with the groups they deem to be irresponsible. That notwithstanding, the Trilateralists had the most explicit agenda for the restructuring of the post-hegemonic global economy in the middle to late 1970s.

The antecedents of the Trilateral Commission were several post-war organizations, including the Council on Foreign Relations, which operated during the war and which had considerable influence over the establishment of the IMF and the World Bank,[30] and the Bilderberg meetings, which began in 1954, whose major objective was the unification of Europe.[31] The Trilateralists, however, were the first such group to include Japan, and, unlike the post-war groups, they actively sought publicity, stated candidly that their intention was to influence public opinion, and commissioned studies on topics of concern to them.

The inclusion of Japan in the Commission was vital to the project. In 1983 Nobuhiko Ushiba, a former minister of external economic affairs, told the commission's plenary session at Rome, "The creation of the Trilateral Commission in the early 1970s was symbolic of this need for more intensive consultation and for the active involvement of Japan as a fully-engaged member of the developed, democratic world."[32]

Many critics viewed the Trilateralists as a conspiracy of the rich against the poor. If conspiracy means the gathering together of a group with like interests to devise means of protecting their privileges, that is a fair charge. The historical parallels are numerous: in the absence of parliamentary government, the kings and courts of European countries did much the same thing, though more crudely. Through the Congress of Vienna and its predessors and successors, strong European states imposed their combined wills on weaker states. (Some have viewed the Trilateralists as a conspiracy of Jewish finance capital in league with communists. For those who are willing to believe this, Henry Kissinger, Pierre Trudeau, and Margaret Thatcher are also closet communists.)[33]

But if a conspiracy is a clandestine organization plotting dramatic events in private, the charge is unwarranted. The rich have other ways of meeting, planning, plotting, conspiring, and otherwise restructuring the world economy; the Trilateral Commission was not a necessary instrument for this. On the contrary, the commission was much more akin to the Japanese *zaikai* at an international level. It was a powerful lobby, a forum within which its members informed themselves of one another's circumstances and interests, deliberated on ways of dealing with problems of mutual concern, and developed means of spreading their message to political and business leaders throughout the world.

In the opinion of one member, the objective of the Trilateral Commission throughout this period was "to seek a private consensus on the specific problems examined in the Trilateral analysis [and] to seek to educate attentive audiences in the three regions so that public opinion in Japan, North America, and Europe will come to reflect the private consensus." [34] The core members were powerful business leaders, together with a smaller number of political, academic, media, and union leaders. The core members had global influence; the others – some three hundred members from the major capitalist countries – influenced public opinion within their own countries. For them, the organization was viewed as the chief bulwark against anarchy. Edmund Wellenstein said at the 1985 meetings. "The trilateral countries are the providers of the world economic order – or what we have of it." [35] The implication was clear: these opinion-makers had the obligation, not merely the privilege, to choose jointly the means of maintaining that order.

While the meetings of the Trilateral Commission were private, commissioned reports and some proceedings were published. These provided a captain's view of the global economy and its problems. From the perspective of its members, participation was reasonable, public-spirited behaviour in the interests of world peace. [36] From an outsider's perspective, this private body of leaders from industrial countries was not elected, was accountable to no one, and had no representation from less developed nations (Mexico was the exception). It outflanked and frequently ignored the United Nations. Its explicit objectives included the propagation of its members' views and action on behalf of its collective interests in the world arena.

The members' views were of two kinds. First, the internal arrangements between governments and populations in the advanced industrial countries had to be restructured. Governments had to be strengthened relative to citizens and democratic interest groups so that they could better create the necessary conditions for the restructuring of economies in a global marketplace. Second, the international organization of states required still greater freedom for transnational capital and a restructuring of the international monetary and trading system to accommodate global capital. By the early 1980s several of the commission's most prestigious members offered advice on how to deal with what they still called Third World debt and the demands of underdeveloped countries for a new international economic order.

One of the first problems tackled by the commission was "excess democracy." Three authors, American, French, and Japanese, each with credentials suitable to the Trilateralist agenda, were commissioned to analyse the "crisis of democracy" and make recommendations.[37] In their report they argued that the democracies had become burdened with overactive minority group representation, too much emphasis on welfare provisions, too much protection of workers, a top-heavy public bureaucracy, and too many critics in academe and the media. Criticism from these last two sources constituted a challenge to democratic government "as serious as those posed in the past by the aristocratic cliques, fascist movements and communist parties."

The heart of the problem lies in the inherent contradictions involved in the very phrase "governability of democracy." For, in some measure, governability and democracy are warring concepts. An excess of democracy means a deficit in governability; easy governability suggests faulty democracy. At times in the history of democratic government the pendulum has swung too far in one direction or the other ... At the present time, it appears that the balance has tilted too far against governments in Western Europe and the United States; in Japan, as yet, this problem is not acute, although it may well become so.[38]

The basic and explicit assumption in this report was that economic growth is essential to progress and democracy. The first recommendation was that all governments should plan for economic growth, and should co-ordinate their planning with one another. To do this, the authors argued, governments would have to be strengthened; they would need to have more centralized authority and less susceptibility to democratic inputs from citizens whose diverse demands undermine efficient planning. The media should be disciplined through stronger libel laws, and governments should be free to withhold information from the media. Mass education should be curbed, since there are already too many educated people for the available jobs; education should be directly related to the job market, and those disciplines most critical of corporate capitalism should be reined in by fiscal restraints. Industry must have the freedom to alter the rules and create new organizations. The authors did not say how workers were to be subdued while this occurred.[39]

The combination of a stronger government and a weaker democratic framework was not a shared objective for the new right; it reflected a world view from the top of the corporate ladder. For others on the new right, the solution was weaker governments altogether. For some, this meant the complete abandonment of democratic institutions.

Other Trilateral Commission publications tackled the range of global issues. In 1973 and 1974 they considered renovating the international monetary system, restructuring North-South economic relations, redirecting world trade, and re-creating a global regime for control of energy.[40] In the mid-1970s they reported on the law of the sea, world commodity markets, international consultation, collaboration with communist countries in managing global problems, and, again, the renovation of the international system.[41] In 1978-9 they addressed East-West relations, malnutrition in developing countries, energy, collective bargaining and employee participation, and industrial policy in the international economy.[42]

The general argument throughout these deliberations was that economic growth is essential, and for the LDCs growth depends on the growth of the developed market countries. The appropriate way to help the poor is to ensure that the rich continue to accumulate wealth. This can be done only in free markets. Separate countries still trade on the basis of comparative advantage calculations; this is appropriate because increasing specialization in production throughout the world will maximize positive trading relations. Mass consumption continues to be the basis of growth.

The Trilateralists noted, as did their opponents, that new consumption patterns were being established in the DMCs because of the new technologies, and new consumer populations were being created in the LDCs. These changes necessitated the restructuring of industry and trade patterns, and there would be temporary dislocations. Member states were urged to co-operate in handling the restructuring and dislocations so that the world order was not upset.

The underdeveloped countries suffered deprivation, the terms of trade for their commodity exports had declined, bank lending had decelerated, and aid concessions had dropped – all of this was conceded in Trilateralist reports of the 1980s. In a 1983 report co-written by the former World Bank president Robert S. McNamara, the problem was stated this way: "The restoration of normal economic conditions in the trilateral countries is closely linked to a return of satisfactory rates of growth in the developing countries."[43] The report advocated more concessional assistance (aid), coherent trade policies, and differential policies for OPEC, the NICs, and the marginal underdeveloped countries. The authors did not deal with private direct investment, which they characterized as "an efficient way of transferring technology and increasing productive capacities." They noted that although such investment was important, they were more concerned with the immediate crisis in the world economy. Nor does the report deal with global negotiations: "The authors are not convinced that these negotiations can have an impact on short- and medium-term problems."[44] In short, the Trilateralists preferred to deal with the North-South conflict in their own forums, not in UNCTAD or the United Nations General Assembly.

Trilateralists perceived the crisis of the LDCs as a consequence of international economic turbulence in the 1970s and the global recession of the 1980s, not as a long-term effect of colonialism, unequal trading relations, or free enterprise ideology. In defence of this position they pointed to the growth of GNP, improvements in health and education, and the construction of physical infrastructures in developing countries before the oil shocks, particularly the second shock of 1978–9. They observed that some governments failed to use bank loans and aid to increase investment or improve income distribution, but instead maintained consumption and subsidized agricultural goods. On this point McNamara and his co-authors were less harsh than some of the left-wing critics who are cited in later chapters. While they took note of these problems, they also argued that most recipient countries used their funds responsibly.

The major concern of the poor countries in the 1980s was that their exports had decreased because the industrial countries had reduced imports and, for the poorest countries, the levels of aid had diminished. The NICs and OPEC, however, were seen as occupying positions substantially different from those of other middle-income and low-income countries. The North-South dichotomy, therefore, was seen as misleading, and Trilateralists were advised to pursue different strategies for these different countries.

The report's chief recommendations were that the Trilateral countries resist protectionism and, "in formulating their trade policies, trilateral governments should take developing countries into account as much as they do their OECD partners." Non-tariff barriers must be recognized and reduced. No solution was to be found for commodity market changes in international schemes to shore up prices artificially; rather, the countries that depended on exports of agricultural and raw material products would have to be encouraged to diversify their economies. GATT would necessarily be involved in dealing with non-tariff barriers, especially in textiles and clothing, footwear, radios, television sets, steel, ships, and chemicals. The NICs would have to be disciplined because they maintained their own protective barriers; it would be unfair if "the GATT rules [applied] to one group of about 20 OECD countries, while all others, regardless of their stage or rate of development, [were] substantially and indefinitely free from international constraints."

The trade issue was related to the debt issue. If these countries could not trade, neither could they pay. As subsequent chapters will show, the Trilateralists' perception of this problem was very different from that of the developing countries: "Protectionist pressures must be resisted if the debt servicing capacity of developing countries is to be maintained and the deflationary impact of the current crisis on the trilateral economies minimized."[45]

Recommendations followed from the assumption that the crisis was one of liquidity rather than solvency, and that it could be solved by greater participation of the IMF and the World Bank in debt rescheduling operations and "reasonable economic adjustments" in the debtor countries.

Finally, the Trilateralists recommended more concessional aid to the poorest countries. The Official Development Assistance (ODA) levels had decreased, and the United States was singled out as the major offender. Its contribution had fallen in 1981 to 23 per cent of total assistance, or 0.20 per cent of GNP, and was far below the "fair US share."

The report concluded that the central objective of economic policy should be "sustainable growth," which could be attained only if the United States economy recovered. Although sustainable growth was not explicitly defined, it did not mean zero growth, as it sometimes does in environmentally conscious circles; the assumption here, as in the earlier report on democracy, was that economic growth was a reasonable and necessary goal for all societies.

A second report in 1983 pursued similar themes, but concentrated on the need for Japan and Europe to share the full burden of sustaining the world economy. The authors argued that "forces outside the trilateral regions will threaten the international political and economic order" in the 1980s, and those forces could have "catastrophic consequences for the trilateral countries" and the rest of the world. "Because of their stakes and their capabilities, the trilateral countries have a special responsibility to act to preserve an acceptable international order."[46] The threatening forces were declining national performances in Trilateral countries; the continuing Soviet threat and "two decades of relentless expansion of Soviet military power"; the poverty of developing countries; and the declining capacity of democratic political institutions to cope with rising expectations and growing political participation (concerns already expressed in the earlier reports on democracy).

These reports and earlier ones on international relations are best understood as the responses of an international investment class (and its "organic intellectuals," as neo-Marxist terminology characterizes the academic and professional support system) to a changing global system in which, though some changes were unnerving and inconvenient, they could still restructure and retain power.

What has changed most significantly over the period since 1950 is the shift from the hegemony of one power to the coalition of three groups. The global reach of Trilateral power has actually increased with the penetration of capital not only into the NICs but also into China and the Eastern European states. In the late 1980s the concerns of the Trilateralists in 1983 about Soviet intentions already sounded dated, but the general assumption was still that they controlled the world and had the obligation to "share the burden" of running it. The assumptions of neo-classical economics – in particular, the arguments for comparative advantage and specialization "in production of those goods it does best" as repeated in the last of the reports – are still the operating assumptions of the global economy. The objective of all this activity is to produce more and more, to expand infinitely, and to create a positive-sum game in which the pie magically grows to accommodate everyone's needs.

The Trilateralists rejected the term "supranational" for their organization. Even so, they provided the forum for the development of supranational policies, and their reports explictly recommended the formation of tripartite advisory bodies on governmental policies in Europe, America, and Japan. Summit meetings of the dominant nations' leaders (five, six, or seven, according to whether Italy and Canada manage to get themselves invited) are among the outcomes. The OECD acts as the secretariat for the summits.[47] The summit participants have made major decisions about exchange rates and IMF and World Bank policies, decisions they are empowered to make because together they control voting rights in those organizations.

The Trilateralists' agenda was to make the private views of members the public views of the governments and peoples of the industrial countries. To a remarkable degree, they have succeeded. The new right, while more concerned with a popular version of the free enterprise market and individualism, and more geocentric in the DMCs, adopted much of the substance of the early Trilateral Commission reports.

This is not to suggest that the "new right" is reducible to the Trilateralists in the sense that its ideology and substance were deliberately created. On the contrary, it had an independent existence, and its gurus, notably Hayek, had published work along these lines long before the establishment of the Trilateral Commission. Rather, I am suggesting that the arguments of the Trilateralists and those of monetarists, supply-side economists, and fanatical libertarians dovetailed in certain crucial respects, and that the various streams of thought offered mutual support. The dovetailing was not perfect. The new right itself was not internally consistent, and diverse or even contradictory versions were promoted under that general label. But there was enough consistency in the basic assumptions to merit its designation as a social movement and to recognize its links to Trilateralism.

From the mid-1970s to the end of the 1980s the new right captured a post-hegemonic global economy in which the particular forms of mass production advanced in the steel age were in decline and the new technologies were not fully implemented. It captured a time at which an élite of the dominant corporate world was consciously striving to reorganize production, the labour force, and its own relationships to nation-state governments and small entrepreneurs were experiencing both the advantages of the new contracting systems and the disadvantages of paying for government services they could no longer afford.

The two agendas noted by Andrew Belsey may be partially understood in terms of these different contributors. Trilateralists did not argue that governments should merely protect property and person, as many libertarians recommend. On the contrary, they assumed that governments were essential to economic growth, provided that governments were not stopped by popular pressure from taking corrective action as the world economy was restructured. By contrast to the libertarians, whose sociological insight was severely constrained, the Trilateralists fully recognized what merchants and early industrialists in Europe had known from the beginning: they could flourish best where governments held a monopoly of force, where a system of rules backed by that force regulated their internal competition, and where a separate institution was charged with the responsibility for social welfare. Capitalism – any system of accumulation – is unable to function without some assurance that rules will be enforced. Accumulators must be able to diagnose, calculate, plan, and predict their economic conditions in order to make decisions and trade goods. The anarchic world proposed by libertarians is not in the interests of corporate capital, even though the morality and general assumptions of the new right are useful underpinnings for the period of restructuring.

WHO PAID FOR ALL THIS? The new right did not emerge simply on the basis of Hayek's books or Friedman's speeches to the media. The ideas had been around for a long time; many of them, after all, are simply those of Smith and Locke. There were a few think-tanks in this mould as early as the 1950s, but they never had a substantial following. The "moral majority" was identified by Reagan and others in the 1960s, but it was little more than a fringe group widely regarded as lunatic. How, then, did the new right agenda become the public agenda in industrial countries by the 1980s?

Seed money for the Trilateral Commission was provided initially by David Rockefeller, and later by the Kettering Foundation, the Ford Foundation, and several other similar groups. Leading corporate executives contributed personally, and General Motors, Sears Roebuck, Caterpillar Tractor, John Deere, Exxon, Texas Instruments, Coca-Cola, Time, CBS, the Wells Fargo Bank, Honeywell, Cargill, Kaiser Resources, Bechtel, and Weyerhauser subscribed funds over the following decade.[48] The numerous institutes in Britain and the United States were also funded by large corporations or by small business and subscriptions.[49] One example from my own region may be useful.

The Fraser Institute, situated in British Columbia, was established in 1972 through a fundraising drive headed by a former vice-president of MacMillan Bloedel. Annual funding was obtained from Eaton's, Molson's, Canadian Pacific, Domtar, BC Packers, Cadillac Fairview, Daon, IBM, Imperial Oil, Placer Development, Imasco, the Canadian banks, Noranda, Pemberton Securities, Genstar, Abitibi-Price, BC Telephone, and other forestry, mining, oil, newspaper, and telecommunications sectors.[50] According to the principal fundraiser, "One could see very clearly what was happening in the private sector in many western countries. Growing inflation and lower private investment. Even in the US, they were eating their own seed-corn. Nowhere could I see effective arguments for a sound economy as opposed to big-scale government intervention."[51]

The Fraser Institute was a corporate response to a perceived vacuum that threatened to be filled by the public sector and more pervasive government jurisdiction. Not only did the institute succeed in promoting the new right ideology through numerous publications and media coverage, it provided the platform for the "restraint" program of the Social Credit government. With slight variations, other corporations (or the same ones in other forms) funded similar institutes across the United States, Western Europe, and Australia.[52] All of the institutes published the same writers on the same themes.

The new right had its own explanation for its emergence as a major ideology of the 1980s. Its defenders argued that public opinion is nothing more than the successful selling of ideas and politicians. People do not demand them until they have been conditioned to want them. Keynesian ideas and the entire "welfare state" to which they gave rise were successfully marketed for thirty years; indeed, they held a monopoly. To wean people from Keynesianism was the task of the new right, and it set about accomplishing this in the same way an innovative entrepreneur would set about supplanting an existing industrial monopoly: by persuading potential customers that they needed and wanted a new product. They had more success in some countries than in others, just as businesses succeed in creating new demands among some clienteles but not among others.

The alternative explanation is that a historical crisis created panic and a search for solutions. As one hard-pressed businessman phrased it, "What we were doing didn't work, so we had to try something new." Liberal democrats, whether of the mildly left or mildly right variety, are reluctant to consider the possibility that public opinion is the creation of marketing experts. Such a view reduces intelligent, literate, and apparently independent people to the level of zombies. Moreover, it raises serious questions about the validity of democratic choice. Yet all politicians and other persons in public life implicitly recognize the element of wizardry in the creation of their own "images," and the element of puppetry in the creation of public attitudes. And we all know that advertising has a great influence on our own economic and political behaviour.

Marketing techniques have long been used by political parties, though the sophisticated use of computerized data banks and techniques based on the knowledge gained from a half-century of opinion polling and marketing experiments is now far more manipulative than Goebbels ever dreamed. Political strategists boast of the successful application of such techniques. Ronald Reagan was viewed by a vast majority of Americans in the 1980s as a father figure, a nice guy, a firm leader; the communists were reviled as the national enemy and the cause of economic problems; recalcitrant neighbours were labelled communist so successfully that a very substantial part of the American public accepted the "right" of Americans to engage in warlike behaviour and even war itself against Nicaragua, El Salvador, and any other country that failed to please. Margaret Thatcher similarly exploited the communist threat, appealed to national patriotism, blamed the poor for poverty, and sustained her popularity until 1989, despite massive unemployment. And while one might well point to the contrary evidence – open class conflict, huge antigovernment demonstrations, and an increasing use of force against dissidents in Britain – the polls continued to show that the majority of the public supported her hard line. The chief marketing adviser to the Social Credit government in the 1983 British Columbia election described his method to marketing students.[53] First, he claimed, he conducted and analyzed extensive public opinion polls. He concluded that people "felt" the economy was in poor shape and that some "strong" government initiatives were required. They also "felt" that the leader of the Social Credit party was unlikeable and un-approachable, whereas they liked the leader of the opposition be-cause he was affable and had a sense of humour. On the basis of this information, the adviser focused on the word "restraint" and created a marketing strategy which "sold" a leader as an unlikeable man because he had the strength to impose "restraint." The leader of the opposition was cast as "too light" precisely because he was so likeable. What "restraint" might actually mean was deliberately omitted from the agenda – in fact, if one accepts Patrick Kinsella's version of events, the government had no idea what it meant. It was merely a word, a saleable product.

These examples appear to support the supply-side argument. Ad-vertising works, and the population of liberal democracies end up "demanding" those things that advertising tells them they should want. Kinsella's admissions are a variation on this theme: the public does have "feelings," and the task of advertising is to shape those vague sensations into specific demands. In the early 1980s the pub-lic's "feelings" were rooted in a long cultural tradition that put private freedoms ahead of social welfare, in a history of free enterprise slogans, and in the bipolar politics of the free world. They were combined with the insecurities, frustrated expectations, and fears that developed with the restructuring of the world economy.

The propaganda capacities of the new international *zaikai* were formidable. The Trilateral Commission's agenda was put in place in little more than a decade; the governments of many of the western democracies adopted the new right's version of the world. Govern-ments "privatized" Crown (state) corporations; "downsized" the public sector; "deregulated" industry and finance; "centralized" gov-ernment decision-making; "restrained" government expenditures selectively, singling out welfare services and those areas of education that were not directly tied to the job market; and took various mea-sures to strengthen business's capacity to restructure operations un-hindered by labour demands and union pressures.

The elimination of borders to investment also proceeded apace. The free trade agreement between Canada and the United States, for example, permits investors in both countries to compete on equal terms in either territory. The agreement covers a wide range of services which were provided by the Canadian public sector. The establishment of the European Community is another example, though it had other and earlier causes.

The traditional left wing was left behind during the 1980s. Where it was once regarded as radical, it now seemed bereft of innovative ideas; it was reduced to defending the welfare state and trying to make public the flaws in the new right's agenda. Intellectuals on the left have produced perceptive and penetrating analyses of that agenda. However, those analyses are too academic: what the new right produced was a populist sloganeering attack on all the groups in society defended by the left – the poor, the handicapped, the unemployed, women in the work-force, the public sector, the welfare state, democracy, majority choice, labour, unions, the underdeveloped nations, impoverished regions, indebted countries, and especially, the intellectuals themselves. In the direct line of fire were the "media" intellectuals, such as the scriptwriters who questioned America's imperial powers and portrayed the domestic consequences of the Asian war; the social scientists who investigated the causes of unemployment and inequality; and the mainline church leaders who openly equated capitalism with exploitation, imperialism with genocide.

PART TWO

A New
International Order

CHAPTER SIX

The Ginza Strip

Japan, Taiwan, and South Korea, all of which had emerged as major participants in the global marketplace since the mid-1960s, had philosophical traditions entirely contrary to the free market ideology. For them the state had always been a major institutional force in the development of the economy, and had been linked in ideology as well as fact with the leading private houses. This divergent history affected their development within the American age; while paying obeisance to the American credo, they retained and adapted the earlier structures of state and capital. And while flattered by the attention of the Trilateralists, Japanese businessmen (an accurate term, since the system remained patriarchal) most reluctantly adopted the forms of an open economy in the 1980s.

In Part One we saw Japan's struggle with the post-war reconstruction. In Part Two we will compare its economic organization with those of the United States and Europe as it coped with success in the 1970s and 1980s, and consider how the leading-edge companies of the new three-ring circus created a modus vivendi.

BRITAIN, JAPAN, AND Taiwan have this in common: industrialization was imposed from the top down. For Britain and Japan the dominant classes of the rural and feudal epoch merged with the rising bourgeoisie or merchant class to promote the structural changes that would destroy the old order. In both cases the new order allowed a dominant class to renew itself, but in another form. Elsewhere, this process occurred slowly or not at all, as a landed aristocracy obstructed social change and refused to align itself with the irresistible forces of the marketplace. In France and Germany industrialization was delayed; in Eastern Europe it was stopped for three centuries; in Latin America today it is obstructed at many turns by agrarian classes that concede nothing to history.

In Britain the price for industrialization was paid largely by the rural peasantry, which was eventually destroyed as agriculture was commercialized and land privatized. In Japan the burden on the rural peasantry was severe, though the process was less sweeping and did not result in an exodus from the farms to the cities. The Japanese peasants remained as tenants, dispossessed but not evicted.[1] The agricultural sector participated in the general prosperity, and at times obstructed the headlong rush towards industrialization. While the modern Japanese state has become, as one observer phrased it, a gigantic business concern, the rural sector has imposed a restraining note and retained the memory of a society that once adhered to a *samurai* code of ethics. In 1940 E.H. Norman wrote,

In Japan there has been a time-lag between the adoption of a new mode of life and the full maturing of its cultural and psychological expression. As long as this lag persists, we have the fascinating picture of a nation whose sky is blackened by the smoke of great industrial centers yet whose fields and villages are peopled by millions with loyalties and emotions which can be quickened by the remembrance of the "Spirit of Old Japan." This spirit is not some inborn endowment; it springs from centuries of acquired training, tradition and habits of thought which two generations of "modernization" that is far from being catholic in its extent cannot obliterate.[2]

Much has changed in Japan since 1940 but the rural society continues to emphasize community over private interests, families over individuals, and long-term relationships over short-term gains. Industrialism and urbanism have diminished those values, but even in the late twentieth century they retain enough validity to make Japan a very different entity from the United States. The harnessing of those values to a corporate accumulation system proved so successful that American corporate leaders became enamoured of the model – but in a very selective way.

AS I ARGUED earlier, American industries operated on the basis of risk-avoidance and profit-maximization throughout the post-war period. They gave relatively low priority to investments in research and development except where the payoff was likely to be quick, and they paid constant attention to the profit margins for every quarter of every year. Labour was still organized on an assembly-line basis. Quality control was still conducted by special investigators and supervisors. Workers were still treated as automatons at their work stations, and unions were seen as impediments to a radical restructuring of the production lines. Industry was dominated by vertically integrated manufacturing firms with layers of subsidiary companies feeding into the main company, producing its raw materials, or duplicating one another's products for regional markets. The authority line was hierarchical, and accountants were more important than scientists and engineers. Unskilled workers outnumbered the skilled, and supervisory personnel constituted a formidable middle layer between labour and management.

This structure could not be transformed rapidly; both management and workers stood in the way of social change. The early semiconductor companies were relatively innovative, entrepreneurial, research-oriented, science-based, and non-hierarchical because their leadership depended on technical knowledge rather than on bureaucratic skills. When the chip manufacturers moved their production outside the United States, they were seeking a cheap labour force, but they also wanted labour that was non-unionized, malleable, and willing to do jobs that industrial labour in advanced countries found tedious; they wanted a solution that would permit their scientific and technical personnel to develop products free of corporate control.

American companies had expanded by vertically integrating their supply, real estate, financial, sales, and service sectors with their manufacturing cores. They bought companies rather than products, and in the process became giant bureaucratic enterprises with numerous component divisions. Some also became conglomerates with more than a single industrial slice included in the same hierarchical organization. Ownership was substantially transferred to institutions, and since the primary motivation for the system was profit rather than stability, the loyalty of shareholders could not be taken for granted.

Japanese corporations organized their enterprises on a different model. With the exception of a few companies which, for technical and marketing reasons, integrated their operations, most Japanese companies concentrated on what they did best and co-ordinated with other companies in complementary sectors. They were joined at the top by interlocking directorates, production and trading relations, and financial arrangements, yet they operated as separate companies.[3] Ownership was institutional, but the banks, insurance companies, industrial companies, and individual shareholders expected stability. The authority structure was hierarchical and outwardly much more authoritarian than in American firms. But the building of consensus at various stages of production, mechanisms for consultation, lifetime employment, and bonuses linked to profitability substantially modified the impacts of hierarchy.

Ronald Dore has compared ownership arrangements in British and Japanese companies. He discovered that in both cases individuals and charities own about 30 percent. In the United Kingdom banks own nothing, and insurance companies own 21 per cent. In Japan banks and insurance companies between them own 38 per cent. In the United Kingdom the third major source of financing is pension funds; no such funds own shares in Japan, but industrial and commercial companies own 26 per cent of other firms. Dore argued that the majority of the Japanese institutional holdings involve a pattern of "mutual obligation-cementing" – that is, relationships of mutual support or the support of a larger firm for a supplier, or of a bank for firms within a *keiretsu* arrangement (described below). Such relationships are established to ensure the stability of the group of companies rather than for the purpose of reaping dividends. They permit companies to engage in long-term planning because they reduce the pressure from shareholders and the need to make short-term profits.[4] Firms that enjoy such secure relationships with financiers are free to diversify, to develop new products, to price aggressively in order to secure a place in foreign markets,[5] and to take other risks that companies organized in the European and North American fashion cannot afford.

The successors to the *zaibatsu* consist of six conglomerates – Mitsui, Mitsubishi, Sumitomo, Fuji (Fuyo, formerly Yasuda), Sanwa and Dai Ichi – each of which owns general trading companies, manufacturing companies, and a central bank or banks. Another half dozen large houses are similarly organized, though less powerful. The six major groups are highly competitive with one another, but they also co-operate through MITI and other arrangements in planning the overall economy. Each group is internally co-ordinated and involved in central planning, but the parts are loosely joined. These six firms, plus three others, are responsible for about 50 per cent of Japan's exports, 60 per cent of its imports, and 20 per cent of domestic wholesale trade.[6]

Mitsubishi is the largest of the groups, consisting of twenty-eight giant core firms and thirty-two closely related companies.[7] The core firms each has a range of dependent companies and subcontractors. A few major financial institutions supply the funds to this group, and the general trading companies take care of exports and imports. Similar arrangements exist in the other conglomerates.

Apart from the banks, which are the real core of these organizations, the general trading companies, or *sogo shosha*, are the most significant entities. They buy supplies from around the globe, and sometimes invest in resource enterprises (though they rarely obtain any more equity than absolutely necessary to guarantee a market commitment for a specified period). They may deliberately establish an oversupply of raw materials by encouraging, through small investments and market contracts, overexploitation in several competing countries. This has occurred with coal (Australia and western Canada being the major sources) and, after the oil shocks, with oil. But the *sogo shosha* do more than procure raw materials: they negotiate with foreign governments, set up sales agencies, and negotiate huge investments in plant and equipment.[8]

Each of the large companies is surrounded by a bevy of subcontractors in a relationship known as *keiretsu*. The subcontractors are formally independent, but they usually have durable and stable connections with a conglomerate. The major company may own shares in the contracting company, but the loans and technological exchanges that maintain the relationships over long periods are more important. Johannes Hirschmeier and Tsunehiko Yui, in a major study of Japanese business, have described *keiretsu* as "intense 'familism'" that is "fostered and extends to the individual workers and employees of the subcontracting firms with the goal of sharing the same 'spirit' and of working for the greater prosperity of the whole group."[9]

Japanese labour is organized around the integrated circuit technology in ways foreign to individualistic Americans. Loyalty, obedience, concern for quality, responsibility for output, and commitment to social groups – family, neighbourhood, corporation, country – are expected of Japanese workers. The state promotes research into technologies and plans social and educational policies so that the labour force is continually restructured in line with future requirements. Assembly lines are evident in Japan as elsewhere, but their alienating effects are somewhat assuaged by cultural norms of obedience to the group and anti-individualism. Workers are socially and emotionally linked to their production organizations, and they adapt relatively quickly to new technologies and divisions of labour.

In the Toyota company system, for example, there are 172 subcontracting companies connected with Toyota (an affiliate of Mitsui); Toyota owns shares in only a few of these. They produce, competitively, most of the parts for the cars. Each contracting firm is responsible for managing its own labour force; Toyota does not have to make long-term commitments to workers. For this reason, the form has won admirers in other OECD countries. In Japan, however, a disengagement from responsibility for workers is not part of the intentional design of these systems. In fact, it may be unwise to use the term "intention," since the *keiretsu* arrangement originated with the ancient *zaibatsu* families, and necessarily involves mutual respect, mutual concerns, and mutual support. The arrangement permits the entire system to restructure around new technologies at a rapid pace, without threatening labour. Many observers have noted the degree of flexibility this arrangement provides to the major companies.

The president of the consulting firm DeWitt, stated the case against the North American model of industrial relations in terms of the labour market's constraints on technological change. He went on to say, however, that "it also had to do with something more fundamental: the increase in risk aversion to redesign and re-engineer the product in the production system; to take as low a risk as possible assured a quest for short-term return, locking into the technology and further reducing the cost of what they consider a low-risk, low-cost solution – this is exactly the thing that contributed to the abandonment of the next generation of products."[10]

The contracting system permits the major Japanese firms to plan another generation of products from the existing technology. The American system, in which all workers are locked into the same firm and engage in union-management negotiations over every aspect of every job, gives the Japanese an inestimable advantage in a swiftly changing technological field. The Americans chose to move offshore to avoid union demands, but in the process they lost the technological edge; they reaped the short-term profits of cheap labour, but not the long-term profits of new designs. The small manufacturers in Japan can efficiently redesign products at relatively low cost.

The American company, which is able to lay off workers when there is a slump or when it installs labour-displacing technologies, contrasts sharply with the Japanese company, which is strongly constrained to keep its workers employed regardless of economic conditions. There is an incentive for Japanese managers to develop new industries for workers who would otherwise be underemployed or displaced by technology. As well, the managers are employed for life; they have to move their company's activities to new sectors since they themselves do not move from company to company.[11]

In the capital-intensive sector and its feeder firms, wages tend to be comparatively high, job security is usually lifelong, unions are in-house, seniority is a major criterion for advancement into man-

agement (though only among the meritorious), and the average level
of education is high. The ratio of technical personnel to factory
workers is five to one in some sectors, and in all sectors engineering,
scientific, and technical personnel predominate.[12] This ratio says a
great deal about the labour force and labour conditions in the capital-
intensive sector. It is a major reason for the manufacturers' ability
to redesign quickly, to adopt new technologies efficiently, and to
keep their costs at commerically viable levels.

THE SHAPING OF business consensus in Japan is the task of the
zaikai. The term is a carryover from the pre-war period, when it
referred to large capitalist families. It now means the organized
power of business. That power is exercised through a number of
employer and trade associations.

In 1946 the Federation of Economic Organizations, or *Keidanren*,
was formed to unite all economic organizations within a single democratic forum to co-ordinate business interests and influence policy
recommendations. It originally included small businesses, but today
is made up of large firms. Chambers of commerce and industry now
represent the smaller enterprises. The *Keidanren* promotes research
on world markets, finance, and employment, and makes political
evaluations relevant to business interests. It engages in conflict resolution when the diverse interests of members collide, and represents its members to government. It is a highly influential body, the
main support of the ruling party (the Liberal Democrats), and the
major influence on MITI. The Federation of Employers' Association,
or *Nikkeiren*, deals with labour relations. The *Nikkeiren* maintains a
low profile, but it has considerable influence on government labour
policies.

Perhaps the word "influence" is inappropriate in the Japanese
context. A Japanese scholar once told me that he found the American
and European literature on the "the state" impenetrable: "They constantly worry about whether government is closely allied with the
ruling class. In Japan that is not a puzzling question. If a ruling class
acts like a ruling class, then it is paternalistic. It protects the workers.
The problem with the American ruling class is that it doesn't act like
a ruling class. So there is no loyalty to it. The *zaibatsu* acts as a ruling
class." The difference is one of ideology as well as reality. In the
North American and European versions of liberal democracy, government is supposed to be entirely neutral and above class interests;
in Japan, no such myth has ever been perpetrated, and there is
acceptance of a forthright, institutionalized co-operative arrange-

ment between the ruling political party and the ruling economic houses. Although the government and the ruling corporations are not immune to criticism, until the late 1980s the Japanese expressed little shock at revelations of collusion. In the Japanese version of democracy, the government is there to ensure that, one way or another, the Japanese population survives. In the aftermath of the war, when the Americans were pushing hard for the dissolution of the zaibatsu, it was not only the Mitsui and Mitsubishi house members who resisted that pressure. With the Recruit scandal of 1989, however, public support for this cosy relationship diminished. The prime minister was obliged to step down, and the ruling party lost credibility; apparently the Japanese electorate and the media were moving towards the European version of appropriate behaviour for politicians.

One critical difference between Japan and North America is Japan's ethnic and linguistic homogeneity. Japanese society has clear class and sex divisions, but because of its homogeneity the demand for equality, and thus the development of an ideology of classlessness, has not emerged as strongly as in Europe and North America. The growth of a meritocracy based on education provides for some permeability in class boundaries. Welfare provisions for the unemployed and unemployable are not notable for their generosity, though various schemes to retrain or otherwise provide an income for displaced workers (as when older industries are phased out) have been adopted from time to time. Monetary compensation has been provided to "victims of adjustment" on the general premise that displaced workers had a right to expect lifetime employment.[13]

As many writers have observed, however, government's major contribution to labour has been indirect – the planning, in consultation with industry, for adjusting the economy. While some workers were displaced at each juncture, or obliged to work at less desirable jobs by their lifetime employer, the overall effect of long-term government planning has been a steadily expanding economy which, in the main, has been able to absorb and retrain workers. Unlike the other OECD countries, Japan has not experienced abrupt cycles of expansion, overproduction, cutbacks, layoffs, closed plants, and unemployment because the government has taken responsibility for the development of national industrial strategies.

Labour evidently recognizes this; although a good deal of sparring takes place in advance of the annual wage-bargaining rites (which occur in one round and bind all workers), a consensus is normally reached that realistically takes into account the rates of economic growth and profits.

IN ADDITION TO the large Japanese companies, they are many relatively small businesses unconnected or only sporadically connected to the main houses. In the agricultural and forestry sectors, small land-owners still predominate. In the rural mountain towns, especially in the Kyoto Prefecture, traditional community life is still very much in evidence. While doing research on the Japanese forestry sector, I observed a system of community obligations and discipline that has no parallel in North America. Forests are nationally, communally, or privately owned; private holdings are, for the most part, very small; and owners regard themselves as custodians of tradition and stewards for the next generation. It would be impossible for a large development company to buy out the land; the local community would collectively resist such a takeover.[14] When one community decided to try to attract outside industry so that young workers who would otherwise migrate to Kyoto could remain at home, the local bank acted as the organizer for the town's businessmen and political leaders; the decision was a community decision. A certain portion of privately owned land was purchased by the community, then sold at a reduced price to an external manufacturing company under conditions that spelled out their community obligations.

Two related problems afflict the rural communities. One is competition from foreign sellers of food and trees, now that Japan has been obliged to open its domestic market; the other is the out-migration of the young. There is a labour shortage in the cities, and rural young people can obtain higher wages and better health and pension benefits from urban employers. In either setting employment is lifelong and employees are not wage-workers in the fashion of other industrial countries. Loggers, silviculturists, planters, sawmill workers, and workers in the specialty mills that turn out Japan's high-quality cedar and cypress poles are all organized within co-operatives. So are forestry owners. One co-operative employs another on contract, and many of the conditions of the contracts are mutually agreed upon through community organizations. The people I interviewed expressed considerable resentment towards the corporate sector and MITI, whose benefits were not shared by the rural regions.

Excluding the primary sectors, 21 per cent of the working labour force in 1981 was made up of the self-employed, employers, and family workers. The largest firms employed about 35 per cent of all workers in the private sector; very small firms employed about 18 per cent.[15] Far more women than men, and more minority group members (of whom persons of Korean descent are the most significant) than native-born Japanese are employed in small businesses in the retail trades and service sectors. As has happened in other industrial countries, the monopoly sector (the large companies) attracts the top-rated recruits and offers them a better material standard of living than rural or small competitive businesses could. A dual economy has developed, and the gulf between employees in the two sectors raises doubts about Japan's happy family image.

The image disintegrates further when one recognizes the sexism and racism that pervade the society. Japan's intense familism has been sustained by a domestic structure that gives women very little independence and few career choices and that relegates outsiders (especially other Asians) to permanent low status. The massive industrial build-up was not accompanied by the development of a welfare infrastructure, and civil rights are not well protected. There is no place in Japanese society for the handicapped, and even the supposedly venerated elders have been largely pushed aside (often into privately financed homes or into the care of already overburdened housewives).

The social structure that provided comfort in the small village can be both oppressive and contrary to community survival when writ large. The "company man" syndrome is no caricature: the corporate employee is so firmly embedded in the corporate culture that he has little else in his life besides his job and after-work drinking with colleagues. Individual initiative has been discouraged for so long that Japan's technological leadership is threatened by a paucity of new ideas because there are no mentors providing the basic frameworks.

The positive features of Japanese society, however, are selectively championed by European and American business writers. They choose to see an authority structure that cements government and private enterprise and promotes worker docility and loyalty. Certain specific features of the Japanese system have been grafted onto American operations already: just-in-time inventory control, contracting out, quality control, and labour-management consultative (but not decision-making) arrangements. To go further, corporations need a different kind of government: not the minimal government that libertarians envision, but more authoritarian government.

JAPAN DID NOT cease to be an imperial power at the end of the Second World War, but its post-1951 imperialism took the form of its mentor, the United States: economic expansion. Indeed, one leading student of Japanese expansion complained that "they have developed a foreign policy more like that of a trading company than of a nation."[16]

After the "normalization" of its relationship with Korea in 1965, Japan's investment increased rapidly, especially in the Masan Free Export Zone and also in Taiwan and elsewhere in Asia. The investments were tied to various aid programs, many of which grew out of the original reparation payments which Japan managed to tie to purchases of Japanese products. By 1974 Japanese investment accounted for 66 per cent of all foreign investments in South Korea and 41 per cent of those in Thailand; Japan was the second-largest investor in Taiwan, Indonesia, and the Philippines.[17] In the early 1970s Japanese companies began to phase out the production of some electronic products in Japan (where wages had risen and the domestic market was becoming saturated, or where the products, such as black-and-white television sets, were becoming obsolete), and moved the production units offshore.

Though Japanese investments in Korea and Taiwan were substantial, the largest direct investments in the period from 1950 to 1977 went first to the United States (us$4.7 billion), then to Indonesia ($3.2 billion), then to Brazil ($2 billion).[18] The objective was to secure markets and evade protectionism even as early as the 1970s. The Indonesian investments were made largely (though not exclusively) in oil and forestry to obtain essential fuels and raw materials.[19] In Brazil the Japanese investment quadrupled between 1970 and 1978 to guarantee the availability of iron ore, aluminum, agricultural products, pulp, and cheap labour for the production of cars and electronic goods for Latin America.

The pattern of offshore production and foreign investment has altered global trading patterns for Japan just as it has for the United States and the EEC. S. Nakajo found that Japanese exports to Asian NIC-located subsidiaries accounted for over 20 per cent of Japanese exports to those countries by 1975.[20] Nearly one-quarter of exports to Japan from the same countries came from subsidiaries. Y. Tsurumi estimated that Southeast and East Asian countries – Taiwan, Korea and the ASEAN countries especially – accounted for two-thirds of total manufacturing investments by number, one-third by value by the early 1970s.[21] Of all investing countries, Japan accounts for the largest share of manufacturing investment in developing areas.[22]

Throughout the Pacific Basin Japan has created a trading bloc of its own companies, exporting component parts and advanced technological machinery as well as a wide range of consumer goods, and importing parts made offshore, resource supplies, and other consumer goods. Japan is not dependent on any single country in this chain; none takes more than 4 per cent of Japan's total exports, and Japan takes no less than 25 per cent of each country's exports.[23] This means that Japanese decisions profoundly affect the Southeast Asian countries, but no other country alone can significantly affect Japan. These trading patterns have a global impact. The proportion of world exports from East Asia and Australasia doubled to 19 per cent between 1962 and 1984, and the proportion was vastly higher for such products as electronics and textiles.[24] The right-wing politician Shintaro Ishihara calls Asia Japan's franchise; most Japanese would use more modest descriptions, but many Japanese foresee the evolution of a "yen bloc" in Asia. By 1988 Japan accounted for about 40 per cent of the total Asian market, and it imported more from Asia than from the United States.[25]

The United States created a similar system throughout the twentieth century, as did Britain during the era of the Pax Britannica. The difference between the earlier systems and the post-war systems is that the latter are much more integrated, and the trades involve the movement of manufactured items in both directions. In 1981 two Australian researchers found that in consequence of these and other advanced nations' trading blocs, about 40 per cent of all world trade was actually trade between component firms of transnational corporations.[26]

Japan is frequently portrayed by Japanese diplomats as a country that was somewhat insecure until its economic success made it a full participant in western democratic society. According to one former minister for external economic affairs, "In the turbulent 1970s, Japan was concerned about its position as a lonely outpost of the advanced, industrial world in Asia." He said that even as Japan was becoming more involved in world affairs, it was not then accepted in the summit inner circle of the United States, Great Britain, France, and West Germany. Only when it began to experience rapid economic growth was it fully included in international consultation and co-operation.[27] By 1987 Japan held the highest corporate rankings in the automotive, communications, consumer electronics, financial, industrial equipment, insurance, office equipment, retailing, steel, textiles, trading, and utility industries in the world. Although General Motors still ranked first in revenue, Mitsubishi was a close second, Mitsui third, and Exxon and Ford far behind as eighth and tenth.[28]

Japanese banks became the leading financial institutions by the mid-1980s (see table 3). At the end of 1985 five Japanese banks were among the largest ten by asset size (compared with one in 1978). A

Table 3
Twenty largest transnational banks, 1978 and 1985 (Ranked by assets)

1985	1978	Bank	*(Number of entities)[1]*		
			DMCs	NICs/LDCs[2]	Total[3]
1	3	Citicorp (USA)	69	160	231
2	8	Dai-Ichi Kangyo (Japan)	24	21	48
3	11	Fuji (Japan)	21	16	37
4	12	Sumitomo (Japan)	25	18	45
5	13	Mitsubishi (Japan)	24	25	53
6	5	Banque Nationale de Paris (France)	58	63	128
7	14	Sanwa (Japan)	17	22	41
9	1	BankAmerica (USA)	62	120	184
10	6	Credit Lyonnais (France)	58	43	103
12	21	National Westminster (UK)	21	7	29
13	18	Industrial (Japan)	22	13	38
14	7	Société Générale (France)	38	40	89
15	4	Deutsche Bank (FRG)	33	32	67
16	19	Barclays (UK)	82	104	188
17	22	Tokai (Japan)	19	16	37
18	24	Mitsui (Japan)	22	24	49
19	10	Chase Manhattan (USA)	41	65	108
20	41	Midland (UK)	45	22	69
24	36	Bank of Tokyo (Japan)	44	54	101

Sources: Extracted from data in UNCTC, *Foreign Direct Investment: The Service Sector and International Banking*, table 7:42; based on "The Top 500," *The Banker*, company reports, and other journals.

[1] Banks without international assets are omitted, including Crédit Agricole (France, ranked 8th in top 500); Norinchukin Bank (Japan, 11th); Mitsubishi Trust and Banking (Japan, 21st); Sumitomo Trust and Banking (Japan, 22d), and others. Assets include subsidiaries, affiliates, branches, and representative offices. Branches and representative offices are counted on the basis of countries and / or cities where they are located. Subsidiaries and /or affiliates of foreign subsidiaries are not counted.

[2] Source labels these "developing market economies."

[3] Total includes entities located in centrally planned economies.

year later Dai-Ichi Kangyo replaced Citicorp as number one, and Nomura Securities supplanted Merrill Lynch (USA) as the world's largest investment firm. These changes occurred because of the appreciation of the yen, Japan's new role as an international creditor, and the growing direct investment by Japanese firms outside the domestic market.[29] There was no doubt that Japan had arrived.

THE SEMICONDUCTOR and electronics industries created a demand in other industries for "strategic partners" with which they could plan global strategies. American firms, having discovered that the organizations of the past were no longer serving them well, experimented in the 1980s with new arrangements. These were not simple moves towards diversification, mergers, or takeovers, as in the past; they were alliances buttressed by mutual minority investments or joint ventures undertaken with a view to mutual development of products and sharing of techologies that even very large firms were unable or unwilling to undertake alone. For example, both AT & T and IBM joined with numerous other firms to maximize their combined strength in computers and communications. IBM bought shares of MCI Communications, and AT & T bought part of Olivetti; in each case the purchase improved the competitive advantages of both parties against the major rival group. IBM undertook a joint venture with CBS and Sears, Roebuck to battle AT & T's combination of Time Inc., the Chemical Bank, and the Bank of America broadcasting, retailing, and banking. This last venture uses AT & T terminal facilities to expand videotex banking. The IBM group, known as Trintex, provides Sears with a credit-card customer base and a data-processing network with videotex billing services. Service industries such as the stock market, airlines, and banking, as well as merchant houses, sought out ways of marrying new communications techniques using broadcast signals, cable television lines, and satellite distribution.[30]

These new alliances involved predictions about the future of the "information society." Some of the predictions are already taking concrete form; others are just around the corner in a society where an information network delivers news, provides video shopping facilities, pays bills, looks after banking needs, controls home temperatures – does everything but walk the dog. Some alliances died on the high-risk table because the giant companies had different corporate styles and needed to learn new ways of co-operating with one another, and because they envisioned ideas that were not quite ready to pay off. IBM, for example, joined with MCA to produce video disks but abandoned the venture in 1982 because the two companies had not yet learned how to work together.[31]

Some of the alliances were more obviously instrumental in producing the major lines of the big companies. For example, IBM purchased 20 per cent of Intel in the Silicon Valley because its personal computers needed microprocessors, and it signed a long-term agreement with Microsoft Corporation in 1985 because the computers needed software and the small West Coast company had what it wanted. Other alliances brought together rivals in the telecommunications industry, just as in the automobile industry. AT & T and

Philips Telecommunications was one such, a marriage of convenience between two giants whose needs were better met by co-operation than by competition.[32]

These alliances were designed to avoid the vertical integration with a manufacturing company that had seemed so important in the post-war period. Corporations had no wish to lock themselves into developing specific products or equipment; technology was changing so rapidly that cheaper or better alternatives might become available at any moment. General Motors claimed that its purchase of Hughes Aerospace Industries was intended to improve its competitive edge in the auto industry, but in fact GM was well on its way to becoming one of the major information companies; automobile manufacturing was yesterday's industry. GM's biggest problem thereafter was that Hughes was tied to the US military.

Japanese manufacturers, once securely into all phases of the spinoff industries, also joined forces for production even while they competed in other and diverse fields. In 1986 Hitachi and Fujitsu announced the joint development of a 32-bit microprocessor that could outflank the US products currently dominated by Motorola (57 per cent of the market), Intel (30 per cent) and National Semiconductor (10 per cent). Only days before this joint venture, it was announced that Fujitsu had merged its semiconductor business with Fairchild.[33] In fact, though the arrangement was called a merger, Fujitsu had offered to buy 80 per cent of Fairchild at a bargain price two years into the slump in semiconductor sales in the United States and with the Japanese yen high against to the US dollar. Fujitsu gained Fairchild's technology and know-how for the bargain price of a couple of factories. While Fairchild (a unit since 1979 of the French-owned, New York-based Schlumberger, an oilfield services and electronics company) was happy with the alliance, other American producers expressed concerns. Said a former head of Fairchild: "We all knew Schlumberger had their problems with Fairchild, but we always thought they would sell to another US company. Now, it's almost as if the handwriting is on the wall for other US semiconductor companies. The question is, who's next?"[34] Actually, there had been previous takeovers: Fujitsu had already purchased 48 per cent of Amdahl, a maker of large mainframe systems. In the end, however, the Fairchild purchase did not go through. A month after the announcement Fujitsu dropped its plans, citing the "rising political controversy" in the United States.[35]

The merger was opposed by the US Defense Department on the ground that it imperilled national security. Fairchild was engaged in about $150 million of government contract work on semiconductors.[36] Its French ownership apparently posed no threat, but a Japanese takeover was deemed unacceptable by the US government. At the time this objection was raised, four US subsidiaries of Fujitsu – one manufacturer of optical-fibre telecommunications equipment and three manufacturers of semiconductors, personal computers, and telephone switching equipment – were already in business, and Fujitsu had announced its plans to build another two plants in Oregon.[37]

While Japanese firms were setting up facilities in the United States, American firms had been less successful in establishing plants in Japan. Texas Instruments set up production facilities there in 1968, but it was 1982 before Motorola and Analog Devices followed. Fairchild began to assemble and test products in Nagasaki in 1984 in anticipation of full production by 1987. The American giants procured chips from Japanese affiliates during the early 1980s, reaping the whirlwind of that practice when it became clear by the mid-1980s that Japanese chip producers could undersell US producers in the United States and Europe (thereby provoking American protectionist threats) and could outstrip American producers in developing a new generation of megachips.

By that time Japanese firms were also beginning to penetrate the semiconductor equipment field. US equipment makers saw their share of the Japanese market drop from 70 per cent to 30 per cent between the late 1970s and the mid-1980s. Japanese equipment was even making inroads in the US market. A Motorola operations manager, noting that Japanese equipment tended to be highly automated and simple to operate, observed in 1985, "We try to support the US industry... but there is no sense putting yourself out of business buying inferior equipment."[38]

In 1986 the US and Japanese governments signed a semiconductor trade agreement which President Reagan hailed as a "landmark pact." The pact grew out of US charges that Japanese companies, particularly Hitachi, were engaged in what the US Justice Department called "predatory pricing," more commonly known as dumping. At that stage Japanese producers accounted for about 45 per cent of all chips sold in the United States.[39] Much of this production came from the affiliates of US companies such as Texas Instruments, IBM, Fairchild, and Motorola. Part of the complaint was that Japan provided generous government grants for research and development to its own companies but not to US affiliates in Japan, and the agreement ensured that those grants would be made equally available to US affiliates. Third-country production was addressed, and Japan promised to monitor their trade in its products. This part of the agreement was invalidated in 1988 by GATT which said that Japan had no right to monitor third countries' trade.[40] Japan accepted with alacrity the United States' suggestion that they join forces (this type of arrangement is called a cartel when the subject is oil) to maintain high chip prices. The integrated Japanese companies could charge cartel prices to outsiders while using their own chips in their own products.

Alliances formed since the mid-1980s include that of IBM with Mitsubishi, and AT & T with Japan ENS. In both cases the Japanese giant was joined by other Japanese companies and banks. In 1986, IBM had slipped to third place in Japanese sales, behind Fujitsu and NEC.[41] In 1987 NEC joined with Honeywell of Minneapolis and Cie des Machines Bull of France in a joint venture.[42] The reason for the US companies' interest is obvious: the American manufacturers who held the lead in this business no longer have guaranteed markets in Japan. Their slow start was not due so much to their own reluctance to establish Japanese firms as to the Japanese government's protection of domestic companies. As Japanese firms, now well established in Japan, seek opportunities to locate production lines in the United States and Europe, their government is coming under pressure to open up its own market. Several US firms have teamed up with partners who previously manufactured chips for them. The Japanese chip makers have gained a reputation for quality, but the competition is tough and US producers are not guaranteed profits from their belated ventures in Japan.

Are the Japanese the inheritors of technological leadership in a global economy? Dr Z.P. Zeman, the Canadian project leader of the Futures Studies Program at the Institute for Research on Public Policy argues that, on the basis of patent patterns, the flow of licences, the number of research and development workers, government guidance and other indices, indeed they are.[43]

In the light of this view, one might interpret in different ways a recent development in Japan. In 1988 the Japanese government appointed a superconductor research consortium led by Shoji Tanaka, a university physicist. This consortium includes scientists from forty-four of Japan's largest industrial concerns, working together to commercialize higher-temperature superconductors before private companies elsewhere – especially IBM and AT & T – can make the product marketable. Superconductors, which some scientists believe will be as revolutionary as the transistor, are substances that carry electricity without resistance and therefore without power loss. The early work on superconductors was slow because they could function only at extemely low temperatures; but IBM made the initial breakthrough,

Tanaka's laboratory made advances, and two University of Houston researchers eventually won a Nobel Prize for creating a ceramic that was superconducting at very warm, and inexpensively obtained, temperatures. Then MITI created the research team, a typical Japanese strategy for obtaining research results with significant technological applications for industry. The cost of participation is high, but all participants will share in the results.

Contrary to usual practice, however, non-Japanese firms, including the major competitors, were invited to join the consortium. In view of the already tense relations between the United States and Japan over technological leadership, the invitation to IBM and other major US companies might be interpreted as a strategy to undermine competitors, co-opt their scientists, or offset a technological lead enjoyed by the American firms. The Japanese, now unable to copy others' technologies, are avoiding the risk by inviting others to share it. IBM refused the invitation, saying the cost was too high and that they expected to make the superconductors commercially viable on their own. Others also refused, although scientists from the United States, Canada, and Europe accepted research positions in the new enterprise.[44]

The Japanese invitations are greeted with some scepticism by North Americans and Europeans, who claim that their own generosity in transferring technology during the 1960s and 1970s led to their eclipse by Japanese and other copiers. Even so, there is evidence that the invitations are sincere and represent a novel approach to international capital. In Japan the words *kukusaika* (internationalization), *kokusai kyoryoku* (international co-operation), and *kokusai kōkan* (international exchange) are often used with reference to science and technology policy. At this point the concern may be more rhetorical than active, but it does indicate a new way of thinking. A report approved by the Prime Minister's Council for Science and Technology in 1985 stated:

We should also realize that Japan's contributions to science and technology should be appropriate for its increasingly significant role in the world community of nations. On this recognition, we should give sufficient consideration to the importance of cooperation with developing countries and to the latest international trends in high technology areas as we seek to internationalize our science and technology personnel, organizations and activities and to promote international exchanges and cooperation.[45]

MITI has echoed this concern, referring to the need for joint research and development projects, technology transfers, exchange of personnel; further, "original R and D – which will be the showcase of future science and technology history – must be performed on an international basis and the results must be disseminated globally."[46]

That this is not all rhetoric is indicated by the MITI plan, made public in 1986, which reverses a century of government policy. The policy has always been that Japan would manufacture domestically all important items and procure from abroad the resources essential for survival so that the country could rest on an export basis with a full manufacturing economy. Now the planners have "unequivocally" announced that horizontal diversification will be pursued and that many domestically produced necessities will be replaced with imported products.[47] This policy change is in part a result of the high exchange value of the yen. Japan will not survive if its exports are so expensive that no one can buy them. Facing the prospect of overcapacity in the science-based and general commodity sectors, Japan is seeking a compromise with other exporting countries. But it does not need to seek a compromise which seriously shares its knowledge: this is a new development. Of the invitation to IBM and other American companies, Tanaka observes that the Americans failed to understand the offer, that it would permit them to penetrate Japan's information network, and that it might reduce US paranoia about Japan's technological lead. Sharing, he argues, would also discipline the Japanese, who "always run to nationalism. That nationalism needs to be strictly controlled."[48]

Japanese patterns of capital ownership, investment, alliances, labour organization, and production are far removed from those of the United States and Europe. The differences arise in dissimilar cultural contexts; Huckleberry Finn would be a sorry outcast in this society. For the moment, the Japanese model achieves greater profits for its investors. But no organizational form can remain dominant forever, and what works in one global economy may be ineffective in another. Japan is affluent, and its people are moving away from the constraints of the paternalistic family and its extensions. Many young people are not enthralled with the spirit of old Japan. Some reject the intense competition for education and status and the drive for business success. Different ethnic groups and classes become more belligerent as affluence permits smouldering anger to surface, and the continuing barriers to women's independence are a cause of increasing out-marriage by educated women. Pollution has become a major problem in industrialized Japan, and there are limits to the practice of moving polluting industries offshore. Technology transfers and the presentation of a developmental model by Japan have already affected the neighbouring countries, several of which – South Korea most notably – have developed their own momentum.

For our purposes, the Japanese model and the example of Taiwan show that the process known as capitalism has many faces and more than a single ideology. Free enterprise is a concept consistent with the European-American cultural heritage, not with that of Japan, though in both regions private property rights and markets are dominant forms of organization. The theoretical tradition inherited from the European industrial revolution does not capture Japanese economic development. But Americans and Europeans want to capture it; they want first to impose on it a free market constraint, and then to adopt those of its practices that are, in fact, least consistent with the free market ideology.

CHAPTER SEVEN

The Travelling Show

We have spoken of the international division of labour. Throughout the 1940s to mid-1960s, the Western capitalist countries were euphemistically known as the First World, the Eastern European centrally managed states as the Second World, and all others as the Third World. This division of space and cultures was a crude means of recognizing that most of the world, especially nations in the southern hemisphere (Japan, Australia and New Zealand excepted), suffered both absolute and relative poverty. Most people entered the cash economy markets, if at all, as providers of raw materials and agricultural goods.

For a handful of the Third World countries the division of labour changed after the mid-1960s. The establishment of the free zones created a new labour force. Young women – in many countries for the first time – were pulled into the paid labour force. They assembled semiconductors and electrical products, or sewed garments for export. They were employed by companies from the industrial countries or by local contractors hired by those companies. Men assembled automobiles and other machinery, and worked in the construction of the megaprojects that were to provide the infrastructure for the companies located in free trade zones. In some countries, new component-manufacturing firms were established on a contract basis.

The free zones and the global production systems continued to operate in the 1980s; some of them even expanded, and new ones were put in place. But a series of further technological and market changes reduced the advantages of offshore production in the semiconductor and related industries. By the mid-1980s firms were altering yet again their internal regional divisions of labour as they continued to restructure their global operations.

In this chapter we will examine first the conditions of employment in the zones from about the mid-1960s to the early 1980s, concentrating on the semiconductor and electrical industries, and then the changes in the international division of labour. The automobile industry is the subject of chapter 8.

IRELAND ESTABLISHED the first free zone in 1958, but the zone established in Taiwan in 1965 became the model for other underdeveloped countries.[1] The Kaohsiung Harbour zone was financed in part by the Japan Export-Import Bank and the Overseas Economic Co-operation Fund, with an infrastructure funded by US aid through the Sino-American Economic and Social Development Fund and government banks. Electronics companies were the major investors, followed by garment, plastics, and metal producers. Among the familiar companies located in the zone by 1975 were Hitachi, Sony, General Electric, Toshiba, Magnavox, ITT, and Harmon Kardon, and the garment manufacturers Van Heusen, Manhattan, and Landmark. US department stores were the major buyers of garments from firms such as these and from Taiwanese contract firms. Of all approved investments in 1975, the largest components were, in descending order, Japanese, Taiwanese, joint ventures with the Taiwanese, European, overseas Chinese, and North American (in most accounts Canadian investments are included with American investments).

Not all of the American and Japanese firms located in zones, but zones rapidly became the model for housing the foreign companies. The United Nations Industrial Development Organization (which actively promoted the zone policy) estimated that by the mid-1970s there were some 120 export zones throughout the world, employing in total about two million workers.[2] A Japanese study counted 468 separate firms in 15 zones in South Korea, Taiwan, the Philippines, Malaysia, Selangor, and Malacca in 1975.[3] India established its first zone in 1965 and another in 1974. Brazil established zones close to São Paulo and the nearby port of Santos, and at Manous on the Western Amazon River, in the late 1960s.

The selected countries of Asia to which investment flowed in the 1970s did not include China, which was still struggling behind closed doors (though some windows had been opened in the mid-1970s). Japan re-established its links with China in this period. After 1979 China, eager to gain access to the science and technology of the advanced countries, opened its doors to foreign investment. Much foreign investment was directed to special economic zones (SEZS) along the east coast. By 1984 numerous joint ventures had been established on a bilateral basis. Hong Kong companies were involved in 71 joint ventures, 33 of which were located in the SEZs; Japan had 56, 9 in the SEZs; and the United States had 38, 8 in the SEZs. Other multilateral joint ventures included those foreign investors as well as European and Singaporean companies. The United States had the highest total foreign investments, followed by Japan and Hong Kong.[4] The industries attracted to China, as elsewhere, were electronics, garments, and relatively low-value items such as toys and leather goods.

The Asian Productivity Organization described the zones in 1975 as enclaves "in terms of customs-territorial aspect and possibly other aspects such as total or partial exemption from laws and decrees of the country concerned."[5] A more graphic definition appeared in the *Philippine Dictionary for Tariff Information*: "[A zone] is an isolated, enclosed and policed area in or adjacent to a port of entry, furnished with the necessary facilities for loading and unloading, for storing goods and reshipping them by land and by water, an area within which goods may be landed, stored, mixed, blended, repacked, manufactured and reshipped without payment of customs duties and without the intervention of customs officials."[6]

In other words, zones were little countries inside other political territories. They were typically guarded by special police, and were sometimes separated from the rest of their societies by barbed wire and concrete walls.

The political implications of these zones deserve attention. In an earlier age an imperial power might have conquered and colonized another country and obliged its people to work in mines or other resource-exploitation activities. In the case of the European imperialist ventures, the subjugated peoples were also the source of unskilled domestic labour. In the silicon age, foreign investors, through their governments, negotiated terms that turned portions of the host countries into international territory, and employed nationals in assembing products meant wholly or largely for export. The workers were not able to migrate because immigration barriers were erected; instead, the metropolitan centres came to them for their labour. The old imperial powers used their own armies to control subject populations; the new ones used local zone police and national armies. The old powers established nations in which they located their armies; the new ones undermined those nations, superimposing on them a transnational economy without respect for national borders.

Foreign capitalists negotiated highly favourable terms for entry into the zones, including exemption from national taxation, waivers of labour and environmental legislation, and, most particularly, cheap and abundant labour supplies. These incentives were advertised by potential host countries as they competed for foreign investment. According to the South Korean Planning Board's *Guide to Investment in Korea* (1974), "South Korea has a highly productive, hardworking, plentiful labor force. The average wage in South Korea is less than one-tenth that of the US, one-eighth of Europe and one-fifth of Japan."[7] In addition to these attractions, legislation was often passed that effectively prohibited strikes at foreign-owned firms.[8]

THE MANAGERS OF THE new factories preferred to hire young women. One study of the Taiwanese zones in 1975, for example, found that 38 per cent of the workforce was made up of women between the ages of 16 and 19; another 33 per cent were women between the ages of 20 and 24.[9] For the most part it was not the desperately poor who were employed in the factories; it was those who had managed to rise above bare subsistence and gain some education. They were not skilled in the urban sense of that term, but they had already acquired the habits essential to an industrial labour force – punctuality, cleanliness, docility.

Youngsters were more easily inducted into wage labour than older and married women; they were inexperienced and malleable, and they were healthy. In particular, they had better eyesight than older women, a matter of great concern for electronics and textile manufacturers because the work involved close attention to minute items (in chip production the work was done under a microscope). Young women are not usually heads of households, and their employment was frequently encouraged by the male heads to whom the wages were sent. For many agricultural families, those wages were the major source of income, though the employers scaled women's wages as if they were secondary sources. Even though their families depended on their factory employment, the women were still embedded in pre-capitalist relationships, and they returned to their family homes during seasonal or other layoffs. While they were employed they lived in company-owned dormitories, and they paid for room and board. Employers acted in loco parentis, treating "the girls" as feudalistic parents would have; in this way the pre-capitalist family was indirectly used to sustain the workers at a low cost.

In a comparative study of zone employment conditions in the early 1980s, Eddy Lee found that 77 per cent of the Malaysian workers put in more than 45 hours per week; all of the workers in the Bataan Zone of the Philippines clocked more than 48 hours per week, and a quarter of them more than 60 hours. Workers put in equally long hours in Sri Lanka.[10] Employees were expected to work quickly, to accept shift work, and to work under constant supervision.

These conditions together with the low wages, have been called "super-exploitation" by Fröbel, Heinrichs, and Kreye,[11] a technical term rather than simply a moral condemnation; the term refers to sub-subsistence wages and exhausting conditions that prevent the worker's reproducing herself without recourse to another source of subsistence funds. Lee pointed out that the same wages and conditions were prevalent outside the zones; this does not reduce the seriousness of the charge, but it does place it in context. It should be noted that outside the zones women were less likely to be employed by firms with relatively high profit margins and access to world markets. Lee also found that the available evidence, while confirming that the wages in zones were low compared either with men's wages or with wages for similar work in industrial countries, did not confirm the more technical argument of super-exploitation; that is, the wages were not below subsistence levels. Even so, they were "pitifully low," the work routines were exhausting, occupational safety and industrial health standards were low, and there was little job security.[12]

In a report on the semiconductor firms in Southeast Asia in the late 1970s, Rachel Grossman noted the strict discipline, the quotas and daily productivity monitoring, the persistent layoffs when quotas were not met, and the extension of factory rules into the private lives of the women workers. She quoted from a workers' manual at one plant in the Philippines: "Do not accept employment by another company, work part time or hold any other job without the consent of the personnel manager and the general manager." Even more telling is the comment of a manager of a Fairchild factory in Indonesia: "What we are doing resembles a family system in which I am not just the manager but also a father to all of those here in Fairchild. This conforms to a very important Indonesian principle, that of the family."[13]

Most studies of these female workers (from any theoretical position) emphasize the widespread socialization practices that train women to be patient, docile, and accepting of male authority. Patriarchal cultures and non-industrial lifestyles also train young women to become manually dextrous, a trait frequently cited by employers as a reason for preferring women over men in textile and electronics work. At the same time employers preferred workers who were already accustomed to fixed working hours, time clocks, and scheduled breaks. To encourage desirable work habits, the education of women throughout Asian countries would have to be upgraded with infusions of foreign investment. Several studies indicated that the young women most likely to obtain employment in the factories of the late 1970s were, on average, better educated than those who remained in rural and domestic service.[14] Though an increasing emphasis was placed on formal education, employers expressed a preference for workers without previous employment histories. This meant that most workers had no standard by which to assess their new factory jobs.[15]

Similar findings were reported in a study of the Santacruz Electronics Export Processing Zone (SEEPZ) in Bombay.[16] In Greater Bombay, as of 1981, 78 per cent of all workers in electronic and semi-electronic industries were male, and in the total non-agricultural labour force of India nearly 90 per cent of all workers were male. This was consistent with the prevailing cultural norms that inhibited women's participation in the labour force. Yet in the same year 90 per cent of the workers in the zone were female. The zone, established in 1974, the second in India, accounted for one-quarter of the country's total electronics exports by 1979. On the basis of interviews with employers and employees, the authors concluded that "low wage considerations thus form an important element in the whole process of recruitment. The choice is then clear step by step, first women, then untrained women and finally the low paid women."[17]

As elsewhere, the employers cited other reasons for recruiting women. One said, "In our advertisement we specify that we need girls who have passed at least ninth standard and have knowledge of tailoring and embroidery work. The reason for this is that such work not only needs concentration but also requires patience to sit for long hours to complete the job." The low wages were tolerated by young girls, and the employers were aided in recruiting them by government contributions to their training. Unions were not in evidence in most firms in the zones, and the workers who were interviewed made it very clear that they were afraid to join, let alone lead, a movement towards unionization.

In the Bombay study the young female workers were predominantly from lower-middle-class, urban, educated families rather than from the enormous population of illiterate families in the slums. They could be induced to overcome the prohibitions of religion and culture by their need for income, and they were likely to have had some training that suited them for urban employment. Most lived in families where a father, brother, or husband earned an income, so that they were inclined to view their own income as supplementary.

In the plants of the 1970s, as the workers matured (in their mid-twenties) they were frequently let go. This was the point at which they began to make adult demands for maternity leave, pension funds, and other social welfare benefits.[18] Their family contexts began to disintegrate, and they could no longer depend upon extended kinship relations for subsistence when they were laid off or in difficulty.

Grossman noted that these women – young, healthy, relatively well educated but with no other work experience, and single when they entered the factories – could be thrown into permanent unemployment when they were fired. Their families could not support them, and their own raised expectations made them unwilling to return to rural lifestyles.[19] A. Lin Neumann found that the women, having been thoroughly immersed in a version of Western culture that emphasized beauty contests and glamourous clothes, were no longer seen as ideal marriage partners either by rural agriculturally based men or by urban unemployed men. Prostitution was frequently the only economic activity open to them. Their customers were tourists and international businessmen who were connected with the Asian factory.[20]

However, other writers have argued that some of these women learned trading skills and languages during their employment and could make use of them in commercial occupations other than prostitution. Linda Lim, in examining other Southeast Asian patterns, argued that the multinationals were able to exploit women's labour most successfully in those countries with strong patriarchal systems. But those women, by virtue of that employment, gained a measure of independence which enabled them to begin the process of casting off their subservience.[21]

For the women who were pushed and pulled into employment in the factories, there may have been a net improvement in income and an increase in independence. Prostitution and poverty undoubtedly were related to the employment practices of the firms, but some women did emerge with new skills and the economy did permit them to enter alternative employment or establish trade-related businesses. Other women found their marriage choices enhanced because they had demonstrated an ability to earn income and, if they had managed to save money during their employment tenure, they had a self-generated dowry.[22]

Several countries on the receiving end of the export-driven assembly economy attempted to institute minimum wage laws, demanding severance pay for women who were fired after several years' work, or promoting other reforms. These countries were burdened with the social and economic problems of a worn-out urban labour force. In addition, though unionization was virtually impossible, and though the young women were typically situated in such strong patriarchal traditions that they accepted extradordinarily oppressive working conditions, there were strikes and some militant responses from women. These were occasionally successful, but they incurred serious risks – especially the risk of the companies' departure.

In China the SEZs had significant impacts on women and on the rural regions in which they were located. Female workers were moved from agriculture to assembly and because the wage structure in the SEZs was high in comparison with local wages (though lower than elsewhere in Asian SEZ locations) the workers enjoyed relatively high status.[23] Incentive schemes and bonuses came into general use, including foreign exchange certificates which permitted workers to purchase imported items in the SEZ. Those imports changed the local cultures and standards of living, and created new differences between SEZ workers and others. The privileged status of the SEZ workers meant that those employees and their children had privileged access to housing and education.[24] Though a reported 97 per cent of all women were in the labour force,[25] China remained a thoroughly patriarchal society. But as women in the SEZ factories gained economic independence, their relative power in domestic society began to increase, just as it had already done in neighbouring countries.

The growth of this labour force in the Asian NICs was rapid through the 1970s and the early 1980s. Everywhere there was a vulnerability to runaway companies that opened low-cost plants where labour conditions were attractive but withdrew overnight if unions were formed or labour strife occurred. The electrical products companies were famous for this behaviour, although the silicon-wafer manufacturing companies were generally more stable. For the makers of consumer products overhead was not a major cost, and new factories in even less developed areas could be established. For the semiconductor plants the overhead costs of air-conditioning and atmospheric control slowed relocation, though the companies were still able to move faster than the heavy industries of the steel age.

The opening of the Chinese labour market and the establishment of export zones in China increased the competition for foreign capital and export-oriented plants throughout the Third World just as the developed market countries (DMCs) were beginning to experience the pains of recession and overproduction in the electrical industries.

AS SOME OF THE NICS flourished, neighbouring countries became reservoirs of migrant labour for their factories. Language, culture, population statistics, men's employment rates, political climates, and geopolitical situations all influenced the flow of capital to Singapore, Hong Kong, Taiwan, and South Korea. As production increased, workers from neighbouring states were allowed to take employment as non-citizen workers. Singapore has imported Malaysian, Thai, Filipina, and Indonesian women as guest workers. These women have no citizenship rights and no civil rights, and are deported if their eyesight or productivity fails to please, or if markets slow down.[26] Hong Kong has imported migrant labour from mainland China and the Philippines. The oil-rich states have imported workers from Sri Lanka, Pakistan, and other South Asian countries.[27]

In the new core countries, the initial phases of industrialization are passing. Since the agricultural revolution and the establishment of factories, a new generation of urban wage-workers has been born. Though the multinationals are not renowned for their training programs, some industrial skills have been transmitted. A good deal of new capital has been infused into the system. National firms have developed subcontracting capacities and have grown into regional production firms. And in each of these "original" factory-zone countries wages have increased. Although the rates are well below those for similar jobs in the United States and Europe, there are significant differences between Singapore and Indonesia, for example, in the level of industrialization and spread effects. In a sense, what happens is that as a few regions become industrialized (even if in a dependent form), they develop the capacity to "export" unemployment and poverty to neighbouring regions by borrowing migrant workers when demand is high and deporting them when it dips. This is the development model Japan followed in its rapid-growth form from the 1950s through to the 1970s.

The use of non-citizens as vulnerable supplies of migrant labour is neither new nor confined to the NICs. In the nineteenth century, as European nations defined their borders and their colonies, a class of stateless people was created. These people were generally members of ethnic minorities ousted from their homelands by political events or by sheer desperate poverty. Statelessness, in contrast to homelessness, is a condition contingent on the universal establishment of nations and the definition of citizenship. It is a curious phenomenon in a world that has created the global assembly line in extraterritorial zones. Nations in the contemporary period are neither one thing nor another, but their citizens have rights that are denied non-citizens, and persons fleeing one nation cannot be admitted to another unless they are deemed to be political refugees. The definition of "refugee" is both highly restricted and politically sensitive. In the post-war United States, migrants had little hope of meeting the criteria unless their homelands were labelled communist. In most DMCs those who were fleeing abysmal poverty were not included on the refugee list except where, as in the Hungarian Revolution, they managed to escape under the umbrella of a political rebellion.

Within this global economy and its increasingly ambiguous political divisions, the stateless ones now include illegal entrants to the industrial economies of both the core countries and the NICs; they compete with one another for poverty-wage jobs and live in fear that they will be caught and deported, even though the industrial economies depend on them to provide service and agricultural labour. Related to them but having legal status are the guest workers, people who are permitted to work for specified times in a country other than their own; they have no civil rights, no citizenship, and no permanent tenure.

Migrant farm workers the world over produce much of what the industrial world eats. Many of these workers are illegal migrants from poor countries – an estimated one-half of the American farm labour force, for example – but the rich countries also use indigenous agricultural workers who move from farm to farm in search of a living. Agriculture is rarely subject to minimum wage legislation, and unions are impotent when the labour force consists of illegal migrants and often of children, when the work is seasonal, and when the employers themselves are often small commodity producers held captive by the market controls of large processing companies.[28]

Illegal migrants are not confined to agricultural work, however, and in the United States vast numbers of them are employed in other sectors. In Silicon Valley, even after the exodus to the NICs, corporations employed illegal migrants to assemble microchips for use in guided missiles and to make printed circuit-boards for personal computers. They provide unskilled labour to companies that produce everything from prosthetics to air conditioners, and much of the southern US economy is completely dependent on cheap and readily available labour from Mexico, Guatemala, and Nicaragua.[29] In Los Angeles nearly half of all workers in the low-wage industries are Mexicans; they earn an estimated 25 per cent less than the US average. In California two-thirds of the garment-industry labour force consists of illegal immigrants. In Silicon Valley between 10 and 20 per cent of the workers are illegal migrants. An immigration official in San Jose admitted that "we'd have a revolution" if they were deported.[30]

Much the same situation, though not yet on the same scale, exists in Japan, which has full employment of its own citizens and faces a labour shortage in the labour-intensive, low-skilled sectors. Japanese employers hire immigrants from neighbouring South and Southeast Asian countries. These immigrants come on tourist or student visas and illegally seek employment. They are essential to the heavy industries of Japan, yet they, like their counterparts in other industrialized countries and in the NICs, have no citizenship status and no civil rights.

Were the gains in selected Asian countries made at the expense of unskilled labour in the metropolitan regions? The debate was intense in the early 1980s. Between 1964 and 1978, the work force in the US electronics industry actually increased by 64 per cent.[31] The impact of the regional shifts was not an overall job loss but a dramatic change in the composition of jobs. In the United States the number of white-collar and technical jobs grew – not a surprising development, since the research, development, sales, and management segments of the firms were located there. At the national level the percentage, though not the absolute number, of production jobs declined in the same period.

Since a high proportion of the production work was performed by women, it follows that the percentage – and, in fact, the absolute number – of women employed in the electronics industry declined. The peak in US employment of both production workers and women occurred in 1966, and since then employment for both groups has almost steadily declined. The employment of women in clerical occupations increased during the same period. There were regional differences in these shifts; the greatest job loss and restructuring occurred in the peripheral production areas of the United States.[32] It can be reasonably inferred that offshore operations in this industry created more skilled jobs for men in the central production regions of the United States while it substituted Asian women in the zones for US women in the unskilled production jobs.

A similar debate has occurred in Germany over offshore textile production. The seminal work of Fröbel, Heinrichs, and Kreye indicated that there was a direct relationship between the decline of employment in Germany and the rise in offshore employment in the textile and garment industries.[33] There, however, there was no equivalent of the high-tech development of a new industry, even though the high-tech machinery is now built into the process. The textile industry relocation did displace workers in all of the industrial countries.

The global economy, then, rests on a shaky foundation of relatively immobile labour in some regions, illegal and easily exploited labour in others, and women whose labour is cheap because of the continuation of patriarchal systems. Full employment in some centres is matched by masses of unemployed and illegal migrants in others. Capital is free to move at will, tapping these various sources of labour, but labour has no corresponding freedom. Unskilled labour has become more competitive on an international scale as workers in some regions lose jobs to workers elsewhere or to the illegal migrants.

THE GROWTH RATES of the NICs as a whole exceeded those of developed economies throughout the 1970s. In boasting of success at attracting foreign investment, Singapore's minister of finance said, "We had no natural resources other than a diligent and enterprising people."[34] By the mid-1980s, political conditions in Singapore were, according to one business publication, "the safest in the world for foreign-owned business and will remain so throughout the rest of this decade."[35] (One of the spinoffs of the restructuring is the creation of information industries that inform global businesses of conditions in the NICs and rate their safety, labour conditions, and financial stability.)

Conditions are still changing, however. Cheap labour was especially attractive in the second phase of the restructuring of industry, before automation was fully underway. Full automation changed the dynamics of capital-labour relations, and for many firms reduced the advantages of cheap labour. Workers sometimes experienced sudden new employment and then abandonment by foreign enterprises within the span of a few years. There was no clear pattern in the moves after 1980, because incentives and disincentives were pulling in opposite directions.

World Bank data show percentage growth changes that suggest gradual improvement for developing countries, or, more specifically, for countries that exported manufactures and low-income countries. Indeed, some countries have enjoyed very high growth rates in both real and per capita GDP. For the period 1965–73 a sample of 90 countries showed real GDP growth rates of 6.5 per cent. Low-income countries had GDP growth rates of 5.5 per cent, middle-income countries rates of 7 per cent. In the period 1980–6, however, the real GDP growth for the same countries was 3.6 per cent; low-income countries registered 7.4 per cent, and middle-income countries 2 per cent. In the interim, oil-exporting countries showed steeply declining growth rates; manufacturing exporting countries showed slightly declining rates; and indebted countries showed nearly negative rates.[36] Growth rates reflect their base as well as changes, and for the low-income countries that base was so low that any growth would have registered strongly.

The wage gap between industrialized countries and the NICs, already wide in 1974, grew significantly wider as the American dollar exchange rate escalated in the 1980s. The gap between the United States and European countries also widened. Hourly pay levels in manufacturing industries shown as a percentage of the US average in 1985 were as follows: Brazil, 9 per cent; South Korea, 10 per cent; Mexico, 13 per cent; and Taiwan, 15 per cent. Spain, Ireland, and Britain showed levels between 37 and 46 per cent, and Japan exactly 50 per cent. The wage rates of the strong European countries ranged from 56 per cent (France) to 73 per cent (Sweden) and 75 per cent (West Germany).[37] In every case there had been a sharp drop in the relative position of other countries between 1981 and 1985. The American dollar, which had climbed some 25 per cent in exchange value between 1982 and 1985, put American workers at a disadvantage; with no or modest real wage increases, they could not possibly compete with European, let alone Third World, workers. Thus, where labour costs remained critical and unskilled labour continued to be useful, the pulls were in the direction of the NICs.

For countries well on their way to industrialization, the other condition that encourages companies to retain their subsidiaries even while locating new plants in the DMCs is a growing consumer population. India's business leaders are now emphasizing this feature in their search for new investments. "We have much poverty, it is true," one speaker at a recent conference in Canada admitted, "but think of it this way: we have many times more people in the middle class than the whole population of your country, and they are ready now to buy your products."[38] R.N. Sharma and Chandan Sengupta observed this trend: "The move is already there to allow 25 per cent of their [export zone companies'] products to be sold in the native market. This will affect the electronic industry outside the zones, or the owners of these industries directly or indirectly will find their place in FTZs. What then will be the relevance of FTZs?"[39]

Assembly lines in the NICs may be automated if there is a potential market for the products. Rather than lose the factories altogether, local goverments may provide still more incentives, and allow their original restrictions on the export of products made under special arrangements to fall by the wayside.

In the zone at Manaus in northwestern Brazil, 251 industrial firms were operating in the mid-1980s. Special zone laws applied to ranching and agriculture in the region, and affected another 67 firms in the interior of Western Amazonia. More than 55,000 workers were employed there in the mid-1980s.[40] Manaus was once the rubber-producing centre of the world. As rubber trees were planted in Indonesia and India and synthetic substitutes for rubber were developed, the town and region rapidly declined. The establishment of the Zone Freia rejuvenated the region. Initially, the zone provided a cheap labour force for assembly-line work using imported parts; but there was also a mandate for expansion into agriculture and new industries, and extensive government support for worker training.

Firms such as Philips, Gillette, Sony, Honda and the many others that seem to occupy the zones all across the globe benefited from that trained labour force. The Manaus authorities offered further incentives as the firms began to automate their lines. In the Honda factory, for example, robots do much of the manufacturing work on motorcycles, and a growing proportion of the motorcycles are now sold on the Brazilian market. The labour force in this plant is predominantly young and male. On a visit to the Manaus zone in the spring of 1987, I observed a group of these young men during their lunch break. They were singing hymns and enjoying the pleasures of a warm day in the parklike grounds. They were clearly far better off than most Brazilians; their working conditions were relatively clean, and their tasks required mainly clerical or fairly simple technical skills. To the outsider, their docility and their almost obsequious reverence for Honda was disquieting, but one had only to look at the unemployed populations elsewhere in Brazil to understand the local government's willingness to accommodate the company. In the same zone Gillette and other manufacturers of small appliances were busy. At one firm hundreds of very young girls stood outside the (guarded) gates awaiting their pay-cheques or seeking employment for the following day. I learned that employment opportunities were declining at the firm, and that its stability was in question.

While cheap labour can still attract some firms, and the potential market in the LDCs or NICs can sustain others, there are forces pulling in the opposite direction. The semiconductor industry has been afflicted persistently with a problem familiar to established industries – an overcapacity that was caused in part by the strategies of offshore production using cheap labour.

By the 1980s this strategy was becoming outdated. The nature of the technology itself and its constant transformation reduced the advantages of offshore production and increased the utility of production in advanced industrial centres. Political uncertainties in some of the underdeveloped countries (Korea and the Philippines particularly), increasing objections by unions and governments in the industrial countries, potential increases in tariffs and other protectionist strategies, and the rising cost of fuel all contribute to the relocation of production.

The companies that had moved abroad were engaged in mass production of standardized commercial chips. In general, their research and development facilities remained in the industrial centres, together with the capital-intensive wafer fabrication lines. These functions required the kind of technical expertise found primarily in industrial countries. The companies could have automated their production lines much earlier, but the cheap local labour had created enough cost savings to make it unnecessary. From the beginning, Japanese chip manufacturers resisted moving their production offshore, preferring to use their own products to automate production lines at home. This strategy paid off in closer ties between research, development, and production departments, and the American producers recognized those advantages when they began to develop very large scale integrated (VLSI) circuits.

The labour-intensive component of semiconductor production decreased with each development; the scientific knowledge, and the cost of science and scientists, steadily increased. More and more of the production work required relatively skilled technicians rarely available in developing countries. One researcher estimated that by 1982 one worker with two weeks' training in an automated plant could replace thirty manual assemblers each with three months' training.[41]

Japanese chip producers had early adopted the Toyota model for just-in-time procurement of parts, thereby eliminating inventory costs. (This topic is discussed in the next chapter.) American producers could adopt this advantageous strategy only by locating chip production close to other production units so that materials could be used at the precise moment and in the precise quantity required without wastage.

Finally, and perhaps most important, the markets for computers, and especially for the VLSI circuits, needed servicing, and it became apparent that the closer the chip production facility was to the customer the better able the company was to service its products. If there were defects in the chips, wastage costs could be greatly reduced by rapid feedback and inventory control. In a competitive industry the cost savings attained through these procedures can mean the difference between survival and decline.

Fairchild moved its digital products division out of Singapore and Indonesia in 1985 and automated the lines: "We think we can make more money doing it here than we can 10,000 miles away."[42] In related industries, similar moves took place in the last half of the 1980s. A Calgary-based manufacturer of cellular telephones, for example, transferred a component-manufacturing firm from South Korea to Lethbridge, Alberta, explaining that it could save up to 10 per cent by automating its assembly plant and abandoning its Korean workers.[43] Some other firms followed suit.

In the mid-1970s the increasing cost of fuel reduced the advantages of air-shipping components, and possibly increased the attractiveness of locations in home or major market countries. As well, threatened tariffs on imported goods provided an incentive for manufacturing more in the industrial countries. The high tariff imposed by the EEC on imported chips induced American companies to locate plants in Britain and Ireland; some of those were transplanted from the NICs.

Relocation and new investment in the industrial countries did not require large numbers of unskilled labourers, and did nothing to offset the growing unemployment of unskilled workers either in Silicon Valley or in other regions in the United States and Europe. In fact, large companies announced layoffs as they automated, moved, or cut back on production of microchips and personal computers because of an oversupplied market. Industry leaders blamed Japanese competition; in the Silicon Valley, observers began talking about "the Detroit syndrome," meaning overspecialization in the production of too few items in a volatile market. IBM experienced sales drops throughout its operations, as did AT & T. New regulations and new products flooded AT & T's telephone production market, and the company responded by cutting nearly two thousand jobs in the United States, though it maintained and even increased employment in Singapore.[44]

Ironically, just as firms were returning to industrial countries or increasing their investments in them, much of the literature on deindustrialization was published. There certainly was some disinvestment and, perhaps more seriously, avoided investment by semiconductor firms from the 1960s until the early 1980s, when the firms moved divisions abroad. But new investments in the United States in the 1980s in that industry did not have the impact on employment anticipated by those who blamed offshore production for the problems. (The automobile industry is discussed in the next chapter). By this time, unskilled workers were not in demand; they had become the victims of the high speed of high-tech. In conditions of overcapacity and declining demand, such companies as AT & T, IBM, Motorola, and National Semiconductor shift their investments from one alliance to another or one product to another, as investments pay off (or fail to) in new technologies that transform whole industrial sectors.

Some job displacement in industrial countries was not related to new technology or direct labour costs. When the Caterpillar Tractor Company moved substantial portions of its production from the United States to Scotland in 1985, it was to avoid the high exchange rate of the US dollar. The Scottish workers were bemused; they noted that their employment depended on financial matters that had little to do with their productivity, and they remembered that Caterpillar had moved its D-8 earthmover production out of the same Scottish town several years earlier when its profits sagged. The plant manager who had had to lay off the workers, many of whom were recruited again in 1985, was called "Neutron" Davis, after the neutron bomb, which takes life but leaves buildings standing. A machinist, apparently reflecting the general opinion of the workforce, said, "American firms is all the same. They drop away, come back. I'm hoping it lasts a little longer this time. I'd imagine we have at least two or three years."[45] A side effect of the moves is apparent in that remark: workers take the jobs that are available because they have little choice, but they have no long-term future with the companies, and they give no long-term loyalty.

The town to which Caterpillar moved, just outside Glasgow, is similar to other regions in Britain, southern Europe, and Ireland, and to the free trade zones of the NICs. Scotland calls one such area "Silicon Glen." The British, like their counterparts elsewhere, offer tax-free rebates to investors, and when the American dollar was high they were able to attract them. The great advantage for American investors in Britain is that they have access both to skilled labour and to the European Common Market.

Thus we have come full circle, and the results are contradictory. The FEZs in the NICs are means of exploiting cheap, and especially female, labour. International capital is the temporary beneficiary. Mass production has penetrated the peripheral regions, bringing with it both the benefits and the defects of American industrial society. These developments have altered trading patterns so that the countries are not wholly dependent on the export of raw materials and foodstuffs (the major Asian NICs are not self-sufficient in agricultural produce). While a generation of young women has been exploited, the process of diminishing patriarchal holds over them has clearly begun. The growth of a global labour pool of unskilled workers migrating from one centre to another in a competitive search for jobs is concurrent with an overall decline in the demand for unskilled labour.

The governments that emerged in this process were typically authoritarian and repressive of civil rights, and it is no coincidence that they made available an oppressed labour force to the transplanted companies. The development of an urban middle class is well underway, however, and that class historically has demanded civil rights and democratic reforms; we have witnessed these demands in South Korea and the Philippines in the 1980s.

The consequences of the globalization of production in the free trade zones, at least in the semiconductor, electrical, and garment industries, cannot be easily labelled either good or evil. One can say with certainty, however, that labour has not had the same freedom as capital, that incentives to companies in the early phases were directly tied to repressive states, and that the integrated circuit of internal markets within large companies operates on considerably less than free market principles.

CHAPTER EIGHT

High-Wire Acts

Huckleberry Finn travelled by raft. Humbert Humbert chased Lolita by car. Across the heavens, leaping over the barriers of the gods, good and evil have been captured forever on American films in endless, mind-numbing car chases ever since. America, the mobile society; America, the great highway for the common man. Labour was mobile at last, chained only by the need to earn money to pay for the wheels. Surely it was the automobile that sustained the mythology of the classless society. Mass production, mass consumption, mass education; there were no lords and ladies in the Ford-managed society.

Then along came computer-assisted design and computer-assisted manufacturing (CAD / CAM) systems, just-in-time inventory organization, and the global production circuit. Like the computer-technology industry, the automobile industry provides us with insight into technological, organizational social, and political change as "globalized" production – and in this case, the image of a global car – first shocked and then transformed the industry that had made America.

IN 1979 SOME 3.6 million people were directly employed in manufacturing automobiles in the United States, Canada, Western Europe and Japan. Nearly one-tenth of the US labour force was in motor-related occupations, and the world's largest automobile companies, General Motors and Ford, were still ahead of Toyota, Nissan, Honda, and Mazda of Japan, and Volkswagen-Audi, Renault, Peugeot, and Fiat of Europe.[1]

But Japanese imports were beginning to gain a substantial share of the North American markets, and the American government imposed quotas in 1981. The Detroit manufacturers were far from unanimous in their support of controls. Ford and Chrysler called for them, but GM demanded "free trade," looking to its Japanese affiliates Isuzu (39.6 per cent owned by GM) and Suzuki (9.7 per cent owned by GM). These stock purchases had been made so that GM could obtain small cars for the North American market. Affiliations with Japanese companies saved GM the immediate capital costs of retooling existing plants for small, fuel-effective cars, and it saved substantially on labour costs. According to GM's internal study of the Isuzu plant in 1981, the differential in production cost over American-made cars was over $2,000 per unit, largely because of reductions in labour costs.[2]

The Japanese manufacturers responded to American protectionism either by setting up their own plants in the United States or, more often, by entering into joint ventures with existing American companies. Mazda, affiliated with Ford, began producing cars in Michigan in 1987. Honda was already established in Ohio. Nissan began producing trucks in a non-union plant in Tennessee in the same year. The non-union Honda plant assembled the Accord model from parts manufactured in Japan, but announced its intention to produce engines and transmission units in the United States.[3]

In 1985 Toyota cars began rolling off the line at a GM plant in California under a 50-50 joint venture agreement. Toyota, Japan's largest company and the third largest in the world at that time, sent parts from Japan for assembly in the United States. The Toyota and Mazda plants were unionized; however, the union – the United Auto Workers – had lost some of its bargaining power in the new production systems, because along with shared ownership arrangements had come computer-assisted manufacturing. An internal GM memo estimated a loss of up to 100,000 jobs by 1990, and in the years between 1979 – when the American industry was at its peak – and 1985, GM laid off about 130,000 workers.[4] In 1987 GM began importing 100,000 cars made by its South Korean partner, Daewoo.

The Ford-Mazda alliance (Ford owned 25 per cent of the shares) involved more than production in the United States or Japan. Mazda's components were used in Ford's Mexican plant in small cars destined for the American market. Mexico and Brazil were the recipients of much of the offshore production for Japanese, American, European, and joint venture automobile firms. Car sales in Mexico and Brazil were relatively high, at one car per 15 or 16 persons, compared with one per 27.6 in Taiwan, 1 per 104.9 in South Korea, 1 per 125 in Nigeria, and 1 per 10,200 in China. Even so, China was viewed as a long-term potential market, and Volkswagen entered into a joint venture with the Chinese government in 1984 to produce Santanas near Shanghai for a Chinese market.[5]

Brazil, with two sophisticated special export zones and some strong domestic-component requirements, played host to Volkswagen, Fiat, Ford and GM, aiming for both the growing domestic market and exports to the industrial countries. Though in general these investments paid off for the foreign companies, the domestic market was variable and in prolonged recession of the mid-1980s the companies faced a lagging demand. In 1987 sales dropped sharply and layoffs were widespread.[6]

Mexico produced low-cost, labour-intensive parts for vehicles assembled in US plants. In addition to Ford-Mazda's operations, GM built pickup trucks in Mexico, and also had a network of twenty-three components plants in the free trade zone near the US-Mexican border. A variation on traditional investment patterns emerged: a corporation could buy up a country's debt at a reduced cost on the condition that it invest in the country. Chrysler, for example, purchased a Mexican bank debt at a 30 per cent discount in return for permission to increase its subsidiaries there. In part this procedure was sparked by the Mexican government's rule that the value of automotive exports equal the value of imports; but the significant incentive was Mexican labour costs. A spokesman for GM's international operations observed, "Their quality of workmanship is quite good and with the proximity, it has a lot of advantages."[7]

In the mid-1980s South Korea was the chief producer of competitive cars, and the GM joint venture with Daewoo was an indication of prospects. The car would be designed by GM's German subsidiary with some additions from Isuzu, GM's Japanese affiliate, made in Korea, and sold in America as a Pontiac.[8] Daewoo was also scheduled to manufacture components for other GM products. These components were labour-intensive, in contrast to engines and transmissions, which would still be produced in automated plants in the industrial countries. Other Korean firms were striking similar deals with Mazda and Chrysler. Mazda, linked to Ford, was also linked to the South Korean truck manufacturer Kia.

Taiwan was another production location. Ford joined with Lio Ho of Taiwan in 1972 (buying 70 per cent of its shares) to produce small vehicles for the local market, and by 1984 a major expansion was undertaken to produce cars for export. Among the exports were subcompacts to be distributed by Ford dealers in Canada. The president of Ford of Canada said, "It has been clear to us for some time that a response was required so that we could effectively compete with the variety of inexpensive small cars being sold in Canada from low labor-cost countries. We have decided that we can best serve our dealers, customers and stockholders by pursuing a strategy of supplementing our North American-produced small cars with products drawn from lower-cost sources."[9]

As the American dollar exchange rate declined relative to the Japanese yen, Japanese manufacturers became more aggressive in establishing plants offshore. Several were located in Canada; others went to Korea, even though it was seen as a potential competitor. Mitsubishi bought cars from Hyundai of South Korea to sell as Mitsubishi products in the United States either under its own name or through joint ventures with Chrysler.[10] Production costs in Japan increased so much that it became profitable, as well as politically clever, to purchase parts in the United States – from Japanese component suppliers. Delta Kogyo, for example, supplied auto seats to Mazda's new plant in Michigan from a nearby plant.[11]

GM, attempting to evade import controls on Japanese models and the rising labour costs associated with the yen, was reported to have negotiated with auto makers in Taiwan, Malaysia, Korea, and Czechoslovakia to arrange resales of their cars under the Isuzu brand names.[12] According to the *Wall Street Journal*, GM's Allante model would end up crossing the Atlantic twice; some components moved from first manufacturing stages in the United States to Italy for assembly, and then moved back to the United States, where further components were added and final assembly took place.[13]

Even more bizarre in the context of the ideology of competition are the unions of opposites. In 1986 Isuzu, which made cars for GM's Chevrolet division, joined with Fuji Heavy Industries, 6 per cent owned by Nissan, to build an assembly plant in Indiana.[14] Japanese, South Korean, and Taiwanese companies are also moving into the European market through exports and investments.

This makes life difficult for European manufacturers. In France, the state-owned Renault company survived through government support. Peugeot (37 per cent owned by the Peugeot family, 15 per cent owned by Chrysler) was marginally profitable, assisted by loans from the government's Industrial Modernization Fund. A government committee report in 1984 concluded that the French motor industry had to lose 70,000 jobs out of a total of 230,000 by 1988, and invest rapidly in new technologies, in order to survive.[15] Renault, attempting to find a way into the American market, began purchasing the stock of American Motors in 1979, but finally sold its controlling interest in 1987 to Chrysler.

Chrysler also held 24 per cent of the shares of Mitsubishi Motors, with which it established a joint venture plant in Illinois. That 1985 agreement worked well for both companies: it allowed Chrysler to get out of the small car market (its Omni and Horizon models were to be phased out when the market demand declines below profitable levels), and gave Mitsubishi a relatively risk-free entry to the American market. Half of the cars were to be sold by Chrysler and half by Mitsubishi, all on the American market.[16] Chrysler had a similar parts-buying agreement with Samsun Group. In addition, Chrysler planned to build a luxury sports car in Italy in a joint venture with Officine Alfieri Maserati (of which it owned 5 per cent).[17]

For the Japanese market, American and European manufacturers linked up with established Japanese firms and with one another – Volvo with Fuji, GM with Isuzu, Peugeot with Suzuki. These connections took various forms, from shareholding to sales consignment, production consignment, and provision of components and knock-down sets.[18]

The Japanese links were supported by Japanese manufacturers, who thus gained access to the American and European markets. By way of explanation, the executive vice-president of Mitsubishi Motors said, "We are not simply giving a helping hand to our rivals: we are seeking greater profits by offering our technology to them and marketing their products."[19] The managing director of Sanyo, referring to similar associations between microchip manufacturers, said, "Joining hands with foreign competitiors is one realistic and viable way of improving our business environment."[20]

Finally, Japanese companies and joint venture capital began moving farther afield in the underdeveloped countries to situate new ventures. Isuzu and Nissan joined Suzuki and an Indian government-owned company in planning joint production of vehicles for India. The Indian government imposed restrictions consistent with its concern about unsafe and crowded roads, and with its worries over indebtedness. It rejected proposals from other manufacturers, a situation that may become more common in a world with overcapacity and intense competition for even small markets.[21]

These moves are not all in the same direction, and the rationale behind them is not the same in each case. The American companies experienced rapid losses in their domestic and offshore markets, blamed high labour costs and union militancy, and began moving abroad or linking up with Japanese competitors. The Japanese companies, fearing protectionism in the United States and European markets, established new plants there. They located plants in Canada in case a continental umbrella was constructed that would give Canada preferential entry to the United States, and in view of the relatively low Canadian dollar, which brought labour costs down.

several Japanese companies invested in plants in the southern right-to-work states.

Once the initial moves were undertaken, there were consequences: a fall in the exchange value of the American dollar, a rise in the value of the yen, and the growing spectre of vast overcapacity. This led to further restructuring: American companies imported Japanese cars from American-Japanese firms, and Japanese firms linked up with Korean capital and capital from other sources to produce offshore for the markets of the industrialized countries. The second phase involved extremely complex production policies for parts; an automobile sold under an American label in Canada might have been assembled through an integrated system that included New Zealand, Korea, Brazil, Japan, India, and Italy.

THE GLOBAL RATIONALIZATION of the automobile industry had a precursor in the continental rationalization of American firms in Canada during the 1960s. Since the 1920s Canada's automobile industry has been dominated by American firms, with GM, Ford, Chrysler, and American Motors in the lead. Until the mid-1960s the industry consisted of two components: the assembly of cars using parts manufactured in the United States, and the manufacture of parts in Canada. In the inter-war years the American car companies produced more cars in Canada than anywhere else other than the United States, but much of this production consisted of assembling components imported from parent companies. Nearly half of the Canadian-assembled vehicles were shipped to British empire markets, where they had preferential tariff entry. Those markets were lost when the preferences disappeared. After the Second World War the Canadian industry ran up a trade deficit in parts imported from its parent firms for relatively small production lines serving the small domestic market. The Canadian component parts manufacturers, which to that point had relied entirely on the Canadian companies for markets, were small, technically unsophisticated, and undercapitalized, but unlike the main industry they were Canadian-owned and they employed Canadian engineers.

In the early 1960s the industry was restructured.[22] The 1966 Auto Pact between the Canadian and American governments removed tariffs on cars and parts. Each major auto maker was to produce a specific range of models for the North American market. Canadian production was specialized, allowing manufacturers to improve economies of scale without duplicating the range of products from their other companies in the United States. Cross-border trade in automobiles increased, a favourable balance of trade for Canada was registered, and Canadian production expanded dramatically.[23] The cost of this reorganization and expansion was the loss or preclusion of research and development capacities in Canada. US firms did all the production engineering and made the production decisions. While there was an increase in assembly-line jobs, there was also a loss of highly skilled technical and managerial jobs in the large firms.

In the component-parts sector of the industry, some sixty new plants were established and over a hundred plant expansions undertaken in Ontario and Quebec between 1964 and 1966. John Holmes estimates that employment increased from 29,000 to 42,000 and productivity rose by more than 50 per cent; however, the volume of "in-house" parts imported from the United States vastly increased and the majority of the new investments were made by American parts producers.[24] The relatively small Canadian auto parts firms, which had previously served only the Canadian manufacturers, lacked experience in the US markets and were generally unable to upgrade their technologies; many were acquired by US firms.

In the mid-1960s, when the Auto Pact was signed, Canadian automobile workers earned an average 30 per cent less than American workers; there was thus a cost advantage to American producers' establishing firms for labour-intensive manufacturing in Canada. The rationalization resulted in a clear regional division of labour: the labour-intensive operations took place in Canadian parts and assembly plants, the more skilled and capital-intensive operations in American plants.[25]

The favourable trade balance lasted less than a decade. By 1970 Canadian plants were losing ground, chiefly because of steadily declining investments in plant and the absence for independent Canadian producers of a parts market in the United States. The major US firms assembled vehicles using parts imported duty-free from their parent firms. Some automotive parts were manufactured in Canada, but 59 per cent of these were produced in subsidiaries (including 36 per cent in "Big Three" subsidiaries). There was no incentive for the American corporations to purchase the products of Canadian independent suppliers.[26]

The problems intensified after the Nixon administration established domestic international sales corporations (DISC), essentially a non-tariff barrier which provided tax incentives to American multinationals to supply foreign markets through American-built parts and machinery. Canadian assembly plants had received 26.5 per cent of continental investment in 1965; that figure dropped to 3.6 per cent in 1972. Investment in parts plants declined from 11.8 per cent to 5.1 per cent in the same period.[27] The American corporations had no interest in expanding investment beyond the stipulated requirements of the Auto Pact. In fact, the Reisman royal commission of 1978 found that US multinational vehicle assemblers and parts manufacturers retained less than half of their earnings in the early 1970s, and sent the remainder to their parent firms.[28]

Trade conducted by the four major auto manufacturers constituted 76.6 per cent of total automotive trade in Canada between 1973 and 1978; most of this comprised intracorporate transfers. The Canadian trade deficit reached $3 billion before the end of the decade, and was a central component of the total trade deficit in 1980 of over $17 billion. The official trade deficit was not even the whole of the financial balance: there were dividends of over $100 million, R & D charges of between $100 and $300 million, and other charges connected to a branch plant organization that had to import its head office management and research expertise.[29]

In 1978 Ohio and Ontario entered a competition for the location of a new Ford engine-production plant. Ohio offered tax incentives. To induce Ford to build the plant in Ontario and create 2,500 jobs, a joint federal-provincial grant of $687 million was awarded. Though Ontario "won," Ford laid off several thousand workers in Canada two years later in response to declining American sales. Simultaneously, the Chrysler company, while blaming government regulations for its crisis, obtained from the Canadian government guaranteed loans totalling $200 million in return for a promise to invest $400 million in Canada and increase the proportion of Canadian jobs. It also obtained guaranteed loans totalling $1.5 billion from the US government. Despite these subsidies and loan guarantees, Canadian vehicle and parts production dropped by some 27 per cent between 1978 and 1981. Sales declined by nearly 30 per cent. Employment declined by 41.1 per cent. After a very brief rally, employment dropped again in the winter of 1981 and continued downward for the next several years.[30]

The Japanese industry had meanwhile become competitive with the North American manufacturers. In 1980 nearly 90 per cent of the Canadian automotive industry's total trade was with the United States, but the growth rate in trade of automotive products with Japan increased by 17.5 per cent per year between 1976 and 1980. Imported vehicles accounted for about 25 per cent of North American sales in 1981, up 15 per cent from the late 1970s; some 80 per cent of those imports were from Japan. The US response to Japanese competition was to negotiate a special agreement by which the Japanese manufacturers reduced their exports by 7.7 per cent in 1981, although parts from Japan were permitted to displace parts from Canadian plants.

Canadian labour costs had risen to American levels, and the Canadian industry was still labour-intensive. The American firms, reeling from the impact of the oil crisis and from more stringent emission-control regulations, were losing their competitive edge even in their own North American market. They began moving offshore, forming associations with their competitors, automating their plants, and creating global production systems. Increasingly, the Canadian auto parts sector suffered deindustrialization as the companies imported parts from elsewhere both directly and via the United States; the parent companies in the United States imported directly from their other subsidiaries or from a new group of subcontractors in the Japanese model of just-in-time production.[31] Canada's share of the American parts market dropped from 70 per cent in the early 1970s to less than 35 per cent by 1980.[32] These events seriously jeopardized employment in the largest of Canada's few manufacturing industries as well as the country's overall export earnings, one-third of which came from vehicles or automotive parts. Government and private studies of the mid-1980s indicated that by 1990 about one-half of all cars sold in Canada would be either assembled from parts made offshore or shipped complete from offshore plants.[33]

The Canadian government responded to these developments in much the same way as it had entered the competition with Ohio to induce the companies to locate in Ontario – by offering incentives to offshore manufacturers similar to those already provided by American state governments. This greatly upset some American legislators and became a contentious item in the bilateral free trade talks between Canada and the United States in the late 1980s. One congressional representative expressed the view that Canada was creating a pincer movement against US auto production, and another seemed annoyed that Canada, in her view "really a trust territory of the US," was acting against US interests. "You'd think Canada would want its own companies," she observed.[34]

The president of Chrysler responded to foreign tax advantages and exchange rate differences: "We've willingly accepted the substantial social costs of doing business in Canada [but] I'm fed up to you-know-what subsidizing the purchase of every import that comes from offshore." He also warned that if Canada did not change its policies, "we do have a plan B, and yes, we will be looking at other places to build cars."[35]

This was in 1986, when Chrysler, which had obtained considerable subsidies from the Canadian government, none the less laid off Canadian workers and had already moved parts of its industry offshore. Chrysler's television campaign, which claimed that the company had the largest network of Japanese auto dealers in Canada, told the tale. While calling for voluntary restraints by Japanese manufacturers on their exports to Canada as well as the United States, Chrysler imported Japanese cars and sold them under its own name. It also formed a joint venture with Mitsubishi to import 20,000 Mitsubishi Colts from Thailand.[36]

Overall, Canada has had more foreign ownership of its industries than other OECD countries. Its dependence on trade with the United States has increased since Britain's entry into the EEC. Its attempts throughout the 1970s to impose limitations through the Foreign Investment Review Agency (FIRA) and to create a National Energy Policy to protect its oil reserves failed, in part because groups within Canada obstructed them at every turn. These groups included the substantial management class employed in American-owned subsidiaries, the investment class that controls Canadian banking and other financial institutions, numerous oil and automobile companies that in one way or another are closely tied to American majors, and Canadian workers who belong to international (American) unions. In the oil industry there were regional animosities, and real regional advantages and disadvantages to a more protective federal stance. Embedded in American society before the Auto Pact came into existence, these groups were unable to disengage themselves when continentalist policies threatened Canadian interests.

During the 1970s and early 1980s the American government objected to attempts by the Canadian government to improve Canadian benefits from the Auto Pact even when (as was frequently the case) the same actions were simultaneously being taken by individual American states. In the brief period when the pact worked in favour of Canada, Washington threatened various sanctions, then reversed its stand as the balance shifted in favour of the United States. In the end, Canada's interests in an integrated industry had no weight, and the United States entered into negotiations with Japan.

Canada and its provinces provided three services to the multinationals – the Auto Pact agreements, direct financial aid, and the legitimation of free trade. Even as late as 1978 Simon Reisman, one of the chief proponents of the pact (subsequently named to a royal commission charged with determining why things were not quite working out, and then appointed Canada's chief negotiator in the bilateral trade talks with the United States in 1986–87) stated, "Despite the hopes and aspirations of the originators, the Auto Pact had failed to provide the stimulus or inspiration to beget similar agreements in its image for the enhancement of international specialization and efficiency in the massive trade between Canada and the USA."[37] The implication was that the fault lay with labour, which had negotiated wage parity with American firms, and with the higher proportion of unskilled workers and the higher labour component in the Canadian parts industry.

The key to this history lies in the assumptions that capital should be unhindered in its mobility, that the task of government is to facilitate accumulation by private capital, and that capital should have no nationality. The American government shared only the first two of these assumptions, though the multinationals advanced all three after the mid-1970s. The demise of the US industry occurred because there was no new plant investment, because the companies had failed to respond to market competition for small and fuel-efficient cars, and because their belated investment went offshore to join their competition rather than face it head-on. It did not occur because of failure of government support or because of government interference in the "free" market, and to lay the consequences at labour's door was, at the least, ungracious.

If we assume that members of government did not deliberately sabotage indigenous industry or intentionally bring about the economic depression which the collapse of the automobile industry presaged, we must conclude either that governments of peripheral states are impotent when multinationals backed by an imperial government penetrate their territory, or that even if some action is possible the dominant class within Canada is so tied into American capitalism that it would prevent behaviour detrimental to US (and therefore to its own) interests. One cannot test these conclusions, since federal governments have rarely attempted to present an independent Canadian option.

A 1978 Canadian Senate report on Canadian-American trade concluded that Canada had "very little leverage for persuading either vehicle manufacturers or the US government to modify the situation."[38] To extricate Canada from the imperial web, both the federal and provincial governments would have to be prepared to take actions that might bring about external sanctions and electoral defeat. A century of behaviour that not only facilitated but legitimated American capitalism pre-empted an appeal to the people on nationalist grounds. Protection for Canadian industry in the 1980s would have violated GATT agreements and caused repercussions in all other industries.

The Canadian auto industry was given a reprieve in the mid-1980s because of the high exchange value of the American dollar. American labour and parts costs were comparatively high again, and Japanese and European manufacturers found it convenient to locate plants in Canada. These plants are assembly operations, but increasingly they are being automated. They offer relatively little new employment, and like their precursors they create no research and development jobs.

The automobile industry is a case study in the operations of the integrated production system. Canada has historically had greater foreign investment levels than any other industrial country, and less research and development capacity than almost all other members of the OECD. But it is no longer unique; Mexico, Brazil, Taiwan, and the many other countries to which capital flows have adopted similar stances in their scramble to attract foreign investment.

THE AUTOMOBILE companies have restructured spatially in response to competition, protectionist threats, labour costs, and changing markets. They have also implemented major technological changes. Flexible manufacturing systems (FMS), based on CAD/CAM, involve a group of clustered machines in a work area; each machine is computer-controlled to handle and produce multiple parts using multiple process steps. Computer-integrated manufacturing (CIM) involves a single computer able to manage a full range of component tasks in a product's life cycle – design, sales, accounting, receiving and shipping, and manufacturing. Just-in-time (JIT) inventory controls, adapted from the Japanese model, rely on a number of subcontractors that feed supplies into the main manufacturing system in sufficient quantity and at the precise moment they are required, thereby reducing inventory to a minimum. This procedure, highly successful in Japan, where Toyota produces cars in Toyota Town through a full system of linked subcontractors,[39] has obvious implications for labour as employment becomes the responsibility of the contractors rather than the main company.

Since the cost of one FMS runs into the millions of dollars, a manufacturer requires substantial capital to obtain this technology. But once it is obtained, the manufacturer can produce variations on a similar product in large and small runs. Economies of scale have not passed into history, but custom runs are no longer luxuries.

Industrial robots are now in place in automobile plants, especially in Japan.[40] Many are simple machines with limited skills and no intelligence, and require human workers to reset and adjust their controls. But each year the number of more intelligent robots increases, and they become more adept at switching tasks and responding to different stimuli. The robotization of plants, together with other computerized systems, requires a reorganization of labour. Many of the "roboticized" jobs are in areas that human workers have long detested: dangerous spray-painting, heavy hauling and lifting, boring and repetitive tasks. Most significant is the move away from individual work stations on the assembly line and towards group workloads. Small teams, charged with responsibility for quality control, with fewer supervisory personnel and more controls embedded in the machinery itself, are now the superior method of organization. Managers speak of this change in glowing terms: they inform workers that at long last workers' initiative, creativity, co-operative capacities, and decision-making skills will be properly utilized. They urge employees to disclaim the "we-them" attitude of earlier industrial unionism in favour of a concerted attitude of "we-ness" towards production in a highly competitive global market. Unions, however, are sceptical, and not without reason. As Robert White, the president of the Canadian Auto Workers, observed, "What is 'new' today is the attempt to recreate the old insecurity and competition between workers in spite of the existence of unions. This has been done by shifting the focus from individual job loss to the possibilities of entire facilities – involving the entire workforce – being closed."[41]

Unions have been affected by closed plants and relocations, and by management's attempts to alter the patterns of collective bargaining and the conditions of employment. In North America, and even more in Europe, bargaining in the larger manufacturing sectors such as automobiles was fairly centralized, encompassing an entire company and often several companies. This pattern has been undermined by plant relocations, by displacement of unionized workers, and by tough bargaining on the part of management.

Canadian auto workers were, until 1983, members of an international union. With the restructuring they recognized a divergence of interests with American workers, and formed a new union, the Canadian Auto Workers. One of the major reasons the new union opposed the free trade agreement with the United States was that, in the CAW's view, it would enable the corporations to move plants and reallocate jobs even more "flexibly" than when the two countries were (at least nominally) separated. The reorganization of labour on the plant floor into work teams may eliminate the absurd job classifications that characterized the mass assembly age, but it will also diminish the capacity of union representatives to closely evaluate all jobs for the purposes of collective bargaining.

Not all automation technology is on the production floor. Production engineers are likely to become redundant as software is developed to inform designers about the strength, temperature resistance, aerodynamics, and other features of potential parts for new products. The demand for managers will also decline as decisions on machines, costs, and quantities are reached automatically. Chrysler has established design work stations connected to mainframe computers that can produce engineering drawings in fifteen minutes instead of three months.[42]

Most North American and European firms have partially adopted CAD/CAM systems. The systems are islands of automation in otherwise old-fashioned plants; the production, engineering, scheduling, and management functions are incompletely computerized. Communication between shop floor and office has often been impeded by an absence of common technical standards and by machine incompatibility. In response, GM persuaded seven computer suppliers, including IBM and Hewlett-Packard, to collaborate in establishing a manufacturing automation protocol (MAP) by which different computers can communicate and thus facilitate the production of cars or any other product. Other manufacturers have followed suit, encouraging CAD systems designers to accept common standards for computerized graphics, technical, office, and other systems.

In the 1980s American car manufacturers talked about recovering their market. GM invested in research and development of new models, but at the same time diversified its investments. In 1984 it purchased Electronic Data Systems and transferred a substantial number of its middle-management staff to the new firm. In 1982 it formed GMF Robotics as a joint venture with Fanuc of Japan. It has also purchased companies in the defence and financial services sectors. Its most startling acquisition was Hughes Aircraft in June 1985. Hughes, a $5-billion-a-year manufacturer of satellites, radar and sonar systems, missiles, and aircraft, turned the largest automobile company into the largest defence-electronics company. (Ford and Boeing were the losing bidders on the deal.) Chrysler had gone after and obtained an option to buy 20 per cent of Gulfstream Aerospace in the same search for high-tech diversification.

Some of these purchases, along with the MAP, are directly related to the improvement in GM's productivity and competitive position

in the automobile industry; several are substantial businesses t
could operate independently should the car market finally succui
to an energy crisis or GM lose its market share to the competition.
The Hughes acquisition places GM in an entirely different set of
industries, and, more significantly, in a high-technology context that
goes far beyond the present stage of automobile manufacturing.

THE SINGLE MOST difficult problem facing the automobile industry
is overcapacity. There are simply too many producers that can produce far too much. Lester Thurow argues that "overcapacity is a
world-wide problem, and it's getting worse. We're still investing as
if the world economy were growing at 4% a year instead of the
actual rate of about 2%."[43] Predictions of surplus production, plant
closings, and job losses in North America were widespread as early
as 1980.[44] Yet a dozen new plants were underway by 1986: four in
Canada (Honda, American Motors, Toyota, and Hyundai), one in
Mexico (Ford), and the remainder in the United States (GM-Toyota,
Toyota US, Honda, Nissan, Mazda, Chrysler-Mitsubishi, and GM
Saturn).[45] South Korean production expanded throughout the decade, but sales declined both at home and in the American market.[46]
By the end of 1989 Ford, Chrysler, and General Motors were closing
Canadian plants. The US trade representative Carla Hills urged the
US and Canadian Automotive Select Panel, established under the
free trade agreement, to consider policies "relative to overcapacity
in the industry."[47] Meanwhile Japan's industry was moving towards
consolidation, as Fuji Heavy Industries (the manufacturers of Subaru
cars) was bailed out by Nissan, and other smaller companies posted
losses.[48]

The American companies are clearly distressed; over half of their
market is now supplied by manufacturers abroad, including their
own joint ventures and subsidiaries. About one-third of the Canadian market fits the same description. In 1990, despite low-cost financing and other incentives, Chrysler's sales fell by 37 per cent
over the previous year; GM and Ford had similar losses. Honda,
Mazda, Volkswagen, Suzuki, and Subaru all reported increases in
sales in North America, but the industry suffered an overall drop
in sales of 23 per cent. Profits for the big American producers were
down by 54 per cent (GM) to 69 per cent (Ford) in the first quarter
of 1990.[49]

It is the employees who are most severely affected; as many as
forty thousand jobs may be lost in Canada, and hundreds of thousands in the United States. But there is also unease in Japan, where

the high yen value, combined with rising labour costs, has impelled manufacturers to produce abroad and to join with Korean and Taiwanese companies in producing for the European and North American markets. Ten per cent of Japanese employment is tied directly or indirectly to the automobile industry.

These contradictory trends are reflected in a joint venture between Suzuki and GM, with Suzuki in the management role and GM providing the marketing expertise, that has situated a new automotive plant in southwestern Ontario. By mid-1990 this plant matched the output of earlier American plants, and employed some two thousand workers. The entire output, including Suzuki, Subaru, Chevrolet, Pontiac, and GM models, went into the North American market.

The move by automobile companies into diverse and technologically sophisticated industries is partly related to the anticipated fallout from overcapacity. Some companies must fail, and those most likely to survive will have something other than automobiles to keep them going. As well, the thinking goes, the high-tech industries may lead to radical changes in transportation, changes that will go beyond mere restructuring and retooling – altogether new means of moving people and things from one location in space to another. But that is in the future.

FOR A CENTURY automobiles were at the leading edge of the American economy. There are some who believe that technology determines social history; they see the decline in the car industry as the explanation for the decline in American power. They might also have seen the decline of Britain as a consequence of the end of the great railway-building era. It is indeed true that each empire seems to have perfected a single technology and to have become fixated at that stage, but fixations are not determined by technology. They are a function of two more fundamental social conditions: the organization of a society around a successful technology, and the decline in risk-taking once success has been achieved.

The United States and Canada, and to lesser degrees Europe and Japan, have been tied to the automobile. Their transportation systems, their social and physical infrastructure, and their mind-sets are based upon privately owned, fuel-consuming cars. Their employment base is tied to mass production factories that either make the cars and parts or are related to automobile production. Their politics, their regional population densities, their suburbs and cities, and their cultures have cars at the centre.

The organization of labour in the car factories and steel industries became the model for the rest of North American society. The division between management and workers was clear, their respective tasks unambiguous. Money could buy labour and labour was prepared to accept money, provided that it was sufficient to give workers the things America produced; the social contract was established between two sides in the production system. American and Canadian labour was silent when North American capital used cheap labour for production of cars elsewhere, so long as the cars were also sold elsewhere and in no way threatened the social contract at home; the balance changed when global production came to mean local unemployment. These patterns of life, this culture, the very cities and towns North Americans inhabited were threatened by the new technologies and then by the new global organizations. But we should focus on the total organization rather than on the technology in explaining the consequences of change.

Without doubt the dislocations involve unemployment and community decline. Yet they also involve the abandonment of an organization of labour on assembly lines and in hierarchical corporate structures that was, by all accounts, soul-destroying. The Fordist organization underlay a society of consumers, a culture-bereft society in which not only capital but labour pursued purchasing power at any cost. The new production techniques raise a spectre of overproduction that cannot be solved by unemployed consumers; thus, a basic contradiction in the system will oblige companies to face the social consequences of their profit-maximization strategies. As well, the overproduction seems bound to induce producers to look to alternatives, to new forms of transportation, for example, which, given the other constraints we are facing in the late twentieth century, may be less polluting and less demanding of space. It may be that this crisis is the essential beginning of the creation of communities that are not merely junctures of highways and conglomerations of service-stations.

CHAPTER NINE

The European Troupe

The notion that all the world would adopt the new right agenda, as pronounced at the end of the eighth decade of this century by Rand Corporation and the us State Department publicist Francis Fukuyama, was not widely accepted in Europe.[1] Both history and ideology resisted their premature termination.

The new right, it is true, had remarkable success in setting the agenda of the 1980s and dismantling the Keynesian consensus. But the development of a united Europe, the establishment of a European Parliament, and the dramatic events in Eastern Europe have modified that agenda. In this chapter we will consider the context of the growth of the new right in Britain, the political policies of Margaret Thatcher's government during the 1970s, and the restructuring of industry and political systems as the new Europe unfolded.

THE DIVISION OF Europe into east and west, communist and free enterprise, was of signal importance for the unification movement. By definition, the western countries had a common enemy. The refugees from Eastern Europe were evidence that communism was oppressive and that it failed to provide economic incentives to its peoples. The imagery sustained the idea that the West, by contrast, was free. However, it did not override class consciousness, historical commitments to Marxist and neo-Marxist ideas, and belief in the viability of socialism and social democracy; it did not make Europe an imitation of the apoliticized United States.

Governments in Western Europe had high profiles throughout the entire post-war period. Comparative data on proportions of industry still under public ownership in 1980 are given in table 4. The United States was unusual in its lack of publicly owned enterprises.

Table 4
State ownership of industries, 1980 (OECD countries)

	Posts	Telecomm.	Hydro	Gas	Oil	Coal	RR	Air	Motor	Steel	Ship
WESTERN EUROPEAN COUNTRIES											
Austria	M	M	M	M	M	M	M	M	M	M	na
Belgium	M	M	2	2	na	0	M	M	0	5	0
Britain	M	M	M	M	2	M	M	5	5	5	0
France	M	M	M	M	na	M	M	5	5	5	0
FRG	M	M	5	5	2	5	M	M	2	0	2
Holland	M	M	5	5	na	na	M	5	5	2	0
Italy	M	M	5	M	na	na	M	M	2	5	5
Spain	M	5	0	5	na	5	M	M	0	5	5
Sweden	M	M	5	M	na	na	M	5	0	5	5
Switzerland	M	M	M	M	na	na	M	2	0	0	na
OTHER OECD COUNTRIES											
Australia	M	M	M	M	0	0	M	2	0	0	na
Brazil	M	M	M	M	M	M	M	2	0	5	0
Canada	M	2	M	0	0	0	5	5	0	0	0
India	M	M	M	M	M	M	M	M	0	5	M
Japan	M	M	0	0	na	0	5	2	0	0	0
Mexico	M	M	M	M	M	M	M	5	2	5	M
S.Korea	M	M	5	0	na	2	M	0	0	5	0
U.S.A.	M	0	2	0	0	0	2[1]	0	0	0	0

Source: Based on data in Cento Veljanovski, *Selling the State*. London: Weidenfeld and Nicolson, 1987, figure 3.1, 50, derived originally from *The Economist* (nd).

Note: M = state monopoly.
    5 = half or more shares under state ownership.
    2 = state ownership between 25 and 49 per cent
    0 = private sector shares over 75 per cent.
[1] including Conrail.

Japan had few businesses so labelled, but, as we have seen, public ownership was not the mechanism for state participation there. All of the European states had large shares in the telecommunications, electrical, gas, railway, and airline industries, and several had stakes in the automobile, steel, shipbuilding, and other sectors.

As outlined in chapter 3, governments necessarily became the financiers and employers in mass production industries at the conclusion of the war. Private capital was insufficient, and the war had destroyed much of the industrial capacity of pre-war Europe. Mass production operations required large capital expenditures and suitable infrastructure: apart from the United States, where private capital monopolies were intact, only public funds and states could provide these. The state operations and infrastructure were essential for the development of new private capital. They created the conditions that made Europe attractive to external investors, especially American companies.

There were also strong ideological reasons for greater state participation in the economic affairs of Europe. Labour, socialist, social democratic, and communist parties had long political histories; class divisions were still manifest; and the political left actively contended for the hearts and minds of European populations. In Britain the Labour party formed the immediate post-war government and was in office from time to time thereafter; in France, Italy, Austria, and Germany social democratic and labour parties were occasionally in power and were always significant forces in the development of policies. In Sweden, Norway, and Denmark social democratic ideas pervaded the institutions of society, affecting conditions of labour, education, health, housing, and social security.

After the Hungarian revolution in 1956, encouraged by the aborted revolutions in Czechoslovakia and Poland, European communists distanced themselves somewhat from the USSR. On the left in general there was a consensus that the form communism had taken in Russia and Eastern Europe was unfortunate but explicable. The Russian communists had inherited a backward society, an impoverished economy, and an autocratic history; much of Eastern Europe had likewise languished in prolonged feudalism before the revolution. Some would argue that that feudalism persisted well into the 1940s. These understandings did not lead to an adoption of the American view that capitalism was unqualified virtue.

Europe enjoyed an economic renaissance in the 1950s, 1960s, and part of the 1970s. The level of state ownership remained high in the European countries even as the GNP and per capita GNP grew over that prolonged boom period (see table 5).

Though all the European states had relatively high levels of public ownership, there were significant differences between them. Britain had lost the economic war in the process of winning two military battles. Its hierarchical, class-divided society retained much of its archaic structure, and although the empire was dismantled the attitudes of imperialism did not dissolve. Its economy grew, but not at the same rate as other European economies. Britain had opened negotiations for entry into the EEC in 1961, as had Eire, Denmark, and Norway, but it was 1973 before Britain's marriage to the EEC was consummated.

The Federal Republic of Germany grew much more rapidly, enhanced by Marshall Plan aid, substantial American investment, and the American military presence. With its plants destroyed, Germany

Table 5
GNP in constant dollars and GNP per capita

| | Total GNP (Billions of 1975 Dollars) | | | |
	1950	1960	1970	1980
World	1,981.5	3,126.3	5,191.9	7,977.8
Trilateral total[1]	1,346.9	2,077.2	3,385.4	4,742.8
USA	671.5	925.6	1,363.0	1,859.1
Canada	48.6	76.5	127.2	187.2
Japan	59.4	136.7	396.8	639.2
Western Europe[2]	567.4	938.4	1,498.4	2,057.3
France	99.0	163.1	280.0	399.5[3]
FRG	113.5	240.1	379.7	501.4
Italy	46.7	99.5	157.7	232.0
United Kingdom	124.5	160.2	212.4	251.1

| | GNP per capita (1975 dollars) | | | |
	1950	1960	1970	1980
World	790	1,027	1,407	1,778
Trilateral total	2,436	3,460	5,100	6,611
USA	4,411	5,122	6,652	8,167
Canada	3,534	4,274	5,972	7,820
Japan	709	1,452	3,804	5,474
Western Europe	1,953	3,051	4,496	5,895
France	2,372	3,569	5,512	7,437
FRG	2,275	4,334	6,255	8,144
Italy	1,135	1,982	2,937	4,067
United Kingdom	2,450	3,057	3,834	4,493

Source: IMF, International Financial Statistics and others, compiled by the Computer Sciences Division of the Harvard Business School, published in Nobuhiko Ushiba, Gramam Allison, and Thierry de Montbrial, Sharing International Responsibilities among the Trilateral Countries: Report of the Task Force on Sharing Global Responsibilities to the Trilateral Commission, 1983.

[1] "Trilateral" totals are a simple addition of the USA, Canada, Japan, and Western Europe totals.
[2] "Western Europe" refers to members of the European Economic Community (EEC): Belgium, Denmark, France, West Germany (FRG), Greece, Ireland, Italy, Luxembourg, the Netherlands, and the United Kingdom; the European Free Trade Association (EFTA): Austria, Finland, Norway, Portugal, Sweden, Switzerland, and Spain.
[3] Estimated where official figures are unavailable.

was able to clear the decks and begin again. New leaders emerged, and new (or, more often, reconstructed) companies became international competitors. While class-based conflict was barely contained in the labour negotiations between unions and companies in

Britain, West Germany created a different kind of social contract whereby labour agreed to no-strike conditions in return for equal participation in a range of employment decisions. Critics argued that labour had been co-opted, but the results were impressive growth statistics and strike-free industries for much of the post-war period.

Six years after the signing of the Treaty of Rome in 1957, continental European firms had increased their share of the *Fortune* 200 top industrial companies from 30 to 41. At the same time the number of American firms dropped from 135 to 123.[2] In a review of the data, Robert Rowthorn and Stephen Hymer argued that by 1969 American growth was on the wane, though not uniformly across industrial sectors. Size was found to be negatively correlated with the growth rate, and European smaller and medium-sized firms were found to have the highest growth rates.[3]

That argument notwithstanding, the *Times 1000 Review* list of major companies in Europe in the mid-1970s showed Du Pont (USA) leading in chemicals, General Motors (USA) in automobiles, IBM (USA) in electrical and computer sectors, and Boeing (USA) in aerospace industries; other US firms among the top ten in their industrial sectors were Union Carbide, Dow Chemicals, Ford, Chrysler, General Electric, ITT, Western Electric, Westinghouse, RCA, and Lockheed. What had changed was the overall composition of dominant companies. There was greater representation of European firms: these included Hoechst, BASF, Bayer, Volkswagen, and Siemens of West Germany; Imperial Chemical Industries (ICI), British Aerospace, and British Leyland of Britain; Renault and Peugeot of France; Philips of the Netherlands; and Fiat of Italy. Toyota, Nissan, and Hitachi of Japan were also on the list.[4] European private capital, then, was becoming more powerful, and was also becoming internationalized.

THROUGHOUT THE post-war period the basic fuel source was oil, supplied mainly by the Middle East through American companies, the Anglo-Netherlands joint company, Shell, and British Petroleum. The Suez crisis in 1956 had threatened supplies moving through the canal. Israeli, British, and French forces invaded Egypt but were obliged to withdraw under pressure from the United States and the USSR. A potential crisis caused by insufficient oil supplies to Europe was overcome by the US government's waiver of antitrust legislation for the major American oil companies in return for the development of new tanker schedules and allocations from alternative sources (primarily Venezuela and US domestic supplies).[5]

The oil crises of the 1970s, however, were not to be solved as easily. For Europe the price increases threatened disaster, since domestic production constituted only 5 per cent of total consumption. Attempts to reduce dependence on Middle Eastern oil had been made after the Suez crisis; import levels from that region dropped from 77 per cent to 52 per cent between 1958 and 1968.[6] Even with increasing quantities of oil imported from North Africa, Nigeria, and Mexico, Europe's industrial growth was in jeopardy. In Robert Keohane's account, Europe regressed immediately to nation-state, competitive behaviour: each country attempted to secure oil supplies through separate agreements. In time, however, this behaviour subsided, and more attention was given to the exploration and development of the North Sea oil and gas fields and to alternative energy sources (hydro-electricity, coal, and nuclear power). The economic boom, which had been based on low-cost fuel, was over in Europe, and companies responded by seeking fuel efficiencies.

Capital had moved to the peripheral regions of continental Europe and Britain during the 1960s, largely to benefit from cheaper labour, weaker unions, and more grateful municipal governments. The oil shocks, combined with the impact of technological change, dictated a return to industrial centres. Companies left the rural communities that had briefly housed them and provided them with workers.[7] This followed the pattern of American capital. Companies were attracted initially to lower-cost labour regions; then, automated and more concerned about fuel costs, they moved closer to suppliers and markets.

Britain's ICI is a case study of the restructuring process undertaken by private capital in those years. Originally formed through mergers in the 1920s, ICI produced a wide range of chemicals, pharmaceuticals, plastics, foodstuffs and other goods. By 1980 the company had factories in over forty countries.[8] Yet as it expanded geographically between 1973 and 1980 ICI reduced its global workforce by 29 per cent, and its UK workforce declined by nearly 40 per cent in the second half of the 1970s.

The job loss in the United Kingdom was not related in any simple way to the offshore location of labour-intensive phases of production, though this did occur to some extent. More important, as J.M. Clarke found, were the rationalization processes through which the company decreased its employment and holdings in declining industrial or heavily oil-dependent sectors, and invested in technological development to improve productivity without increasing employment in more profitable sectors. In sectors where overcapacity affected profits for all firms, ICI, like other large companies, reduced the number of manufacturing units, strategically dropping older plants, those with least access to large markets, or those in regions with higher fuel costs.

The relationships between companies in different industrial sectors plays a part in decisions to restructure. The decline of the textile industry in Britain, for example, had repercussions for ICI and other dye manufacturers. Similarly, the market decline for British cars reduced demand for numerous ICI products, and the company responded by moving to West Germany, close to the Volkswagen plant. The relative cost and availability of fuels became a critical factor after 1973, and among the advantages of locating in the United States was the ready supply of natural gas.[9] ICI purchased Stauffer Chemical of Westport, Connecticut, in 1988, thereby gaining the company's pesticide operations. It then sold the parts of Stauffer that did not fit in with its rationalization plans to Akzo NV of the Netherlands and RhoÔne-Poulenc SA of France.[10]

Other companies, such as Hoechst of West Germany, also established plants in the United States in the late 1970s and 1980s. They were driven by fluctuating currency values and by the need to gain shares of the vast North American market before threatened import controls were put in place. Some firms also entered into joint ventures in the United States to gain access to international marketing techniques.

While private sector restructuring was going ahead, Britain and other European states continued to be major participants in industry. As some of the private steel-age businesses declined, countries nationalized their properties (for example, British Rolls Royce in 1971, the French steel industry in 1978) to keep them alive and to sustain communities and employment. After the oil crises of the 1970s, these nursing habits became more dubious; the cost of propping up sick industries was possibly an even sicker overall economy.

In fact, by this time numerous flaws were evident in the economic fabric. The same problems that confronted American private capital were confronting both state-owned and private firms in Europe. They too were burdened with obsolete steel-age industries and rigid, hierarchical bureaucratic structures. Much more than in the United States, their workers were organized both in the workplace and in political parties. Transnational capital, expanding everywhere and uncontainable within national borders, was moving towards the new knowledge-intensive service sectors. Those sectors were not tied to specific locations and resident labour pools. They were mobile, and they had low overhead costs. Financial institutions were clamouring for larger shares of international wealth. The new industries demanded the removal of non-tariff barriers between European states, the de-regulation of the financial and service sectors, and more flexible relationships with labour.

In addition to these problems, the European states that had established colonies in their earlier periods now had to cope with post-colonial relationships to newly independent states. For some – in particular France, Britain, and Holland – there was an influx of immigrants from former colonial territories that brought with it mixed benefits and burdens. Though the immigrants, like the masses of stateless migrants whose numbers constantly increased over the nineteenth and twentieth centuries, provided cheap labour to expanding industrial economies, they also made demands on the Keynesian states for housing, social services, and citizenship rights. The phenomenon of the *gastarbeiter*, or guest worker, became a fixture in Germany; workers from poor countries obtained employment for fixed periods, but enjoyed no citizenship privileges and could be fired and deported when they were no longer needed. In Britain the competition for employment and a persistent shortage of adequate housing for workers created the underlying conditions for open racism. Preferential trading relationships with former colonies created other demands, many of which were in conflict with the interests of European states as they moved towards unification.

Throughout Western Europe these tensions were manifested in the student rebellions of the late 1960s, the increasingly bitter labour strikes of the 1970s, and the persistent separatist struggles and ethnic strife in many countries where ethnic minorities were excluded from economic and political power.

In summary, then, the Europe of the late 1970s was moving towards unification. It was striving to reduce its dependence on oil, and it was no longer tied to the American oil regime. Its private companies were growing, restructuring, internationalizing, and actively competing with American capital, but they were also merging with American and, subsequently, Japanese capital, so that the distinctions between these pools were becoming blurred. State-owned industries in Western Europe (excluding the Scandinavian countries, where the relationship between state and capital was not based on the same free enterprise model) were in decline and becoming technologically obsolete. Labour was organized and militant, and both class and ethnic conflicts were manifest. Colonial empires had been dismantled, and former imperial powers were burdened with their legacy of immigrants from empire territories and preferential trading relationships with former colonies.

The Trilateral Commission was firmly established by this time, and European leaders were major participants in the development of its agenda. New right publications and institutes were present in continental Europe, but were much more visible in Britain. And it was in Britain that the new right achieved its greatest political success in the form of Margaret Thatcher's Conservative government.

MARGARET THATCHER CAME to power first as leader of the Conservative party in 1975 and then as prime minister of Britain in 1979. The defeat of the likely winner in the first of these contests was interpreted by many astute observers as a rejection not so much of Edward Heath personally as of more experienced politicians generally, politicians whose knapsacks seemed to hold no new tricks for reversing the country's economic deterioration.

Hayek and Friedman, celebrated intellectuals of a new right, were joined by a member of Thatcher's cabinet, Sir Keith Joseph. Joseph was active in the Centre for Policy Studies, where he and his colleagues urged British voters to reject public ownership, state managerialism, and everything else that for him, as for Thatcher, constituted socialism. The election victory may have represented some support for that view, but it also represented a groundswell of discontent with the status quo. Britain's fortunes were widely felt to be in decline, inflation was growing, employment was dropping, investment capital was leaving, and even the previous Labour government had quietly adopted a monetarist approach and a reduction in public expenditures.

In the 1960s and 1970s, Britain had added substantially to its publicly owned properties and state services. The nationalized sectors continued to expand their areas of influence. Its opponents grumbled that "the National Coal Board manufactures bricks, produces chemicals, builds and lets houses, and prospects for oil ... No nationalised industry, it seeems, would be complete without its subsidiary activities ... To put it another way, the nationalised industries have between them a controlling interest in over one hundred apparently private concerns, and, with minority holdings taken into account, are involved in about seven hundred companies of all types and descriptions."[11]

The objections on economic grounds were backed up by a growing anger and frustration with the bureaucratic structure that managed this enormous state. Among the disenchanted were private industries interested in moving to higher-technology applications; they claimed that the bureaucratic management of state science funding for research inhibited their initiative. In particular, they complained that the government rather than industry was in control of the direction research might take: "The dangers of a small body of individuals spending other people's money in ways they think industrially useful are all too obvious."[12]

While these frustrations were fanned by special interest lobbies, right-wing think-tanks, and the Conservative party (when Labour was in power), one could not attribute the general unease solely to supply-side provocateurs. Harold Wilson's Labour government had been defeated in 1970 after a wave of strikes and the imposition of moderate but mandatory restraints on unions' rights. His Conservative successor, Edward Heath, promised greater economic competition. He brought Britain into the Common Market but found no solution to the impact of the fuel shortage, and his new industrial relations act exacerbated rather than relieved labour strife. The return of a Labour government in 1976 coincided with continuing economic decline, strikes, unemployment, inflation, and political disaffection. Though their interpretations of the causes differed, commentators of all political positions converged in their belief that Britain was in crisis. Because of their high profile, the unions bore most of the blame.

What matters for our purposes is how the economic restructuring of Thatcher's new right government took form, but we must keep in mind that these policies were always advanced under the banner of a mighty moral crusade. Britannia would rule again (especially after the Falklands / Malvinas war); her children would stand tall (a favourite phrase in Thatcher's speeches); and personal choice and private property would take their rightful places in the New Jerusalem. The impact of mobile international capital, the maldistribution of income, and the two million who lived in poverty despite the welfare state were largely ignored, while unions, bureaucracy, and impediments to entrepreneurialism were blamed for Britain's illness.[13]

A new right platform was announced by Thatcher's government in 1979 and greatly expanded in the ensuing years. Its stated objectives were to increase economic competition, reduce government's participation in industrial decision-making, permit private capital to raise funds in the capital market on commercial terms, reduce government expenditures, and raise revenues.[14] As well, workers were to become shareholders in their companies and owners of their dwellings.

During her first years in power, Thatcher made a modest attempt at implementing monetarism. The second oil shock of 1979 and external events, especially the American crises, deepened the recession in Britain. Unemployment rose and inflation was not curbed, even though it was targeted as the government's major issue. In spite of numerous assurances that taxes and public expenditures would be reduced both actually increased between 1978 and 1983.[15]

Before the 1983 election, public housing expenditures were reduced by offering many council houses for sale to their occupants. Those who were able to purchase their homes through this policy were enthusiastic; the many who could not were perhaps the first victims of privatization. As subsidies were cut back, the quality of public housing deteriorated after 1981.[16]

The first phase of privatization (1979–83) involved the sale of twenty-five enterprises, most of which were potentially competitive and profitable in the private sector. They included part of the government's holdings in British Petroleum; half of the equity of British Aerospace and of Cable and Wireless, Britoil, Associated British Ports; most of British Rail's hotels; some assets of British Airways and British Steel and the National Enterprise Board; and all holdings in Amersham International.[17]

After the 1983 election the pace and nature of the privatization process accelerated. Public monopolies were replaced by private ones, raising questions about the absence of competition. New regulatory agencies had to be established to monitor prices and performance.[18] Members of the government argued that private monopolies were more efficient than public ones, and that abuses of power could be controlled through regulatory agencies and competition law.

The privatization measures taken after 1983 included further sales of shares in the companies initially affected in the first phase, as well as sales of Enterprise Oil, British Gas, British Airways, Rolls-Royce, British Telecom, and parts of other transportation, energy, and shipbuilding concerns. Overall, between 1981 and 1987, Thatcher's government sold public holdings in gas and oil, aerospace, telecommunications, seaports, transportation services, car manufacturing, chemicals, and hotels.[19]

After the 1987 election the government began to privatize water and sewerage services, and announced the privatization of British Steel. Public housing continued to be privatized throughout the entire period. Between 1979 and early 1988, approximately 40 per cent of the state-owned industries were transferred to the private sector.

The private sector, in turn, grew substantially not only in the proportion of GDP for which it was responsible, but in the number of shareholders and private owners in the population. By one accounting, about 10 per cent of the adult population owned shares, compared with 7 per cent in 1979. One of the major objectives of the privatization program was being achieved – an increase in the number of property owners in Britain.[20]

The sale of properties was accompanied by the privatization of numerous social services formerly provided within the public sector. The housing sales were part of the privatization of services. Services formerly provided by or for the National Health Service, including domestic, catering, and laundry services, were turned over to private enterprise, and greater participation of the private medical sector in health care was permitted. After 1980 local government authorities were required to run labour-intensive operations as separate trading bodies in competition with the private sector, and to show a profit. Further legislation over the 1980s required that highway works, sewerage construction and maintenance, garbage collection, janitorial and other services for public buildings, and catering services for schools be open to public tender. A 1987 bill specifically prohibited local authorities from circumventing competition provisions. Police services were reduced, and many component parts were parcelled out for competition.

Part of the privatization program involved an expansion of contracting-out arrangements. Following the example of private industry, the National Health Service was required to contract out such component tasks as nursing care for elderly patients, laboratory work, staff accommodation, training, computer services, janitorial services, and food preparation. The Metropolitan Police of London was required to contract out vehicle services, vehicle and other repairs, parking control, and the same range of general services as the NHS – janitorial, computer, food, and laundry.

Education was also transformed as universities and schools were systematically deprived of adequate funding; they had to reduce wages, cut back on employment, and contract out services. The objective was to reduce the capacity of public institutions to provide high-quality education so that the public would create private alternatives. Since the state also imagined a future capitalism built on applied science, private companies were encouraged to fund research projects most likely to enhance future profits.

The British government also removed various restrictions on private business in a series of deregulation policies. Thatcher's opponents pointed out that there was no coherent strategy: deregulation and privatization were introduced together with new regulatory bodies and more reliance on competition law. There seemed to be no long-term objectives other than to rid the state of its properties.[21] The opponents, however, saw Thatcherism as an ideological movement; they failed to grasp the significance of the global changes affecting Britain, including the growth of international trade in services, the impact of the technological revolution, and the political implications of mobile, transnational capital.

The same effects were experienced elsewhere in Europe. The British experiment in dealing with them was influential as a model, though elsewhere the rhetoric was muted and the new right agenda, while evident in solutions, was less frequently expressed in words. Privatization occurred throughout the 1980s in the Netherlands, Italy, Finland, Germany, and France. Matra, the French defence and electronics group, privatized in 1988, was purchased by General Electric of Britain (not related to GE of the United States), Daimler-Benz of West Germany, and the Wallenberg Group of Sweden. The purchasers anticipated increasing co-operation in weapons development throughout Europe.[22] In Germany the Bonn government sold its shares (20 per cent) in Volkswagen and the energy giant Veba (30 per cent). The proceeds were to be used to balance state budgets and reduce fiscal deficits. France became extremely active in privatizing state corporations after 1986. However, this activity should be understood in context; whereas British state ownership and management had gradually grown over the period from 1945 to 1978, France had experienced a substantial increase in nationalization in the early 1980s. Austria, with a lengthy history of state-owned corporations, undertook some privatization in the late 1980s.

Benefiting from deregulation, financial services companies internationalized their operations. No longer serving local businesses, they sought out clients in the underdeveloped countries. One manifestation of these changes was the growth of the Eurobond market. In the early 1980s, companies, countries, governments, and individuals could raise billions cheaply through international underwriting syndicates. American firms soon moved in; in 1984 American banks arranged the biggest share of new offerings for countries and corporations in the Eurobond market. Four of the top five underwriters of Eurobonds in 1985 were American firms (and the fifth, Credit Suisse First Boston, was actually 35 per cent owned by First Boston of New York, though it considered itself a British merchant bank).[23] The market vanished abruptly in 1987 when the dollar's decline made international investors reluctant to buy dollar-denominated bonds, and borrowers moved to newly deregulated markets in the United States and Japan. American tax laws were part of the reason for the shake-out; in 1984, tax changes for foreign bondholders made domestic bonds, especially US Treasury notes, more attractive to international investors. As well, and perhaps most critical to the abrupt drop in Eurobond values, was the wave of mergers and leveraged buyouts by American firms. Large international financial companies were the unusual losers in this game. Merrill Leckie, Morgan Stanley, Salomon, and others were caught with unmarketable bonds.[24] While the enthusiasm lasted, however, European governments accommodated the changing financial system through deregulation and in numerous other ways facilitated the development of new kinds of global service industries in the financial sectors.

The new industries included postal services (electronic mail, facsimile, couriers), health care (everything from janitorial services to whole hospital staffs transported on contract to LDCs), and education (the establishment of specialized schools and private universities catering to foreign nationals). Other industries, already established but now internationalized and vastly expanded, included advertising and transportation companies that provided extensive touring and hotel services. The common thread throughout was the communications technology that permitted commercial groups to capture markets around the globe, provided that they were not impeded by local non-tariff barriers or preferences accorded citizens by local and national governments.

How much of this was understood or predicted by the planners of the British new right strategy is not known: possibly very little. It is more likely that external conditions, including the rapid transformation of private industry and its high mobility, exerted pressure on the nation-state to dismantle tariffs and other barriers in the service sector as in others. A willing government took up the cause, provided the public rationale, and proceeded to create the desired conditions.

The success of privatization is not measurable on any single dimension. If expansion of ownership rights were the measure, Britain would have succeeded. If revenue for the exchequer were the measure, or a reduction in state participation in industrial decision-making, then too it must be regarded as successful. If industrial efficiency and increased competition were the measures, the record is much more ambiguous. Private monopolies of very large utilities such as British Telecom and British Gas obliged the government to introduce regulatory bodies to guard against the very behaviours that privatization was supposed to eliminate. If monopolies are by their nature bad – as Adam Smith, for one, believed – a private monopoly is no better than a public one; and if the public interest is what matters, sensible arguments can be made (whether or not one agrees with them) that public monopolies are preferable. The concerns about private versus public monopolies are greatest where the monopolies in question are in sectors whose technology could harm the environment or human health, such as water-works, sewage treatment, and nuclear power stations.[25]

For many it is not economic considerations that best measure the impact of privatization and deregulation but rather the escalating unemployment rates. There were 1.1 million unemployed in 1979; and 1.9 million in 1989. Inflation was reduced from 10.3 per cent in 1979 to 7.9 per cent in 1989, but that figure was still twice the average for Europe. North Sea oil exports and the massive restructuring of large companies notwithstanding, Britain had a deficit of $100 million per day in 1989, and income taxes still consumed a third of the British pay-check.[26] London's subways and alleys become permanent dwellings for homeless people. There were stark differences in affluence between the industrial heartlands and the peripheries of Britain. The gulf between the haves and the have-nots grew, as had the number of people on the dole and the proportion of the total population living (officially) below the poverty line. Industry had restructured, but the education system was starved, and retraining of the unemployed never took place.

Contrary to its stated intention of dismantling an intrusive state, Thatcher's government has increased the power of the central government over taxation, education, and social policy. In 1990 local councils were deprived of their traditional right to establish business property tax rates, and personal property taxes were eliminated in favour of a head tax. Primary and secondary schools, traditionally managed by local school boards, were brought under the control of the central government. Thatcher attempted to control information by invoking and then attempting to redraft the Official Secrets Act. She lost two celebrated court cases with the media over her attempts to muzzle the press. Since the passing of the Police and Criminal Evidence Act in 1984 police intervention in industrial disputes and race riots has increased. British police practices, including telephone-tapping, corporal punishment, and treatment of mental patients and minority groups, have frequently violated the European Convention on Human Rights. Market freedom, it appears, has not resulted in greater private freedom; paradoxically, it has culminated in more authoritarian central government. This is not surprising in view of the contradictions inherent in the new right ideology; once the democratic and regional institutions that provide the counterbalance to centralized government are gone, once a single view of morality is superimposed on all activity, the central power itself becomes authoritarian.

Thatcher was a nationalist, resolutely opposed to much of the merging tendencies of the EC. She resisted those forms of integration that appeared likely to "soften" British sovereignty or culture. She complained that much of what she privatized in the 1970s and early 1980s was reclaimed and re-regulated by EC decisions made in Brussels. But her opposition to the European Parliament's growing power became less important as the Parliament itself gained independence from national government leaders. In 1989 the British electorate voted Labour representatives to the European Parliament, and public opinion polls in Britain strongly indicated a rapid decrease in Thatcher's popularity. Already an explicit social contract covering the rights of workers was on the agenda of the Commission of European Communities; in time, the problem of universal rights of many other kinds will come up for debate. In 1990, Thatcher resigned when the polls showed that she could not retain her party's leadership or win another election.

The British new right, then, appears to have exhausted its popularity and its mandate. Yet there is no doubt that between 1979 and 1989 the consensus in favour of the Keynesian solution and welfare state was terminated. The task of the new right was to change the ideological climate. That done, both Britain and the rest of Europe will move on to the new task of organizing a restructured international economy in a marketplace that never runs according to the simple laws of supply and demand.

WHILE BRITAIN languished, West Germany prospered. In 1985 German exports accounted for 35 per cent of GNP, and overall German-source exports accounted for nearly 10 per cent of global sales (comparable to 12 per cent for the United States and nearly 10 per cent for Japan). The major market for these goods was the rest of Western Europe, but during the early 1980s, when the Deutschmark was low against the US dollar, sales to the United States climbed steadily.

West German companies are major investors in the global circuit, and, as part of that phenomenon, they are increasingly international in their shareholdings. Daimler-Benz, said by its chairman to be "an international technological concern,"[27] is now about half owned by non-German investors. Since 1980 it has acquired several large electronics, aircraft parts and engine companies. One of these, AEG, has one of the largest electronics research facilities and is a leader in radar technology; its researchers are currently trying to redesign a transportation system capable of warning drivers about potential traffic congestion. Companies such as AEG, now established on a global scale often have chequered histories. Bayer, BASF, and

Hoechst, for example, were once united as I.G. Farben, a giant chemical cartel whose directors supported and financed Hitler's regime and used slave labour at the Auschwitz extermination camp for their synthetic coal-oil and rubber plant.[28] The combination was split by the Allies after the war, and foreign holdings were confiscated. But each of the component firms was rebuilt around traditional areas of expertise and vertically integrated, and by the 1970s the companies had moved into new industrial sectors.

German banks have not been subject to strong restrictions. They have operated on various levels as chartered banks, trust companies, insurance firms, and investment dealers, without limitations on their industrial holdings. They have become, in consequence, major shareholders in industrial companies. Deutsche Bank, for example, owns over 25 per cent of Daimler-Benz. In the mid-1980s the Flick group of companies underwent dismemberment after being purchased by Deutsche Bank. Its major companies – Feldmühle in paper and packaging, Duynamit Nobel in chemicals, and Buderus in steel engineering – were sold piecemeal at a high profit.

German auto makers concentrate on export markets. Audi, for example, exports nearly two-thirds of its cars (compared with less than 3 per cent of cars made in North America). Porsche sells 55 per cent of its output in North America, concentrating on the upper end of the market and advertising its quality and exclusivity. In the domestic market Volkswagen continues to hold the largest share at 22 per cent; General Motors (as Opel) has 16 per cent; Ford of Germany and Daimler-Benz compete at about 10 per cent each. But Japanese imports are gaining greater shares of the market, and now account for about 15 per cent of domestic sales.[29] As the full European union approaches, Germany's auto- makers are attempting to restructure in anticipation of Japanese competition in the luxury end of the market.[30]

While politicians talk about Europe's becoming a counterweight to the power of Japan and the United States, Germany's largest company, Siemens, demonstrates the inconsistency of that position in the reality of a global marketplace. In 1985 Siemens signed an agreement with Toshiba in connection with production of a four megabyte chip. And West German companies have exhibited guarded enthusiasm for participating in the American strategic defence initiative research program, aware that such programs have technological spinoffs from which they could benefit. The EC will provide a large market, and its populations will experience both wealth and poverty as its diverse regions prosper and wane, but the EC will not be, as the political version anticipates, a self-contained unit. Political boundaries, even for so large a unit, have become rather like the Wall of China in keeping out armies that no longer travel by horse.

Ideological boundaries are non-existent in the age of mass media. The new right's impact on Germany was less obvious and less celebrated than in Britain. Both centre-right and social democratic governments adopted some features of the new right agenda, but avoided much of the rhetoric. Political analysts attribute the resurgence of ultra-right-wing political parties and of neo-Nazi political movements to a renewed nationalism, and dismiss them as unimportant.[31] Green parties have had greater electoral success, it is true, but that combination of extreme right-wing politics and nationalism is worthy of further examination. The restructuring of economies on a transnational scale and the restructuring of Europe's political map threaten identities in Britain, France, and Germany. In all three countries the backlash has taken the form of right-wing nationalism.

On 3 October 1990, the Federal Republic of Germany added 16.6 million East Germans to its population of 61 million. France (with a population of 56 million;) Britain (57 million), and Italy (58 million) are smaller powers within the European Community. They are less burdened, however, with the problems of low living standards, productivity, and capital investment. Though East Germans have flooded Berlin's shopping-malls, and though capitalism is judged a success by a population long starved of consumer goods, it seems unlikely that East Germans will eagerly adopt the free-market ideology. The gap between the prevailing ideas of West Germans and the beliefs, experiences, and social conditioning of East Germans is huge, and the likely outcome of the re-creation of Deutschland is a rethinking of both ideological extremes. Market-oriented state enterprises are among the possible instruments for developing East German and other East European economies.

WHILE GERMANY MUST struggle with the addition of a relatively impoverished population from the East, other European Common Market countries are struggling with additional populations from their southern peripheries. Greece, Spain, and Portugal became members in the early 1980s, swelling the EEC population to about 320 million. Turkey applied for admission in 1988. Prospects for this enlarged market were mixed: aggregate demand will be strong, and internal resources will be plentiful, but there will be pressure on the richer countries to provide for the poorer ones, and industries in the poorer regions will need protection. The 1986 annual economic report of the Commission of European Communities indicated that between 1983 and 1986 growth in GNP and industrial-production averages were well below Japanese and American rates; unemployment rates were substantially higher, and the EC was ahead of the United States only on trade balances, largely because these included all internal transactions. [32]

Of the continuing high unemployment rates, the commission observed that "certain segments of the labour force still pose specific problems." The entry of Spain and Portugal raised the overall unemployment level for the community, but unemployment was already increasing in Britain and continental European countries. The commission recommended more investment, stable monetary policies, moderate growth in real wage costs, modernization of production structures, and similar conventional measures for improving employment rates. Its recommendations could be implemented only with the reintroduction of strong, centralized states, or, ultimately, the establishment of an overarching super-state. That does appear to be the destination, though not one likely to be achieved by 1992.

By that date the EEC will have dismantled virtually all intra-European trade barriers. Money, labour, trucks, services, and goods will all flow through Europe unimpeded by national borders. Anticipating this, France's minister of industry, Alain Madelin, argued: "Europe has no choice but to become a third pole of equivalent weight [to Japan and the U.S.]. Or else, poor in raw materials, politically divided, technologically dependent, it will fast become nothing more than a subcontractor for the other two." [33]

Simultaneously, Europe's monetary system is being centralized. A ten-year-old plan for a unified system incorporating a European Central Bank and European Currency Unit (ECU) is expected to be established by 1992. The basic ingredient in this would be, as described by the former French president, Valéry Giscard d'Estaing, "the complete freedom of movement of capital within the community." On the same note, the former West German chancellor, Helmut Schmidt, argued that there was no longer such a thing as a national stock market or a national money market. "Nobody is in charge," he said, "and this is very dangerous." His proposal was to establish three centres of economic management in the US Federal Reserve Bank, the Bank of Japan, and the European Central Bank. [34]

Meanwhile, Japanese companies are moving into the lower-cost regions of Europe to produce competitive cars, electronic products, cameras, and the same general line of goods Japan produces in the NICs of Asia. Since joining the EEC, Spain has been the chief recipient of Japanese investment by Nissan, Suzuki, Fujitsu, and Sanyo. Other

EEC countries had retained protectionist tariffs against Japan, despite their clamour on other fronts about the need for free markets.[35] With reductions in internal tariffs, these national tariffs against Japanese products become irrelevant, just as tariffs between the nations became irrelevant, because international companies produce goods within the tariff borders. Spain's relatively low wages make it an attractive entry point to the EEC market, where Japanese cars will compete more effectively with Renault, Fiat, and Volkswagen.

As it moved towards unification, Europe was already manifesting the same general trends that had occurred in other nations. Some regions were becoming more marginalized, others overendowed with industry as investment funds sought out private profits. Workers, now encouraged by common market policy to become mobile, had to move from their home countries in search of jobs and migrants from peripheral regions were becoming major components of labour forces in the highly industrialized countries. These workers won some social security benefits, but they remained in the category of guest workers without citizenship rights. And unemployment rates climbed steadily in all regions.

The entry of Spain and Portugal to the Common Market increased the regional disparities within the union, and the addition of Turkey would test the federation to its limits. Turkey, strategically situated, growing economically, democratic, and part of the western military alliance system, applied in 1988 to join the EEC. An associate member since 1963, Turkey's renewal of relations with Greece has eliminated the one barrier to its membership. But Spain, Portugal, and Turkey, all relatively poor agricultural nations with high unemployment, and high birth rates, would weigh down the community. The already controversial farm policies of the community could become impossible, and the growth in the number of unemployed workers flooding into continental Europe could wipe out the gains of the past several years. Whether Christian Europe could tolerate Islamic Turks is a question that is muted in public discourse. Turkey has very little choice: if the European Community establishes its full union by 1992, Turkey will be disadvantaged in its market and increasingly marginalized in global trade. Turkey had threatened to withdraw from NATO if the EC refused to grant it entry, but with the recent astonishing changes in Eastern Europe NATO itself has become an alliance with a dubious future.

THE NEW RIGHT assumed, even deliberately retained, the bipolar world of free enterprise versus communism. West Germany prospered and East Germany declined, proof indeed that markets were superior. But events in the USSR and its satellites at the beginning of the new decade upset the balance of power. The East was won; but what could the West do with it?

Perestroika and *glasnost* in the USSR opened the exit doors for Poland, Hungary, East Germany, Czechoslovakia, and Romania. The Baltic states demanded absolute independence, and the internal regions of the Russian empire were no longer stable. West Germany had to cope with an influx of thousands of East Germans seeking employment, housing, and social security benefits; France experienced the reawakening of fears of a strong and united Germany. How were all these new countries to fit into the global economy? If they tried to join the EC, it would become an unmanageable political unit, and the economic costs to the more affluent western democracies would be exorbitant. But if they were not accommodated by the market economies, their own power vacuum and their internal ethnic and class divisions could throw the entire region into revolt.

Western corporations were invited to reconstruct the Eastern European economies, but there was a catch: the populations were not prepared to adopt the whole circus of capitalism. They wanted parliamentary democracy; they wanted food in stores, and clothes, and western television; but they did not want massive unemployment or the abrupt removal of their social safety nets. Mikhail Gorbachev opened the gates and allowed the Wall to be turned into tourist souvenirs, but he made it clear that he – and with him Russia – would remain socialist.

The new right had dismantled much of Keynesianism. Now, however, the captains of capitalism were faced with the insuperable problem of providing social security to an enormous world population when no "evil empire" contested their ability to satisfy human wants. Instead, the evil empire offered a challenge to the ingenuity of all these entrepreneurs: find a way to sell in this market with its very different history and culture. European banks were already established in Eastern Europe, but doing business there, as many eager business people quickly discovered, would not be easy.

In mid-1990 the Warsaw Pact voluntarily ended its military role. Its member countries announced that it would dismantle its joint command at a pace to be determined by the pace of progress in negotiations with NATO over troop and conventional arms reductions. NATO at this stage was still considering how it could include a united Germany within its own alliance, and it was still far from recognizing that it was an anachronism. The final communiqué from the Warsaw Pact leaders described the notion of "the enemy" as obsolete: "The concepts of East and West have now regained their purely geographical meaning."[36] This swift demilitarization will have an especially heavy impact the United States, which is still entrenched in a military-industrial economy.

Inevitably, the combination of changes in both Eastern and Western Europe are creating ideological repercussions. The debate is about every feature of social, economic, and political life. The new right was an organized force in Europe; but unification and the assimilation of Eastern European immigrants can provide the nexus and the bodies with which to refashion social democratic ideologies and policies. Further, though the corporatist new right envisioned and strategically planned for much larger political units than nation-states, it was in the nation-states that the new right had its successes. The small business leaders who adopted the extreme laissez-faire stance in national circumstances are being swept aside by history; their support for European integration, let alone for a European Parliament, is at best lukewarm. Like Thatcher, they repeat a message that has lost much of its currency.

The debate now focuses on the nature of a European social charter. At issue are such large matters as how to dismantle the military institutions that supported the East-West hostilities; how to strike a new balance between market forces and the public interest; how to deal with distinctive cultures while amalgamating them into a new society; how to ensure individual freedoms while guaranteeing social security.

Where Thatcher could speak in 1988 of a Europe of nation-states, the president of the Commission of European Communities, Jacques Delors, spoke in 1989, of the evils of a new mercantilism, of the need for ethics, and of the defects of excessive nationalism and individualism; he asked, "What sort of society are we building?"[37]

In the Penny Arcade

"The gringos believe in formalities, we have to
understand them," Emilio Arevalo said. "They're
happy with the General and all they ask is that
democratic forms be preserved. With Odria as an
elected president, they'll open their arms to us and
give us all the credit we need."

Mario Vargas Llosa, *Conversation in the Cathedral*

American and European banks are overexposed in Latin America;
their outstanding loans far exceed their capital. If Argentina, Brazil,
and Mexico repudiated their debt, two of Britain's largest banks
(Lloyds and Midland) and a good dozen of the largest US banks
(including Citicorp, Chemical, and First Interstate) would court in-
solvency.

The passage from simple dependency to integrated circus has been
fraught with ironies, the most prominent being the political outcomes of the economic theory of the free market. The banks of the
industrial countries took Rousseau literally: they would force the
rest of the world to be free. In the process they obliged it to fall
under the control of military juntas and dictators. In the United
States the private banks and corporations, always reminding their
government that they should be free to seek profits according to
market principles, brought their own country into the debt crisis
and disabled its attempts to find solutions.

THE UNDERDEVELOPED countries constitute some 70 per cent of the
world's population, but receive only 30 per cent of the world's income. The disparities are compounded by internal inequalities. The
industrialized countries, members of the OECD, have within them
great pockets of poverty as well as an extremely wealthy minority
and a large middle class of affluent citizens. The less developed
countries have a small wealthy élite, but a vastly larger segment that
is impoverished. As well, the LDCs no longer form a homogeneous
group that can be generally classified (as in the "Third World" terminology). They include the handful of NICs, the few oil-rich states
of the Middle East and other members of OPEC, the countries that

Table 6
Economic performance of developing and industrial countries, 1965–86
(Average annual percentage change)

Country group and indicator	1965–73	1973–80	1980–86
DEVELOPING COUNTRIES			
Real GDP	6.5	5.4	3.6
Low-income countries	5.5	4.6	7.4
Middle-income countries	7.0	5.7	2.0
Oil exporters	6.9	6.0	0.8
Exporters of manufactures	7.4	6.0	6.0
Highly indebted countries	6.9	5.4	0.6
Sub-Saharan Africa[1]	6.4	3.2	−0.4
Merchandise export volumes	4.9	4.7	4.4
Manufactures	11.6	13.8	8.4
Primary goods	3.7	1.2	1.3
Merchandise import volumes	5.7	6.1	0.8
INDUSTRIAL COUNTRIES			
Real GDP	4.7	2.8	2.3

Source: Derived from World Bank, World Development Report, 1987, tables 2.1 and 2.5, 16 and 26.
Published for the bank by Oxford University Press.
Note: All growth rates for developing countries are based on a sample of ninety countries.
[1] Excluding South Africa

have resources though they remain poor, and others that are resource-poor as well as poor in all other senses. In the more favoured regions a middle class has emerged. Overall, about half of the world's population survives at a bare level of existence, and about a quarter is impoverished to the point of chronic hunger.[1]

Between 1950 and 1975, the growth rate in the LDCs as measured by GNP was slightly higher than that of the industrialized countries (5 per cent compared with 4.2 per cent overall), though growth rates in per capita incomes were lower in the LDCs, where the population densities were much higher than in the industrialized countries (see table 6).[2]

There were some positive achievements in the LDCs in the 1960s and 1970s: literacy rates increased, death rates declined, and agricultural productivity improved. Counterbalancing these gains were outflows of skilled migrants, high population growth, and the rise of an unemployed and impoverished urban fringe population. The "green revolution" temporarily improved agricultural output rates, but also created chemically induced soil erosion and new pests and pushed poor agricultural workers off the land and into the cities, where the capital-intensive factories could not absorb them.

Table 7
Growth of GDP per capita, 1965–86 (Annual percentage change)

Country group	1965–73	1973–80	1980–6
DEVELOPING COUNTRIES	3.9	3.2	1.5
Low-income countries	2.9	2.5	5.4
Middle-income countries	4.4	3.3	−0.3
Oil exporters	4.3	3.2	−1.8
Exporters of manufactures	4.8	4.1	4.3
Highly indebted countries	4.2	2.9	−1.8
Sub-Saharan Africa[1]	3.6	0.3	−3.4
INDUSTRIAL COUNTRIES	3.7	2.1	1.6

Source: World Bank, World Development Report, 1987, table 2.6, 26. Published for the bank by Oxford University Press.
Note: all growth rates for developing countries are based on a sample of ninety countries.
[1] excluding South Africa

The differences between developing and underdeveloped countries increased after the mid-1970s. Growth rates continued to be high in a few NICs where the manufacturing of garments, electronics, and other consumer goods had become firmly established. Singapore, Thailand, and Indonesia had continuing improvements in GDP and per capita income. The oil-exporting regions declined, and the debtor countries suffered steadily deteriorating conditions (see table 7).

The fate of these regions has been shaped by both internal and external agents, though it is virtually impossible to determine where one begins and the other leaves off. We have noted in connection with the industrialization of Britain and Western Europe, Japan, and Taiwan the importance of the commercialization of agriculture in the countries' formative stages of development. The landed class and the peasantry were disbanded or absorbed and the feudal social relationships dissolved. Barrington Moore saw this early demise of feudal relations as the essential condition for the subsequent development of democracy,[3] and it appears to be the essential condition for successful industrialization.

In the United States, Canada (except Quebec), Australia, and New Zealand no landed classes took root, and those societies therefore began with the essential condition. Most other societies were obliged to rid themselves of those classes before they could develop urban and capitalist markets. This occurred in Meiji Japan. It also happened in Taiwan, initially under Japanese control and later under the Kuomintang. For various historical and cultural reasons, most of

Latin America has been unable to rid itself of feudal landed classes, which have obstructed change in many ways and constitute an internal barrier to development.

In view of these facts, it would be wrong to blame the crisis of the 1980s entirely on the world's banks and transnational extensions, but they certainly have been at the core of the problem. Some would argue that the failure of land reforms in some Latin American countries, and the continued significance of the military in most, are directly attributable to the policies of the international banking community. That is not the argument here, but one must concede that the policies of the banking community have exacerbated the difficulties in Latin America and elsewhere by putting countries in positions where they are forced to accept government by juntas and dictators.

PRESIDENT HARRY S TRUMAN'S Point Four program of 1949 called for assistance to the LDCs, but the US foreign aid program was initially submerged under the Marshall Plan for Europe. The foreign aid programs subsequently put in place – the United Nations Development Program (UNDP), the World Bank, and other agencies of the United Nations – became entangled in the political battles of the cold war. This political context was beneficial to countries regarded by the industrialized countries as strategic for geographical, political, or economic reasons, which became the major recipients of aid. However, as the cold war thawed slightly during the 1960s and early 1970s, the flow of aid declined.

Evan Luard has shown aid levels from 1960 to 1980 declining, for the United States, from 0.53 per cent of GNP to 0.18 per cent and, for France, from 1.3 per cent to 0.59 per cent. The trend is similar for Britain and West Germany. Japan maintained a level of about 0.25 per cent throughout the period. Only the Netherlands and Sweden increased their aid as a proportion of GNP.[4] Aid flows have tended to be directed to strategically located regions – Israel and Egypt receive substantial US aid, for example – or to countries in a state of emergency that have attracted media attention; in these latter cases the aid tends to be short-term.

BANK LOANS AND foreign direct investment are more important sources of funds than outright aid. Following the Second World War, individuals gave way to companies, banks, governments, and international agencies as major lenders or investors. Loans came from three sources: the World Bank and the IMF or other intergovernmental bodies, national government agencies through bilateral loans, and private banks.

The Keynesian plan for dealing with trade imbalances was to create a central clearing union to be known as Bancor. The mechanism Keynes proposed would have inhibited mounting debts, but it would also have required the wealthier countries to contribute to the maintenance of the union. The United States, then anticipating that it would retain a surplus in balance of payments, rejected this proposal, countering with what became known as the White Plan. The weaker countries were burdened with deficits while the richer countries provided deficit loans. The IMF was modelled on the White Plan; it was designed to provide short-term credits to reduce balance of payments deficits. The World Bank was designed to provide longer-term development aid to those countries that conformed to IMF rules. The rules ensured open borders to capital, a fixed exchange rate, and limitations on government interference in the market in debtor countries. Article 1, ("Purposes") of the IMF charter includes (1) providing consultative machinery on international monetary problems; (2) facilitating balanced growth of international trade, which would promote and maintain high levels of employment and real income and develop productive resources;[5] (3) assisting in the establishment of a multilateral system of payments and in the elimination of foreign exchange restrictions; (4) providing means to correct maladjustments in balance of payments; and (5) shortening the duration and lessening the degree of disequilibrium in the international balances of payments of members.[6]

Voting power in the IMF was weighted in favour of the lending countries by quotas based on the international pecking order of 1945 or, more generally, on contributions. While the quotas have been revised from time to time, in the 1980s the United States still held 20 per cent of the shares and the United Kingdom just under 7 per cent, with West Germany, France, and Japan following. The USSR withdrew from the IMF as it had from GATT; but other Eastern European countries rejoined GATT and finally, in the late 1970s and early 1980s, applied for membership in the IMF. The developing countries as a whole now hold just over 34 per cent of the votes, but the combined voting power of the industrial countries greatly outweighs theirs.[7] Only in the United Nations, where each nation has one vote, have they been able to organize and oppose the industrial countries. But even there they are finally countered by the veto powers of the dominant countries.

The OPEC countries gained greater influence in international finance after 1973, securing 3.5 per cent of voting rights in the IMF and becoming major contributors to the funds. The funds were then lent to other LDC countries whose relative positions abruptly deteriorated because of the rise in oil prices.

Voting power in the World Bank is held according to shares. This has given the United States enormous power and veto strength, though US shares have gradually declined as Japanese and European shares have increased.[8] The World Bank has a greater flexibility in its lending program, but because it draws its resources from private sources it is constrained by private interests in its practices. Even with the addition of the International Development Association (IDA) in 1960 in response to growing frustration among Third World countries, loans remain subject to the interested direction of US financial and government leaders, and borrowers are subjected to surveillance to ensure that they conform to IMF and World Bank rules.

Keynes expected the IMF to act as the world's financial policeman, but the fund's interpretation of that role differed from his.[9] The IMF determines through investigation whether a borrower country is creditworthy, and requires the borrower to sign documented plans outlining how the money will be used to achieve "stabilization." Other lenders depend on the IMF seal of approval, and debtor countries are virtually obliged to conform to IMF demands if they wish to borrow not only from the IMF but from other sources. The IMF does not divulge the nature of its demands, and borrower countries rarely make them public. They become known in retrospect, and there is no opportunity to determine before the fact whether the demands are in the interests of the people in the borrowing countries.

The terms of IMF and World Bank loans create a Catch-22 situation. On the one hand, the recipient is obliged to remove all restrictions to the "free market"; on the other hand, because it must open its borders to foreign investment and imports it is unable to develop independent momentum as an industrial country. The IMF increasingly views inflation as the paramount problem of underdeveloped countries, and its demands are pegged to that perception. In this respect, the power of the IMF and the ideological leadership of the Trilateralists and the right-wing think-tanks around the world combine to impose a particular view not only of how the global economy should function but of social and cultural priorities.

Typical demands made by the IMF are devaluation, restrictions on domestic credit, reductions of budget deficits, and dropping of subsidies for public goods. These requirements effectively strip national governments of their capacity to intervene in the economy so as to respond to local cultures, population needs, or their own visions of a more humane society. They also make the borrower countries more dependent on external agencies, more in need of foreign currencies, and thus more supportive of direct investment from industrial countries. And they encourage dictatorships and military juntas, since democratic governments are unable to impose the stringent and often cruel restraints that the IMF requires.

The World Bank ties its financing to competitive bidding on bank projects. In 1962 a concession to recipient countries provided an allowance for preference bidding of up to 15 per cent for local companies, but international suppliers took up the remainder. On all projects, but especially on the mega-energy projects that the bank enthusiastically supported in the aftermath of the energy crises, international suppliers benefited enormously and host countries became major importers of supplies. Local industries were unable to obtain a foothold, and debt escalated even as loans increased. A bank spokesman explained, "We have to take into account that the providers of our capital are very interested and we have to strike a balance between the interest of exporters of equipment and goods and recipients of loans."[10]

The World Bank engaged in remarkable double-think on this score. In 1985, with the United States talking about the need for the World Bank to act as a police force against countries that failed to uphold the free market, the bank argued that its loans were already conditional on "dismantling controls or improving efficiency of public-sector management. They aim at increasing competition and helping private-sector activity ... In most oil and gas ventures, the Bank has been a catalyst for major private-sector participation."[11] In the same defence, the acting information director of the World Bank noted that the bank "focuses on poverty alleviation anchored in sound policies," though it was not in a position to police human rights violations; further, "growing markets in Third World countries mean greater exports and more jobs in industrial countries." There, finally, was a bottom line.

THE IMF AND THE World Bank, buttressed by GATT and the dollar-based fixed exchange rates of the 1945–70 era, did provide a measure of stability to the world, even if it involved uneven and dependent development for the poor countries. Not envisioned in the original institutional organization was the rapid growth of private commercial banks. Between 1970 and 1982 loans made through the international agencies (called concessional loans in financial jargon) decreased as a proportion of the total, while non-concessional loans grew at a rapid pace. Of the $536 billion increase in total external

debt between 1971 and 1982, about 80 per cent ($440 billion) con-
sisted of commercial loans. In 1971 commercial loans had accounted
for under one-fifth of all debt; by 1982 they comprised almost half.[12]
In Gerald Helleiner's view, The Eurocurrency banks in particular
"came to function in international lending essentially unregulated,
unsupervised, outside the borders of their own countries, expanding their credit at a rate of over 20 per cent a year for the last
ten years ... What happpened in the 1970s was that the basic monetary function for which the IMF was created in the post Second-
World-War years was taken over by the international commercial
banks."[13]

Referring to the world's investment banks, *The Economist* said that
"the world is their oyster," which does not mean they are pearls;
rather, they harvest the gems in a very competitive, aggressive business which, like the silicon wafer firms, has became "globalized" as
well as deregulated.[14] The private banks have become a more important source of funds for the LDCs since the oil crisis. Petrodollars
banked by OPEC countries were used to provide long-term bank
loans at variable interest rates. The loans were made because the
banks aggressively pursued Third World customers and because the
developing countries, frustrated by the IMF terms and conditions
and believing that despite high fuel costs they would succeed in
increasing their shares of world markets, took risks.

In addition, banks provided very expensive short-term loans, for
which there is no international accounting system: it is estimated
that they made up 20 per cent of LDC total debt in 1980–2 and about
14 per cent by 1984 as the banks tightened up on credit in view of
the growing risk of default.[15] In June 1983 the share of debt attributable to short-term loans to Brazil, Argentina, Chile and Turkey
was about 19 per cent; to Mexico, Peru, South Korea, Columbia,
and Nigeria, between 27 and 32 per cent; to the Philippines, 38 per
cent; and to Venezuela, 45 per cent.[16]

Those private debts are crucial components of the debt crisis. The
variable rates and servicing costs spiralled upwards, and then, very
suddenly, two impossible conditions interrupted the process. First,
the export markets sharply declined, leaving the debtor countries
with no way of obtaining funds to pay the servicing on their debts;
second, the banks abruptly cut back on their credit. Before we deal
with these developments, we should consider the third source of
funds – direct investment.

DIRECT INVESTMENT in the LDCs in the 1950s accounted for only
20 per cent of total US foreign investment, and was overwhelmingly

located in the resource sectors. Exports from these countries consisted chiefly of agricultural products (76 per cent in 1955) and minerals (13 per cent).[17] In the 1960s, however, there was a gradual
increase in direct foreign investment in factories that produced goods
to be consumed in the host countries. Then, from the mid-1960s on,
investments in the manufacturing of goods designated for export to
the developed countries grew in what were now NICs, which constituted a separate part of the Third World, but overall the growth
was modest. Some writers anticipated a general pattern of increasing
investment in manufacturing on the basis of the trends of the
1960s.[18] However, the events of the 1970s – the oil crisis, the growing
militancy of labour in the industrial countries, and the decline of a
hegemonic system, together with the changes in technology and
production systems – have not borne out these hypotheses, except
in the few NICs that were sufficiently advanced by 1973 to withstand
the shocks. Investments in the manufacturing sectors of Indonesia,
Singapore, and Panama grew while investments in resource-extrac-
tion services declined, but the pattern elsewhere was uneven, and
no trend could be identified.

The central investment agencies in the manufacturing sectors are
transnational corporations, and their capital has gone largely to certain research-intensive industrial sectors such as chemicals and electrical products and to the labour-intensive phases of production of
lighter goods. In Mexico during the early 1970s, 67 per cent of the
outputs of the chemical industry, 84 per cent of the rubber industry,
and 63 per cent of the electrical machinery industry were produced
by foreign-owned transnationals. Similarly, in Brazil 51 per cent of
the chemical industry and 64 per cent of the rubber industry outputs
were produced by the transnationals; and in Argentina as well these
industries were substantially controlled by foreign investment corporations.[19] The industries are research-intensive, but the research
is done in the industrial centres, not in the host countries.[20]

The service sector has also grown in the LDCs since the late 1960s.
Banking and insurance firms constitute a large part of this sector;
indeed, the growth of banking has been greatest in the developing
countries.

By region, the major recipient countries in 1967 were Brazil
(11.3 per cent of all direct investment), Venezuela (10.6 per cent)
Mexico (5.5 per cent), Argentina (5.5 per cent) and India (4.0 per
cent). In 1976 Brazil was still the largest recipient (13.1 per cent),
followed by Indonesia (7.4 per cent) and Mexico (6.8 per cent). In
international terms the percentage of investment in the NICs appears
low, but in terms of actual dollars relative to population size and

established infrastructure, the investments in Singapore, Taiwan, South Korea, and Hong Kong and the Philippines had all risen from under 1 per cent to over 2 per cent of the total, and continued to rise until the 1980s. Japanese investment in Asia expanded greatly from the mid-1960s to the mid-1970s, while investments in Latin America, especially by Japanese companies, declined.[21]

THESE DIVERSE SOURCES of funds cannot be treated separately if we are to gain an understanding of the debt crisis. IMF and World Bank funding, bilateral government loans, private bank long- and short-term credit, and direct investment occurred simultaneously, one influencing the other.

Brazil, Mexico, and Chile were among the earliest recipients of IMF loans in the late 1940s. Before 1959, Brazil was the largest borrower from the World Bank.[22] A populist government in the mid-1960s had attempted to introduce land reform, income redistribution, nationalization of US corporate subsidiaries (especially ITT), and restrictions on transfers of profits by transnationals. The World Bank, together with US private and public financial institutions, imposed a credit boycott that lasted from 1959 until 1964, in the wake of which the Brazilian army staged a successful coup. While the historian Thomas Skidmore notes that there was no evidence of active US involvement in the coup, he remarks on the alacrity with which the American government expressed its support for the new military regime. Even though a democratically elected government had been overthrown President Lyndon Johnson sent this message immediately following the events: "The American people ... have admired the resolute will of the Brazilian community to resolve these difficulties within a framework of constitutional democracy and without civil strife."[23] The curious amalgam of military rule with limited, constantly changing, and highly contrived democratic appendages reached agreement with the IMF very soon after the coup. This included an attack on wages, acceptance of profit transfers, and repression of protest and dissent by way of guaranteeing political stability. The American government co-operated in providing financial assistance, and the Brazilian government became strongly pro-American in its foreign policy. The production of arms as well as of consumer goods was advanced. The intention was to implement import-substitution policies, but that required imported machinery. Foreign corporations, with their global procurement and export policies, acted in the interests of their shareholders, not in the interests of the Brazilian people, when they imported capital-intensive machinery. The imports contributed to mounting debts and trade deficits.

Dependence on oil imports grew as truck transportation increased. After the oil crisis, development bank loans and a series of megaprojects in the energy sector, intended to reduce dependence on oil imports, further increased the debt. These projects required imports of capital-intensive goods and used sugar-cane land in the development of alcohol as a substitute fuel for cars. The second oil price shock in 1979 was the coup de grâce. The industrial nations became more protectionist, and the high interest policies of the United States made it harder for Brazil and other countries to pay the interest on their debts. The IMF was prepared to negotiate loans, but IMF stabilization policies were regarded as unacceptable by the Brazilian government. Even so, Brazil was finally forced in 1980 to accept most of the IMF guidelines in order to regain its creditworthiness in the eyes of the international banks. The emphasis now was on exports, and industrialization and import-substitution policies were waived in a desperate attempt to stop the slide into debt.[24]

Of particular interest here is the relationship between international development aid for the megaprojects and the participation of large foreign corporations in their construction and servicing. When aid is conditional on open borders, imports by foreign contractors cannot be stopped and import-substitution policies cannot be implemented. According to Richard Newfarmer, "international aid finances more than 80% of heavy electrical equipment purchases for hydroelectric projects (including generation, transmission, and distribution and equipment such as hydraulic generators, turbines, transformers, and cables). About three-quarters of the funding now comes from the Interamerican Bank and the World Bank."[25]

Another aspect of the aid to Brazil and other countries is its hidden effect in exploiting new territory. While loans may be made for hydro-electric dams or smelters, mills, and plants in resource regions, they carry with them sufficient funds for the construction of roads and communications links. The infrastructure is industry-specific – that is, it is designed for the extraction of certain materials or the development of certain projects, not for general development or general population needs. It frequently allows for greater government control of indigenous populations, and provides a means of eradicating non-industrial uses of land and forests. The Trans-Amazonian Highway is an example.

Cheryl Payer has studied the relationship between a transnational corporation and Brazil's industrialization through World Bank financing.[26] The Hanna Company of Cleveland, Ohio, participated in several World Bank-aided mining projects in Latin America. It was discomfited by a law requiring Brazilian firms to exploit subsoil minerals, and fought the law in the late 1950s and 1960s in its attempt to extract iron ore deposits in the region of Minas Gerais. An expropriation decree was ordered in 1962 by the Brazilian president. The order was appealed, and the case was in the courts when the military coup took place. Shortly after the coup Hanna received approval to build loading facilities, a deep-water harbor, and local rail cutoffs, and the right to exploit the iron ore deposits.

A few years later Hanna, now joined to one of Brazil's largest holding companies (CAEMI) and Nippon Steel of Japan, created a new iron-ore company (MBR) and entered joint ventures with Alcoa Alcominas to extract bauxite for the aluminum industry. Meanwhile, Alcominas had obtained a World Bank loan. It may be worth noting that the head of Hanna Mining was an ex-US. secretary of the treasury and an ex officio US governor of the IMF and the World Bank, and that the first president of the World Bank was acting as Hanna's counsel in Brazil.

The IMF and the World Bank take pride in their apolitical stance. But as the Brazilian case exemplifies, their fundamental concern with their monetarist version of stabilization leads them to be very political indeed, and their politics show a marked preference for military juntas, dictators, and other governments that are prepared to let the free market of the outside world in while preventing the population from exercising any substantial freedom of its own.

Chile is an obvious second example. In the mid-1960s Chile's copper accounted for about 75 per cent of export earnings, and the copper industry was dominated by the American companies Anaconda, Kennecott, and Cerro. The 1964 election was fought on the issue of nationalization of the industry; the Christian Democrats, who advocated a program of partial ownership, won the election. Takeovers with 75–25 splits and generous compensation to Kennecott and Cerro, along with a 51–49 split for Anaconda, were arranged. As well, Chile imposed a surtax to capture larger profits, and in other respects, including its land reform policies, was moving towards greater national control of resources and economic planning before the 1970 election. Stephen D. Krasner's study of American policies on Chile until that election indicates that no hostile action was taken to prevent the takeovers or other reforms. None the less, the United States was very much involved in Chilean politics: the CIA had provided over half of the Christian Democrats' campaign funds in the 1964 election, and American per capita aid to Chile was higher than for any other Latin American country.[27]

The central objective of US foreign policy was to prevent the left, under Salvador Allende, from attaining power. While one may suppose that this coincided with the long-term interests of capital in sustaining open borders for investment, it is clear that the nationalization and land reform policies introduced by a liberal government were contrary to the interests of the copper companies. Thus US foreign policy was not unambiguously defensive of American capital in place, but it was defensive of capitalism as a system. Allende, despite US opposition, won the 1970 election and nationalized the copper companies. His government also took over Chitelco, the Chilean telephone company owned by International Telephone and Telegraph, Bethlehem Steel, several American banks, and other American firms. Economic pressures were exerted by the companies (especially ITT) and by the US State Department. Bilateral aid and Export-Import Bank credits were stopped, the World Bank refused to make loans, and, perhaps most important, a surplus of copper was put on the market through increased sales of US stockpiles. Imports of machine parts were impeded, and opposition within the country, including particularly army and truckers' factions, was financed by the CIA.[28] The Allende government was ousted in 1973 by General Augusto Pinochet (the CIA's role in the coup was later documented in Congressional and Senate hearings). Pinochet quickly obtained the World Bank loan that had been denied Allende.[29]

Only 4 per cent of US copper supplies were imported from Chile. Krasner argues that American behaviour cannot be adequately explained in terms of corporate economic interests or national resource supplies security; he quotes the CIA's Directorate of Intelligence as explaining that the United States was responding to the "definite psychological advance [of] the Marxist idea."[30] Ironically, the "Marxist idea" is considerably advanced by this history: the US government attempted to act in the long-term interests of capital, even where that action involved short-term losses. At the same time it does appear that the US government, especially the CIA, developed an anti-communist momentum far in excess of what was needed to protect corporate interests.

These examples are not atypical. South Africa continued to obtain loans after the UN General Assembly had voted against aid and demanded that any future aid be conditional on its ending the apartheid system in 1982. Nicaragua received no loans after the overthrow of Anastasio Somoza; yet the Somoza family had obtained loans (and, apparently, pocketed them without penalty).[31]

The banking community's preoccupation with free enterprise stands in stark contrast to the financial aid, corporate settlements, and political support given to strategically located countries that strayed far from free enterprise ethics – notably Taiwan. Dominated by a foreign army and occupied by foreign firms, Taiwan is regarded as second only to Japan as an economic miracle. In addition to the companies mentioned in earlier chapters, many American firms are located there: oil companies (Gulf, Mobil, Standard), Union Carbide; chip, computer, and electrical industries (RCA, ITT, IBM, Zenith, General Instrument, Motorola, Texas Instruments); chemical companies (Du Pont, Chemical Corp., National Distillers); and Ford Motors. Japanese investors include Hitachi, Mitsubishi, Matsushita, Sanyo, Nippon, Asahi, Sony, and Mitsui.[32] The public sector share in manufacturing has declined, but government remains dominant in heavy machinery, steel, shipbuilding, petroleum, engineering, aluminum, and semiconductors; the banks are still state-owned, and the state strictly supervises financial industries in general.[33] The extent of government control in the Taiwanese economy has not harmed the island's credit standing; only Singapore and Saudi Arabia were rated as more creditworthy than Taiwan in 1984. This was so even though Taiwan's membership in the IMF was transferred to the People's Republic of China in 1980. Taiwan is not in need of world bank funding: it can easily obtain money from the private markets. As a final irony of history, its industrialists are now investing in China. The original reason for industrializing Taiwan was to develop its military capacity to conquer China; that notion has become only the dream of old and worn-out warriors. Free enterprise, when directed by a military junta and backed by enormous foreign aid and foreign capital, can conquer a country without a single shot.

IN 1981 THE OECD countries experienced a recession and inflation. Their monetarist response was to increase interest rates and concentrate on policies aimed at reducing inflation. The prices of raw materials declined, immediately lowering the export revenues of the LDCs. The banks, recognizing that the risk of indebtedness was escalating, began to stem the flow of fresh capital to LDCs. The LDCs then had to reduce their imports in order to continue paying their debt charges. By 1982 they had become net capital exporters. Short-term loans were obtained to pay service costs on older long-term loans, and the total cost skyrocketed while export income declined.

There are several reasons for the mounting indebtedness – the falling rate of relative market prices for the raw materials exported by underdeveloped countries, the rising cost of fuel, and most particularly, the extraordinarily high cost of debt servicing for private bank loans. But the behaviour of the privileged, the politicians, and the middle classes in the indebted countries is also to blame. Those who controlled capital moved it out of risk-ridden locations to safe havens in Europe and the United States. That money finds its way back to the very banks that hold the outstanding debts. *Time* estimated the capital flight from Mexico, Venezuela, and Argentina for the period from 1979 to mid-1984 at $63 billion;[34] other estimates for Latin America as a whole but the figure at $130 billion, a third of the total debt.[35] Various estimates for the decade beginning in 1973 are between $15 and $20 billion for Brazil, $5 to $10 billion for Peru, and about $8 billion for Chile. Mexico holds first place: the former president, José Lopez Portillo, informed the Mexican Congress in his final address of 1982 that some $42 billion had been exported in the previous few years.[36] "I also have to add that Mexican investment in the United States during the last few years has been higher than the total foreign investment in Mexico throughout its whole history."

In addition to capital outflows of this kind, there were numerous excesses and wasteful uses of funds in recipient countries. The élites and the middle classes developed appetites for foreign travel, foreign education, and high standards of living similar to those enjoyed in the industrial countries. These behaviours were connected to employment in the corporate sector, and were encouraged by the free market ideology. Imported luxury goods contributed to the mounting debts. Foreign companies also imported parts which became components of the debt. Finally, the debtor countries invested in military build-ups and standing armies far beyond any sensible defence needs.

THE DEBT CRISIS exploded in 1982. At first there were expectations that it would ease with the passing of what was then believed to be a temporary recession. But it intensified, and the major commercial banks cut back further as debt-ridden countries began defaulting on the servicing of debts they could never pay off. Their situation deteriorated steadily as interest rates rose in the United States. Capital ceased to flow into the NICs. Now such countries as Mexico, Brazil, and Argentina no longer attract foreign capital in the form of loans or investments. They still have enormous debts, and the debt servicing obliges them to send out more capital than they receive. Since 1982, for example, the seventeen nations in the World Bank's list of highly indebted countries have had a net outflow of $130 billion (us) in service charges on the $80 billion in loans and investments that flowed in between 1978 and 1982.[37]

Countries so deeply indebted cannot afford social services, housing, or new capital expenditures necessary for development. Because their people cannot purchase the goods of the industrial countries, their imports drop. This occurs even when they desperately accept the IMF's loan conditions. Brazil, after resisting IMF conditions for nearly a year, finally accepted them because the major us banks refused loans until the IMF agreements were signed. The cruzeiro was devalued by 30 per cent before the IMF approved a new loan in 1983, with terms that included policies to facilitate profit transfers by transnational corporations, abandonment of wage indexation, increases in domestic interest rates, cuts in state subsidies to agricultural sectors, and removal of export duties and import controls.[38]

The consequences were severe: there were riots, strikes, and raids on food stores, and the tempo of repression steadily increased. The IMF was targeted as public enemy number one in Brazil; even the national industrialists were angered by terms that so clearly favoured transnational capital at their expense. The middle class was under attack, the public sector was severely downsized, and the poor were pushed beyond endurance. The Catholic church spoke out against the IMF's policies, and government ministers resigned rather than implement them. But even when they were implemented, even when further loans were desperately sought with still more onerous conditions, even with a favourable balance of trade in 1984, Brazil, too heavily burdened with debt-servicing, could not begin to repay the loans. Nor could Mexico, nor could the other countries that were likewise entrapped. A *Globe and Mail* correspondent calculated that "an increase of one percentage point in the us prime rate, for example, means that Brazil's annual debt-service costs automatically swell by roughly $1 billion, Mexico's by about $900 million, Argentina's by $450 million, Chile's by $200 million."[39]

The growing trade deficits and indebtedness of the United States have added to the problems in Latin America. The liberalized trade policies initiated by the United States after the war and developed further in the GATT negotiations were largely directed at relations between the developed countries. As the effects of offshore production and the industrialization of the LDCs were experienced in the United States, particularly after the OPEC oil embargoes, the United States and other industrialized countries became considerly less enthusiastic about open borders. Trade policies grew more complex, on the one hand praising the advantages of free trade and on the other restricting imports from the LDCs. The 1974 US Trade Act introduced a generalized system of preferences for duty-free access to the US market from designated LDCs, but added a list of limitations and ineligibilities that increased the barriers to exporting goods to the United States. These included prohibitions on countries that nationalized property without immediate compensation, and on goods that constituted over half the quantity of US imports. Even more damaging, they included a range of products, especially shoes, textiles, electronic goods, and other products – almost all in the labour-intensive category – deemed to be "import sensitive." Tariffs remained lowest for resources, and escalated with the amount of value added to the product, thereby inhibiting the development of manufacturing in the LDCs.

These policies notwithstanding, the United States continued to incur mounting deficits and debts of its own. The US economy was still twice the size of the Japanese economy, and its productivity was still the highest in the world, but the zenith of American power had come in 1973, and the nation was past its peak. The two debt problems are related, though not in a simple way. To some extent the inability of the debtor countries to import goods affects the industrial countries because it means a persistent drop in exports. The impact of such drops on an export-dependent country such as Canada is severe; between 1980 and 1984, for example, Canadian exports to Latin America declined by 23 per cent ($670 million).[40] Banks in the industrial countries are armed with insurance, and they can deduct some losses from income tax, but ultimately these are paid for by shareholders and taxpayers.

The impasse has been reached: Latin American debt cannot be repaid, and further development is stalled as long as the private banks of the DMCs and the international organizations insist on the payment of servicing debts. Without industrialization the OECD countries, and especially the United States, since it is the chief lender through its private banks, lose investment, new opportunities, and export markets; and as long as the banks, already in receipt of the funds that escaped illegally or at least unethically, insist on repayment, the United States loses credibility and courts political disaster throughout South America.

The United States proposed in 1985 that world commercial bankers and the international development banks increase their lending on the condition that the developing nations radically alter their economies to accommodate the "free market." How much more of it they could accommodate was in question, since the free market had

Table 8
Latin American debt, capital flight, World Bank loans, and IMF credits, by country, 1986 (Billions of us dollars)

	External debt			Capital flight		World Bank loans	Use of IMF credit		
	Total	Owed to banks	Owed to us banks	Deposits for banks	Net flow in 1983–5	Net disbursements in 1985	Loans outstanding	Potential borrowing	Repayments scheduled for 1986–8
Argentina	49.0	26.6	8.1	8.2	0.1	0.075	2.31	3.45	1.33
Bolivia	4.2	0.7	0.2	0.4	0.3	-0.001	0.05	0.37	0.05
Brazil	103.9	77.9	23.8	8.5	6.6	0.351	4.62	3.13	2.30
Chile	21.1	13.4	6.6	2.2	-0.6	0.212	1.09	1.25	0.70
Colombia	13.1	6.9	2.7	2.6	0.7	0.424	0.00	1.73	0.00
Ecuador	7.7	5.0	2.2	1.3	0.6	0.016	0.36	0.40	0.22
Mexico	96.7	71.8	25.8	15.3	16.2	0.505	2.97	2.15	0.91
Peru	14.0	5.5	2.1	1.5	1.1	0.091	0.70	1.05	0.42
Uruguay	4.7	2.0	1.0	2.0	0.2	0.011	0.35	0.49	0.19
Venezuela	31.9	25.1	10.6	12.6	5.5	-0.022	0.00	6.03	0.00

Source: "World Financial Markets," compiled by *Latin American Weekly Report*, 1986:11, 14 March 1986. *Latin American Weekly Report*, 9 February 1989, indicates current situations for Argentina, Bolivia, Brazil, Paraguay, Peru. Venezuela, Mexico, and Guatemala, and includes negotiations and attempts to reschedule debts. No new negotiations are reported for Chile, Colombia, Ecuador, or Uruguay.

clearly failed them. The proposed solution simply reinforced the image of a banking community blind to poverty and hunger and unable to recognize that the debt problem would be their own undoing.

The *Latin America Weekly Report*, widely regarded as a reliable source, showed the relationships in 1986 between bank debt, world bank loans, IMF credit, and capital flight deposits (see table 8). One year later Brazil announced that it would indefinitely suspend the payment of interest on the $68 billion in medium- and long-term loans it owed to commercial banks. It also froze $15 billion in short-term trade and interbank credits to prevent retaliation and further capital flight.[41] *The Economist* added up the figures and concluded that the major losers would be the banks, with Citicorp, Chase Manhattan, Bank of America, and Manufacturers Hanover at the top of the list.[42] With little to gain from compliance and much to lose, Peru followed Brazil, defaulting on part of the servicing of $14 billion in debts. By this time the level of indebtedness totalled over $1 trillion. In 1988 the director of international economics at the World Bank admitted that no solution was in sight.[43]

Other bankers began to suggest political solutions. The Bank of Nova Scotia has proposed one of several solutions that involve new lending arrangements on a country-by-country basis. What is significant about these proposals is that in every case, they require a world political order with some kind of global organization that has the authority to impose conditions on both the lenders and the borrowers. The Bank of Nova Scotia proposals, for example, recommend the establishment of a new international financial institution linked to the IMF and the World Bank that would examine each country's ability to pay interest and then negotiate interest rate levels accordingly. A contributory insurance scheme would be established by creditors, ultimately backed by governments through an agency such as the World Bank. "The considerable difficulties of negotiating an innovative and comprehensive solution to the debt problem cannot be overcome without political leadership and an act of international statesmanship of the sort that led to the Marshall Plan or to the founding of the World Bank."[44]

Many of the bankers' solutions are similar to the IMF's notions free market solutions to poverty. But slowly they are beginning to recognize that a true solution will require a new international economic order instituted through a new political order. This is precisely what the Trilateralists propose. It is not the same international economic order dreamed of by the developing countries. It is not a solution to the problems of the LDCs that the bankers are seeking, but a solution to the bankers' problems.

PART THREE

Beyond the Market

CHAPTER ELEVEN

Economic Reality

In fact some gentlemen of the Holy Office have
recently been almost shocked by this new picture of
the universe, compared to which our accepted one is
only a miniature such as could be hung round the
enchanting necks of certain young ladies. They are
worried because, in the case of such enormous
distances, a prelate and even a cardinal might easily
go astray.

The Inquisitor, in Bertolt Brecht, *The Life of Galileo*

In a free market there is no room for an interventionist state. Yet
leaders of the LDCs can see that the industrial countries are extremely
active in protecting the rights of their nationals elsewhere, even
while strongly arguing for the moral as well as the economic virtue
of non-intervention and of pure market forces. They see too that in
a free market where property rights are overwhelmingly held by
nationals of rich countries the poverty of their own people not only
persists but increases.

A MODEST REJECTION of received economic theory was mounted in
the 1960s by Raúl Prebisch,[1] the former head of the United Nations
Economic Commission for Latin America, and by leaders of the non-
aligned countries. The developing and underdeveloped countries
pulled into the orbit of the alliances that adopted this position were
for the most part former colonies or peripheries, and many of them
had achieved their independence only in the early 1960s.

Prebisch had long been an advocate of import substitution as an
industrial strategy for Latin American countries, but his studies led
him to change his mind. He noted that the colonial pattern of trade
persisting into the post-war period, in which primary commodities
were imported tariff-free to the industrial countries while manufactured goods attracted import tariffs, ensured that the developing
countries would be unable to compete for markets. Demand for
primary goods did not increase as did demand for manufactured
goods, and in some sectors it actually decreased because technical
progress reduced the raw material content of the end products.
Prebisch argued that an increasing proportion of increments to income would always be spent on imported manufactured goods es-

sential to industrialization, since the price of these would continue to rise relative to the prices of commodities. For example, if manufactured goods from underdeveloped regions were to compete with those of the developed countries, they would have to be produced by similar technologies, and the technologies would have to be imported because the underdeveloped countries had no access to the science and no capital to undertake their own research and development or to pay for patents under licence. There was a trade gap between the core and peripheral countries that would continue to grow unless the industrial countries actively altered their trading system to accommodate manufactured goods from the LDCs.[2] Prebisch's analyses had a substantial impact and led to the establishment of the United Nations Conference on Trade and Development (UNCTAD 1) in 1964, with Prebisch as its first secretary general.[3]

The non-aligned countries' agenda dovetailed with the concerns about economic conditions in the southern countries. These Asian and African countries had formed an alliance in 1955, and more formally in 1961, to resist becoming embroiled in the East-West conflict and to focus their attention on national sovereignty and self-determination, peaceful coexistence, disarmament, the strengthening of the United Nations, and disbandment of military bases on their territories. They were also allied in their opposition to apartheid. Their concerns up to that point had been largely political, but by the early 1960s were perhaps best expressed in economic terms.

UNCTAD WAS ESTABLISHED because the GATT institutions were unable to deal with the problems of the developing countries. The entire GATT system was geared to trade between the industrial nations, and GATT did not have the authority to supercede national legislation. The industrial countries were already organized apart from the United Nations within the OECD, which provided them with statistical backup, economic analyses, and the institutional nexus for co-ordination of their trade policies. The developing countries did not benefit from the OECD, and they did not have a similar institutional backup.

During the 1960s, these countries – far more diverse in language, culture, and economic conditions than the OECD members – gradually managed to develop institutional links. The importance of organization can hardly be overstated: without it, the diverse nations had no way of identifying their common ground or resisting the collective forces of organized stronger nations. With organization they also developed an ideology which (far more trenchantly than the analyses by Prebisch) blamed the northern industrial economies for the underdevelopment of the southern hemisphere. Though the precise mechanisms of this relationship were ambiguous, being located in colonialism for some nations and in trade practices for others, the ideology had a powerful motivating capacity.

The Group of 77 – its numbers grew to 120 over the next decade – emerged from UNCTAD 1 as a loose coalition of African, Asian, and Latin American states, together with Yugoslavia. The developed countries formed a second group, and the centrally planned economies of COMECON a third. Several states, including South Africa and Cuba, were not members of these unofficial groups. UNCTAD, then, was numerically dominated by a coalition of LDCs, though over half of its budget was underwritten by the northern industrial countries.[4] Despite their majority, the Group of 77 was unable to obtain changed terms of trade through majority votes in UNCTAD or UN meetings as long as the major developed countries had veto powers; but they did develop closer ties with one another, and formed the Industrial Development Organization (UNIDO) to unite UN aid programs.

The emerging ideology may be glimpsed in the statement of the Colombian representative: "[UNCTAD] will show whether the developed countries are capable of discharging the obligations imposed on them by their wealth. It will also require them to renounce their traditional policy of passively accepting the supremacy of market forces."[5]

The UNCTAD argument was based initially on the straightforward observation that, contrary to the neoclassical arguments on comparative advantage and long-term tendencies towards equilibrium in world markets, there was in fact a continuous polarization of economies, a persistent international division of labour that benefited the core industrial countries. The inequality could be countered only through international and national action directly opposed to free trade principles.

The reforms outlined at UNCTAD 1 were rejected by the industrial countries (indeed, they thought UNCTAD was unnecessary; they argued that GATT could have handled these matters more effectively). The United States voted against five of the fifteen general principles, including the principle of equality of states, the assertion that trade and development were global concerns, and particularly the idea that every state had the right to select its own economic system and control its own natural resources.

From the perspective of the United States, the Third World was trying to exploit the developed world and trying to reduce the prosperity that had been earned through hard work. In the opinion of us representatives to the United Nations, the Third World was unwilling to expend the blood and sweat required for industrialization, and was simply trying to get it on the cheap through aid from the developed countries. The Americans were also concerned about the leadership of underdeveloped countries. In a revealing article Tom Farer noted, "Our conflict is not with huge, anonymous masses whose demands have to be aggregated through fairly uncertain representational arrangements. For the most part, Third World elites are even less committed to human equality as a general condition of humanity than we are. They are talking about greater equality between states. And in their largely authoritarian systems, the state is they."[6]

The alternative to international trade, articulated by Julius Nyerere of Tanzania and promoted by the non-aligned countries of Africa and Asia, was to concentrate on import substitution and protectionism, developing the domestic market, and achieving self-reliance. Some people, especially African nationals, saw China and Yugoslavia as models of "self-reliant" development. These models suggested at that time that opting out of the international economic system was a viable alternative.[7] To develop self-reliance meant finding a common approach to foreign direct investment and transnational corporations. At the 1970 Lusaka Summit of the non-aligned countries, the participants pledged "to ensure that external components of the developmental process further national objectives and conform to national needs; and in particular to adopt so far as practicable a common approach to problems and possibilities of investment of private capital in developing countries."[8]

This position differed from that of other underdeveloped countries whose local economies were being transformed by American, European, and Japanese capital. The argument for most underdeveloped countries at this stage still reflected the "world trade" set of assumptions, though this divergent approach influenced the way in which those assumptions were integrated into a general ideology of underdevelopment.

In the late 1960s Robert McNamara, who was just beginning his presidency of the World Bank, appointed the former Canadian prime minister Lester Pearson to head a commission on international development needs. Pearson's report received considerable support from the Group of 77, especially with respect to its argument that the rich nations had a moral duty to aid the poor. Pearson argued, and most Third World nations agreed, that the central problem was a "lack of political will" in the developed nations, which, with a public opinion campaign, might be mobilized to accept the responsibility for providing aid to the poor nations. The United Nations allocated funds to such a campaign, and LDC representatives began to clarify their analysis for consumption in the developed countries.

This strategy had two major defects. The Pearson Report, though compassionate and well-intentioned, was not sophisticated in its structural analysis of poverty. First, the expectation that matters would change if only everyone was informed about the existence of poverty was at best rather innocent. Further, even if attitudinal changes would have been enough to change the behaviour of the developed countries, the LDCs soon discovered that clarifying their analysis was virtually impossible as swiftly changing investment and aid programs altered their situations in diverse ways.

Former colonies, especially in Africa, based their analysis on the consequences of colonial exploitation, and their demands tended to reflect their belief that compensation for plunder was appropriate. Developing countries, especially in Latin America and Asia, were primarily interested in changing the terms of trade. Differential treatment by the IMF, the World Bank, governments involved in bilateral arrangements, and private banks, and the very different direct investment patterns of transnational corporations, had divided the underdeveloped world into several groups: the oil producers and a few others with highly marketable resources; the NICs and the semi-developed Latin American countries; and the former colonies, especially those in Africa. The underdeveloped world was much less unified in 1970 than it had been in 1964. If nothing had changed in their interactions with the developed countries, this impasse might not have been overcome.

AS TRADE DEFICITS grew and genuine competition between the developed countries began to undermine the Pax Americana, the United States adopted more restrictive trade and aid policies. The devaluation of the US dollar and abandonment of fixed exchange rates had an immediate impact on underdeveloped and developing countries. Their ability to purchase American-produced goods declined when their foreign currency was devalued, and trade restrictions only added to their difficulties. These events united the developing countries in a denunciation of the United States and the EEC and in a renewal of their demands for reform. There were calls for a new monetary system that would avoid the debt-crisis potential inherent in the Bretton Woods system, and for coalitions of raw material producers to improve the terms of trade.

While the international debate on these actions was taking place, OPEC finally coalesced and created the fuel crisis of 1973. This was the first time that resource-producing countries had formed a successful cartel to press their demands beyond resolutions at the United Nations. (Earlier attempts by producers of commodities such as sugar and coffee had failed). This, together with the disintegration of the Bretton Woods regime, was interpreted by many in the underdeveloped countries as the beginning of the end for the Pax Americana.

OPEC money was partly invested in the World Bank and in American and European banks, and partly given in aid to Arab allies to strengthen opposition to Israel. But substantial loans and aid grants were also made to African countries; according to World Bank data, Saudi Arabia, Kuwait, the United Arab Emirates, and Nigeria all provided aid at a considerably higher proportion of GNP than the OECD countries in the middle to late 1970s.[9] This selective aid pattern did not do much to unite the underdeveloped countries, but the model of a cartel sparked some admiration. Though the LDCs without oil were pushed into further indebtedness by the OPEC strategy, they tended to see the OPEC success as indicative of what could be accomplished using economic weapons.

At this stage the developed market economies were highly dependent on the LDCs for raw materials. According to UN statistics for 1974, 48.1 per cent of all raw materials used by the industrial nations were imported from the LDCs. Japan and the United States both imported nearly 64 per cent of their raw materials from LDCs. In the fuel, minerals, and related materials sector, the overall proportion increased to 78.5 per cent; Japan imported 87.4 per cent and the United States and Europe just short of 80 per cent from the LDCs.[10] Producers of certain materials, including bauxite, copper, rubber, coffee, cocoa, and sugar, had formed associations in hopes of copying the OPEC strategy.[11]

In reaction to the oil embargoes, the United States invited the major oil-consuming countries to a Washington conference in 1974. The Algerian president Houari Boumediène, on behalf of the non-aligned countries, responded by asking the secretary general of the United Nations to convene a special session on raw materials and development. The Sixth Special Session, convened in 1974, was the outcome.

UNDERDEVELOPED countries had shifted from subsistence farming to cash-crop production after 1950, becoming dependent on market demand in industrial countries for such goods as cocoa, sugar, coffee, bananas, rubber, vanilla, and grain crops. Once a community is organized around the production of cash crops, it is not easy to reorganize infrastructures and people to return to subsistence farming when markets decline because of increased competition or because synthetic substitutes are developed (as for rubber and vanilla).

The paradox of overproduction in some regions and hunger in others is not simply a function of hoarding or similar practices. It involves the anarchic behaviour of markets and nation-states. This is demonstrated in the agricultural policies of the United States during the 1970s. Before 1972, the United States exported less than one-fifth as much and imported twice as much food as Latin America; after that date US exports increased dramatically. In the 1970–2 period, US exports were valued at $2,950 million; in the 1973–5 period, at $28,230 million. [12]

There was a terrible famine in Africa in 1972 and 1973, and one might expect that the increase in exports from the United States was related to this situation. But that is not the case: there were increases in aid programs, but most of the exported food went to Japan, the EEC, and the USSR. A group of researchers organized as the International Federation of Institutes for Advanced Study conducted a three-year study of the African drought beginning in 1972, and concluded that it was the changed international market rather than the drought that explained the widespread famine. [13] They disagreed with United Nations, the US Academy of Sciences, the Rockefeller Foundation, and other groups which maintained that the African famine was caused by drought. The researchers noted that there had been a drought in Great Britain in 1976 from which no one died. (In 1988 there was drought on the Canadian prairies and the western plains of the United States, but no famine or deaths.) Explanations that attribute to nature a causal effect of this kind stop short of inquiring into the socio-political structures underlying such events. Equally unsatisfactory, from the researchers' perspective, were explanations that treated superficially the effect of the world commodity markets for food. As an example, they quoted the following passage from a popular account: "In the early seventies the soaring demand for food, spurred by both continuing population growth and rising affluence, has begun to outrun the productive capacity of the world's farmers and fishermen." [14]

FAO data for world production of food grains show a very slight drop in 1972 (2.2 per cent) and a long upward curve with peaks in 1971 and 1973. The increases after 1965 were so great that they far outstripped the United Nations' own estimates of what would be required to feed the world's population. The small drop in 1972 can be explained not by the vagaries of climate and weather but by the reduction in productive acreage in the United States after the surpluses of 1971. Further, explanations resting on crop failures in the USSR and its increased purchases on world markets are inadequate, as are those citing increased demand in developing countries. I will not review all the statistical data here. What emerges is the recognition that the world's supplies of grain are directly influenced not by problems of world food security, but by world prices for grains. Thus statements such as that made by the director general of the FAO in 1974 are deficient in their factual basis: "For the third consecutive year the world food and agricultural situation must be viewed with grave concern ... Although there was a substantial recovery of production in 1973, very large harvests were needed in 1974 if a beginning was to be made in returning to any reasonable degree of security in world food supplies."[15]

In the opinion of the researchers, the various crises in the American economy exerted pressure to maintain a level of food exports and prices that were counter to offering grains either as aid to developing countries or at prices they could pay. As well, the United States had been maintaining costly reserves of grains and paying subsidies to farmers, thereby keeping down food prices in their domestic market. Protectionist policies in the EEC and Japan were perceived as obstacles to exports of both agricultural and manufactured goods, and the United States began to exert pressure on those regions to liberalize trade; simultaneously, it began to develop taxation, subsidy, and export policies to increase its own share of international markets for specific agricultural products, even though these would be competitive with the exports from developing countries.

The United States developed a new agricultural exports policy in the early 1970s, following a report by the Commission on International Trade and Investment Policy. The report recommended expansion of both imports and exports of agricultural products on a more specialized basis, consistent with comparative advantage calculations. The calculations suggested the export of soybeans and feedgrains, and the import of more labour-intensive crops. US food exports constituted 22 per cent of total export earnings in 1974, when the country was striving to counteract the increased cost of oil and reduced exports of manufactured goods. The US director of the Office for Food Policy stated that higher food costs at home would increase wage and price structures throughout the economy; therefore, controls on supplies were justified, and shortages (with their resulting high prices) "were helpful in swelling our export proceeds for these commodities."[16]

For the USSR, the explanation seems to lie in its holding of US currency reserves, which lost value because of the devaluation of the American dollar; the two countries were in a period of détente which allowed them to use the grain market for their respective purposes – the United States to maintain the price of grain and reduce its reserves without loss, the USSR to maintain its exports to Comintern countries and rid itself of US dollars. There was a grain shortage that year in the USSR, but that does not account for the extent of purchases from Canada and the United States.

In short, the underdeveloped exporting regions faced a changed market structure in which their grain products were suddenly competing with products from the United States. They continued to have strong markets in labour-intensive agricultural products – dairy, vegetable, and fruit – but overall the increase in US exports and the decrease in imports created a shortfall in foreign currency holdings and a deficit in trade balances for the underdeveloped producing regions. For the drought-stricken countries with no surplus grain or other subsistence crops, adequate international aid was not forthcoming; the underdeveloped countries were unable to help, and the developed countries were preoccupied with improving their terms and shares of the grain trade.

If the developed nations had been interested in making sure that the poor countries benefited from improved agricultural methods, no one would have starved. But that was not their priority, and the frequently heard argument that the objective of science and technology is to improve the human condition is contradicted by reality. Technological advances in agriculture are directed towards improving the condition of the privileged.

The events in Africa in the 1970s were just the beginning of a global food crisis. Television audiences in the developed world were shocked to learn that Africans were dying of starvation, but information is a commodity like any other, and television sets can be turned off. Sporadic relief efforts were organized and generous aid programs were mounted, but at the same time the market continued to dominate agricultural exchanges. As the American economy spun downward, as the players of the high-tech game reinvented competition, as Japan and the EEC became industrial powers again, the United States was trying to recoup its market losses by selling raw materials and food, and the post-war international division of labour became a victim of the new economic reality.

The world food market of the 1980s was still dominated by the industrialized countries. Agricultural subsidies in the United States, Canada, and European countries maintained this system, while the governments of these countries and the international lending agencies continued to insist that underdeveloped countries engage in free trade in agricultural products. Since the industrial countries are net exporters of grains, all of which are capital-intensive crops, the underdeveloped countries strive to find their market niche in plantation crops such as coffee, tea, cocoa, sugar, cotton, and bananas. These crops are labour-intensive, and their price on world markets has steadily declined.[17]

AT THE UNITED NATIONS General Assembly in 1974, formal resolutions calling for the establishment of a new international economic order (known by its acronym, NIEO) were put forward. At this and subsequent meetings the developing countries pressed their demands for better terms of trade for primary and manufactured goods and for a reorganization of international financial and managerial institutions. Now the key terms were sovereignty, autonomy, and non-intervention. The declaration of the Sixth Special Session begins:

We, the Members of the United Nations ... solemnly proclaim our united determination to work urgently for THE ESTABLISHMENT OF A NEW INTERNATIONAL ECONOMIC ORDER based on equity, sovereign equality, interdependence, common interest and co-operation among all States, irrespective of their economic and social systems which shall correct inequalities and redress existing injustices, make it possible to eliminate the widening gap between the developed and the developing countries and ensure steadily accelerating economic and social development and peace and justice for present and future generations.[18]

More specifically, the declaration called for greater capital and technology transfers to the LDCs, the expansion of markets in the developed countries for LDC products or acceptance of LDC import-substitution programs, and changes in property rights in national industries and seabed resources. International commodity agreements, producer cartels, regional trading blocs, and a code of ethics for transnational corporations were recommended. As well, the declaration called for redistribution of voting rights in the IMF and the World Bank, for an expansion of previous agreements between the EEC and former African, Caribbean, and Pacific (ACP) colonies, and a third UN Conference on the Law of the Sea (UNCLOS 3).[19] These demands were all based on the assumption that international trade was the motive force for economic development, an assumption shared by the developed countries and contrary to the ideology of self-reliance. Indeed, the term "self-reliance" was now tied to the ideas of national sovereignty over natural resources, the right of states to nationalize properties, and protectionist trade policies in defence of employment on national territories. It was argued that all nations should have the right to determine how they should develop, and other nations should not be permitted to interfere in the internal affairs of any of their members.

Growing out of the NIEO demands, and in the context of the new energy situation, the EEC moved toward new negotiations with ACP nations. The Yaoundé Convention of 1963, renewed in 1969, was replaced by the Lomé Convention of 1974. Each of these agreements provided access to the European market for former colonies. The Lomé Convention assured ACP participants of financing in return for guaranteed access to raw materials. It provided considerably more decision-making power than earlier agreements over the uses of aid to the ACP, and the terms of assistance were modified. Most important, the agreement provided improved terms of trade on a wide range of goods, both primary and manufactured.[20] This agreement was hailed as a victory by the NIEO advocates, and taken as a model for trade relations between other LDCs and developed countries. The renegotiation of Lomé in 1978 was also hailed as a breakthrough because it reaffirmed the commitment of a rapidly changing European Community to trade, aid, and development of former colonies in Africa, the Caribbean, and the Pacific.

Another outcome of the demands of developing countries was unsuccessful. The 1977 Conference on International Economic Cooperation (CIEC) was to deal with development issues and especially with high energy prices. This was reluctantly agreed to by the United States, and participation was limited to Saudi Arabia, Algeria, Iran, and Venezuela as oil exporters; the EEC, the United States, and Japan as industrial countries; and India, Brazil, and Zaire as oil-importing LDCs. The first meeting ended in a stalemate when Algeria demanded full consideration of all commodities trade and the United States refused to consider commodities other than oil. When OPEC failed to fall apart quickly, the US attitude softened somewhat, and a second meeting between twenty-seven countries was convened. This too ended without agreement, though for a different reason: the United States successfully outmanoeuvred the LDCs by separating OPEC from the NIEO countries. A telegram from Secretary of State Henry Kissinger to the US delegation was leaked to the press: "In our view, the connection which some OPEC officials have made between CIEC and OPEC is more rhetorical than actual ... it is unlikely that OPEC countries view CIEC as a major factor in a decision on oil price increase."[21] This tactic, together with the very real decline in oil purchases by the industrial countries and development of new oil sources elsewhere, apparently worked: OPEC negotiated smaller increases than feared, and the CIEC ended with no resolution.

At the UN General Assembly's Seventh Special Session in 1975, the NIEO program was developed further. Proposals were drafted on food and agriculture, technology transfer and science policy, international monetary reforms, international trade, and the restructuring of the economic and social sectors of the United Nations system.[22]

On trade and commodities, the NIEO countries argued that close to two-thirds of the exports from non-OPEC countries were primary commodities, with food and raw materials accounting for one-half and fuels for much of the remainder.[23] In the period since the 1950s their share of world trade had declined (from 31 per cent in 1950 to 18 per cent in 1972; the figures improved only when the value of OPEC oil exports increased in 1973). Prices for raw materials had declined relative to manufactured goods (World Bank and UNCTAD data were strong evidence of this). Foreign exchange was essential to LDCs to develop their industrial, transportation, communications, and other sectors, but when they were dependent on single commodities and declining prices they could not obtain supplies of foreign currency. Their situations would improve immediately if more of the processing and fabrication of end products were located in their territories.

The transnational corporations' control over strategic raw materials (including bauxite), however, made it impossible for the NIEO countries to develop their own processing industries; the companies extracted the resource and shipped it to their manufacturing plants elsewhere. The countries were locked into trading patterns that made them dependent on single markets in one or a very few other nations. The data on this point were overwhelming. For example, "approximately 60 percent of Surinam's exports are made up of bauxite; of these 90 percent are shipped to the United States and 10 percent elsewhere. What these figures disguise is that all transactions are initiated by affiliates of Alcoa and Royal Dutch / Shell, and that most of the exports are sent to affiliates of these companies."[24]

The NIEO program argued for stabilization of commodity trade prices and export earnings, diversification of production capacities, improved market access, expansion of processing, and encouragement of research and development in the developing countries. Specific recommendations were made for buffer stocks and development of core primary products.

On debt and financial aid, the NIEO countries pointed to the failure of the international financial system to provide adequate funding for development, the desperate turning to private capital markets, and the need for relief from servicing of the accumulated debt of non-oil-producing countries. On science and technology, the NIEO countries argued that virtually all world research and development expenditures were made in northern countries, and while education levels were rising in many LDCs, a brain drain of scientists had also occurred. Again, this was associated in part with the dominance of the transnational corporations, whose research units were located in the industrial countries. The NIEO countries' recommendations concentrated on the protection of intellectual property, technology transfer mechanisms, technical co-operation, and the establishment of facilities in developing countries.

The response of the industrialized countries to this extensive program for change was lukewarm. The US representative associated his country with "the larger objectives," but then went on to say that "the United States cannot and does not accept any implication that the world is now embarked on the establishment of something called the 'new international economic order.'" He expressed reservations about the international monetary system and the decision-making in international financial institutions: "We support an evolving role for developing nations. We believe, however, that participation in decision-making in international financial institutions must be equitable for all members and take due account of relative economic positions and contributions of resources to those institutions, as well as of the need for efficient operational decision-making."[25] Much the same position was taken on industrialization: "Redeployment of industry should be a matter of the evolution of economies rather than a question of international policy or negotiation."

Earlier, however, the United States had announced some changes in the American position on agriculture. Though reforms in this sector were welcomed, the Americans made no moves to recognize the demands for trade in manufactured goods and technology transfers. By sharp contrast, Norway announced that it would introduce adjustment assistance policies for its own citizens to compensate workers whose industrial jobs were lost because of competition from LDC imports.[26] Norway recognized that LDC growth was essential to continued prosperity in Europe; the United States argued that the LDCs would benefit if US development resumed at its earlier pace.

Germany also voiced objections. Its ambassador to the United Nations (who later became the president of the Thirty-fifth General Assembly and the president of the Security Council), Baron Rudiger von Wechmar, expressed his disapproval: "We cannot create a better and more equitable international economic order by totally destroying the existing one. We shall achieve our aims only by constantly improving the existing system, notably where imbalances warrant change, and by preserving those elements that have worked well to the advantage of all and that have proved their efficiency."[27] He argued that producers' cartels in basic commodities would weaken the position of Europe and Japan and strengthen the positions of Canada, Australia, South Africa, the USSR, and the United States, all of which have raw materials, and would not be in the economic or political interests of the developing countries.

In summary, the leading industrial countries were unwilling to alter existing institutions or to deviate from free trade principles, although a few nations, especially the non-EEC Scandinavian countries, were sympathetic to the NIEO countries; overall, the NIEO agenda was rejected. The politicization of the Third World was interpreted as a shocking development by many American and European participants. The American ambassador to the United Nations spoke of "the tyranny of the majority," and referred to the NIEO program as a "steamroller."[28] The developed countries, especially the United States and the leading industrial countries of the EEC, believed that the LDCs needed strong industrialized countries to which they could sell their goods. Much of the debate of the late 1970s echoed positions taken by the Trilateralists.[29]

The analogy between the development of welfare states in the rich nations and the demand for a new economic order at the international level by poor nations was attacked by libertarian and new right writers. They argued that emphasis should be placed on poor individuals rather than on poor states, and that strengthening authoritarian regimes would not enable individuals to become prosperous or to achieve protection of their human rights.[30]

The Club of Rome's reports on the limits to growth were interjected into this history after 1976. In response to the recommendations of the third report,[31] Peru proposed that the NIEO program include a clause requiring that nations disarm and direct the funds saved by reduced military budgets to the economic development of the LDCs. As well, the Club of Rome's recommendations on the way

in which negotiations between the LDCs and the industrialized nations should take place were reiterated in the General Assembly by
the Secretariat and the NIEO representatives, especially in a debate
on the disappointing failure of the CIEC negotiations. Essentially,
the argument was that negotiations between any group of states
should be conducted within a framework earlier negotiated by all
states. Buttressing these arguments was a US government report
which predicted that the United States would become increasingly
dependent on growth elsewhere;[32] but even with this the United
States was unable to accept equality in partnership with the LDCs.

The LDCs had taken two steps forward and one step back, it
seemed, and the early 1980s, though filled with rhetoric and stim-
ulated by the report of the Brandt Commission,[33] failed to produce
any real changes in the situation, though the Lomé Convention was
regarded as a positive development for the ACP nations.

The Brandt Commission, like its predecessor the Pearson Commission, was initiated by Robert McNamara. Its task was to propose
means of reducing North-South tensions. The first report was controversial, less because it proposed large injections of developmental
aid, minimum prices for raw materials exported by LDCs, and other
ways of improving the relative position and reducing the absolute
poverty of the LDCs than because its reasoning was sloppy and open
to rational objections even by those who shared its general assumptions.[34] While none of its recommendations was adopted by
the DMCs, the report had the merit of creating a larger audience for
these international issues. It stated the South's case with occasional
eloquence: "The North-South debate is often described as if the rich
were being asked to make sacrifices in response to the demands of
the poor. We reject this view. The world is now a fragile and interlocking system, whether for its people, its ecology or its resources."[35]

By now there were numerous commission reports, independent
policy institutes, and recorded debates on the NIEO; of these, several
important ones originating in the northern industrial countries had
taken positions supportive of the NIEO. But no further progress was
made. In 1980 the Brandt Commission suggested that North-South
negotiations take place in summit meetings. To general surprise,
the new American president, Ronald Reagan, agreed to such a meeting at Cancun, Mexico. The meeting turned into a general but unsuccessful attempt to persuade British Prime Minister Margaret
Thatcher, West German Foreign Minister Hans-Dietrich Genscher,
and President Reagan to accept the Peruvian proposal for negotiations leading to a new economic order.

The NIEO had politicized the élites of the LDCs, and perhaps had expanded an awareness of the common bonds between the poor of many nations, but it had not offered a solid strategy for change. Its failure to persuade the leaders of the industrial countries to alter their basic philosophical stance was evident in the 1980s as economic conditions deteriorated, exchange rates altered relative advantages within the OECD, and the debt crisis grew ever more ominous. In May 1987 the seven leading industrial nations declared that all countries should promote the integration of their economies into the world economy. What does this mean in real terms? For those who advocate it, it means the further development of "free enterprise" markets, a seemingly paradoxical concomitant of a demand for greater control by a central world government. The proposed controls would be imposed on the LDCs, on the debtor nations, to oblige them to deregulate their economies and to oblige their governments to withdraw from industrial activity.

CRITICS OF THE NIEO were not all cast in the Trilateralist mould. Similar dismissals of the program came from the left, which argued (as had a prominent conservative economist) that this was not new, not international, not economic, and not an order.[36] To the left, however, the NIEO was a demand for equal participation in a world system that by its very nature creates poverty, disorder, inequality, and exploitation. In other words, if the NIEO was implemented there might be a slight alteration in the distribution of benefits, but the capitalist system would continue to victimize the poor. It was argued, first, that the NIEO could succeed only if the industrial world maintained its rate of expansion and consumption so that primary commodities and manufactured goods coming from the LDCs would be purchased at higher cost. Second, what was desired was nothing more than the creation in the LDCs of societies identical to those of the enemy, including a wealthy class that exploited the poor. Third, the attempt to solve the problems of hunger, poverty, habitat, energy, and resource degradation through consultation and "rational" discussion between élites was unrealistic. Ultimately, said the critics, power structures would have to be dismantled and force would be required. Fourth, the NIEO was based on a "statocratic" concept of international relations whereby the state retained primacy. States, they argued, are unequal, and the chief beneficiaries of present state systems are élites, bureaucrats, military juntas, and others whose control of state machinery allows them to exploit their own people.[37] In the critics' view, the representatives of the countries who argue for the NIEO are simply arguing for a larger slice of the capitalist pie. The increase, of which they themselves will be the chief beneficiaries, will not help their people or change the international distribution of capital based on the labour power of the poor.

Another interpretation of this history utilizes class theory in a somewhat different fashion. Among the effects of industrialization everywhere are two significant events: the growth of a middle class and an often abrupt decline in birth rates. When it is under the absolute control of international capital, subservient to the international banks, and vulnerable to the predations of transnational corporations, the middle class is suppressed. As long as there is an infinite supply of cheap labour, external capital and its extensions in the subordinate state can maintain order through military and autocratic governments. But eventually, as the supply of cheap labour begins to decline with the birth rate, and as the new middle class begins to identify itself and its interests, the state begins the process of transformation. The middle class demands its share of decision-making power and becomes the champion of democracy. (The Philippines and South Korea were examples of this process in the 1980s.) These developments push forward a new class of leaders, many of whom are attached to state enterprises and ideologically attached to the growth of states. They may adopt positions congruent with international capital's interests when they perceive these to be in the interests of their territorial states, but they may also diverge when they see them as incompatible. Their measure of what is good is their perception of what constitutes the development of their states: that is in their self-interest, just as the expansion of state programs is in the interest of the state-employed classes in the industrial countries. But their self-interest in this sense is not antithetical to the economic development of their countries or to the redistribution of income to the poor.

These new leaders have few options. They might attempt to develop their regions through autonomous policies along the lines adopted by China in the 1950s and 1960s. Ideally, this would involve co-operation with other LDCs and the development of "collective self-reliance" policies. But though this path has been discussed, it has also been discarded as unrealistic and unworkable. Small may be beautiful, but China concluded in the early 1970s that it could not support its population, even as it was finally becoming stabilized, without more extensive industrialization. Industrialization finally leads a country back into the world marketplace, seeking technology, machinery, fertilizers, capital, and markets.

Taking the view that they do not have a realistic option, these leaders instead seek some means of improving their lots within the existing order. Through political means they attempt to modify rather than genuinely transform that order. Since their starting-points differ and their internal resources and cultural and political histories diverge, no single theory of "the state" is applicable. The state within the marketplace necessarily facilitates the accumulation of capital, and in that sense the critics are correct, but the question is not whether that is the case; rather, it is how the state can direct the accumulated capital into projects most suitable for development (and not simply growth) and most capable of overcoming the poverty of citizens.

The example of Eastern European states, with their centrally managed economies, has not been inspiring. Theoretically, a state acting as the accumulator and investor has great advantages for the people, but only if its priorities are theirs, and if it does not create its own oppressive class structure. History (as opposed to theory) suggests that a monopolistic state does indeed create its own classes, and that the state bureaucrats became as oppressive in their own way as the transnational corporate management class. As well, and perhaps most problematic, there is apparently a distinct limit to the economic development possible within the framework. The growing participation of the Eastern European countries in the world marketplace, and even more, the penetration of their territories by the transnational corporation of the Western countries, suggests that the limit was reached and that the need for external funds and organization dictated a change in policy.

Apart from this analysis, for those whose ideological bent coincides with that of the left-wing critics, there is the problem that those critics offer no programmatic alternatives. If the state is an absolute evil, and the marketplace Beelzebub incarnate, how does a poverty-stricken country, already unevenly pulled into the world economy, proceed? If it nationalizes foreign properties, turns everything over to popular control, and hopes that somehow a technically unskilled population will produce its own subsistence, it will quickly run into two barriers: first, organized interest groups within the population itself may rebel (the truckers' strike in Chile is a tragic model); second, international capital, backed by the very states that most unctuously demand non-intervention from their clients, will impose economic sanctions (again, consider Chile, where in 1974 the CIA, the copper companies, and other transnational corporations and state agencies imposed food boycotts and market controls on copper exports). For these countries export-driven policies may be an unfortunate compromise, but when survival of so many is at stake, compromises are generally preferable to revolutions.

For the underdeveloped countries entering the world system as new nations in the 1960s and 1970s, the alternatives were limited;

they tried to carve out a course between extremes, a course that modified but did not transform the market economy, that used the state as an instrument of reform but not as an instrument of repression. As we have seen in previous chapters, their attempts in this direction were persistently frustrated by the states most strongly attached to the free market ideology, and by policies that persistently favoured authoritarian states. The American obsession with freedom bred repression.

CHAPTER TWELVE

The Environmental Dimension

"All these factories, they give us life, but they kill us at the same time," said a Brazilian mother in Cubatão.[1] In her town, one of the most polluted on earth, half the inhabitants are thought to suffer from respiratory diseases. In 1985 the state-owned Petroleo Brasileiro refinery had an accident that killed about six hundred inhabitants of a slum neighbourhood. The Brazilian companies are reported to be the worst offenders in air and water pollution; American companies such as Monsanto and Union Carbide are more conscious of environmental impacts, especially after the Bhopal tragedy in India. In the end, it does not matter which of the two dozen or so multinational and local companies clustered in a narrow valley between São Paulo and the port of Santos is most to blame; the environment has become a cesspool.

The mother's dilemma is the subject of this chapter. It is a dilemma shared by the rest of the world's population, though its immediate effects are much grimmer in the underdeveloped countries than in the developed ones. And it is a problem that puts the free market theory to its most severe test.

THE BOTTOM LINE of the free market argument is the preservation and unlimited expansion of private property rights. The "tragedy of the commons" analysis advanced by Garrett Hardin is frequently used by others to sustain those rights.[2] Hardin argued that common property was anything to which no one had a claim, that no one could be denied access and use, and that common property was therefore unprotected. He refered to the English commons, which was part of the demesne land of a manor and was used for roads and common pasture. He claimed that the commons was overgrazed and abused because each farmer calculated only his own benefits in adding grazing stock. By extension, he argued, our population problems were caused by each couple's increasing its family size solely with reference to its own needs and without respect for the earth's carrying capacities. The solution, in his view, was the extension of private rights.

One might note in passing that Hardin's argument is historically false. The commons was not overgrazed by tenant farmers who used it as community property; it was exhausted only when it was brought under private ownership by the yeomanry and landed classes to graze sheep for the wool trade. The tragedy of the commons was not the abuse of land, but the abuse of the peasants who depended on the land for their livelihood. [3]

Before the enclosures, the commons involved group management of pasturage. The same pattern of communal responsibility has been found throughout the world among herding and hunting groups. There is no evidence that such groups typically mismanaged their lands or their fishing territories. The problem of mismanagement does not arise until there are dense populations, resources are treated as commodities rather than subsistence foods, and private property rights push aside community rights.

Property is a social relationship stipulating the rights of some against the rights of others. It does not exist in a social vacuum; things are not property unless they are socially so designated. [4] There is no such thing as non-exclusionary common property. What Hardin might have addressed, and apparently meant to address when he ventured into unfamiliar history and sociological territory, was the problem of a global ecosystem in which no identified managers are charged with caretaking responsibility. He ended up defending private property as the only solution, but private property rights have inhibited rather than advanced solutions to such problems as drought, famine, and air and water pollution.

Missing in his defence, as in so many others from the industrial world, is the concept of the commons as a positive set of rights and responsibilities. In a global economy measured by growth in GNP, where the major consuming nation is locked in a battle to stay in first place against a competitor, the rights of others, of those who have little on no property, have no status. The history of privatization, first from the commons and then from the state, is a history of brutality against the poor and against the planet itself.

The underdeveloped countries are caught in an impossible dilemma. Pulled into the world accumulation vortex by choice or by force, they cannot escape by running backwards. Populations have been pushed from the land and pulled into cities, and must be fed through industrial production combined with commercial agriculture. Foreign currencies are needed to purchase machinery for industrialization, and foreign companies bring the currencies, establishing factories that employ the workers and at the same time extract local resources and impose their own demands on ecological systems. The countries are much too weak and much too dependent on the companies to enforce pollution controls. They are further constrained by the IMF, the World Bank, private banks, and other international agencies which demand free market conditions that are not consistent with governmental regulation of industrial production.

Large population densities in cities combined with large production organizations inevitably pollute water, air, and land. In São Paulo, for example, the daily emission of pollutants is estimated as "500 tons of particle materials (70 per cent from industry), 900 tons of sulphur dioxide (90 per cent from fuel combustion), 5000 tons of carbon monoxide (90 per cent from motor vehicles), and 1200 tons of hydrocarbons and hydrogen dioxide (mostly from motor vehicles)."[5] Pesticides, energetically promoted by transnational chemical corporations and widely used in the developing countries, are toxic and frequently lethal. World Health Organization data document the lethal effects of pesticide use, including cancer, infertility, genetic defects, and absorption of poisons in the maternal placenta and more generally in the ecosystem itself. Products prohibited in the home countries of chemical firms continue to be manufactured there, resulting in such sad ironies as US import restrictions on chemically treated agricultural products coming from Mexico and South America. As Jacobo Schatan noted, "The moral of this story is quite clear: the profits of pesticides can enter the US but not their noxious effects; these must be totally absorbed by the people living in the South!"[6]

Pollution from industrial production in the developing countries is accompanied by environmental damage and resource depletion. Mining was the earliest resource industry to move abroad from Europe, first under the aegis of Spain in South America. Extraction of gold and other minerals transformed agricultural people into slaves and destroyed nearby forests for fuel. Water and soil were polluted in the process, and soil erosion followed deforestation.

Industries from the developed countries have moved their extractive operations elsewhere, both because they have exhausted the supplies in their home countries and because they wish to conserve domestic supplies. The forest industry is an example of the first process. As the softwood forests of the northern countries were depleted by overcutting and acid rain, companies invested in research on new species and transformation technologies. By the late 1970s species that had previously had limited commercial use, especially eucalyptus but also many hardwoods and new pine species, could be transformed into high-grade pulp. The companies began investing in new mills and plantations in southern climates. The oil industry is an example of the second process. In fact, it was American government policy to conserve domestic supplies while extracting oil elsewhere.

The commercialization of agriculture further eroded soil and contaminated water. The cash crops introduced by the large coffee and sugar companies in the late nineteenth and early twentieth centuries devastated lands in Central and South America. More recently, the "green revolution" has introduced new seed varieties, disease controls, chemical fertilizers, pesticides, irrigation, and intensive cultivation to agricultural countries. Food production has increased (there is an annual growth rate of 2.7 per cent in cereals, for example), but at an enormous environmental cost – overuse of chemical fertilizers and pesticides, nitrate pollution of aquifers, and soil erosion from overcultivation. At the same time, less land is available for production. The United Nations Environment Programme has estimated that over the next two decades some 600 million hectares of agricultural land will be eroded or pulled into urban use; this is nearly half of all agricultural land that was under cultivation in 1975.[7]

Industrialization and the commercialization of agriculture in underdeveloped countries were undertaken in the expectation that they would provide the basis for economic growth. Economic growth is supposed to lead to an improved quality of life. That was the promise of science and of proponents of the free market. Yet the result does not match the promises. In much of the world poverty has increased both absolutely and in relative terms, and both famine and insufficient food supplies are endemic in many countries. The world produces more food today than at any previous time, and the production levels have outpaced population growth. Yet some 730 million people are malnourished.[8] In a study of world agriculture, John W. Warnock noted, "In 1985 world grain reserve stocks were at a peak of 190 million metric tonnes. Total world grain production in the 1983–84 crop year was estimated at 1,612 million metric tonnes. That alone was more than enough to provide every man, woman, and child in the world with 3,000 calories and 65 grams of protein per day."[9] Yet in that year famine was widespread, and there were food riots in urban centres in Brazil, Chile, and other NICs, as well as throughout rural Africa and Asia.

OVERPOPULATION IS frequently seen by the rich populations as the cause of underdevelopment and poverty. Rural societies everywhere have higher fertility rates than urban industrial societies. Overpopulation afflicts the underdeveloped countries today, just as it did the European countries of an earlier age. Europe solved its population pressures by exporting surplus people to colonies in the new world. Indonesia has tried a similar solution through its "transmigration" project, the movement of urban families from overcrowded Java to rural regions of the less inhabited islands. Brazil has tried moving poor people to the Amazon region, where they are expected to farm land formerly occupied by the tropical rain forest. The transmigration project has had some success, at least in areas where the new land can support agriculture and agribusiness. The Amazon settlements have merely spawned terrible poverty.

Most countries have no place to send their poor. Their numbers grow, and betterment for the many becomes less possible as the many increase. Overpopulation, then, is a problem, but by itself it is not a satisfactory explanation of underdevelopment or poverty; nor are high birth rates in themselves an explanation of population pressures. More significant are declining mortality rates, especially in children. The poor have as many children as they have always had, but many more survive to adulthood.[10] The Pax Americana brought numerous and contradictory changes to the LDCs; an emphasis on cash crops and an erosion of subsistence cultures, but also malaria control, vaccinations, improved public sanitation, and medical aid programs. More people survived; but since the benefits of the developed world were not otherwise dispersed, more survived in poverty.

Those who express Malthusian concerns about population growth frequently ignore the socio-cultural dynamics of fertility. We have observed over the last century a steady decline in birth rates wherever human communities enjoy adequate food supplies and reasonable physical security. In particular, there is a relationship between urbanization and declining birth rates. Since the late 1950s – a single generation – the birth rate in Quebec has gone from the highest in North America to the lowest. The same trend has occurred in Singapore. Both societies are alarmed at this development, as are European and North American societies generally. They are no longer reproducing themselves through natural increase, and governments are now offering incentives to family growth in the form of "baby bonuses" and tax relief. The phenomenon is not genetic and is not peculiar to any one religious or cultural population: immigrants to these societies demonstrate the same decline in family size within a generation, regardless of their place of birth or heritage. It seems self-evident that the higher birth rates in impoverished countries must be related to poverty itself, and specifically to rural poverty.

Poverty breeds hopelessness. Apart from raising children, there is little one can do; there is no future to plan for. The future can only be worse without children who might earn wages or work in the fields and eventually care for their elderly parents. Moreover, the patriarchy is strongest in poor countries, and wherever women are treated as property they have no or limited control over their own fertility. Concomitant with the patriarchy are status systems that provide greater security for men, and thus for families with male children.

It seems to follow from these observations that the two best solutions to overpopulation are substantial increases in wealth in poor countries and economic independence for women. The latter solution would reduce fertility very rapidly, both because women would have options and because the advantages of having more male offspring would disappear. In urban industrial areas, the advantages of having many children decline with the opportunities available to prospective parents.

Urbanization, however, brings with it severe environmental degradation. Some countries have tackled this problem through government policies that provide special benefits to rural populations. Indonesia has attempted to redistribute its urban poor to rural areas, giving them land and other benefits and simultaneously providing information, encouragement, and incentives to engage in family planning (However, the transmigration project has serious adverse effects on tropical forest lands.) The better-known experiment is the Chinese "one child per family" plan.

The Chinese approach has been to redistribute wealth to rural areas rather than to import the poor to cities. Land reclamation, health care, controlled internal migration, and priority support for rural populations in China have been accompanied by raising the legal marriage age, distributing contraception information, and making abortion easily available. Because of the ancient preference for male children and the continuation of a patriarchal culture that could not be destroyed through government dicta, a massive advertising campaign has been mounted by the Chinese government. Billboards show the happy family as two healthy parents and one female child. Severe legal penalties are imposed on those who kill or abandon female children – a legacy of patriarchy that is found in many underdeveloped countries, but which has become more marked with the one-child policy in China.[11] For conforming parents there are tremendous benefits in accommodation, employment, and general prosperity; for most Chinese, the threat of social ostracism alone is a sufficient deterrent.

The Chinese government claims that its policies are working, and that birth rates have declined (statistics are not readily available, and the one-child policy is too new to measure accurately in any case). We do not need statistics, however, to see the effects of health care in China: children and adults who live in towns and rural regions throughout that enormous country are very obviously in better health than the vast majority of people in the underdeveloped (and many of the developed) countries. None the less, even with one-child policies, population pressures are exceeding any government's capacity to solve China's problems – or those of the other developing countries.

It is paradoxical that DMCs deplore their declining population while LDCs have the reverse problem. Canada and Australia complain that they lack domestic market power because of their low population density, while China, India, and Brazil have gigantic markets but lack the capital to develop them. One might venture to suggest the obvious: that DMC immigration policies are part of the problem in both regions. The freedom of capital to move has not been accompanied by a similar freedom for labour.

Labour has been a controlled commodity, permitted to move only in response to identified shortages in richer regions. With declining birth rates in the DMCs, there may be, as there has been in the past, controlled importation of labour from the LDCs, but the new technologies decrease the demand for unskilled workers. So far, in the remaining sectors that use such labour, the solution for capital has been to locate in the LDCs. European industrial centres will solve their labour shortages through internal expansion of the political unit, and American industrial centres through illegal migration from Central America. The vast numbers of poor and unskilled people in the rest of the world will remain where they are.

IT IS THE SMALL populations of developed countries, not the large ones of the poor areas, who consume the world's resources and pollute its atmosphere and its water. The United States, with 6 per cent of the world's population, consumes about 50 per cent of all raw materials, and spews forth acid rain and carbon monoxide in great quantity. Japan, wealthy beyond most of the world's imagination, is mired in air pollution. The industrial strip running from

Aoyama, near the top of Honshu Island, as far south as Hiroshima is daily blanketed in smog.

Acid rain and contaminated water supplies have become major problems throughout the world. Air pollution and the possible destruction of the ozone layer have finally convinced industrial populations that their environment is truly threatened, and that they are on a suicidal course if they continue to produce and consume at their present rates. Yet we still measure the goodness of a society by its annual increase in GNP.

In the most northerly regions of North America, the marginalized "Fourth World" peoples are ill adapted to the industrial society. The same is true for the Dayak of Indonesia, and for countless other indigenous peoples throughout the world. The most significant aspect of their "failure" is their continued interaction with nature on the basis of a different cultural understanding. Their traditional culture does not assign greater importance to humans than to the rest of nature; the notion of humankind's conquering nature does not make sense. In his report on the proposed oil and gas pipelines from Alaska and northern Canada, Justice Thomas Berger observed, "The decisions we have to make are not ... simply about northern pipelines. They are decisions about the protection of the northern environment and the future of northern peoples."[12] By stark contrast, industrial societies regard nature as a commodity to be consumed and an external antagonist to be conquered.

There is no absolute limit to consumption.[13] There are always more commodities that we might be persuaded to want, and each innovation spins off additional demands. A massive advertising industry is devoted to persuading people that they must have more. And as the consumption pattern increases, sustaining this affluent lifestyle becomes more and more dependent on the exploitation of resources and the control of exchange values in the world marketplace. The few satisfy their wants at the cost of survival for others.

This process will not end until nature's ability to regenerate itself is finally exhausted, but nothing in the ideology of industrialism and its contemporary expression in the free market ideology permits us to anticipate such an outcome: nature, after all, is not our loving mother; it is merely a passive context for industrial expansion.

The acid rain produced in northeastern North America and in western Europe destroys lakes, air, forests, and soils throughout the northern hemisphere; the destruction of tropical forests depletes the entire earth's oxygen supplies. Pollution of water anywhere eventually affects the earth's water supplies everywhere. The poisoning of land or water sets up a grim cycle of toxicity throughout the whole world. In 1972 the Club of Rome published its first report, which dramatically announced that if consumption and growth patterns continued to increase at their present rate, within a century the earth's resources would be exhausted; food and energy would become so scarce that much of the world's population would not survive.[14] The oil crisis occurred on the heels of this publication. The projections, calculations, factual basis, and general arguments of that report and of a second issued in 1974[15] were strongly contested in the following years. Businesses argued that growth was essential; the left was equally blind, treating environmentalism as liberal nonsense. And as Warnock observed, "The group venting the most outrage were the orthodox economists. Their critiques of *The Limits to Growth* bordered on hysteria."[16]

In the mid-1970s the chief outcome of the reports (entirely at odds with their intentions) was policies aimed at ensuring that the nations best placed to do so would limit the impacts of scarcity on themselves. All primary commodities began to rise in value. Taking advantage of this trend, underdeveloped countries began to coalesce in producers' cartels or under trade agreements that would improve their collective bargaining power in the sale of primary commodities; but since their basic commodities were controlled by external capital, they had little success, apart from the OPEC rebellion. The industrialized countries began to restructure energy-intensive industries or move them offshore, and to examine and secure their sources of other essential resources.

Alternatives have been explored: most of these are centred on zero, steady-state, or sustainable growth. The idea of the "conserver society" has been advanced. The Club of Rome's first report addressed these ideas, and they had been discussed earlier at some length by a group of African and Asian countries which sought a self-reliant rather than a world-integrated mode of development. As well, before the Club of Rome reports, a few economists and scientists had broken with the conventional wisdom that growth was good for its own sake. On agriculture, Eugene P. Odum argued that attempting to increase the yield of agricultural crops involved increases in energy subsidies that would deplete the earth in another way.[17] Many other experts have demonstrated that monoculture cash crops require fossil fuel subsidies and increase the genetic vulnerability of seeds and soil. Scientists contributed to this literature in cautious documents linking drought, desertification, acid rain, and the greenhouse effect to the mindless extraction and processing of resources.

The overdeveloped industrial countries have studiously avoided or repudiated at every turn an obvious solution: to reduce consumption on every front. If consumption were reduced by 50 per cent in these countries, the population would still be infinitely wealthier than most of the rest of the world. If, for example, North Americans cut their energy consumption in half, they would still consume four times more fuel than most other countries. Apart from resisting on straight self-interest grounds, opponents of reduction point out that the rest of the world depends on selling its fuel, food, and other resources to the rich countries. If the developed countries suddenly – in a remarkable exercise of rational judgment – stopped purchasing so much, the surplus would not automatically feed the poor elsewhere. Much of what we consume is not subsistence food (one cannot survive on coffee), and urban populations need cash to buy food. This dilemma arises because it is assumed that the only possible way of organizing the global economy is on the basis of self-interest or, at most, national interest, as expressed through a free market. The alternatives have yet to be explored.

THE EARTH IS VALUED in free market theory only for the commodities it produces. The extreme new right version of the theory argues that if environmental (or community, aesthetic, or any other unprofitable) values matter, people should be prepared to pay for them. The measure of how much they want to uphold them is how much they are willing to pay (i.e., what they are willing to forgo). The mechanism for expressing such preferences should be voluntary combinations of individuals. If some individuals want to uphold those values but others do not, the measure is the break-off point at which those espousing one set of values are prepared to be bought out by the others. For example, fishers who want unpoisoned fish should bargain with pulp mills and mines so that they either buy out or are bought out by them. This example illustrates the numerous flaws in the theory. First, fishers have few resources relative to pulp mills, and could never win such a contest. Second, even if they received compensation for their loss of livelihood, fishers cannot be compensated for the loss of a way of life they prefer. Third, many individuals who have stakes in the outcome are not included, and for sheer physical reasons could not be included, in the bargaining. Consumers of fish and recreational users of the lakes and oceans are among these; so are the cities that depend on clean water supplies. Even if all of these individuals were somehow brought together and were fully informed of the options and the probable effects of making a choice, how could the votes be counted? Majority rule is not acceptable in the theory because it necessarily involves the involuntary submission of the minority. As Kenneth Arrow argued, there are no logically possible ways of solving common problems through individual preferences alone in a non-dictatorial voting system.[18]

The issue goes beyond individual preferences. A preference for profits over human health or the safekeeping of the earth is not in the same category as a preference for strawberries over raspberries. Preferences that preclude the possibility of others ever expressing their own preferences are not dealt with by free market theory. Yet they occur all the time, and the dilemma of the mother in Cubatão is one of their manifestations. How would she express her preferences? Indeed, how would she be able even to form preferences? She could choose to starve herself and her children rather than live where she can find employment. She could not choose to have a clean environment in the valley, because there is no way that she, alone or in free and voluntary combination with others, could buy out the polluting industries. She is effectively deprived of her individual right to choose a healthy environment.

The free market enthusiast might answer that this situation occurs because the government of Brazil has interfered in the marketplace by providing subsidies and infrastructure to both Brazilian and foreign companies. In a sense this is true, but it is equally true that the government has few options. The companies that so strongly urge governments to obey free market principles also demand incentives to create employment for local workers. Among those incentives are lax rules against pollution, and a cheap, immobile labour force.

Some who espouse environmental causes have accepted the ground rules of a free market economy. They have turned the health of the environment into a marketable product. They advertise, solicit subscriptions to mount legal and public relations battles, and try to sell human safety and survival. They have had some success at this. "If the market for biodegradable plastic takes off, we will also make the stuff," says a spokesman for Mobil. "We have to stay in business."[19] At the moment, however, chemical companies still contribute to advertising campaigns against environmentalists.

The campaign and the response are occasioned by modest government controls in the United States and Europe on plastic packaging, disposable diapers, and plastic grocery bags. The chemical companies have recognized the trend, and while it does not immediately threaten their bank accounts, they can see that it may be the beginning of a changed consumer environment. One Dow

Chemical company manager noted, "If we don't solve the solid-waste problem, it will hurt our bottom line. We're going to suffer as an industry."[20] Another industry participant observed that "legislation will ultimately make [product safety] a big business."[21]

Current responses to the problem of solid wastes in plastics are not yet solutions. Decaying plastics, for example, create chemicals that may contaminate groundwater, and some give off gases such as methane, which may be flammable in large concentrations. There are other concerns about toxicity. The problems might be solvable, but the main impediments to a solution at this stage are the cost of production – which includes the cost of retooling factories – and the cost of new advertising messages. The chemical industry has built up consumer desires for strong plastics; a move to biodegradables would require reindoctrination, which is expensive. In fact, Dow Chemicals developed a photodegradable plastic some years ago. However this might endanger the market for conventional plastic. Dow says it will sell the plastic only for use in connector rings (which hold together six-packs of beer) so that birds will not strangle – a development brought about by pressure from environmentalists and wildlife specialists. But even Dow admits that it is obliged to invest in alternatives now that environmentalism is a more popular cause.

Like any other commodity, environmentalism has to be sold. And it has to be sold in a marketplace where the sellers are unequal, where groups funded by individual contributions are pitted against such enormous corporations as Mobil and Dow. Every product has to be scrutinized separately, and scientific evidence has to be provided to prove beyond doubt that there are dangers to human beings in items that create employment and profits. The argument that nature should be preserved does not carry much weight in a free market understanding of the world.

LET US CONSIDER an example in which the victims are not poor. In our study of Japan we encountered the rural forestry towns of the Kyoto Prefecture. In the past, the private forest owners, none of whom owned huge tracts of land, co-operated to thin, nurture, selectively cut, and replant trees. As Japan became a major industrial power, it was obliged to open its markets for trees as well as for other goods. The free market works well for Japan's pulp and construction industries, which can now import logs from Canada and the United States more cheaply than the private forest owners of Japan can produce them. The local owners cannot reduce their prices unless they reduce the wages of the workers (already below wages paid to comparable workers in industry), reduce their silvicultural treatments (thereby diminishing the quality of the trees and the beauty of the forest), and either clear-cut trees or stop replanting them. None of these options is desirable; also not desirable is depopulation and the gradual erosion of subsistence opportunities in rural towns. At the same time, millworkers in Canada and the United States are angered by the export of logs to Japan, which deprives them of processing and finishing work.

North American logs are cheaper for several reasons. First, the forests in the exporting countries are clear-cut; the forests are less intensively managed than in Japan and thus the costs of production are lower. Second, Japan's industrial growth has raised the average wage levels above those of the exporting countries. Third, the exporting regions (British Columbia and the northwestern United States in particular) produce very few value-added wood products; with Japan's high demand for logs and low demand for lumber, they can sell the raw material at a better price than dimensional lumber.[22]

The "green gold" of fir, red cedar, balsam, hemlock, pine, and spruce has enriched generations of loggers in the Pacific Northwest.[23] The softwood forest is now so depleted that companies log lodgepole pines, once regarded as trash, and the pulp mills are looking to the boreal aspen forests for new fibre supplies. The managers of these mills continue to repeat their catechism: nature would burn up the forest in a century or two anyway. Indeed it would; it would also replant the forest in its own time and in ways best suited to sustain wildlife. But the catechism is most interesting for what it omits: the tree left standing would live for at least a century; the tree felled and pulped will be turned into a newspaper or, at best, a frame house that will stand for a few decades. The living tree nurtures fauna and flora that cannot survive without it.

All of this demonstrates the operation of a free market. Without government interference in either the exporting or the importing countries, we can expect that the rural communities of Japan will continue to decline and that the trees of North America will continue to be shipped out as long as they last. According to free market theory, this is the most beneficial result for all parties. The problem is that it is not beneficial if the measurement of benefit is anything other than money. Since the theory has no other measure, such values as healthy forests and flourishing communities are lost. One might answer that Japan chose to be an industrial power, and that wealth was worth more to its people than trees and communities. That may be a fair assessment for the industrial cities; but, as is typically the case in these trade-offs, those who pay the price are not those who benefit from the trade.

The genetic engineering is partly related to forest depletion in the northern temperate climates. In North America settlement, industry and overcutting have reduced the stock of accessible timber. However, the more crucial variable is the length of time required to grow temperate-climate forests; a century compared to three to ten years for the eucalyptus or eighteen to thirty years for pines. Even where replanting is extensive, as in Sweden, the crop cannot be harvested for a long time. Forest companies invested in bio-technicological research, and the characteristics of the new species are matched to new pulping technologies. Some of the plantations displace tropical forests; others are located on marginal land often land already deforested by ranching or other activities.

One might think that these events would bring prosperity to underdeveloped regions, but for two caveats: much of the plantation forestry is dominated by external companies or by consortiums of their buyers; and where tropical forests have been destroyed, they are irreplaceable. Clear-cutting changes the local ecology so dramatically that no new tropical forest can be planted. The plantations, while profitable in the short run, do not provide environmental protection to native populations (who, in the main, have been pushed off the land and forcibly resettled far from their natural habitats), to wildlife, or to the planet, which depends on the oxygen generated by tropical forests.

To be fair to plantation forestry, it may be less damaging than other activities that have destroyed tropical areas, including settlement, ranching, earlier plantation crops, mining, hydro-electric installations, road-building, and railways. Forty per cent of Southeast Asia's tropical forest has disappeared since 1950.

In Indonesia and Malaysia, transmigration and logging are displacing the tribal hill peoples. The Penan of Sarawak have attempted to prevent further logging on their traditional hunting and agricultural land, but without success. They, like the Dayak of Indonesia, have been forced to relocate in makeshift camps. FAO statistics suggest that Malaysia could lose all of its forests by the turn of the century.[25] Plantations do not provide a forest cover for people who hunt and practice swidden agriculture. World Bank, FAO, and other subsidized plans for afforestation are intended to create plantation forestry, not to protect the subsistence of the indigenous forest-dwellers.

In Thailand, the indigenous tribes who practice shifting cultivation are being blamed for the massive deforestation of watershed regions. Shifting cultivation, when too intensively practised by large groups, causes soil erosion and sedimentation of downstream rivers. Watershed areas cannot adequately absorb rainfall and release it gradually. There is no doubt that the (paradoxically) increasing populations of tribespeople have caused substantial soil erosion, but they are not solely responsible for the reduction in tropical cover from 53 per cent of the total land area in 1961 to 29 per cent in 1985. Thailand's economy was much enriched by the export of logs in the early 1980s. Over six hundred companies had logging concessions covering a vast area.[26] Reforestation was much discussed but seldom practised, and many watershed areas were abandoned after being clear-cut. After many deaths from massive flooding, logging was banned in February 1989. However, Thai logging companies immediately obtained concessions in Burma, where the whole process is being re-enacted.[27]

THE CHINESE METHOD of reducing population pressures raises the problem of private freedom. It would be absurd to call China a free country, and the argument that curtailment of private freedoms is always in the public interest is of dubious validity. When any one group – especially an aging oligarchy – defines the public interest without reference to the public itself, the result can be (and was, in China in 1989) a means of sustaining the power of that group. We see a parallel in Iran's theocracy, or Argentina's junta after Peron, or the USSR under Stalin to Brezhnev.

Yet the dilemma cannot be solved by turning over everything to private interests and market forces. The tragedy of the commons is precisely that there is no commons left, nothing sacrosanct that belongs to all and is managed in the public interest. We have not devised mechanisms to translate the public interest into policies. Voluntary mechanisms are insufficient when the participants are unequal in power and wealth. They are logically impossible when the potential effects of private decisions have a global impact. They are socially impossible when the potential participants are not all members of the same community and engaged in face-to-face interaction or at least obliged to share the consequences of a decision.

The logical and social problems of the free market are combined with the paradoxical effect of highly selective government interference. As was noted in earlier chapters, the food and agricultural trade crises have been exacerbated by government policies in the industrial countries. The industrial countries subsidize their farmers, encouraging the production of surplus which is then given as aid or sold on international markets. While food riots occur elsewhere, the American, Canadian, and EEC governments debate how best to reduce their grain surpluses, even paying farmers not to produce because the market prices are too low.

The United Nations World Commission on Environment and Development (the Brundtland Commission) argued in favour of an end to subsidies (or further subsidies to stop production) in industrial countries: subsidies "depress international prices of products, such as rice and sugar, [which] are important exports for many developing countries and so reduce exchange earnings of developing countries. They increase the instability of world prices. And they discourage the processing of agricultural commodities in the producing countries."[28] The commission suggested that the solutions would involve radical changes in the terms of trade to favour farmers in the developing regions through pricing policies and government expenditure reallocations, land allocation policies, and global co-ordination of policies on forests, watersheds, and the ecosystem.

These are far-reaching reforms; others might involve differential pricing for food products in the industrial and developing countries. Among the effects of higher food costs in the industrial countries would be a reduction in expenditures on non-essential items, so resistance to such global policies would be mounted by many groups besides farmers. Similarly, higher oil prices would reduce the advantages of petroleum-based fertilizers and increase the cost of food production in the industrial countries.

Food costs would also rise if farm labour and family farm owners were paid rates consistent with wages for industrial workers and corporate managers or self-employed professionals in the industrial countries. Ironically, much of the production of surplus food is done by unpaid family labour or migrant labourers working for subsistence wages. This cannot be attributed to government intervention, because the agricultural sector in most industrial countries is exempt from minimum wage laws.

Government intervention, as this suggests, is highly selective. The policies that interfered with free market processes in agricultural trade intensified the problems of underdeveloped countries. But from that one cannot deduce that the free market, left alone, would have adequately fed and maintained those populations. When the governments of rich countries are concerned with the welfare of only a part of their own populations, and when a problem affects the entire world, government actions complicate an already tragic situation but do not cause it. To address the problem, a level of supranational government participation is necessary. Further, this supranational government would have to be given the exclusive right to impose conditions and sanctions on all countries, thus infringing not only on private property rights but on sovereign national rights.

History shows us that nation-states were established in part for the purpose of creating a central power capable of imposing common rules on contesting economic powers. That was in the interests of the private property owners themselves. No free market could have survived without those rules and those governments. Now we have problems that cannot be solved by the same type of territorial organization, and we must move towards larger units. Initially, such units are carved out by existing property holders to enhance their market opportunities and expand their accumulation base. But when further expansion becomes impossible because the planet's resources are reaching the point of exhaustion, the expanded governments may limit our appetites by imposing new rules on us all.

Such global government is probably essential to the solution to many global problems. However, some problems will never be solved by larger territorial units. Throughout the history of capitalism and nation-building we have seen small communities die and regional populations disperse. Industrialism is an urban phenomenon that tends to destroy all other forms of life. The values that small communities espouse are not consistent with free markets; if such communities are to be retained, the global society must alter its values very substantially.

If the earth's survival is no more than another commodity dependent on the advertising funds available for its sale to consumers who might prefer strong garbage bags, the earth may well be inherited by the meek – that is, by whatever insects can survive inside plastic bags. Willy Brandt called it established disorder; I call it the integrated circus. Either way, the problems of the restructured world economy cannot be solved by gung-ho free enterprise and free markets.

CHAPTER THIRTEEN

Conclusion

So no, not the millennium. Not yet. Just a unique
moment in history when, in order to be a realist, it is
necessary also to be an idealist; when the improbable
is happening every day, and the impossible every
week; and where human imagination, and human
creativity, unleashed in time, may yet sweep us
above the slough of hopelessness to which we have
been condemned too long.

John Le Carré, quoted in the *Globe and Mail*,
29 September 1989

The world is undergoing several revolutions at the same time. The technological revolution initiated by the development of the silicon chip is one dimension; the agricultural revolution with its mixed results in underdeveloped countries is another; the astonishing conclusion of the cold war and the beginning of East-West co-operation is a third. As we move towards another century, we are beginning to understand that the earth is fragile, and that what we do in one region has impacts on all other regions. Perhaps that is the most fundamental change in our time – a change that takes place in our hearts and minds and obliges us to reassess our basic values.

The new right, however, was not a response to environmental crises, and it emerged before the dissolution of the Russian empire. It was a response to the decline of American hegemony, to the rise of Japan and a united Europe, to the technological changes that were taking place in the 1960s and 1970s, and to the mobility of capital. It provided the ideological basis for a massive restructuring of industry and labour in all countries, and it provided the rationale for the dismantling of the Keynesian welfare state in the industrial countries. Although its impact remains strong in the 1990s, world events have outstripped this response, and populations everywhere have mounted opposition to applications of laissez-faire economic principles. Before we move beyond the history of the new right, let us briefly review the events of its era.

THE TRANSISTOR TECHNOLOGY the late 1940s led to the integrated circuit technology of the 1960s, which would render obsolete much mass-production, steel-age industry. By the mid-1970s, with American power in decline for other reasons, this new technology was providing the foundation for wholly new political and economic alliances. Like other technological developments, but now on a vast and sweeping scale, the technology was initiated because its original backers – in this case the American military, the American government, private corporations, and privately employed scientists – anticipated benefits. Not for the first time in history, the technology turned out to be bigger than its inventors, and they lost their position of leadership as it grew.

American economic power had become linked to the growth of transnational corporations, enormous organizations that straddled the globe, shifting production and assembling operations as short-term profits dictated, exploiting communities and labour at home, creating new (but temporary) industrial capacity elsewhere, playing the financial markets along with the investors who gave them so little loyalty. The corporations adapted the new technologies to their communications systems, the better to move capital efficiently and develop a service industry; but they failed to advance the industries that actually produced the goods to be serviced. The established corporations did not invest enough money in research and development, new plants, or the retraining of the domestic labour force. Their offshore production policies created a new labour force and a new international division of labour.

Linked to American investment habits was the power of the military in the United States. An increasing share of national wealth was devoted to military maintenance, to wars, and to stockpiling for an imagined future conflict with the USSR. The integrated circuit technology was initially funded and advanced by military interests, but this impetus to its development also became the impediment to its commercial applications.

Japan's re-emergence as a major industrial power was made possible by the Korean War, and was advanced by the war in Vietnam. Japan's growth was sustained by an organization of state and economy quite unlike the American model. State planning, public investment in research and development, and the assumption of leadership by the national *zaikai* created a massive business machine.

By the late 1960s American products were overpriced relative to other countries': the dollar exchange ratio fixed at Bretton Woods could no longer be sustained. Anticipating revaluation, currency speculators intensified the problems. In 1972 the United States unilaterally devalued its dollar and thereby set in train a chaotic international money market.

The Vietnam War dragged to a close, and the defeated and dispirited American soldiers came home. The United States had lost its moral and political leadership in battles that seemed to have neither point nor end. Superman had been beaten, and for the first time his followers were unsure about his right to combat evil wherever it occurred.

The OPEC price rises of 1973–4 and the Iranian revolution of 1979 signalled the end of American control over the world's oil supplies. That control, like control of the monetary system, was a vital aspect of American hegemony; without it, America's allies were more independent of the giant, and the OPEC countries became – though only for a short period – significant investors on the money markets. Their wealth, together with capital in transit from American and European investors, was lent to less developed countries through American and European private banks. Striving to enter the industrial world, constrained in their projects by IMF and World Bank directives, the poor countries invested in massive dams and other megaprojects that provided infrastructure for the subsidiaries of transnational corporations.

Political organization in the mass-production, mass-consumption era under the Pax Americana revealed a paradox: the more the industrial nations imposed free enterprise – or rather their version of freedom – on the rest of the world, the more centralized and authoritarian local governments became. Local populations were not perverse in their response to freedom; the phenomenon was inherent in the market demands. Poor societies could not be internally free and still accommodate the global marketplace, and they could not choose to opt out.

The newly industrializing countries played host to transnational capital invested in semiconductor assembly operations and the manufacture of garments, small machinery and electrical products, and automobiles. Their free enterprise zones offered tax holidays, cheap and unorganized labour, and duty-free export of locally assembled products to the markets in the developed countries. They became the much-vaunted competition in the American domestic market.

Once the integrated circuit technology was established, and after the oil price increases, economies of scale became less decisive in determining profit rates, and fuel efficiency became important for the first time. Companies began to restructure their operations, divesting themselves of units that were relatively less profitable, too burdened with old technology, or too fuel-intensive. In the 1960s and early 1970s, when the technological revolution was only beginning, they had shifted labour-intensive operations out of industrial centres. By the 1980s the advantages of low-cost, unskilled labour had declined, and companies brought some of the offshore units back to industrial regions where they could automate production and provide highly skilled services in what were now extremely competitive businesses.

In Europe, governments had taken the lead in restructuring their national economies after the war. They too now found themselves burdened with obsolete steel-age industries. Transnational capital, expanding everywhere and uncontainable within national borders, began to organize new kinds of industries in the knowledge-intensive service sectors, and the financial industries changed. They were no longer tied to specific locations and resident labour pools, and they had low overhead costs. Following the Japanese model in form though not in spirit, American and European industries organized their operations as a system of subcontracting units. They were re-creating small business as a service sector tied to international capital. Unions could not penetrate these small operations, and were largely unable to affect the service trades of the large ones.

These were the diverse but related components of the fall in American power. In the early 1970s, as the turmoil began, neither Japan nor Europe was ready to assume world leadership, and the international mechanisms in place were inadequate to the task. The new right, in its corporate form, identified the dilemmas and established a strategic plan for dealing with them. This plan was radical in many ways, and it was directly counter to the prevailing social consensus in industrial countries. Through funding and ideological leadership the planners advanced their objectives by arguing for a more libertarian environment. The organization and message of the new right became the medium for the restructuring of national economies, and a selective version of Japanese culture became the model for the restructuring of industry.

By 1980 the new right had political power in Britain, under Prime Minister Margaret Thatcher; in the United States under President Ronald Reagan; and in various forms, though with less new right rhetoric, in other OECD countries. In that decade the new right's message provided the ideological explanations for the dismantling of the Keynesian state. Small business captured state contracts in place of subsidies; unions lost the power of collective bargaining, and their members lost privileged employment in large corporations. Equality and democracy took on a disreputable aspect, and both were blamed for the economic upheaval that restructuring had brought about.

The introduction of privatization programs was in large part a consequence of capital mobility and the forced labour mobility that followed it. Privatization was impeded by the existence of the welfare state, and even more by the large public sector bureaucracies that had been put in place to service societies based on mass production and mass consumption.

Other policies implemented in Britain, advanced in the United States, and adopted in varying degrees and with differing levels of enthusiasm elsewhere partly (but never wholly) embodied the agenda of transnational capital or state responses to the agenda. There were modifications to accommodate the interests of territorially located smaller property owners, and much of the rhetoric of the new right was representative of those interest groups. Unions were weakened but not destroyed, and some government policies responded to their objections and demands. The net results were not internally consistent, and we should not attempt to devise artificially a one-to-one relationship between what the global investment class wanted and the state policies that were put in place. While avoiding that pitfall, however, we may recognize that the interests of private property owners, and more specifically of transnational capital, were advanced by the privatization programs of the 1980s, and the interests of the unpropertied, for whom the state had become a guardian, were substantially pushed aside.

The ancillary changes at the international level included the full development of the European Market with a European Parliament; the bilateral trade agreements between Australia and New Zealand and between Canada and the United States; and the Association of Southeast Asian Nations (ASEAN) and its somewhat testy relationship which Japan. These agreements are much larger than trade and tariff contracts; they effectively regulate, and assume the privatization of, many services previously performed by national and local governments. They establish the groundwork for political unions beyond (and possibly in place of) national states. In the 1980s these agreements facilitated private property interests, and probably will continue to do so through the 1990s. However, they have the capacity to reintroduce issues of public interest, and the EC, despite Thatcher's opposition, has indicated a renewal of concern for the quality of life for its component populations.

OPPOSITION TO THE new right in the early stages was mounted by democrats and traditional left-wing or liberal-left political parties, together with unions. Their opposition had been anticipated, and the new right think-tanks were well-stocked with verbal ammunition.

The left had settled for Keynesian solutions even though it thought them inadequate. It had concentrated on reforms and expansion of welfare systems. It had not anticipated the impact of restructuring, and it had not developed an international strategy to cope with massive social change. Now it found itself on the defensive, trying to save the remnants of the welfare state. For the first time since the war, the left appeared to be the defender of tradition and the right appeared radical and innovative.

Unions were a primary target of the new right. Within the context of the free enterprise ethic and the private institutions that effectively controlled the American and other economies, a labour force had emerged that, like its employers, was primarily concerned with short-term interests and persistently transient in pursuit of personal happiness – or at least better jobs. The unpleasantness of large corporations and repetitive work on the assembly line was offset, during the age of affluence, by high wages and welfare cushions; but when the corporations pulled out of their host communities, there was little left. The steel-age industries had created unions and institutionalized class conflict; with their passing, the unions were becoming anachronisms. They were unable to reorganize themselves, unable to adjust to the changes imposed on them, and either uninvited or unwilling to co-operate in a gradual adoption of new technologies and work patterns. Their opposition was anticipated, and the tactics of international capital were effective in abandoning more often than directly confronting industrialized labour. When confrontations did take place, notably between Thatcher's government and the mining unions and between Reagan's government and the air-traffic controllers, it was the unions that lost power.

Public sector unions were also vilified. They had little sympathy from members of traditional trade unions, who thought they were cushioned in tenured jobs. Their traditional support for expansion of state services and their anticipated opposition to the dismantling of the welfare state brought them into the line of fire. They were effectively portrayed as defenders of privilege or as parasites on the public purse, and thereby separated from other workers.

Even as right-wing governments articulated the new right agenda, social democratic and labour governments were equally pressed by the restructuring process. Just as in the 1940s conservative as well as labour governments had nationalized industries, so in the 1980s labour as well as conservative governments privatized, deregulated, and downsized state operations. The process took place in Australia, New Zealand, and throughout Europe; governments were trying to cope with an economic change that was not controllable at the national level.

A harsh blow to left-wing opposition came from an unexpected source – Eastern Europe. With the fall of the huge, bureaucratic, centralized states, Marxist, neo-Marxist, socialist, and even social democratic ideologies came under attack by the populations that had experienced communist governments. Monopoly government was clearly not an acceptable instrument for containing the excesses of market economies, and traditional opposition parties that had advocated strong interventionist governments were not popular.

But as the new right agenda became better understood, and as the restructuring actually materialized, a wider population entered the debate. The middle class rejected the idea that all property rights were vested in private corporate capital. Some public services, particularly health care, turned out to be sacred. Only in the United States was health care still in the private sector, and the US model was widely understood as much more expensive and less effective than public services. With each step the Thatcher government took towards dismantling the British National Health Service in the late 1980s, popular support for the government declined.

Among the casualties of the restructuring were many regions that for various reasons were not attractive to private companies. Many companies that had located plants in the peripheral regions in the 1960s subsequently relocated. Britain became more sharply divided by region as well as by class into haves and have-nots. Some European regions (Spain, for example) improved their situations; many others went into decline. By the late 1980s, anger at these developments was accumulating almost as fast as private profits.

Other casualties were all too evident in the major cities of Europe and America among populations without employment or inadequate sources of subsistence. What had been called the Third World became manifest at home, and the employed as well as the unemployed demanded that the government pay attention to the deterioration of the social fabric.

As capital became genuinely global, the welfare of the developing countries could no longer be easily ignored. Their plight was linked, especially in the report of the Brundtland Commission, with environmental crises that directly affected the industrial countries. The destruction of the Amazon rain forest attracted the world's attention not because it threatened the cultural genocide of indigenous peoples, not because it meant the loss of a tropical forest, but because the industrial populations learned for the first time that its existence was essential to their oxygen supply.

Small communities caught up in this process of transnationalization and growth of political units had become voiceless. A rural municipality, or even a metropolitan centre, can do very little to control its own resources, improve its quality of life, or maintain its local culture. Indeed, small communities have difficulty maintaining their own population base as workers, especially the young, move to cities in search of jobs. Persistent geographical mobility, an absence of community and long-term relationships, and the growth of unemployment are all manifestations of deeply troubled societies, and by 1990 those societies were less easily persuaded that free markets and entrepreneurs would save them.

The policies of the new right provided the means for the reconstruction of national economies and the international framework, but the issue of public versus private property rights remained unresolved by 1990. Reconstructed national economies continued to be awkward combinations of groups and interests. For the issues of the 1990s – the continuing debt crisis, the exit of capital from underdeveloped and developing countries, genuine competition in the marketplace, unemployment and poverty in the urban centres of both industrial and industrializing countries, growing international terrorism and fundamentalist movements, and a global environmental crisis – the new right had no solutions.

The issues are manifest in both the industrial countries where the new right became important and the underdeveloped or developing countries where external capital wields great power over the populations and governments of relatively weak states. The more global capital becomes, the more intimately connected are the rich and the poor countries. What happens in one country – an environmental disaster, a debt crisis – immediately affects the rest of a now self-consciously global society. Yet it is also evident that no global crisis can be solved by national states with no jurisdiction over international capital, or by the extension of unlimited property rights.

The working out of new right policies in the industrial centres has its ironic twists. Privatized utilities turn out to need regulation, for without it public anger boils over when costs rise and corporate accountability diminishes, and those angry consumers are often other companies. For example, reduced spending on education eventually affects the very companies that condemned the public education systems: either they must provide training for a highly skilled labour force at their own cost, or they must enable governments to do so. They discover, as the bourgeoisie of the fourteenth century discovered, that knowledge cannot be neatly confined to what is immediately useful and supportive of the status quo.

The libertarian right, the wing that was in political office in Britain and the United States, finally encountered the central contradiction of its public stance: if it was to cope with the problems of a society without state intervention, a more centralized and more directive state structure would be required. The new right reduced the obstacles to authoritarian government through an ideology that condemned democracy and removed the state from its protective functions. Privatization turned out to be a way-station rather than an end result. Privatized monopolies had to be regulated, if only in the interests of capital. The state had to support the development of new high-tech industries, sometimes to the point of establishing and funding them. Either the national state or the new suprastates and international organizations had to become the large purchasers of many of the products and services produced by both transnationals and small companies.

As we entered the final decade of the century, the global economy was no more manageable than it had been in 1970. The more integrated it became, the less it could be controlled by the corporate structures that had planned and orchestrated the show. If history is a guide, corporate leaders should worry: as Tocqueville has noted,[1] a clear signal that the aristocracy had lost its power in industrialized Europe came when its wealth was most vigorously attacked. When the authors of reports for the Trilateral Commission worried about the loss of faith in corporate and political leaders, they did not look to history. The new right may have been the rear guard of a fading class defence of privilege.

MOST OF THIS BOOK IS concerned with specific historical events that occurred between the 1940s and 1990. But my more general argument throughout is that the resurgence of a laissez-faire ideology was connected to a continuing tension between two kinds of property claims: public and private.

Privatization, in the sense of rendering private that which was in the public or community domain, is not a new idea. The progressive privatization of nature from the commons is the history of market economies since at least the twelfth century. The enclosures movements in Britain (that is, the appropriation of common land) and corresponding actions in Europe more generally are but the more celebrated forms of privatization in this history. Though the privatizations of state properties in the 1980s were not transfers from the commons, they similarly challenged the contemporary understanding of the "public interest" and property rights. Privatized properties include services previously regarded as essential but unprofitable to capital.

When Locke and Smith spun their theories, the private owners they defended were individuals, families, and small firms, and their economic system was normally limited to the borders of their own states, though they may have marketed goods elsewhere. In the contemporary world, these people and businesses are small players in the economic system. The power belongs to the transnational corporations. The term "private enterprise" remains, but the activities to which it refers are no longer really private or enterprising. They are undertaken in the private interests of shareholders, but they have dramatic consequences for labour, communities, and nations; and while they may compete with one another, they do not constitute a marketplace of entrepreneurs buying and selling on equal footing.

When "property" referred primarily to fixed resources such as land, and even when it came to mean fixed industrial assets, territorial boundaries for political jurisdictions coincided with and were advanced by private property owners. Thus, in a territorially located population there were classes – the propertied and the propertyless – but they shared space and necessary mutual interests. Over the post-war era, and especially since about the mid-1960s, property rights have been claimed and effectively extended to non-material things. The right to a return on investment, the right to profits, and the right to move capital out of regions where it was accumulated were among these. Such rights exceed their territorial location. Governments that are fixed in space and property rights that exceed that space no longer form a coherent political and economic unity.

Rights claimed by fixed populations – the right to collective bargaining, to income security, to employment and job tenure, to child care, to health care, and to adequate food, education, and accommodation – infringe on the rights of private capital. All these claims were advanced in the Keynesian era, and many became established in law. The new right was very much concerned with dismantling these infringements on the private liberty of corporate actors; and since those rights were the results of democratic political processes, it was democracy that became the focus of attack.

Other rights were claimed on behalf of humanity or the planet: the right to clean air and water and to oxygen-generating forests, for example. These claims became more pressing near the end of the 1980s, and each claim infringed on the right of corporations to establish plants and produce goods in the places and by the means they thought best. What was economically efficient for the producers was socially inefficient for citizens or environmentally destructive for the earth, and it was here above all that the conflict between private and public rights was evident. The political forum had served workers well, if slowly, as they gained rights, and it had begun to serve citizens more generally; now it was tested to its limits as the environmentalists claimed yet more comprehensive rights.

Separate national governments became less and less able to deal with these diverse claims. Their control over international capital diminished, their material base declined, and their ability to cope with demands from so many diverse sources was limited. Many claims were by their nature universalistic, and any such claims must rest on an agreement about the nature and boundaries of the universe. As capital moved around the globe, labour was obliged either to follow or to fall into poverty; the boundaries of the universe for universal services were being erased. National governments were out of their depth, and those who argued that resources apparently rooted in any one territory were in fact the property of the earth and all its inhabitants had no political organization capable of transforming that idea into policy.

Transnational governments, though established for quite other purposes, may be an essential means of re-creating public rights, universal rights, and environmental protection. The struggles played out in national forums will inevitably regain momentum as the new structures are established. As they have since the inception of modern governments, these struggles will pit citizens against capital, public interests against private interests, political governance against economic governance. The weakness of socialism is not terminal; a renewed resistance to the predations of capitalism will grow in the new international forums. It will, however, be a different kind of socialism; a socialism that is necessarily informed by a greater understanding of global society; a socialism that is less likely to reduce the universe to two opposing classes, less likely to advance state ownership as the vehicle of change, and more concerned with the fates of small communities in which "workers" are the minority and work itself is in need of redefinition.

THE US GOVERNMENT began to search for a new security policy in 1988. The containment of communism and the Soviet Union was wearing thin. *Glasnost* had begun in the USSR; McDonald's fishburgers were the hottest item on the Japanese fast food menu; South Korea had elected a government; Ferdinand Marcos had been deposed in the Philippines; and as the Reagan era wound down, both presidential candidates were more concerned with economic policy than with the crusade of the American century. Not that the blinders had been removed altogether: Vice-President George Bush asserted, without a blushing glance at American post-war behaviour, that "economic growth is now as much a matter of foreign policy as it is of monetary policy."[2] As the new president he tapped a popular feeling in calling for a "gentler America." By 1990, with America still considering the meaning of that phrase, the cold war had been pronounced dead by Gorbachev and the Warsaw Pact countries.

The containment of communism had become the equivalent of free trade, free enterprise, the free market, and the free world. Americans had caged themselves behind these shibboleths while half the world's smaller nations obtained arms (purchased from the industrial countries and their free enterprises), and the revolutionary threat from armed militants elsewhere became more immediate than a tepid battle with an aging communist bureaucracy. Japan, by far the greatest economic combatant, had nothing invested in strategic nuclear warheads, and her best scientific minds were engaged in commercial research.

Environmental problems, unexpected and unplanned for, were of concern in industrial societies. In the Canadian election of 1988 public opinion polls revealed that a majority of the electorate thought environmental issues were the most pressing, even though the candidates focused entirely on "free trade" with the United States. The report of the Brundtland Commission entered the debate, and while it suggested only partial solutions, mostly consistent with a free market, its impact on public opinion went considerably beyond its modest recommendations. Margaret Thatcher announced her intention to put environmental issues at the top of her agenda, thus tapping a well of public opinion that had not been created by the new right.

In the last decade of the century, the division of the world into "free" and "communist" is clearly absurd. The real cleavage is between rich and poor. Yet this cleavage is not adequately described in simple class terms. It has regional and ethnic dimensions that do not neatly overlap class lines, and it has a gender dimension that cannot be comprehended at all in class terms.

Nationalist movements have sometimes adopted the label "communist" as the only available defence against the predations of capitalism. But another set of ideologies has gradually supplanted communism for such opponents: fundamentalist religions, each of which bears a distinctive ethnic or nationalist stamp, each of which is utterly intolerant of non-conforming ideas. The highly unequal distribution of the world's wealth feeds the fundamentalists' hostility to the industrial countries.

The numbers of the dispossessed continue to increase. In most of the world, refugees flee their homelands because they are starving or under threat of torture. The United Nations High Commission for Refugees numbered political refugees at 15 million in 1990, and estimated that another 100 million were "economic" refugees. These figures included the 5.6 million Afghans who fled a civil war and lived in camps in Pakistan and Iran; the 3 million who fled both wars and famine in Africa; 2 million Palestinians; and the thousands of Indochinese, Cambodians, and Vietnamese whose poverty and fear has driven them to refugee camps in neighbouring countries.[3] The phenomenon of statelessness, first noted when the European states were established, has now become an epidemic.

Hunger and poverty live together with fundamentalism and intolerance. Communism, if that term means central management and the growth of a huge state bureaucracy, is no answer, and few would now advance it as a solution. But capitalism, particularly unfettered free markets that determine the allocation of all resources, is likewise a failure and cannot solve these massive problems.

What is the optimum balance between markets and social controls, between private properties and public interests? These are the questions originally asked by Locke and Smith, and we necessarily return to them. We have tried the extremes in both directions, and now we are faced with the more difficult task of finding the median.

Populations in industrial countries could choose to redefine property so that critical resources and essential life processes are protected by democratic governments at both regional and global levels. As the dimensions of the environmental crisis become better understood, it seems likely that the United Nations will take on more legislative responsibility, and that nation states will surrender some of their rights to achieve a safer global environment. Rich nations will have to co-operate with poor nations in new ways. Redistribution is an obvious trade-off for a clean atmosphere; reduction of consumption in the rich countries is a reasonable trade-off for an increased life expectancy.

Within existing regional blocs and the remnants of nation-states in industrial regions, there are alternatives to unfettered market forces and authoritarian governments. Sweden has implemented a mixed economic system over the past century, and has succeeded in sustaining a generally better quality of life and employment standard than the rest of Europe. Worker-managed firms are alternatives to the present system of institutionalized industrial conflict. Community co-operatives, if accompanied by state-run product-marketing agencies, are viable enterprises. Profit-sharing is a means of combating unemployment and inflation; it requires state participation through tax incentives and other supports.[4] There are, in short, numerous mixed systems of market and state regulation which allow for private property rights, but inhibit their pre-eminence over all other values.

The world economy cannot be restructured through haphazard experiments in worker participation or co-operatives while values remain unchanged. If we retain the notion that private freedom is always and everywhere of such primary importance that all else must give way, then no alternative organization of the global society will work, and an environmental disaster is inevitable. At some point we have to agree that public interests exist, and that there are numerous dimensions of life that cannot be measured in GNP and other economic indices.

That which properly lies in the public realm needs to be determined, a process of negotiation and democratic decision-making that is frustrating but essential; and when it is determined, it must be set above the market. The health of a population, the education of its children, and the preservation and conservation of the land, water, and air are matters of such urgency that they cannot be left to market forces.

Society as a whole has to examine the vehicles of contemporary capitalism. These do not even remotely resemble the small enterprises defended so eloquently by Locke and Smith. Transnational corporations are larger than most nation states, and have far more control of capital and labour than any nation state has ever had. Sometimes these corporations have produced goods and services efficiently. But like their predecessors, the Hudson's Bay Company and the East India Company, they have passed their peak of utility for a global society. Like the science they have harnessed, they have become ends in themselves, and they cease to serve human society as they expand their own domain.

Life – the life of the planet and of all the species in and on it – is under threat. The threat comes not from nature, but from the impact of humans on nature. Enthralled by their capacity to invent technologies that conquer and displace nature, humans have become captive to their own inventions. The mother at Cubatão, agonizing over the awful choice between death from poverty or death from pollution, is its symbol.

Neither the advances of science nor the enormous wealth its applications have brought to selected populations of the earth have provided the mass of humanity with a better quality of life. Fundamentalist religions and fanatical nationalism appeal to people who are materially or spiritually dispossessed. The spiritual poverty of our age is the paradox, for surely we know more than people have ever known, and have more means of communicating knowledge than have ever before existed.

The ancient myth of the Garden of Eden, a myth that long predates Christianity, captured the paradox: knowledge that does not begin with the cherishing of life itself is destructive. We have knowledge, but we have no sense of the sanctity of life. The centralized bureaucracies of Eastern Europe were as bereft of that spiritual dimension as the boardrooms of the capitalist corporations. Neither those who are rushing towards market societies nor the market societies already in place can recreate human existence through the laws of supply and demand.

Judging the worth of a society by the single value suggested by Hayek and Nozick – private freedom – is a testament to our spiritual poverty. Human beings exist in communities and a natural environment. They cannot survive alone and in a vacuum. Liberty is absolutely meaningless outside a social organization, and social organization by its very nature implies restraints on human activities. Human beings have to decide how much and what kind of restraint is essential and beneficial for the world as a whole. They can decide this only through political activity. The decision cannot be made by science, for science is not about human values. If the decision is made by the most powerful constituents of a society – in our time the transnational corporations, in an earlier time the aristocracy – their liberty is unrestrained while the very survival of others is in jeopardy.

Political activity, meaning public participation in determining mutual restraints and choosing the means by which both private and public interests are to be realized, is itself severely constrained – indeed, virtually precluded – when the global economy is outside the range of debate. It is impossible to sustain democracy while a privileged class of investors and corporate directors is permitted to decide what will be produced, by whom, and where. Adam Smith's little world has no analogue in this global economy. To invoke his dicta on the relationship between each man's pursuit of selfish interests and the magical achievement of the common good is to admit that in the twentieth century the science of economics has lost all sense of reality.

The measure of any economic system is its effectiveness in providing for the sustenance of the earth and of human populations. By this measure the free market system is deficient. Keynesian correctives were not adequate; they left intact the power structure that ultimately destroyed their effectiveness in modifying market forces. We face the challenge of dismantling that power and replacing it with a system that maintains a fine balance between global controls and small community controls. The new right may have had its most useful role in creating a global economy; we must now transcend it to create a global society that respects the diversity of its component communities.

Notes

CHAPTER ONE   INTRODUCTION

1 Ronald Bailey, reprinted in the *Globe and Mail*, 17 March 1989. The book under review was *The Other Path: The Invisible Revolution in the Third World* by Hernando de Soto, translated by June Abbott (New York: Harper and Row, 1989). The argument is that Latin American states have impeded the growth of economies.
2 Arrighi, "A Crisis of Hegemony," 55–108.
3 Bluestone and Harrison, *Deindustrialization of America*.
4 Reich, *New American Frontier*, 141.
5 Bowles, Gordon, and Weisskopf, *Beyond the Wasteland*.
6 Lipietz, "Crisis of Fordism," and "International Division of Labor"; Aglietta, *Capitalist Regulation*.
7 Fröbel, "Current Development of the World Economy."
8 World Bank, *World Development Report*, 1986, iii–iv.
9 *Globe and Mail*, 19 June 1989; source: Deutsche Bundesbank.
10 *Forbes*, June 1987.
11 United Nations Conference on Trade and Development, "Indexation" and "Action on Export Earnings."
12 Trilateral Commission reports, based on Harvard Business School research and data, are sources of such information, though their interpretations differ from mine. See, for example, Ushiba, Allison, and de Montbrial, *Sharing International Responsibilities*.

CHAPTER TWO   THE INVISIBLE HAND

1 Locke, "Second Treatise on Civil Government," 32.
2 Smith, *Wealth of Nations*.
3 Ibid., chapter 2, paragraph 2.

4 Ibid., chapter 5, paragraph 1.
5 Ibid., chapter 8, paragraph 6.
6 Moore, *Dictatorship and Democracy*, 487.
7 Braudel, *Wheels of Commerce*.
8 Ibid., 52–3.
9 Moore, *Dictatorship and Democracy*, 20–9.
10 Braudel, *Wheels of Commerce*, 265–72.
11 Bentham, *Principles of the Civil Code*, chapter 8 ("On Property").
12 Ibid., chapter 3 ("Relations between These Ends").
13 Mill, *Principles of Political Economy*, chapter 2.
14 For a discussion of these relationships see Laski, *Political Thought in England*, and Macpherson, *Possessive Individualism*.
15 Rousseau, "Second Discourse."
16 Macpherson, *Property*, 29.
17 Rousseau, "Second Discourse," quoted in Macpherson, *Property*, 31. A slightly different translation is given in Crocker, 211–12.
18 Marx and Engels, *Manifesto*, 82–3.
19 Veblen, "The Natural Right of Investment."
20 Tawney, *Equality*, and "Property and Creative Work."
21 Cohen, "Property and Sovereignty," in Macpherson, *Property*.
22 Macpherson, "The Meaning of Property, in *Property*; see also Macpherson, *Possessive Individualism*.
23 Tilly, *Formation of National States*, 20–9.
24 See Arendt, *Origins of Totalitarianism*.
25 Locke, "Second Treatise on Civil Government."
26 Arendt, *Origins of Totalitarianism*, 17.
27 Polanyi, *Great Transformation*.
28 Marx, *Class Struggles in France*, 69–70.
29 Marx and Engels, *Manifesto*, 33.
30 Engels, *Origins of the Family*, 155–7.
31 This argument originally formed the basis of my lecture "The Uncertainty Principle," presented to the Canadian Sociology and Anthropology Association in the John Porter Lectures, 1984–1987, 62–72.
32 Ludwig Feuerbach, *History of Modern Philosophy from Bacon of Verulam to Benedict Spinoza*, from *Collected Works*, quoted in Leiss, *Domination of Nature*, 48.
33 Bacon, *The New Organon: Works*, IV, 115, quoted in Leiss, *Domination of Nature*, 50
34 Leiss, *Domination of Nature*, chapter 3. Leiss's work on this subject is most helpful, and I have drawn on it in this chapter.
35 Ibid., 76–7.
36 Heisenberg, *Physics and Philosophy*, 196–7.

37 I am indebted to Geordon Marchak for debating this issue with me, making me more conscious of the positive side of science than I might otherwise have been.

38 Service, "The Law of Evolutionary Potential," in Sahlins and Service, *Evolution and Culture* 97.

39 Minshull, *The New Europe*, 3.

40 Luard, *World Economy*, table 1.2.

41 Kalecki, *Capitalist Economy*; Keynes, *Collected Writings*, vol. 7.

CHAPTER THREE   PAX AMERICANA

1 Luard, *World Economy*, 7.

2 Brett, *International Money*, 36, and Horsefield et al., *International Monetary Fund*, vol. 3, 33.

3 By the 1970s the twenty-four member states included Australia, Austria, Belgium, Canada, Denmark, the Federal Republic of Germany, Finland, France, Greece, Iceland, Ireland, Italy, Japan, Luxembourg, the Netherlands, New Zealand, Norway, Portugal, Spain, Sweden, Switzerland, Turkey, the United Kingdom, and the United States.

4 This section is based on the account by Keohane, *After Hegemony*, and Anderson, *Aramco*.

5 Anderson, *Aramco*, 96.

6 Keohane, *After Hegemony*, 154, and Anderson, *Aramco*, 78 n17 (quoting Acting Petroleum Adviser James Sappington, 1943: "If Middle Eastern oil should enter the United States to meet the postwar need for oil imports, the result should be a further conservation of the reserves" of the western hemisphere).

7 Keohane, *After Hegemony*, 185.

8 Tivey, *British Industry*, 17.

9 P.L. Yates, *40 Years of Foreign Trade* (London: Allen and Unwin, 1959), data reprinted in Luard, *World Economy*, chapter 3.

10 International Monetary Fund data, annuals, and US Department of Commerce, *Survey of Current Business*, annuals cited in Piore and Sabel, *Second Industrial Divide*, at 185.

11 Servan-Schreiber, *American Challenge*, 35.

12 I have discussed the impact of US policy during the cold war on Canada in Marchak, *Ideological Perspectives on Canada*, 3d ed. (1987).

13 Halliday, *Japanese Capitalism*, 200–2.

14 Hirschmeier and Yui, *Japanese Business*, 295.

15 Ibid., 277.

16 Amsden, "Taiwan's Economic Development," 91.

17 Myers, "Agriculture in Modern China."

18 For a discussion, see Amsden, "Taiwan's Economic Development."

19 Zenger, "Taiwan," 88–9.

20 As used, for example, by Easton, *Analysis of Political Life*.

21 Examples of this line of thought may be found in Auster and Silver, *The State as a Firm*, and Deutsch, *Nerves of Government*.

22 Dahl, *Who Governs?*; Parsons and Smelser, *Economy and Society*; and Almond and Verba, *The Civic Culture* exemplify this line of reasoning.

23 Dahl, *Polyarchy*, 2. See also Dahl, *Who Governs?* and Dahl, *Democratic Theory* for earlier formulations of pluralist theory.

24 For further and mostly similar views, see Alford and Friedland, *Powers of Theory*.

25 See, for example, Moore, "Motivational Aspects of Development."

26 Rostow, *Stages of Economic Growth*. See also Horowitz, *Three Worlds of Development*, and Eisenstadt, *Tradition, Change, and Modernity*.

27 See Freeland, *Origins of McCarthyism*.

28 See Krasner, *National Interest*. Krasner examined US foreign policies affecting procurement of raw materials. He found that while policies at certain periods and in certain countries could be unambiguously explained as defence of economic interests, other actions of the American state were the result of ideological beliefs held by American political leaders. Especially in the post-war period, Krasner argues, American government interpretations of "the national interest" took precedence over material interests in such notable cases as Cuba and Vietnam.

CHAPTER FOUR   THE COCA-COLA STALL

1 Galbraith, *The Affluent Society*.

2 Naisbitt, *Megatrends*.

3 Siegel, "Delicate Bonds," 2, citing Leonard Weisberg, in industrial technology hearings, US Senate Committee on Commerce, Science, and Transportation, 30 October 1978, 74–5, and John E. Tilton, *Diffusion*, 76–7. See also Keller, "Division of Labor in Electronics," 346–50, for an extended discussion of the Pentagon's role; and Snow, "International Division of Labor," for a relevant examination of employment trends. The market share held by the Pentagon dropped after 1965.

4 Siegel, "Delicate Bonds," 4, citing Don Hoefler's study in *Electronic News*, 11, 18, and 25 January 1971. A subsequent study was published as "Silicon Valley Genealogy" by the Semiconductor Materials Institute (SEMI).

5 Siegel, "Delicate Bonds," 7.

6 Ibid.; and Siegel and Grossman, "Fairchild Assembles an Asian Empire."

7 Muto, "Free Trade Zone," 16, citing US Senate, *Multinational Corporations and the United States Foreign Policy Hearings before the Subcommittee on Multinational Corporations of the Committee on Foreign Relations,* part 3, p. 23.

8 Snow, "International Division of Labor" provides a detailed examination of employment statistics for Silicon Valley workers.

9 Muto, "Free Trade Zone," 14; the source of the data is Bank of Japan, *Foreign Capital Industrial Trends in Asian Countries,* September 1976.

10 Siegel, "Delicate Bonds," 7.

11 Ibid., 13.

12 Ibid., 12. See also Bello, "Marcos and the World Bank," 8–9.; and Bello, Hayes, and Zarsky, "500-Mile Island."

13 Payer, *The World Bank,* 160.

14 Sayer, "Industrial Location," 110.

15 United Nations Center on Transnational Corporations, *Transnational Corporations in the International Semiconductor Industry,* 34.

16 "Can Semiconductors Survive Big Business?" *Business Week,* 3 December 1979.

17 Ibid.

18 Sayer, "Industrial Location," 113–14, and United Nations Center on Transnational Corporations, *Transnational Corporations in the International Semiconductor Industry,* 275.

19 Baranson, "Japanese Challenge."

20 Sayer, "Industrial Location," 117–18.

21 Ontario, *Ontario Study of the Service Sector,* 9. In Canada, the service sector accounts for 75.7 per cent of employment and 72.4 per cent of GDP; in the United States the figures are 76.8 per cent and 73.3 per cent respectively.

22 Ibid., 7, citing Statistics Canada's figures on employment, earnings, and hours (catalogue no. 72.002, CANSIM Matrix 8363.

23 Free Trade Agreement, chapter 14, 194.

24 Landefeld and Young, "US Trade in Services," table 5.2, 97.

25 Ibid.

26 United Nations Center on Transnational Corporations, *Foreign Direct Investment,* 32–5.

27 Ibid., 27.

28 Ibid., table 5, 26.

29 Canada, Task Force on Trade in Services, *Background Report,* 15.

30 Statistics Canada, *International Transactions in Services,* table 1, 17.

31 Bhagwati, "International Trade in Services," 24–5.

32 Reich, *Next American Frontier.*

33 Bluestone and Harrison, *Deindustrialization of America.*

34 Ibid., 145–6.

35 Ibid., 145–8. Their account is based on a then unpublished study by Jemadari Kamura, "Plant Closings and Apartheid: The Steel Connection," and Holland and Myers, "Profitability and Capital Costs."
36 Reich, *Next American Frontier*, 141.
37 Thurow, *Zero-Sum Society*.
38 Bowles, Gordon, and Weisskopf, *Beyond the Wasteland*.
39 Saul, "Secret Life." For background see Clement, *Continental Corporate Power*; Niosi, *Canadian Capitalism*; and Marchak, *In Whose Interests*.
40 Bellon and Niosi, *Decline of the American Economy*, 157.
41 Blackaby, *De-industrialization*.
42 Fröbel, Heinrichs, and Kreye, *International Division of Labour*.
43 Jordan, *Mass Unemployment*.
44 Massey and Meegan, *Anatomy of Job Loss*.
45 Kennedy, *Rise and Fall*.

CHAPTER FIVE
THE NEW RIGHT AGENDA

1 Hospers, *Libertarianism*.
2 Sawer, "Libertarianism in Australia," 2.
3 Gunn, *Revolution of the Right*, 21. See also Levitas, *Ideology of the New Right*, and Crawford, *Thunder on the Right*, for descriptions of the institutes and publications.
4 Belsey, "The New Right," 197.
5 Tocqueville, *Democracy in America*.
6 Hayek, *Constitution of Liberty*.
7 Ibid., 203.
8 Ibid., 106.
9 Ibid., especially chapter 8.
10 Hayek, *Knowledge, Evolution and Society*, 19.
11 Seldon, *The New Right Enlightenment*, xii.
12 Harris, *End of Government?*, 11.
13 Ibid., 34–6.
14 Gilder, "Supply Side," 14.
15 Gilder, *Wealth and Poverty*, chapter 4.
16 Gilder, "Supply Side," 15.
17 Ibid., 23.
18 Hayek, *Constitution of Liberty*, 103–17.
19 Kristol, *Two Cheers for Capitalism*, 16.
20 Ibid., 38–9.
21 In, for example, *Capitalism and Freedom*, and, with Rose Friedman, *Free to Choose*.
22 Nozick, *Anarchy, State and Utopia*.

23 For further examples, see Seldon, *Emerging Consensus?*, Harris, *Radical Reactionary*, and Scruton, *Meaning of Conservatism*. Joseph, who became Margaret Thatcher's chief intellectual adviser, wrote *Reversing the Trend* and *Stranded on the Middle Ground*.

24 Kavanagh, *Thatcherism*, 87. See also chapters 3 and 4 for further details on these institutes.

25 Published as *The Omega File* in 1985; see Kavanagh, *Thatcherism*, 87–8.

26 For example, Alan Crawford, the author of *Thunder on the Right*, is a conservative who believes that the new right will destroy conservatism. A different perspective is that of the contributors to Sawer, *Australia and the New Right*. Both books provide strong social critiques.

27 Among the most interesting of these is Schotter, *Free Market Economics*.

28 Arrow, *Social Choice*, 2–5, 9.

29 Schotter, *Free Market Economics*, 71.

30 Shoup and Minter, "Shaping a New World Order," 135–56.

31 Thompson, "Bilderberg," 157–89.

32 Plenary session, "The State of Trilateral Relations," *Trialogue* (Trilateral Commission), Spring 1983, 12.

33 Thompson gives examples in "Bilderberg," note 57.

34 Gerard C. Smith, ambassador-at-large for non-proliferation matters, in *Atlantic Community Quarterly* (Fall 1974), 350, quoted in Sklar, *Trilateralism*, xii.

35 Wellenstein, "Domestic Moods: A Trilateral Perspective," Plenary Conference of the Trilateral Commission, Tokyo 1985, *Trialogue* (37), 27.

36 Spoken in self-defence by David Rockefeller, *Wall Street Journal*, 30 April 1980.

37 Crozier, Huntington, and Watanuki, *Crisis of Democracy*.

38 Ibid., 6–7.

39 Ibid., 173.

40 Ibid., 173–87.

41 Trilateral Commission, *Task Force Reports* 1–7.

42 Trilateral Commission, *Task Force Reports* 15–19.

43 Watanabe, Lesourne, and McNamara, *Facilitating Development*, 2.

44 Ibid., 4.

45 Ibid., 119, 120

46 Ushiba, Allison, and the Montbrial, *Sharing International Responsibilities*, 2.

47 Novak, "Trilateralism and the Summits," 190–211.

48 Sklar, "Purpose, Structure, and Program" in Sklar, *Trilateralism*, 86.

49 Crawford, *Thunder on the Right*, examines the finances of several American groups.

50 Stainsby and Malcolmson, *Fraser Institute*; Fraser Institute, *Annual Reports*.
51 Doug Collins, quoting Pat Boyle, in "The Guiding Light of the Corporate Right," *Province Magazine* (Vancouver) 17 June 1984, 3, 10.
52 See Sawer, *Australia and the New Right*, 1–19, and Crawford, *Thunder on the Right*, 3–41.
53 Patrick Kinsella, speech to Simon Fraser University Student Marketing Association, as reported in the *Vancouver Sun*, 29 November 1984.

CHAPTER SIX   THE GINZA STRIP

1 Norman, *Modern Japanese State*, 243–73.
2 Ibid., 116.
3 Tsurumi, *The Japanese Are Coming*, 11; and Edgington, "Japanese Transnational Corporations," 15. See also Young, *The Sogo Shosha*.
4 Dore, *Flexible Rigidities*, 62–72.
5 United Nations Centre on Transnational Corporations, *Transnational Corporations in the International Semiconductor Industry*, 286.
6 Young, *The Sogo Shosha*, xix; Edgington, "Japanese Transnational Corporations," 19.
7 Hirschmeier and Yui, *Japanese Business*, 322–33.
8 Ibid., 339–43.
9 Ibid., 337.
10 Baranson, "Japanese Challenges," 9–20.
11 Dore, *Flexible Rigidities*, 72.
12 Baranson, "Japanese Challenges," 13.
13 Dore, *Flexible Rigidities* 127.
14 This account is based on my field notes (May 1989).
15 Dore, *Flexible Rigidities*.
16 Hellman, *Japan and East Asia*, 8.
17 See Nakano, "Investment Patterns," 33–50, for data on Japanese overseas investments. See also the annual publications of MITI on direct investment and company profile data, published as *Japan Company Handbook*.
18 Kitazawa, *Brazilian Economy*, 1.
19 AMPO: *Japan-Asia Quarterly Review* 12 (1980) special issue on Japanese transnational enterprises in Indonesia.
20 Nakajo, "Japanese Direct Investment." The discussion is extended by Roger Hayter, "Canada's Pacific Basin Trade."
21 Tsurumi, *The Japanese Are Coming*, chapter 3.
22 Murakami, "Japanese Foreign Investment," 71. See Edgington, "Japanese Transnational Corporations" for further discussion.

23 Nakajo, "Japanese Direct Investment," 470; Helleiner, "Manufactured Exports" and Hayter, "Canada's Pacific Basin Trade," 42–3; Edgington, "Japanese Transnational Corporations," 27.

24 A detailed account of trade data can be found in *The Economist*, 3 May 1986.

25 *Globe and Mail*, 4 September 1990.

26 Hamilton and Linge, *Spatial Analysis*, vol. 2, 65.

27 Ushiba, "Trilateral Relations," 12.

28 *Forbes*, July 1988.

29 United Nations Centre on Transnational Corporations, *Foreign Direct Investment*, 40–6.

30 *Wall Street Journal*, 8 November 1985.

31 Ibid.

32 Ibid.

33 Ibid., 28 October 1986.

34 Ibid., 27 October 1986. See also, for background, *Wall Street Journal*, 1 August 1986.

35 Ibid., 17 March 1987.

36 Ibid.

37 *Globe and Mail*, 10 December 1984.

38 *Wall Street Journal*, 9 January 1985.

39 Ibid., 1 August 1986.

40 Ibid., 25 March 1988.

41 *New York Times*, 9 August 1985.

42 *Globe and Mail*, 19 March 1987.

43 Zeman, *Men with the Yen*, 1984, chapter 2.

44 *Wall Street Journal*, 29 April 1988.

45 Recommendations in response to inquiry no. 23, "Re: General Guidelines for Science and Technology Policy," 3 December 1985, cited in Harris, "Japanese Science."

46 MITI report in *Kogyo Gijutsu*, April 1986, in Harris, Japanese Science, 3.

47 Tsusan Janaru, August 1986, cited in Harris, "Japanese Science," 5.

48 *Wall Street Journal*, 29 April 1988.

CHAPTER SEVEN
THE TRAVELLING SHOW

1 The idea for zones in Taiwan is credited to Professor Paul F. Keim of California State University, whose recommendations in 1958 included an international trade zone in the harbour area of the Kaohsiung Harbor Expansion Project. The second zone, Natze, was situated on a

former sugar cane field owned by the Taiwan Sugar Company (a government enterprise). The third was located in central Taiwan. See Zenger, "Taiwan," 84.

2 United Nations Industrial Development Organization, "Redeployment of Industries," 419. See also idem, "Women in the Redeployment of Manufacturing Industry."

3 Tsuchiya, "Introduction," 1–5. The figures are based on UNIDO data.

4 Organisation for Economic Co-operation and Development, "Delegates' Survey Report," shown in graphic form in Oborne, *China's Special Economic Zones*, annex 2. This was brought to my attention by Therese Mair, "Technology Transfer in China."

5 *Survey of Duty-Free Export Processing Zones in APO Member Countries*, Asian Productivity Center, July 1975, cited in Tsuchiya, "Introduction," 1.

6 Ohara, "Bataan Export Processing Zone," 93.

7 Government of the Republic of South Korea, Economic Planning Board, *Guide to Investment in Korea*, cited in Tsuchiya, "Masan."

8 Matsuo, "Masan Free Trade Zone," 71–2; and Ngiam, "Industrialization in Singapore," 145–7 detail the rulings in South Korea and Singapore respectively.

9 Zenger, "Taiwan," 86.

10 Lee, *Export Processing Zones*.

11 Fröbel, Heinrichs, and Kreye, *International Division of Labour*, 359.

12 Lee, *Export Processing Zones*, 16–18.

13 Grossman, "Women's Place," 5.

14 O'Brien, "Effect of Industrialization," 26. See also Lim, "Capitalism."

15 Byrne, "Educating Third World Women," 45–59.

16 Sharma and Sengupta, *Women Employment*.

17 Ibid., section III.

18 This feature of employment is widely reported; see, for example, Fröbel, Heinrichs, and Kreye, *International Division of Labour* 339–402; Sivanandan, "Imperialism in the Silicon Age," 31, 38; and Grossman, "Women's Place," 2–17.

19 Grossman, "Women's Place," 2–17.

20 Neumann, "Hospitality Girls," 18–23.

21 Lim, "Capitalism," 82.

22 I know of no published study on this. The observation was made to me in Bombay by women doing research on employment in the electronics firms and by several women so employed.

23 Oborne, *China's Special Economic Zones*, 147, table based on ILO *Yearbook of Labour Statistics, 1983* together with other sources of wage statistics. Oborne expresses these figures, in 1982 Hong Kong dollars: Japan $3,950; Hong Kong, $1,356; Singapore, $1,247; South Korea,

$1,115; Shenzhen SEZ, $540; Shantou SEZ, $400; Xiamen SEZ, $400; Guangzhou, PRC, $200; Philippines, $197; China (average), $175.

24 Oborne, *China's Special Economic Zones*, 144–8.
25 Hooper, "China's Modernisation," 72–89, and Currie, "Women and Work," 90–102.
26 *Pacific Research* 9:5–6 (1980) 17.
27 Sivanandan, "Imperialism in the Silicon Age," 36, 28
28 For one account see *Wall Street Journal*, 7 May 1985.
29 Ibid.
30 Ibid.
31 Palmer, "Women's Employment," 29–44.
32 Snow, "New International Division of Labor," 52–5.
33 Fröbel, Heinrichs, and Kreye, *New International Division of Labour*, 49–156.
34 Agnelli, "Singapore," 27.
35 *Country Risk Update*, February 1985, 27
36 World Bank, *World Development Report*, 1987, tables 2.1, 2.5, and 2.6.
37 *Wall Street Journal*, 17 July 1985.
38 Asia-Pacific Conference on Prospects for Business in India, Vancouver, 18 May 1988 (my notes).
39 Sharma and Sengupta, *Women Employment*, last paragraph of section XIII.
40 Brazil, Ministry of the Interior, *Basic Legislation of the Free Zone of Manaus*, 3.
41 Juan F. Rada, *Structure and Behaviour of the Semiconductor Industry* (New York: UNCTC, 1982), cited in Sayer, "Industrial Location," 115.
42 *Wall Street Journal*, 21 August 1985.
43 Novatel Communications Ltd. as reported in *Globe and Mail*, 4 May 1988. As noted in the report. "The factors that allowed Novatel to produce more efficiently in Alberta included redesigning the product so it has fewer components and requires less labor to produce." The Lethbridge workforce, according to Novatel's vice-president of computer-integrated design and manufacturing, "is head and shoulders above what you'd find offshore in terms of an intelligent, motivated work force."
44 *Globe and Mail*, 22 August 1985.
45 *Wall Street Journal*, 10 April 1985.

CHAPTER EIGHT   HIGH-WIRE ACTS

1 *The Economist*, 2 March 1985, "Motor Industry Survey."
2 Ibid.
3 Ibid.

4 Ibid.
5 Ibid.
6 *Globe and Mail*, 30 June 1987.
7 Ibid., 29 October 1986.
8 *The Economist*, 2 March 1985.
9 *Globe and Mail*, 1 October 1985.
10 *Wall Street Journal*, 28 October 1985.
11 Ibid., 16 December 1986.
12 Ibid.
13 Ibid., 28 October 1985.
14 Ibid., 16 December 1986.
15 *The Economist*, 2 March 1985, with reference to the Dalle Committee Report.
16 *Wall Street Journal*, 16 April 1985.
17 Ibid., 10 and 11 March 1987.
18 *Japan Economic Journal* vol. 26, no. 1310, 30 April 1988.
19 Ibid.
20 Ibid.
21 *Globe and Mail*, 18 October 1986.
22 See Perry, *Canada's Auto Industry*, 3–27, for a detailed history of the industry after 1965.
23 For a detailed analysis, see Holmes, "Industrial Reorganization."
24 Ibid., 262.
25 In addition to Holmes, see Macdonald, *The Future of the Canadian Automotive Industry*, and Reisman, *Canadian Automotive Industry*.
26 Perry, *Canada's Auto Industry*, 8–12.
27 Laxer, *Canada's Economic Strategy*, 136; see also Clarkson, *Canada and the Reagan Challenge*, 128.
28 See Perry, *Canada's Auto Industry*, 8–13, with reference to the 1978 Reisman Commission.
29 Clarkson, *Canada and the Reagan Challenge*, 128–31.
30 Laxer, *Canada's Economic Strategy*, 138–46; Clarkson, *Canada and the Reagan Challenge*, 129–34. The subsidies to Ford incurred the wrath of Washington, which launched a complaint with reference to both the Auto Pact and the 1976 OECD statement on international incentives. The ensuing bilateral negotiations meandered through to 1980, when the Americans backed off because of other negotiations with Japan by then in progress.
31 Ameringen, "Canadian Automobile Industry," 167–87.
32 Ibid., 281.
33 Shantz, "Creation of Jobs," 4.
34 *Globe and Mail*, 23 July 1986.
35 Ibid., 20 February 1986.

36 For the Japanese sales firms' reaction to this, see ibid., 15 May 1987.
37 Reisman, *Canadian Automotive Industry*, 236.
38 Clarkson, *Canada and the Reagan Challenge*, 132, citing the report of the Standing Senate Committee on Canada-United States Relations.
39 Hirschmeier and Yui, *Development of Japanese Business*, 307–9.
40 See *The Economist*, 5–11 April 1986, for contemporary data from the Japan Industrial Robot Association.
41 White, "Old and New," 8.
42 *The Economist*, 5–11 April 1986.
43 *Wall Street Journal*, 9 March 1987.
44 Ibid.
45 *Wall Street Journal*, 14 February 1986.
46 *Wall Street Journal*, 2 March 1990.
47 *Financial Post*, 1 December 1989.
48 *Wall Street Journal*, 24 April 1990
49 *Globe and Mail*, 4 May 1990.

CHAPTER NINE
THE EUROPEAN TROUPE

1 Fukuyama, *End of History*.
2 Holland, *Uncommon Market*, 69.
3 Rowthorn and Hymer, "The Multinational Corporation," 57–91.
4 *Times 1000 Review*, industrial comparisons by sales, 1975–6.
5 Keohane, *After Hegemony*, 169–74.
6 Minshull, *The New Europe*, 26.
7 See, for example, Watts, "West German Multinationals."
8 This description is based on Clarke, "International Division of Labour."
9 Ibid., 104–9.
10 *Globe and Mail*, 1 January 1988.
11 O'Sullivan and Hodgson, "The Expanding State," 14–15.
12 Henfrey, "Science and the Market Place," 59.
13 For one discussion of the context in Britain, Calvocoressi, *The British Experience*; for a range of perspectives, see Kramnick, *Is Britain Dying?*
14 Veljanovski, *Selling the State*, 8, argues that the initial objectives were financial and managerial but the government subsequently acquired further intentions.
15 There are numerous reviews of this period. One of the more succinct assessments is Riddell, *The Thatcher Government*, especially chapter 4.
16 Riddell provides a detailed account of housing sales and repair costs; see ibid., 157–9.
17 Detailed listings are given in Fraser, *Privatization*, 9–14.

18 Veljanovski, *Selling the State*, 3–7.
19 These included British Aerospace; Cable and Wireless; Amersham International; National Freight; Britoil; Associated British Ports; International Aeradio; BR Hotels; British Gas Onshore Oil; Enterprise Oil; Sealink; Jaguar; British Telecom; British Gas; British Airways; British Technology Group / ICI / Fairey / Ferranti / Inmos: see Veljanovski, *Selling the State*, 5.
20 Fraser, *Privatization*, 14.
21 See, for example, Kay and Thompson, *Privatisation and Regulation*, and "Privatisation: A Policy in Search of a Rationale," *Economic Journal* 96 (1986) 18.
22 *Wall Street Journal*, 23 February 1988.
23 Ibid., 25 February 1985.
24 Ibid., 29 March 1988.
25 An assessment for each privatized sector relative to the industrial efficiency measure can be found in Vickers and Yarrow, *Privatization*.
26 These data are from the *Globe and Mail*, 2 May 1989; the article, "Thatcher's Economic Miracle Dwindling," was part of a series on Britain by Edward Greenspon.
27 *Financial Post*, 1 November 1986.
28 For a description of I.G. Farber's role during the war, see William L. Shirer, *The Rise and Fall of the Third Reich*, 664–5.
29 Ibid.
30 *Globe and Mail*, 19 June 1989, Special Report on West Germany.
31 For a discussion, see Patricia Clough's article, in the *Vancouver Sun*, 20 April 1989.
32 Commission of the European Communities, *Annual Economic Report, 1986–87*, graphs 2 to 5, at 22.
33 *Wall Street Journal*, 23 February 1988.
34 Ibid.
35 Ibid., 8 April 1985 and 24 May 1988.
36 As reported in the *Globe and Mail*, 8 June 1990.
37 *Financial Post*, 23 October 1989; speech delivered in Bruges, October 1989.

CHAPTER TEN   IN THE PENNY ARCADE

1 Boulding, "Cartels," 61.
2 Pratt, "International Bankers," 15.
3 Moore, *Dictatorship and Democracy*.
4 Luard, *World Economy*, table 2.4, 48.
5 The reference to productive resources was inserted through the efforts of India, and is occasionally used by way of urging the IMF to be

more concerned with the matter. The Indian proposal originally was stronger – that the IMF should "assist in the fuller utilization of the resources of economically underdeveloped countries" (cited in Horsefield et al., *International Monetary Fund*, vol. 1, 93).

6 See Korner et al., *IMF and the Debt Crisis*, 44.

7 Ibid., 46.

8 For a detailed account of the voting structure, see ibid., chapter 2.

9 The operation is outlined ibid.; this account is based on chapter 2 of Korner et al.

10 In Rubin, *Foreign Development Lending*, 219; see also Payer, *World Bank*, 37.

11 H. Martin Koelle, acting information director, World Bank, in letter to editor, *Wall Street Journal*, 21 October 1985.

12 World Bank, *World Development Report*, 1985; Organization for Economic Co-operation and Development, *External Debt of Developing Countries*, annual surveys; and, for an analysis, Schattan, *World Debt*.

13 Helleiner, "Rise and Decline of the IMF," 47.

14 *The Economist*, International Banking Survey, 16 March 1985.

15 Organisation for Economic Co-operation and Development, *External Debt of Developing Countries*, 1984, 35; and see Korner et al., *IMF and the Debt Crisis*, based on calculations from IMF, World Bank, and OECD data.

16 As cited in Korner et al., *IMF and the Debt Crisis*, 8.

17 Cohen and Frieden, "Impact of Multinational Corporations," 149, table 9.1.

18 The three stages of direct investment are examined in Leff, "Investment in the LDCS."

19 Cohen and Frieden, "Impact of Multinational Corporations," 151.

20 Ibid., 152, citing documentation in F. Fajnzylber and T.M. Tarrago, *Las empresas transnacionales en la industria mexicana* (Mexico City: CONACYT / CIDE, 1975); Newfarmer and Mueller, *Multinational Corporations*; and Willmore, "Direct Foreign Investment."

21 Cohen and Frieden, "Impact of Multinational Corporations," 157–8.

22 For the background events leading to the coup, see Schneider, *Brazil*. See also chapter 3 of Korner et al., "Impact of Multinational Corporations" for a brief account of the role of financial institutions and the American government.

23 Skidmore, *Politics in Brazil*, 327.

24 Korner, et al., "Impact of Multinational Corporations," 76–7.

25 Newfarmer, *Transnational Conglomerates*, 295, and Payer, *World Bank*, 36–7.

26 Payer, *World Bank*, 171–5. Her references include R.F. Mikesell, "Iron Ore in Brazil: The Experience of Hanna Mining Company," in Mike-

sell (ed.), *Foreign Investment*, 345–64 (sympathetic to Hanna); and Edie Black and Fred Goff, "The Hanna Industrial Complex," NACLA *Newsletter* 3 (1968) (critical).

27 Krasner, *National Interest*, 231.

28 Ibid., 307–10. This role of the CIA has been widely reported. See, for example, the US Congress, Senate, Select Committee to Study Governmental Operations with Respect to Intelligence Activities, *Covert Action in Chile, 1963–1973*, Committee Print, 94th Congress, 1st Session, 1975.

29 Korner et al., "Impact of Multinational Corporations," 61; also Morrell and Biddle, *Central America*, 7. There is some confusion in these accounts between the IMF and the World Bank. The United States strongly opposed loans from the bank and credits under the IMF special facilities for compensating countries for fluctuations in export earnings. The bank made no new loans between 1970 and 1973. As well, Export-Import Bank credits were stopped in 1971, bilateral and aid grants dropped sharply, as did private bank financing.

30 Krasner, 312, citing US Congress, Senate, Select Committee to Study Governmental Operations with Respect to Intelligence Activities, *Alleged Assassination Plots Involving Foreign Leaders*. Interim Report, report no. 94–95, 94th Congress, 1st session, 1975.

31 Korner et al., "Impact of Multinational Corporations," 61–2.

32 Zenger, "Taiwan," 90–1, table 6.

33 Amsden, Taiwan's Economic Development," 91–2.

34 *Time*, July 1984.

35 Schatan, *World Debt*, 45, citing *Excelsior*, 12 July 1984.

36 Cited in Schatan, 46.

37 C.E. Ritchie, *Globe and Mail*, 19 February 1988.

38 *IMF Survey*, 7 March 1983; *Fortune*, 11 August 1983; Korner et al., "Impact of Multinationals," 77.

39 Oakland Ross, *Globe and Mail*, 19 December 1984.

40 *Globe and Mail*, 8 October 1985, Archibald Ritter and David Pollock of the North-South Institute.

41 *Wall Street Journal*, 3 March 1987.

42 *The Economist*, 28 February 1987.

43 C.E. Ritchie, quoted in *Globe and Mail*, 19 February 1988.

44 Ibid.

CHAPTER ELEVEN   ECONOMIC REALITY

1 See, for example, Prebisch, "Economic Development of Latin America."

2 Prebisch, "Commercial Policy"; di Marco, "Prebisch's Economic Thought."

3 See Dell, "The Origins of UNCTAD."

4 Jones, *North-South Dialogue*, 29.

5 Alphonso Patino, 1963, quoted in Murphy, *NIEO Ideology*, 59.

6 Farer, "The United States and the Third World."

7 Murphy, *NIEO Ideology*, 93–6, provides a synopsis of this position.

8 Sauvant, "The Origins of the NIEO Discussions," in Sauvant, *Changing Priorities*, 18.

9 World Bank, *World Development Report*, 1981, table 16, 164–5; summarized in Jones *North-South Dialogue*, 49.

10 United Nations, *Yearbook of International Trade Statistics*, 1977, vol. 1, table A, 22–9.

11 Martner, Producers-Exporters Associations, reprinted in Sauvant, *Changing Priorities*, table 1.11.

12 García, *Not Guilty*, table 2.3, 54; the table is based on data compiled from United Nations Conference on Trade and Development, *Handbook of International Trade and Development*, 1976, and *Supplement*, 1977.

13 García, *Not Guilty*. See also the two further volumes of *Drought and Man*.

14 Brown and Eckholm, *By Bread Alone*, quoted in García, 14.

15 Food and Agriculture Organization, "Foreword," vii.

16 Quoted in García, *Not Guilty*, 29–30.

17 Warnock, *Politics of Hunger*, 139–48, surveys the trade data for the 1980s. He arrives at the same conclusion as the International Federation of Institutes for Advanced Study.

18 Preamble, Resolution 3201 (S-VI), *Declaration on the Establishment of a New International Economic Order*, Sixth Special Session of the United Nations General Assembly, reprinted in Sauvant, *Changing Priorities*, as appendix A.

19 Sixth Special Session of the United Nations General Assembly. Declaration on the Establishment of a New International Order, 3201 (S-VI) 2229R Plenary Meeting, 1 May 1974, as reprinted in Sauvant, *Changing Priorities*, appendix A, 170–2.

20 For a discussion, see Stevens, *EEC and the Third World*; and Directorate-General for Development of the Commission of the European Communities, *Ten Years of Lomé*.

21 Quoted in Jones, *North-South Dialogue*, 60. See also Frey-Wouters, *European Community*, 241–5.

22 Resolution 3362 (S-VII), Seventh Special Session of the United Nations General Assembly, reprinted in Sauvant, *Changing Priorities*, Appendix A(C).

23 The following draws on Sauvant, *Changing Priorities*, and the NIEO statements at the Sixth and Seventh Special Sessions reprinted in the appendices to Sauvant.

24 Sauvant, *Changing Priorities*, 89. These data are based on United Nations, "Problems of Availability and Supply of Natural Resources, Survey of Current Problems in the Fields of Energy and Minerals: The World Mineral Situation. Report of the Secretary-General" (E/C 7/51), 13 February 1975, annex.

25 United Nations, *Official Records of the General Assembly, Seventh Special Session*, part II, annexes, document A/10232, "Report of the Ad Hoc Committee of the Seventh Special Session" 14–16; reproduced in Sauvant, *Changing Priorities*, appendix A, 235–7.

26 This general account is based on the description in Murphy, *NIEO Ideology*, of the official records of the General Assembly, Seventh Special Session, 127–37, and on the appendices in Sauvant, *Changing Priorities*.

27 Wechmar, "Industrialized Countries," in Sauvant, *Changing Priorities*, 159.

28 *New York Times*, 13 December 1974, reprinted in Sauvant, *Changing Priorities*, 79.

29 As enunciated, for example, in Richard N. Cooper, Karl Kaisa, and Masataka Kosaka, "Towards a Renovated International System," New York: Trilateral Commission Triangle Paper #14, 1977.

30 See, for example, Little, "Distributive Justice."

31 Tinbergen, *Reshaping International Order*.

32 US Council on Environmental Quality and Department of State, *Global 2000 Report to the President*.

33 Independent Commission on International Development Issues *North-South*.

34 For various critiques, see Jones, *North-South Dialogue*, 92–3; Henderson, "Survival"; Ward, "Another Chance"; and the panel debates in *Encounter*, vols 55 (1980) and 56 (1981).

35 Independent Commission on International Development Issues, *North-South*, 33.

36 The sentiment is credited to the economist Harry Johnson by Roy Preiswerk in "Hidden Dimensions," 33.

37 Preiswerk, "Hidden Dimensions," 31–48.

CHAPTER TWELVE
THE ENVIRONMENTAL DIMENSION

1 Quoted in *Wall Street Journal*, 15 April 1985.

2 Hardin, "Tragedy of the Commons." See also Hardin, "Denial and Disguise," and Crowe, "Commons Revisited."

3 I have argued this case in "What Happens When Common Property Becomes Uncommon?" The historical evidence is discussed in some detail in Moore, *Dictatorship and Democracy*.

4 See C.B. Macpherson, "The Meaning of Property," in Macpherson, *Property*.

5 Schatan, *World Debt*, 85.

6 Schatan, *World Debt*, 87.

7 Ibid., 88. See also Harrison, *Inside the Third World*.

8 United Nations, World Commission on Environment and Development, *Our Common Future*, 118–19.

9 Warnock, *Politics of Hunger*, xi.

10 Schnaiberg, *The Environment*, chapter 2, reviews the literature and statistics on the population debate.

11 This information was obtained through interviews with Chinese academicians in Beijing; any visitor who observes a typical pre-school population will see that there are markedly more males than females. The problem is admitted by officials, and the billboard campaign represents government policy.

12 Berger, *Northern Frontier*, vii.

13 See Hirsch, *Social Limits to Growth*, for argument on this position.

14 Meadows et al., *Limits to Growth*.

15 Mesarovic and Pestel, *Turning Point*.

16 Warnock, *Politics of Hunger*, 33, with references to summaries in Luten, "Ecological Optimism," and O'Riordan, *Environmentalism*.

17 Odum, *Fundamentals of Ecology*, 411–13.

18 Arrow, *Individual Choice*.

19 *Wall Street Journal*, 21 July 1988.

20 Karl Kamena, manager of state and local regulatory affairs for Dow Chemicals, quoted in *Wall Street Journal*, 21 July 1988.

21 Lawrence Powers, chairman of Spartech Corporation, quoted ibid., 21 July 1988.

22 My field notes, May 1989. See also Yoshiya Iwai, "Movement of the Lumbering Industry."

23 I have described this industry up to 1980 in *Green Gold*.

24 Details are reported in Marchak, "For Whom the Tree Falls." Background data are provided in numerous sources, including Brady, *Indonesia Forestry Project*; Kathleen Hendrix's articles in the *Los Angeles Times*, 19 March 1990; Government of Australia, "Developments in the Forest-Based Industries of Indonesia, Malaysia and the Philippines, Implications for Australia," 1982; Plumwood and Routley, "World Rainforest Destruction"; and Schneider, *Deforestation*.

25 *World Wood*, October 1987; see also (1985) 15 *The Ecologist*, no. 5 / 6, 40–1.

26 Arbhabhirama et al., *Thailand Natural Resources Profile*, 142–78.

27 See details in Marchak, "For Whom the Tree Falls." See also *World Wood*, October 1987.

28 United Nations, World Commission on Environment and Development, *Our Common Future*, 123, with specific reference to FAO, *Commodities Review and Outlook 1984–85* (Rome 1985).

CHAPTER THIRTEEN CONCLUSION

1 Tocqueville, *The Old Regime and the French Revolution*, part 2, chapter 1, 22–41.
2 *Wall Street Journal*, 11 August 1988.
3 Figures from the United Nations High Commissioner for Refugees, as reported by Victor Malarek, *Globe and Mail*, 31 March 1990.
4 For an extended discussion of this point, see Weitzman, "Profit-Sharing Capitalism."

Bibliography

Ackerman, Frank. *Reaganomics: Rhetoric versus Reality*. Boston: South End Press, 1982

Addo, Herb (ed.). *Transforming the World Economy?* London: Hodder and Stoughton, 1984

Aglietta, M. *A Theory of Capitalist Regulation*. London: New Left Books, 1979

Agnelli, Bernard F. "Singapore: Boom Town." *Columbia Journal of World Business* 6:6 (1971) 27–32

Alford, Robert R., and Roger Friedland. *Powers of Theory: Capitalism, the State, and Democracy*. Cambridge: Cambridge University Press, 1985

Almond, Gabriel A., and Sidney Verba. *The Civic Culture: Political Attitudes and Democracy in Five Nations*. Princeton, NJ: Princeton University Press, 1963

Amin, Samir. *Accumulation on a World Scale: A Critique of the Theory of Underdevelopment*. Translated by Brian Pearce. New York: Monthly Review Press, 1974

AMPO Japan-Asia Quarterly Review 12 (1980). Special issue on Japanese transnational enterprises in Indonesia.

Amsden, Alice H. "The State and Taiwan's Economic Development," in Peter B. Evans, Dietrich Rueschemeyer, and Theda Skocpol (eds.). *Bringing the State Back In*. Cambridge: Cambridge University Press, 1985

Anderson, Irvine H. *Aramco, the United States and Saudi Arabia: A Study of the Dynamics of Foreign Oil Policy, 1933–1950*. Princton: Princeton University Press, 1981

Arbhabhirama, Anat, Dhira Phantumvanit, John Elkington, and Phaitoon Ingkasuwan. *Thailand Natural Resources Profile*. Singapore: Oxford University Press, 1988

Arendt, Hannah. *The Origins of Totalitarianism*. Cleveland: World Publishing, 1958

Arrighi, Giovanni. "A Crisis of Hegemony," in S. Amin et al. *Dynamics of Global Crisis*. New York: Monthly Review Press, 1982

Arrow, Kenneth J. *Social Choice and Individual Values*. 2d ed. New York: Wiley, 1963

Asia-Pacific Conference on Prospects for Business in India. 1988 conference proceedings (unpublished notes). Vancouver, British Columbia.

Auster, Richard D. and Morris Silver. *The State as a Firm: Economic Forces in Political Development*. The Hague: Nijhoff, 1979

Baldock, Cora, and Dorothy Goodrick (eds.). *Women's Participation in the Development Process*. Proceedings of the Women's Studies Section, ANZAAS Congress, May 1983, Perth, Western Australia

Baranson, J. "Japanese Challenges to US Technological Leadership," in Zavis P. Zeman and David Hoffman (eds.). *The Dynamics of the Technological Leadership of the World*. Montreal: Institute for Research on Public Policy, 1980

Bello, Walden. "Marcos and the World Bank." *Pacific Research* 7:6 (1976) 1–15

Bello, Walden, Peter Hayes, and Lyuba Zarsky. "'500-Mile Island': The Philippine Nuclear Reactor Deal." *Pacific Research* 10:1 (1979) 1–29

Bellon, Bertrand, and Jorge Niosi. *The Decline of the American Economy*. Translated by Robert Chodos and Ellen Germaise. Montreal: Black Rose, 1988

Belsey, Andrew. "The New Right, Social Order and Civil Liberties," in Ruth Levitas (ed.). *The Ideology of the New Right*. Cambridge: Polity Press, 1986

Bentham, Jeremy. "An Introduction to the Principles of Morals and Legislation," in *The Utilitarians*. Garden City, NY: Doubleday, 1961

– "Security and Equality of Property," in C.B. Macpherson (ed.). *Property: Mainstream and Critical Positions*. Toronto: University of Toronto Press, 1978

Berger, Thomas R. (Commissioner). *Northern Frontier, Northern Homeland: The Report of the Mackenzie Valley Pipeline Inquiry*. Vol. 1. Toronto: James Lorimer, in association with Publishing Centre, Supply and Services Canada, 1977

Bhagwati, Jagdish. "International Trade in Services and Its Relevance for Economic Development," in Orio Giarini (ed.). *The Emerging Service Economy*. Oxford: Pergamon Press, 1987

Bisson, T.A. *Zaibatsu Dissolution in Japan*. Berkeley: University of California Press, 1954

Blackaby, Frank Thomas (ed.). *De-industrialisation*. National Institute of Economic and Social Research, Economic Policy Paper 2. London: Heinemann, 1979

Bluestone, Barry, and Bennett Harrison. *The Deindustrialization of America: Plant Closings, Community Abandonment, and the Dismantling of Basic Industry*. New York: Basic Books, 1982

Boulding, Kenneth E. "Cartels, Prices, and the Grants Economy," in Edwin P. Reubens (ed.). *The Challenge of the New International Economic Order*. Boulder, Colo.: Westview Press, 1981

Bowles, Samuel, David M. Gordon, and Thomas E. Weisskopf. *Beyond the Waste Land: A Democratic Alternative to Economic Decline*. Garden City, NY: Anchor Press, 1983

Bowles, Samuel, and Herbert Gintis. "The Crisis of Liberal Democratic Capitalism: The Case of the United States." *Politics and Society* 11:1 (1982) 51–94

– *Democracy and Capitalism*. New York: Basic Books, 1986

Boyson, Rhodes (ed.). *Goodbye to Nationalisation: A Symposium on the Economic, Political and Social Failure of the "Publicly" Controlled Industries and the Need to Return Them to a Competitive Framework*. Enfield, Middlesex: Churchill Press, 1971

Brady, Michael A. *Indonesia Forestry Project Working Paper*. Rome: FAO / World Bank Co-operative Programme Investment Centre, 1985

Brannigan, Augustine, and Sheldon Goldenberg (eds.). *Social Responses to Technological Change*. Westport, Ct: Greenwood Press, 1985

Brasil, Ministério do Interior, superintendéncia da zona franca de Manáos. *Basic Legislation of the Free Zone of Manaus*. Translated by Minerva Makarem.

Braudel, Fernand. *The Wheels of Commerce*. Vol. 2 of *Civilization and Capitalism 15th–18th Century*. Translated by Sian Reynolds. London: Fontana, 1982

Brett, E.A. *International Money and Capitalist Crisis: The Anatomy of Global Disintegration*. London: Heinemann, 1983

Brown, Lester R., with Erik P. Eckholm. *By Bread Alone*. New York: Praeger, 1974

Byrne, Eileen. "Educating Third World Women for Development – An International and Regional Perspective," in C. Baldock and D. Goodrick (eds.). *Women's Participation in the Development Process*. Proceedings of the Women's Studies Section, ANZAAS Congress, May 1983, Perth, Western Australia.

Calvert, John. *Government Limited: The Corporate Takeover of the Public Sector in Canada*. Toronto: Canadian Centre for Policy Alternatives, 1984

Calvocoressi, Peter. *The British Experience, 1945–1975*. New York: Pantheon, 1978

Camps, Miriam, in collaboration with Catherine Gwin. *Collective Management: The Reform of Global Economic Organizations*. New York: Council on Foreign Relations / McGraw Hill, 1981

Canada. *The Canada-US Free Trade Agreement. Trade: Securing Canada's Future*. Ottawa: External Affairs, 1989

Canada. *Task Force on Trade in Services Background Report*. Ottawa: Industry, Trade and Commerce, 1982

Cassen, Robert, Richard Jolly, John Sewell, and Robert Wood (eds.). *Rich Country Interests and Third World Development*. London: Croom Helm, 1982

Castle, Leslie V., and Sir Frank Holmes (eds.). *Cooperation and Development in the Asia-Pacific Region Relations between Large and Small Countries*. Tokyo: Japan Economic Research Center, 1976

Channon, Derek F. *The Strategy and Structure of British Enterprise.* London: Macmillan, 1973

Clarke, I.M. "The Changing International Division of Labour within ici," in Michael Taylor and Nigel Thrift (eds.). *The Geography of Multinationals: Studies in the Spatial Development and Economic Consequences of Multinational Corporations.* London: Croom Helm, 1982

Clarkson, Stephen. *Canada and the Reagan Challenge: Crisis in the Canadian-American Relationship.* Toronto: James Lorimer, 1982

Clement, Wallace. *Continental Corporate Power: Economic Elite Linkages between Canada and the United States.* Toronto: McClelland and Stewart, 1977

Cohen, Morris. "Property and Sovereignty," in C.B. Macpherson (ed.). *Property: Mainstream and Critical Positions.* Toronto: University of Toronto Press, 1978

Cohen, Robert, and Jeffry Frieden. "The Impact of Multinational Corporations on Developing Nations," in Edwin P. Reubens (ed.). *The Challenge of the New International Economic Order.* Boulder, Colo.: Westview Press, 1981

Cole, H.S.D., Christopher Freeman, Marie Jahoda, and K.L.R. Pavitt (eds.). *Thinking about the Future: A Critique of "The Limits to Growth."* Sussex: Sussex University Press, 1973

Commission of the European Communities. *Annual Economic Report, 1986–87,* no. 30. Brussels, 1988

Country Risk Update, vol. 2 (3). New York: irm (usa) and beri / sa, February 1985

Crawford, Alan. *Thunder on the Right: The "New Right" and the Politics of Resentment.* New York: Pantheon, 1980

Crowe, Beryl L. "The Tragedy of the Commons Revisited," in Garrett Hardin and John Baden (eds.). *Managing the Commons.* San Francisco: W.H. Freeman, 1977

Crozier, Michel J., Samuel P. Huntington, and Joji Watanuki. *The Crisis of Democracy: Report on the Governability of Democracies to the Trilateral Commission.* New York: New York University Press, 1975

Currie, Jan. "Women and Work in Australia, China and India," in C. Baldock and D. Goodrick (eds.). *Women's Participation in the Development Process.* Proceedings of the women's Studies Section, anzaas Congress, May 1983, Perth, Western Australia

Cutajar, Michael Zammit (ed.). *UNCTAD and the South-North Dialogue: The First Twenty Years.* Oxford: Pergamon, 1985

Dahl, Robert A. *A Preface to Democratic Theory.* Chicago: University of Chicago Press, 1956

– *Who Governs? Democracy and Power in an American City.* New Haven: Yale University Press, 1961

– *Polyarchy: Participation and Opposition.* New Haven: Yale University Press, 1971

Dell, Sidney. "The Origins of UNCTAD," in Michael Zammit Cutajar (ed.). *UNCTAD and the South-North Dialogue: The First Twenty Years*. Oxford: Pergamon, 1985

Deutsch, Karl W. *The Nerves of Government: Models of Political Communication and Control*. Glencoe: Free Press, 1963

di Marco, Eugenio (ed.). *International Economics and Development: Essays in Honor of Raúl Prebisch*. New York: Academic Press, 1972

Directorate-General for Development of the Commission of the European Communities. *Ten Years of Lomé: A Record of ACP-EEC Partnership, 1976–1985*. Brussels: Centerick, 1986

Dore, Ronald. *Flexible Rigidities: Industrial Policy and Structural Adjustment in the Japanese Economy, 1970–80*. Stanford: Stanford University Press, 1986

Easton, David. *A Systems Analysis of Political Life*. New York: Wiley, 1965

Edgington, David. "Japanese Transnational Corporations and the Economic Integration of Australia and the Asian-Pacific Region." Working paper no. 15, University of Sydney Transnational Corporations Research Project, 1983

Edgren, Gus. "Spearheads of Industrialization or Sweatshops in the Sun?" in Eddy Lee (ed.). *Export Processing Zones and Industrial Employment in Asia: Papers and Proceedings of a Technical Workshop*. Bangkok: International Labour Organisation Asian Employment Programme, 1984

Ehrlich, Paul R., and Anne H. Ehrlich. *Population, Resources, Environment: Issues in Human Ecology*. San Francisco: W.H. Freeman, 1970

Eisenstadt, S.N. *Tradition, Change, and Modernity*. New York: John Wiley, 1973

Elster, Jon, and Karl Ove Moene (eds.). *Alternatives to Capitalism*. Cambridge: Cambridge University Press, 1989

Engels, F. *The Origin of the Family, Private Property, and the State* (1884). New York: International Publishers, 1968

Evans, Peter B., Dietrich Rueschemeyer, and Theda Skocpol (eds.). *Bringing the State Back In*. Cambridge: Cambridge University Press, 1985

Farer, Tom J. "The United States and the Third World: A Basis for Accommodation." *Foreign Affairs* 54 (1975) 79–97

Food and Agriculture Organization. *The State of Food and Agriculture 1974: Report of the Director-General*. Rome: FAO, 1975

Frank, André Gunder. *Capitalism and Underdevelopment in Latin America*. New York: Monthly Review Press, 1967.

– *Dependent Accumulation and Underdevelopment*. New York: Monthly Review Press, 1979

Frank, Isaiah. *Foreign Enterprise in Developing Countries: A Supplementary Paper of the Committee for Economic Development*. Baltimore: Johns Hopkins University Press, 1980

Franko, Lawrence G. "Multinationals: The End of US Dominance." *Harvard Business Review* 56:6 (1978) 93–101

Fraser, Robert (ed.). *Privatization: The UK Experience and International Trends.* Harlow, Essex: Longman, 1988

Fraser Institute. *Annual Reports.* Vancouver, 1972–

Freeland, Richard M. *The Truman Doctrine and the Origins of McCarthyism: Foreign Policy, Domestic Politics, and Internal Security, 1946–1948.* New York: Schocken, 1974

Frey-Wouters, Ellen. *The European Community and the Third World: The Lomé Convention and Its Impact.* New York: Praeger, 1980

Friedman, Milton. *Capitalism and Freedom.* Chicago: University of Chicago Press, 1962

– "Market Mechanisms and Central Economic Planning." Warren Nutter Lecture in Political Economy to the Thomas Jefferson Center Foundation. Washington, DC: The American Entreprise Institute, 1981

Friedman, Milton, and Rose Friedman. *Free to Choose: A Personal Statement.* New York: Avon, 1980

– *Tyranny of the Status Quo.* San Diego: Harcourt Brace Jovanovich, 1984

Fröbel, Folker. "The Current Development of the World Economy: Reproduction of Labour and Accumulation of Capital on a World Scale," in Herb Addo (ed.). *Transforming the World Economy?* London: Hodder and Stoughton, 1977

Fröbel, Folker, Jürgen Heinrichs, and Otto Kreye. *The New International Division of Labour: Structural Unemployment in Industrialized Countries and Industrialization in Developing Countries.* Cambridge: University Press, 1980

Galbraith, John Kenneth. *The Affluent Society.* Boston: Houghton Mifflin, 1958

Garcia, Rolando V. *Nature Pleads Not Guilty.* Vol. 1 of *Drought and Man: The 1972 Case History.* 3 vols. Oxford: Pergamon Press, 1981

Gauhar, Altaf (ed.). *Third World Strategy: Economic and Political Cohesion in the South.* New York: Praeger, 1983

Giarini, Orio (ed.). *The Emerging Service Economy.* Oxford: Pergamon Press, 1987

Gilder, George. *The Political Economy of the Welfare State.* London: Macmillan, 1979

– *Wealth and Poverty.* New York: Basic Books, 1981

– "The Supply-Side," in Richard H. Fink (ed.). *Supply-Side Economics: A Critical Appraisal.* Frederick, Md.: Aletheia, 1982

– *The Spirit of Enterprise.* New York: Basic Books, 1984

Gramsci, A. *Selections from Prison Notebooks.* New York: International Publishers, 1971

Greene, T.H. *The Principles of Political Obligation.* London: Longmans, 1955

Grossman, Rachel. "Women's Place in the Integrated Circuit." *South-East Asia Chronicle* no. 66 (July-October 1978)

Grunwald, Joseph, and Kenneth Flamm. *The Global Factory: Foreign Assembly in International Trade*. Washington, DC: The Brookings Institution, 1985

Gunn, Simon. *Revolution of the Right: Europe's New Conservatives*. London: Pluto Press, 1989

Hadley, Eleanor H. *Antitrust in Japan*. Princeton: Princeton University Press, 1970

Halliday, Jon. *A Political History of Japanese Capitalism*. New York: Monthly Review Press, 1975

Hamilton, F.E.I., and G.J.R. Linge (eds.) *Spatial Analysis, Industry, and the Industrial Environment*. 2 vols. Chichester: John Wiley, 1981

Hardin, Garrett. "The Tragedy of the Commons" and "Denial and Disguise," in Garrett Hardin and John Baden (eds.). *Managing the Commons*. San Francisco: W.H. Freeman, 1977

Harris, Ralph. *The Challenge of a Radical Reactionary*. London: Centre for Policy Studies, 1980

– *The End of Government ...?* London: Institute of Economic Affairs, 1980

Harris, Martha Caldwell. "The Internationalization of Japanese Science and Technology." Unpublished, c. 1987. Available through Office of Technology Assessment, Washington, DC

Harrison, Paul. *Inside the Third World: The Anatomy of Poverty*. Harmondsworth: Penguin, 1981

Hayek, Friedrich. *The Road to Serfdom*. London: Routledge and Kegan Paul, 1944

– *The Constitution of Liberty*. London: Routledge and Kegan Paul, 1960

– *Law, Legislation and Liberty* 3 vols. London: Routledge, 1973–9

– *Law, Legislation, and Liberty: A New Statement of the Liberal Principles of Justice and Political Economy*. 3 vols. London: Routledge and Kegan Paul, 1982.

– *Knowledge, Evolution, and Society*. London: Adam Smith Institute, 1983

Hayter, Roger. "Canada's Pacific Basin Trade and Its Implications for the Export of Manufactures in BC and Alberta." Working paper no. 14, "Canada and the Changing Economy of the Pacific Basin." Vancouver: University of British Columbia Institute of Asian Research, June 1983

Heisenberg, Werner. *Physics and Philosophy*. New York: Harper and Row, 1962

Helleiner, F. "Manufactured Exports from Less-Developed Countries and Multinational Firms." *Economic Journal* 83 (1973) 21–47

Helleiner, Gerald K. "The Rise and Decline of the IMF," in Jill Torrie (ed.). *Banking on Poverty: The Global Impact of the IMF and World Bank*. Toronto: Between the Lines, 1983

Hellmann, Donald C. *Japan and East Asia: The New International Order*. New York: Praeger, 1972

Henderson, P.D. "Survival, Development and the Report of the Brandt Commission." *World Economy* 3 (1980) 87–117

Henfrey, Anthony. "Science and the Market Place," in Rhodes Boyson (ed.). *Goodbye to Nationalisation*. Enfield, Middlesex: Churchill Press, 1971

Hirsch, Fred. *Social Limits to Growth*. Cambridge: Harvard University Press, 1976

Hirschmeier, J., and T. Yui. *The Development of Japanese Business 1600–1980*. 2d ed. London: George Allen and Unwin, 1981

Hobbes, Thomas. *Leviathan*. London: Dent, 1957

Holland, Daniel, and Stewart Myers. "Profitability and Capital Costs for Manufacturing Corporations and All Nonfinancial Corporations." *American Economic Review* 70:2 (1980) 320–5

Holland, Stuart. *Uncommon Market: Capital, Class and Power in the European Community*. London: Macmillan, 1980

Holmes, John. "Industrial Reorganization, Capital Restructuring and Locational Change: An Analysis of the Canadian Automobile Industry in the 1960." *Economic Geography* 59:3 (1983) 251–71

Hooper, Beverly. "China's Modernisation: Are Young Women Missing Out?" in C. Baldock and D. Goodrick (eds.). *Women's Participation in the Development Process*, Proceedings of the Women's Studies Section, ANZAAS Congress, May 1983, Perth, Western Australia

Horowitz, Irving Louis. *Three Worlds of Development: The Theory and Practice of International Stratification*. New York: Oxford University Press, 1972

Horsefield, J.K., et al. *The International Monetary Fund, 1945–1965*, vol. 1, *Twenty Years of International Monetary Co-operation*, and vol. 3. *Documents*. Washington: IMF, 1969

Hospers, John. *Libertarianism: A Political Philosophy for Tomorrow*. Los Angeles: Nash, 1971

Ihara, Tetsuo. "The Contours of Tomorrow's Robotic Society" in Keiji Ikehata et al (eds.). *Industrial Robots: Their Increasing Use and Impact*. Tokyo: Foreign Press Center, 1982

Independent Commission on International Development Issues (the Brandt Commission). *North-South: A Programme for Survival*. London: Pan, 1980

– *Common Crisis: North-South: Co-operation for World Recovery* London: Pan, 1983

Inglehart, Ronald, and Jacques-Réné Rabier. "Europe Elects a Parliament: Cognitive Mobilization, Political Mobilization, and Pro-European Attitudes as Influences on Voter Turnout," in Leon Hurwitz (ed.). *Contemporary Perspectives on European Integration*. Westport, Conn.: Greenwood Press. 1980

International Labour Organization. *Yearbook of Labour Statistics*. Geneva, 1935–6

Iwai, Yosiya. "The Movement of the Lumbering Industry in the USA and Its Influence on Japanese Forest Industry." Unpublished, 1989.

Japan, Ministry of International Trade and Industry. *Japan Company Handbook*. Tokyo: Toyo Keizai Shinposha / Oriental Economist, 1974–

Jones, Charles A. *The North-South Dialogue: A Brief History*. London: Frances Pinter, 1983

Jordan, Bill. *Mass Unemployment and the Future of Britain*. Oxford: Basil Blackwell, 1982

Joseph, Sir Keith. *Reversing the Trend: A Critical Reappraisal of Conservative Economic and Social Policies*. London: Barry Rose, 1975

– *Stranded on the Middle Ground? Reflections on Circumstances and Policies*. London: Centre for Policy Studies, 1976

Kalecki, M. *Selected Essays on the Dynamics of the Capitalist Economy, 1933–1970*. Cambridge: Cambridge University Press, 1971

Katz, Naomi, and David S. Kemnitzer. "Fast Forward: The Internationalization of Silicon Valley," in June Nash and María Patricia Fernández-Kelly (eds.). *Women, Men, and the International Division of Labor*. Albany: State University of New York Press, 1983

Kavanagh, Dennis. *Thatcherism and British Politics: The End of Consensus?* Oxford: Oxford University Press, 1987

Kay, John, Colin Mayer, and David Thompson (eds.). *Privatisation and Regulation: The UK Experience*. Oxford: Clarendon, 1986

– "Privatisation: A Policy in Search of a Rationale." *Economic Journal* 96 (1986) 18–32

Keller, John F. "The Division of Labor in Electronics," in June Nash and María Patricia Fernández-Kelly (eds.). *Women, Men, and the International Division of Labor*. Albany: State University of New York Press, 1983

Kennedy, Paul. *The Rise and Fall of the Great Powers: Economic Change and Military Conflict From 1500 to 2000*. New York: Random House, 1987

Keohane, Robert O. *After Hegemony: Cooperation and Discord in the World Political Economy*. Princeton: Princeton University Press, 1984

Keynes, J.M. *The Collected Writings of John Maynard Keynes*, vol. 7, *The General Theory of Employment, Interest and Money*. London: Macmillan, 1973

Kitazawa, Yoko. *Japanese Inroads into the Brazilian Economy: Development as Dependence*. Tokyo: Pacific-Asia Resources Center, 1980

Korner, Peter, Gero Maass, Thomas Siebold, and Rainer Tetzlaff. *The IMF and the Debt Crisis. A Guide to the Third World's Dilemma*. Translated by Paul Knight. Avon: Bath Press, 1986

Kramnick, Isaac (ed.). *Is Britain Dying? Perspectives on the Current Crisis*. Ithaca: Cornell University Press, 1979

Krasner, Stephen D. *Defending the National Interest: Raw Materials Investments and US Foreign Policy*. Princeton: Princeton University Press, 1978

Kristol, Irving. *Two Cheers for Capitalism*. New York: Basic Books, 1978

Landefeld, J. Steven, and Kan H. Young. "US Trade in Services: 1970–1985," in Wray O. Candilis (ed.). *United States Service Industries Handbook*. New York: Praeger, 1988

Langford, John W., and K. Lorne Brownsey (eds.). *Politics and Government in Asia Pacific Nations*, 2d ed. Victoria: Institute for Research on Public Policy, Institutions of Governance Research Program, 1987

Laski, Harold J. *Political Thought in England, Locke to Bentham*. London: Oxford University Press, 1920

Laxer, James. *Canada's Economic Strategy*. Toronto: McClelland and Stewart, 1981

Lee, Eddy (ed.). *Export Processing Zones and Industrial Employment in Asia: Papers and Proceedings of a Technical Workshop*. Bangkok: International Labour Organisation Asian Employment Programme, 1984

Leff, Nathaniel. "Investment in the LDCs: The Next Wave." *Columbia Journal of World Business* 4, no. 6 (November-December 1969) 44–8

Leiss, William. *The Domination of Nature*. Boston: Beacon Press, 1974

– *The Limits to Satisfaction: On Needs and Commodities*. London: Maron Boyars, 1978

Levitas, Ruth (ed.). *The Ideology of the New Right*. Cambridge: Polity Press, 1982

Lim, Linda Y.C. "Capitalism, Imperialism, and Patriarchy: The Dilemma of Third-World Women Workers in Multinational Factories," in June Nash and María Patricia Fernández-Kelly (eds.). *Women, Men, and the International Division of Labor*. New York: State University of New York Press, 1983

– "Labour and Employment Issues in Export Processing Zones in Developing Countries," in Eddy Lee (ed.). *Export Processing Zones and Industrial Employment in Asia: Papers and Proceedings of a Technical Workshop*. Bangkok: ILO Asian Employment Programme, 1984

Lipietz, Alain. "The Globalization of the General Crisis of Fordism, 1967–84," in John Holmes and Colin Leys (eds.). *Frontyard, Backyard: The Americas in the Global Crisis*. Toronto: Between the Lines, 1987

– "New Tendencies in the International Division of Labor: Regimes of Accumulation and Modes of Regulation," in Allen J. Scott and Michael Storper (eds.). *Production, Work, Territory: The Geographical Anatomy of Industrial Capitalism*. Boston: Allen and Unwin, 1986

Lipset, Seymour Martin. *The First New Nation: The United States in Historical and Comparative Perspective*. New York: Basic Books, 1963

– "Radicalism in North America: A Comparative View of the Party Systems in Canada and the United States." *Transactions of the Royal Society of Canada* series 4, vol. 14 (1976) 19–55

Little, I.M.D. "Distributive Justice and the New International Order," in Peter Oppenheimer (ed.). *Issues in International Economics*. London: Routledge and Kegan Paul, 1978

Locke, John. "Two Treatises on Government: Second Treatise on Civil Government," in *Social Contract: Essays by Locke, Hume and Rousseau*. London: Oxford University Press, 1960

Luard, Evan. *The Management of the World Economy*. London: Macmillan, 1983

Luten, Daniel B. "Ecological Optimism in the Social Sciences: The Question of Limits to Growth." *American Behavioral Scientist* 24 (1980) 125–51

Macdonald, N. *The Future of the Canadian Automotive Industry in the Context of the North American Industry*. Ottawa: Science Council of Canada, 1980

Macpherson, C.B. *The Political Theory of Possessive Individualism: Hobbes to Locke*. London: Oxford University Press, 1962

Macpherson, C.B. (ed.). *Property: Mainstream and Critical Positions*. Toronto: University of Toronto Press, 1978

Maier, Charles S. (ed.). *Changing Boundaries of the Political*. Cambridge: Cambridge University Press, 1987

Mair, Therese. "Technology Transfer in China." Unpublished.

Marchak, M. Patricia. *In Whose Interests: Multinational Corporations in a Canadian Context*. Toronto: McClelland and Stewart, 1979

– *Green Gold: The Forest Industry in British Columbia*. Vancouver: University of British Columbia Press, 1983

– "The State and Transnational Corporations in Canada," in Robert B. Stauffer (ed.). *Transnational Corporations and the State*. Sydney: University of Sydney, 1985

– *Ideological Perspectives on Canada*. 3d ed. Toronto: McGraw Hill-Ryerson, 1987

– "What Happens When Common Property Becomes Uncommon?" BC *Studies* no. 80 (Winter 1988–9) 3–23

– "For Whom the Tree Falls: The Restructuring of the Global Forest Industry," paper presented to joint meetings of Canadian Political Science and Canadian Anthropology and Sociology Associations, Victoria, BC, May 1990; published in *BC Studies* 90 (Summer 1991): 3–24

Martner, Gonzalo. *Producers-Exporters Associations of Developing Countries: An Instrument for the Establishment of a New International Economic Order*. Geneva: IFDA, 1978

Marx, Karl. *The Class Struggles in France, 1848–1850*. New York: International Publishers 1937

Marx, Karl, and Friedrich Engels. *The Communist Manifesto*. New York: Washington Square Press, 1970

Massey, Doreen, and Richard Meegan. *The Anatomy of Job Loss*. London: Methuen, 1982

Matsuo, Kei. "The Working Class in the Masan Free Export Zone," in AMPO: *Japan-Asia Quarterly Review*. Tokyo: Pacific-Asia Resources Center, 1977

Meadows, Donella H., et al. *The Limits to Growth: A Report for the Club of Rome's Project on the Predicament of Mankind*. New York: Universe, 1972

Mesarovic, Mihajlo, and Eduard Pestel. *Mankind at the Turning Point: The Second Report to the Club of Rome*. New York: E.P. Dutton, 1974

Mikesell, Raymond F. (ed.). *Foreign Investment in the Petroleum and Mineral Industries*. Baltimore: Johns Hopkins University Press, 1971

Mill, John Stuart. "Utilitarianism" and "On Liberty," in *The Utilitarians*. Garden City, NY: Doubleday, 1961

– "Principles of Political Economy with Some of Their Applications to Social Philosophy, in John M. Robson (ed.). *Collected Works of John Stuart Mill*, vols. 2–3. Toronto: University of Toronto Press, 1965

Minshull, G.N. *The New Europe: An Economic Geography of the EEC*. New York: Hodder and Stoughton, 1978

MITI. See Japan, Ministry of International Trade and Industry

Moore, Barrington. *Social Origins of Dictatorship and Democracy*. Boston: Beacon Press, 1966

Moore, Wilbert. "Motivational Aspects of Development," in A. Etzioni and E. Etzioni (eds.). *Social Change: Sources, Patterns, and Consequences*. New York: Basic Books, 1964

Morrell, Jim, and William Jesse Biddle. *Central America: The Financial War*. Washington: Center for International Policy, 1983

Murakami, A. "Japanese Foreign Investment – Problems of Large Home Country," in L.V. Castle and F. Holmes (eds.). *Cooperation and Development in the Asia Pacific Region: Relations between Large and Small Countries*. Tokyo: Japan Economic Research Centre

Murphy, Craig. *The Emergence of the NIEO Ideology*. Boulder, Colo.: Westview Press, 1984

Muto, Ichiyo. "The Free Trade Zone and Mystique of Export-Oriented Industrialization," in *AMPO: Japan-Asia Quarterly Review*, special issue on free trade zones and industrialization of Asia. Tokyo: Pacific-Asia Resources Center, 1977

Myers, R.H. "The Commercialization of Agriculture in Modern China," in W.E. Willmott (ed.). *Economic Organization in Chinese Society*. New Haven: Yale University Press, 1970

Naisbitt, John. *Megatrends*. New York: Warner, 1982

Nakajo, Seiichi. "Japanese Direct Investment in Asian Newly Industrializing Countries and Intra-Firm Division of Labor." *Developing Economies* 18 (1980) 463–83

Nakano, Kenji. "Japan's Overseas Investment Patterns and FTZs." *AMPO: Japan-Asia Quarterly Review*, special issue on free trade zones and industrialization of Asia. Tokyo: Pacific-Asia Resources Center, 1977

Neumann, A. Lin. "Hospitality Girls in the Philippines." *South-East Asia Chronicle* no. 66 (1979) 18–23.

Newfarmer, Richard. *Transnational Conglomerates and the Economics of De-*

pendent Development: A Case Study of the International Electrical Oligopoly and Brazil's Electrical Industry. Greenwich, Conn.: JAI Press, 1980

Newfarmer, Richard W., and Willard F. Mueller. *Multinational Corporations in Brazil and Mexico: Structural Sources of Economic and Noneconomic Power.* Washington, DC: US Government Printing Office, 1975

Ngiam, Peng Teck. "Industrialization in Singapore," in *AMPO: Japan-Asia Quarterly Review,* special issue on free trade zones and industrialization of Asia. Tokyo: Pacific-Asia Resources Center, 1977

Niosi, Jorge. *Canadian Capitalism: A Study of Power in the Canadian Business Establishment.* Translated by Robert Chodos. Toronto: James Lorimer, 1981

Norman, Herbert. *Origins of the Modern Japanese State: Selected Writings of E.H. Norman.* Edited by John W. Dower. New York: Pantheon, 1975

Novak, Jeremiah. "Trilateralism and the Summits," in Holly Sklar (ed.). *Trilateralism: The Trilateral Commission and Elite Planning for World Management.* Montreal: Black Rose, 1980

Nozick, Robert. *Anarchy, State, and Utopia.* Oxford: Blackwell, 1975

Oborne, M. *China's Special Economic Zones.* Paris: OECD, 1986

O'Brien, Leslie. "Class, Sex and Ethnic Stratification in West Malaysia." PHD dissertation (Monash University 1979)

– "The Effect of Industrialization on Women: Western and Current Southeast Asian Experiences," in Cora Baldock and Dorothy Goodrick (eds.). *Women's Participation in the Development Process.* Proceedings of the Women's Studies Section, ANZAAS Congress, May 1983, Perth, Western Australia

O'Connor, James. *The Fiscal Crisis of the State.* New York: St Martin's Press, 1973

Odum, Eugene P. *Fundamentals of Ecology.* 3d ed. Philadelphia: Saunders, 1971

Offe, Claus. "The Theory of the Capitalist State and the Problem of Policy Formation," in L.N. Lindberg et al. (eds.). *Stress and Contradiction in Modern Capitalism, Public Policy and the Theory of the State.* Lexington, Mass.: D.C. Heath, 1975

Ohara, Ken. "Bataan Export Processing Zone: Its Development and Social Implications," in *AMPO: Japan-Asia Quarterly Review,* special issue on free trade zones and industrialization of Asia." Tokyo: Pacific-Asia Resources Center, 1977

Ontario, Ministry of Treasury and Economics. *Ontario Study of the Service Sector.* Toronto: The Ministry, 1986

Ophuls, William. *Ecology and the Politics of Scarcity: Prologue to a Political Theory of the Steady State.* San Francisco: W.H. Freeman, 1977

Organisation for Economic Co-operation and Development. "Sino Trade Association, Delegates" Survey Report on the Investment Environment in China." October 1984

– *External Debt of Developing Countries.* Annual surveys.

O'Riordan, Timothy. *Environmentalism*. London: Pion, 1976

O'Sullivan, John, and Patricia Hodgson. "The Expanding State," in Rhodes Boyson (ed.). *Goodbye to Nationalisation*. Enfield, Middlesex: Churchill Press, 1971

Palmer, Ingrid. "Women's Employment and Economic Change in Asian Developing Countries," in Cora Baldock and Dorothy Goodrick (eds.). *Women's Participation in the Development Process*, Proceedings of the Women's Studies Section, ANZAAS Congress, May 1983, Perth, Western Australia

Parsons, Talcott, and Neil Smelser. *Economy and Society*. Glencoe: Free Press, 1956

Payer, Cheryl. *The World Bank: A Critical Analysis*. New York: Monthly Review Press, 1982

Pearson, Lester B. *Partners in Development: Report of the Commission on International Development*. New York: Praeger, 1969

Perry, Ross. *The Future of Canada's Auto Industry: The Big Three and the Japanese Challenge*. Toronto: James Lorimer, 1982

Piore, Michael J., and Charles F. Sabel. *The Second Industrial Divide: Possibilities for Prosperity*. New York: Basic Books, 1984

Plumwood, Val, and Richard Routley. "World Rainforest Destruction – The Social Factors." *Ecologist* 12:1 (1982) 4–22

Polanyi, Karl. *The Great Transformation*. Boston: Beacon Press, 1944

Poulantzas, Nicos. *State, Power, Socialism*. Translated by Patrick Camiller. London: New Left Books, 1978

Pratt, R. Cranford. "International Bankers and the Crisis of Debt," in Jill Torrie (ed.). *Banking on Poverty: The Global Impact of the IMF and World Bank*. Toronto: Between the Lines, 1983

Prebisch, Raúl. "Commercial Policy in the Underdeveloped Countries." *American Economic Review* 44 (1959) 251–72

– "The Economic Development of Latin America and Its Principal Problems." *Economic Bulletin for Latin America* 7 (1962) 1–22

Preiswerk, Roy. "Hidden Dimensions of the So-Called New International Economic Order," in H. Addo (ed.). *Transforming the World Economy?* London: Hodder and Stoughton, 1984

Pryke, Richard. *The Nationalised Industries: Policies and Performance since 1968*. Oxford: Martin Robertson, 1981

Redclift, Michael. *Development and the Environmental Crisis: Red or Green Alternatives?* London: Methuen, 1984

Reich, Robert. *The Next American Frontier*. New York: Penguin, 1983

Reisman, Simon. *The Canadian Automotive Industry: Performance and Proposals for Progress*. Ottawa: Ministry of Supply and Services, 1978

Repetto, Robert (ed.). *The Global Possible: Resources, Development, and the New Century*. New Haven: Yale University Press, 1985

Reubens, Edwin P. (ed.). *The Challenge of the New International Economic Order*. Boulder, Colo.: Westview Press, 1981

Ricardo, David. *The Works and Correspondence of David Ricardo*. 10 vols. Edited by Piero Sraffa. Cambridge: Cambridge University Press, 1951–65

Riddell, Peter. *The Thatcher Government*. Oxford: Martin Robertson, 1983

Roberts, John G. *Mitsui: Three Centuries of Japanese Business*. New York: Weatherhill, 1973

Roberts, Paul Craig. "The Breakdown of the Keynesian Model," in Richard H. Fink (ed.). *Supply-Side Economics: A Critical Appraisal*. Frederick, Md.: Aletheia, 1982

Rostow, W.W. *The Stages of Economic Growth: A Non-Communist Manifesto*. Cambridge: Cambridge University Press, 1960

Rousseau, Jean-Jacques. *The First and Second Discourses of Rousseau*. Edited and translated by Roger D. and Judith R. Masters. New York: St Martin's Press, 1964

– *The Social Contract and Discourse on the Origin and Foundation of Inequality Among Mankind*. Edited by Lester G. Crocker. New York: Washington Square Press, 1967

Rowthorn, Robert, and Stephen Hymer. "Multinational Corporations and International Oligopoly: The Non-American Challenge," in Charles P. Kindleberger. *The International Corporation*. Cambridge: Harvard University Press, 1970

Rubin, Seymour J. (ed.). *Foreign Development Lending – Legal Aspects*. Dobbs Ferry, NY: Oceana, 1971

Sahlins, M.D., and E.R. Service (eds.). *Evolution and Culture*. Ann Arbor: University of Michigan Press, 1960

Saul, John Ralston. "The Secret Life of the Branch Plant Executive." *Report on Business Magazine*, January 1988.

Sauvant, Karl P. "The NIEO Program: Reasons, Proposals, and Progress," in Sauvant (ed.). *Changing Priorities on the International Agenda*. Oxford: Pergamon, 1981

Sauvant, Karl P. (ed.). *Changing Priorities on the International Agenda*. Oxford: Pergamon, 1981

Sawer, Marian (ed.). *Australia and the New Right*. Sydney: George Allen and Unwin, 1982

Sayer, Andrew. "Industrial Location on a World Scale: The Case of the Semiconductor Industry," in Allen J. Scott and Michael Storper (eds.). *Production, Work, Territory: The Geographical Anatomy of Industrial Capitalism*. Boston: Allen and Unwin, 1986

Schatan, Jacobo. *World Debt: Who Is to Pay?* London: Zed, 1987

Schnaiberg, Allan. *The Environment: From Surplus to Scarcity*. New York: Oxford University Press, 1980

Schneider, Aaron (ed.). *Deforestation and "Development" in Canada and the*

Tropics: The Impact on People and the Environment. Sydney, NS: University College of Cape Breton Press, 1989

Schotter, Andrew. *Free Market Economics: A Critical Appraisal*. New York: St Martin's Press, 1985

Scruton, Roger. *The Meaning of Conservatism*. Harmondsworth: Penguin, 1980

Seldon, Arthur (ed.). *The New Right Enlightenment: The Spectre That Haunts the Left*. Sevenoaks, Kent: Economic and Literary Books, 1985

Seldon, Arthur (ed.). *The Emerging Consensus ... ?* London: Institute of Economic Affairs, 1981

Servan-Schreiber, Jean-Jacques. *The American Challenge*. Translated by Ronald Steel. New York: Avon, 1971

Sewell, John W., Richard E. Feinberg, and Valeriana Kallab (eds.). *US Foreign Policy and the Third World: Agenda 1985–86*. New Brunswick, NJ: Transaction, 1985

Shaikh, Anwar. "An Introduction to the History of Crisis Theories," in Union of Radical Political Economists. *US Capitalism in Crisis*. New York: URPE, 1978

Shantz, Allan. "Creation of Jobs in the Automotive Industry, Past, Present, and Future." *Atkinson Review of Canadian Studies* 4:1 (1986) 4–7

Sharma, R.N., and Chandan Sengupta. *Women Employment at SEEPZ Bombay*. Report prepared for Indian Council for Research on International Economic Relations, Bombay, 1984

Shirer, William L. *The Rise and Fall of the Third Reich: A History of Nazi Germany*. London: Secker and Warburg, 1961

Shoup, Laurence H., and William Minter. "Shaping a New World Order: The Council on Foreign Relations' Blueprint for World Hegemony," in Holly Sklar (ed.). *Trilateralism*. Montreal: Black Rose, 1980

Siegel, Lenny. "Delicate Bonds: The Global Semiconductor Industry," *Pacific Research* 11:1 (1980), special issue, 1–8

Siegel, Lenny, and Rachael Grossman. "Fairchild Assembles an Asian Empire." *Pacific Research* 9:2 (1978) 1–8

Sivanandan, A. "Imperialism and Disorganic Development in the Silicon Age." *Race and Class* 21 (1979) 111–26

– "Imperialism in the Silicon Age." *Monthly Review* 32:3 (1980) 24–42

Skidmore, Thomas E. *Politics in Brazil, 1930–1964: An Experiment in Democracy*. New York: Oxford University Press, 1967

Sklar, Holly (ed.). *Trilateralism: The Trilateral Commission and Elite Planning for World Management*. Montreal: Black Rose, 1980

Smith, Adam. *An Inquiry into the Nature and Causes of Wealth of Nations* (1776). London: Methuen, 1961

Schneider, Ronald M. *The Political System of Brazil: Emergence of a "Modernizing" Authoritarian Regime, 1964–1970*. New York: Columbia University, 1971

Snow, Robert T. "The New International Division of Labor and the US Work Force: The Case of the Electronics Industry," in June Nash and María Patricia Fernández-Kelly (eds.). *Women, Men, and the International Division of Labor*. New York: State University of New York Press, 1983

Stainsby, Cliff, and John Malcolmson. *The Fraser Institute: The Government and a Corporate Free Lunch*. Vancouver: Solidarity Coalition, 1982

Statistics Canada. *Canada's International Trade in Services, 1969 to 1984*. Catalogue 67–510. Ottawa: Statistics Canada, 1986

– *Canada's International Transactions in Services, 1986 and 1987*. Catalogue 67–203. Ottawa: Statistics Canada, 1988

Stevens, Christopher (ed.). *EEC and the Third World: A Survey*. vol. 4. Renegotiating Lomé. London: Hodder and Stoughton, 1984

Stohl, Michael and Harry R. Targ (eds.). *The Global Political Economy in the 1980s: The Impact of the New International Order*. Cambridge, Mass.: Schenkman, 1982

Tawney, R.H. *Equality* (1931). London: Unwin, 1964

– "Property and Creative Work," in C.B. Macpherson (ed.). *Property: Mainstream and Critical Positions*. Toronto: University of Toronto Press, 1978

Thompson, Peter. "Bilderberg and the West," in Holly Sklar (ed.). *Trilateralism*. Montreal: Black Rose, 1980

Thurow, Lester. *The Zero-Sum Society: Distribution and the Possibilities for Economic Change*. New York: Basic Books, 1980

Tilly, Charles. *The Formation of National States in Western Europe*. Princeton: Princeton University Press, 1975

Tilton, John E. *International Diffusion of Technology: The Case of Semiconductors*. Washington: The Brookings Institution, 1971

Tinbergen, Jan (co-ordinator). *Reshaping the International Order: A Report to the Club of Rome*. New York: E.P. Dutton, 1976

Tivey, L. *Nationalisation in British Industry*. London: Jonathan Cape, 1966

Tocqueville, Alexis de. *The Old Regime and the French Revolution*. Translated by Stuart Gilvert. Garden City, NY: Doubleday, 1955

– *Democracy in America*. Vol. 1 (1835). Translated by Henry Reeve. New York: Schocken, 1961

Tolba, Mostafa Kamal. *Development without Destruction: Evolving Environmental Perceptions*. Dublin: Tycooly International Publishing, 1982

Tomlinson, Jim. *The Unequal Struggle? British Socialism and the Capitalist Enterprise*. London: Methuen, 1982

Trilateral Commission (see also by authors' names for commissioned reports). *Task Force Reports 1–7: The Triangle Papers*. New York: New York University Press, 1977

– *Task Force Reports 9–14. The Triangle Papers*. New York: New York University Press, 1978

– *Task Force Reports 15–19: The Triangle Papers*. New York: New York University Press, 1981

– *Trialogue: The Trilateral Commission's Quarterly of North American and European-Japanese affairs.*

Tsuchiya, Takeo. "Introduction" and "Masan: An Epitome of the Japan-ROK Relationship." *AMPO: Japan-Asia Quarterly Review.* Tokyo: Pacific-Asia Resources Center, 1977

Tsurumi, Yoshi. *The Japanese Are Coming: A Multinational Interaction of Firms and Politics.* Cambridge, Mass.: Ballinger, 1976

United Nations. *Transnational Corporations in World Development: A Re-examination.* New York: United Nations, 1978

– *Official Records of the UN General Assembly, Sixth Special Session (1974).* New York: United Nations, 1976

– *Official Records of the UN General Assembly, Seventh Special Session (1975).* New York: 1977

– *Yearbook of International Trade Statistics.* New York: United Nations, published annually until 1982. Thereafter, see *International Trade Statistics Yearbook.*

United Nations Centre on Transnational Corporations. *Transnational Corporations in the International Semiconductor Industry.* New York: UNCTC, 1986

– *Foreign Direct Investment, the Service Sector, and International Banking.* Series A:7 New York: UNCTC, May 1987

United Nations Conference on Trade and Development. "Indexation: Report by the Secretary-General of UNCTAD." TD/B/563, 7 July 1975

– "Action on Export Earnings Stabilization and Developmental Aspects of Commodity Policy: Report by the UNCTAD Secretariat." TD/229, 8 March 1979

United Nations Environment Programme. *The World Environment, 1972–1982: A Report.* Edited by Martin W. Holdgate, Mohammed Kassas, and Gilbert F. White. Dublin: Tycooly International Publishing, 1982

United Nations Industrial Development Organization. "Redeployment of Industries from Developed to Developing Countries." *Industrial Development Conference Papers,* 4/9 3 October 1979

– "Women in the Redeployment of Manufacturing Industry to Developing Countries." *UNIDO Working Papers on Structural Change, No. 18.* Vienna: UNIDO/ICIS, 1980

United States. Commission on International Trade and Investment Policy. *United States International Economic Policy in an Interdependent World.* Washington: US Government Printing Office, 1971

United States. Council on Environmental Quality and Department of State. *Global 2000 Report to the President: Entering the 21st Century.* 3 vols. Washington: US Government Printing Office, 1980

Ushiba, Nobuhiko. "The State of Trilateral Relations," *Trialogue,* July 1983

Ushiba, Nobuhiko, Graham Allison, and Thierry de Montbrial. *Sharing International Responsibilities among the Trilateral Countries: Report of the Trilateral*

Task Force on Sharing Global Responsibilities to the Trilateral Commission. New York: The Commission, 1983

Van Ameringen, Marc. "The Restructuring of the Canadian Automobile Industry," in Duncan Cameron and François Houle (eds.) *Canada and the New International Division of Labour*. Ottawa: University of Ottawa Press, 1985

Veblen, Thorstein. "The Natural Right of Investment," in C.B. Macpherson (ed.). *Property: Mainstream and Critical Positions*. Toronto: University of Toronto Press, 1978

Veljanovski, Cento. *Selling the State: Privatisation in Britain*. London: Weidenfeld and Nicholson, 1987

Vernon, Raymond. *Exploring the Global Economy: Emerging Issues in Trade and Investment*. Cambridge: Harvard University Center for International Affairs, 1985

Vernon, Raymond, and Yair Aharoni (eds.). *State-Owned Enterprise in the Western Economies*. London: Croom Helm, 1981

Vickers, John, and George Yarrow. *Privatization: An Economic Analysis*. Cambridge, Mass.: MIT Press, 1988

Wallerstein, Immanuel. "Crisis as Transition," in Samir Amin et al. *Dynamics of Global Crisis*. New York: Monthly Review Press, 1982

Ward, Barbara. "Another Chance for the North?" *Foreign Affairs* 59 (1980–1) 386–7

Warnock, John W. *The Politics of Hunger: The Global Food System*. Toronto: Methuen, 1987

Watanabe, Takeshi, Jacques Lesourne, and Robert S. McNamara. *Facilitating Development in a Changing Third World*. Report of the Trilateral Task Force on Strategies for Assistance to Developing Countries to the Trilateral Commission. Triangle Paper 27. New York: Trilateral Commission, 1983

Watts, H.D. "The Inter-regional Distribution of West German Multinationals in the United Kingdom," in M.J. Taylor and N.J. Thrift (eds.). *The Geography of Multinationals: Studies in The Spatial Development and Economic Consequences of Multinational Corporations*. London: Croom Helm, 1982

Weber, Max. *The Protestant Ethic and the Spirit of Capitalism* (1904). Translated by Talcott Parsons. New York: Scribners, 1958

– *Economy and Society: An Outline of Interpretive Sociology*. Edited and translated by Guenther Roth and Claus Wittich. New York: Bedminster Press, 1968.

Wechmar, Baron Rudiger von. "The Position of the Industrialized Countries," in Karl P. Sauvant (ed.). *Changing Priorities on the International Agenda: The New International Economic Order*. Oxford: Pergamon, 1981.

Weitzman, Martin L. "Profit-Sharing Capitalism," in John Elster and Karl Ove Moene (eds.). *Alternatives to Capitalism*. Cambridge: Cambridge University Press, 1989

White, Robert. "The Old and the New: Workplace Organization and Labour Relations in the Auto Industry." *Atkinson Review of Canadian Studies* 4 (1986) 8–10

Whitehead, Christine (ed.). *Reshaping the Nationalized Industries*. New Brunswick, NJ: Transaction Books, 1988

Williams, Gwyneth. *Third-World Political Organizations: A Review of Developments*. 2d ed. London: Macmillan, 1987

Willmore, Larry. "Direct Foreign Investment in Central American Manufacturing." *World Development* 4 (1976) 499–517

World Bank. *World Development Report*. New York: Oxford University Press, published annually

– *Environmental Considerations for the Industrial Development Sector*. Washington, DC: World Bank, 1978

World Commission on Environment and Development (the Brundtland Commission). *Our Common Future*. Oxford: Oxford University Press, 1987

Young, A.K. *The Sogo Shosha: Japan's Multinational Trading Companies*. Boulder, Colo.: Westview Press, 1979

Young, Oran R. *Natural Resources and the State: The Political Economy of Resource Management*. Berkeley: University of California Press, 1981

Zeman, Z.P. "The Dynamics of the Technological Race," in Zavis P. Zeman and David Hoffman (eds.). *The Dynamics of the Technological Leadership of the World*. Montreal: Institute for Research on Public Policy, 1980

– *The Men with the Yen: Some Foreseeable Future Developments of Japan Relevant to Canada*. Montreal: Institute for Research on Public Policy, 1984

Zenger, J.P. "Taiwan: Behind the Economic Miracle," in *AMPO: Japan-Asia Quarterly Review*, AMPO, special edition on free trade zones and the industrialization of Asia. Tokyo: Pacific-Asia Resources Center, 1977

Index